GW00456531

The Definitive NORTHAMPTON TOWN F.C.

A statistical history to 1995

Statistics by Frank Grande
Production by Tony Brown

Volume 2 in a series of club histories, published by Tony Brown, on behalf of the Association of Football Statisticians.

First published in Great Britain by Tony Brown, on behalf of the
Association of Football Statisticians, 22 Bretons, Basildon, Essex
SS15 5BY.

© Frank Grande and Tony Brown, 1996

All rights reserved. No part of this publication may be
reproduced, stored in a retrieval system, or transmitted in any
form, or by any means, electronic, mechanical, photocopying,
recording or otherwise without the prior permission in writing of
the Copyright holders, nor be otherwise circulated in any form or
binding or cover other than in which it is published and without a
similar condition including this condition being imposed on the
subsequent publisher.

The owners of the copyright of the photographs used have not
been traced. The AFS would be pleased to hear from anyone
whose copyright has been infringed unintentionally.

Other volumes in this series (some in preparation) are:

ISBN 1 899468 02 1

FOREWORDS BY TOMMY FOWLER ......

Tommy Fowler played 521 League games for the club, from the resumption of soccer after the Second World War, to season 1961/62. He played in 237 consecutive games between 1952 and 1956.

Two games stand out for me; one in January 1958, when we beat Arsenal 3-1 in the F.A. Cup at the old County Ground. Then, away to Liverpool in the next round. Although we were beaten 1-3, on a surface covered by an inch or two of snow, the boys did themselves proud.

My lasting memory was the presentation by the Club, out on the pitch, of a gold watch, when I had completed 500 games.

Tommy Fowler

..... AND BY CLIFF HOLTON

Cliff Holton scored 50 League goals in just 62 matches in the early 1960s, helping Northampton on their way from the lower divisions to the highest.

Cliff in Charlton's colours in 1966

Manager Dave Bowen persuaded me to join Northampton; my most vivid recollections of that period are the friendly attitude of the club and directors, plus the fact that the old County Ground was open on one side due to the cricket square. I found the latter most odd to come to terms with when playing!

My most notable game was the initial match, versus Crystal Palace away. The "Cobblers" had made a poor start to the season, while the "Glaziers" were in fine form. I dithered about making my debut in this match. Dave, with his lucky suit on, assured me it was a very favourable venue for him. I signed the transfer agreement at 4.30 pm and made my debut that evening. We won 4-1, which fortuitously included a hat trick or me. Supported by a talented squad of players, goalscoring continued throughout my congenial stay, enabling me to yield a record season.

Cliff Holton

INTRODUCTION BY THE AUTHOR

After writing the history of Northampton Town some ten years ago and then following up with the "Who's Who" a couple of years later, I have been somewhat stagnant when it comes to producing anything else on the club. I have had several ideas, but that was all they were, added to which there has been a lot of talk of other parties bringing out publications on the club; hence I have taken a back seat.

When Ray Spiller approached me with the idea of a "Definitive" record I jumped at the chance, especially as it is being produced by the A.F.S., of whom I proudly boast to being one of the early members.

It has taken myself, and my fellow Cobbler's statistician John Harley, some years to put together these records. Some of the early line ups do not agree with those in the national press, but we had an agreement early on that we would always go with the local press, as local reporters would know the players better. All the statistics have been checked, and double checked, and although we can prove our records with cuttings and programmes, we cannot prove that these articles are correct! It is always a nightmare for the statistician and historian.

My thanks go to John Harley, who checks all the facts with the finest of tooth combs, to the A.F.S. who came up with the idea, to the supporters of Northampton Town, who patronised my earlier publications, and to my wife Tina, who has always been helpful and supportive all through our married life, and has put up with "Northampton Town F.C.", the other love of my life!

Frank Grande, January 1996

Frank joined Northampton Town as a youngster, while they were a struggling fourth division side. He became a prolific scorer, breaking all the club records, and it was his goals that lifted the club to the First Division. Turning down many offers from top clubs here and abroad, he took over as player manager and led Northampton into Europe, winning all the major cup competitions. The only time they did not win the European Cup, Frank was helping England win the World Cup, scoring goals against the Brazilians. He retired at the age of 47, after F.I.F.A. asked him to stand down, to give others a chance.

This happened in his dreams! In reality, the author is just another supporter, having watched the club for 40 years. He can bore people with the names of every player who has played for the club since the war, every opponent, and the club's league position every season since their formation. Riveting stuff!

PRODUCTION NOTE

Mention 1966 to most Englishmen, and they will start to reminisce about the World Cup win at Wembley Stadium. I was there (funny how many say that, but I've got the ticket stub to prove it!). There was another highlight for me in 1966; unfashionable Northampton Town were playing in Division One! OK, so they didn't stay there for long, but it's nice that that the League structure allows the smaller clubs to rise from their slumbers and challenge the giants. Long may it continue to be so! Though our "Definitives" deliberately restrict themselves to the "bare" statistics, if you read them carefully you will find they tell their own story of the clubs' rise and fall.

Thanks first of all to Frank for his courtesy and swift response to my questions. Michael Joyce's player database saved me hours of work on the player section, and Brian Tabner kindly extracted the official attendances from the records of the Football League.

Tony Brown, January 1996

NORTHAMPTON TOWN RECORDS PAGE

PLAYERS:

Most Appearances	Tommy Fowler, 552 (521 League, 31 FAC)
	Peter Gleasure, 412 (344, 25, 25 FLC, 18 other)
	Joe Kiernan, 352 (308, 19, 25)
	William Watson, 352 (326, 26)
Most Goals	Jack English, 143 (135 League, 8 FAC)
	Ted Bowen, 120 (114, 6)
	Bert Dawes, 103 (82, 16, 5 other)
Most League Goals in a Season	Cliff Holton, 36, 1961/62
Most Goals in a League Game	5 by R Hoten v. Crystal Palace, 27/10/1928

THE CLUB:

Best League Performance	21st in Division 1, 1965/66
Best F.A. Cup Performance	5th round 1911/12, 1933/34, 1949/50, 1969/70
Best League Cup Performance	5th round; 1964/65, 1966/67
Most League Points	68, Division 4 1975/76 (2 points for a win)
	99, Division 4 1986/87 (3 points for a win)
Most League Goals	109, Division 3(S), 1952/53
	109, Division 4, 1962/63
Most League Wins in a Season	30, 1986/87
Best League Win	10-0 v. Walsall, 5/11/1927
Best F.A. Cup Win	10-0 v. Sutton, 7/12/1907
Best League Cup Win	8-0 v. Brighton, 1/11/1966
Best League Run Undefeated	21, from 27/9/1986
Undefeated League Games Home	29; from 20/2/1932 and 28/3/1975
Undefeated League Games Away	12; from 30/9/1986
Best Run of League Wins	8, from 27/8/1960
Longest Run of League Draws	6, from 18/9/1983

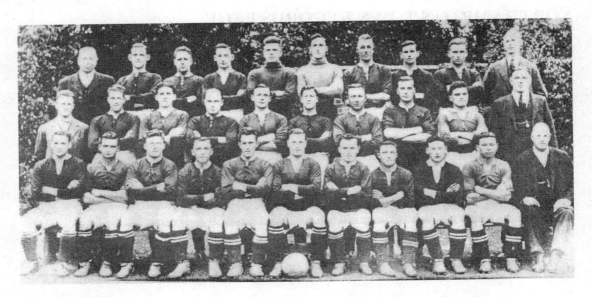

1929/30 *Back: F.C. Gillitt (Director), Andrews, Hoten, Wells, Hammond, Cave, Maloney, A Dawes, F Dawes, Newman (trainer). Centre: J Tresadern (manager), Bowen, Brett, Smith, Anthoney, Russell, Odell, Wilson, Eyre, Mellors (trainer). Front: Sissons, Berridge, Allon, McNaughton, Loasby, Watson, Shaw, Waite, Weston, Riches, Mr. R.P. Seal (Diector).*

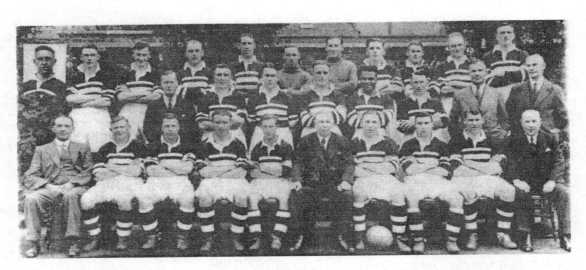

1938/39 *Back: Gunn, Barron, Platt, Tilson, Allen, Jones, Gormlie, Cuff, Rodgers, Hewitt, Russell. Centre: McKinnell, (assistant trainer), Ford, Dickenson, McCullogh, Parris, Postlethwaite, Mr. E.C. Hawtin (Director), Newman (trainer). Front: Mr. J.H. Marlow (secretary), Hurel, O'Rourke, Bosse, King, Mr. T.C. Gillitt (Chairman), Lauderdale, Blunt, Thayne, Mr. G. Hooton (Director)*

1950/51 *Back: Newman (assistant trainer), Woollard, Duckhouse, Garrett, Collins, Candlin, Ansell, Freeman, Hughes, Solomon, Croy, Docherty, McCulloch, Jennings (trainer). Centre: Coley, Smalley, Southam, Adams, Jeffrey, J Smith, Davie, Briscoe, Maxwell, Fowler. Front: Mitchell, Dixon, Murphy, D Smith, English, Hargrave, T Smith, Burn.*

1962/63 *Back: Dave Bowen (Manager), Jennings (coach), Ashworth, Leck, Large, Brodie, Branston, Kurilla, Cockcroft, Ray Osborne (secretary), Joe Payne (trainer). Front: Everitt, Hails, Ray Smith, Foley (captain), Lines, Reid, Mills.*

NORTHAMPTON IN PRE-FOOTBALL LEAGUE SEASONS

Northants League

		P	W	D	L	F	A	Pts
1897/98	4th	14	7	1	6	33	35	15
1898/99	Champions	16	13	2	1	49	17	28

Midland League

		P	W	D	L	F	A	Pts
1899/1900	3rd	24	16	2	6	66	36	34
1900/01	3rd	26	13	7	6	65	43	33

Southern League

		P	W	D	L	F	A	Pts
1901/02	11th	30	11	5	14	53	64	27
1902/03	8th	30	12	6	12	39	48	30
1903/04	15th	34	10	7	17	36	69	27
1904/05	12th	34	12	8	14	43	54	32
1905/06	18th (last)	34	8	5	21	32	79	21
1906/07	20th (last)	38	5	9	24	29	88	19
1907/08	8th	38	15	11	12	50	41	41
1908/09	Champions	40	25	5	10	90	45	55
1909/10	4th	42	22	4	16	90	44	48
1910/11	2nd	38	18	12	8	54	27	48
1911/12	3rd	38	22	7	9	82	41	51
1912/13	10th	38	12	12	14	61	48	36
1913/14	3rd	38	14	19	5	50	37	47
1914/15	5th	38	16	11	11	56	51	43
1919/20	19th	42	12	9	21	64	103	33

INTRODUCTION TO THE STATISTICS PAGES

The season by season grids show the results of games in the Football League, F.A. Cup, Football League Cup, Associate Members' Cup and the Third Division (South) Cup. Games which were expunged from the records because of the resignation of a club are not included, nor are the results of the 1939/40 season which was abandoned on the outbreak of World War Two. However, details of these games can be found in a later section.

Home games are identified by the opponents name in upper case, away games by the use of lower case. Northampton's score is always given first. Attendances for League games are taken from the official Football League records since 1925/26; before that, estimated attendances based on newspaper reports have to be used.

Substitutes have the numbers 12 and 14. 12 is used if only one substitute appeared (no matter what number was on the player's shirt).

A full player list is provided for every player who made a League appearance. Date and place of birth are shown, where known, and the year of death. Players with the same name are given a (1) or (2) after their name to avoid confusion. The next two columns, "seasons played", act as an index to the season by season grids. The years shown are the "first year" of the season; for example, 1971 is season 1971/72. The two columns show the season in which the player made his League debut; and the final season that he played. However, if he only played in one season, the second column is blank. An entry of "1994" in the second column does not imply that the player has left the club, but means that he appeared in this "final season" of the book.

Note that some players also made F.A. Cup appearances before 1921 and in 1945/46. If a player also made a League appearance his F.A. Cup appearances from these seasons are included in the list.

Previous and next clubs show where he was transferred from, and the club he moved to. Non league club information is included when known.

The appearance columns have separate totals for the League, F.A. Cup, Football League Cup and miscellaneous tournaments. In Northampton's case, the latter category includes the Third Division North Cup, the Football League Trophy and the Associate Members' Cup (played under a variety of sponsors' names). "Goals scored" are also shown under the four headings.

If a player has had more than one spell at the club, a consolidated set of appearance and goals are shown on the first line. Subsequent lines show the seasons involved in his return, and his new pair of previous and next clubs.

A full record of meetings against all other League clubs is included. Some clubs have played in the League under different names, but the totals are consolidated under the present day name in this table. Other pages show the club's record in the F.A. Cup in non League seasons and the list of managers.

1920/21

14th in Division 3 (South)

	Date	Opponent	Score	Scorers	Att.	Thorpe T	Sproson A	McKechnie JP	Hewison R	Jobey G	Tomkins EF	Pease WH	Whitworth GH	Lockett WC	Thomas WS	Freeman E	Watson WJ	Bellamy BW	Grendon FJW	Smith HC	Churchman E	Tysoe J	Weston CA	Burnard WT	Chambers L	Bedford SG	Hawtin LC
1	Aug 28	Grimsby Town	0-2		12000	1	2	3	4	5	6	7	8	9	10	11											
2	Sep 2	Queen's Park Rangers	2-1	Lockett 2	10000	1		3	4	5	6	7	8	9	10	11	2										
3	4	GRIMSBY TOWN	4-1	Whitworth 2, Lockett, Freeman	10000	1		3	4	5	6	7	8	9	10	11	2										
4	6	QUEEN'S PARK RANGERS	0-3		6000	1		3	4	5	6	7	8	9	10	11	2										
5	11	WATFORD	0-1		9000	1		3	4	5	6	7	8	9	10		2	11									
6	13	MILLWALL	0-2		6000	1	2	3	4	5	6	7	8	9	11			10									
7	18	Watford	1-7	Pease	7000	1	2	3	4	5	6	7	8	9	10	11											
8	25	SWANSEA TOWN	2-0	Whitworth, Lockett	6000	1			3	5	6	7	8	9	10	11	2		4								
9	Oct 2	Swansea Town	2-2	Whitworth 2	12000				3	5	6	7	8	9	10	11	2		4	1							
10	9	PORTSMOUTH	1-0	Jobey	7000	1			3	5	6	7	8	9	10	11	2		4								
11	16	Portsmouth	0-2		15000	1			3	5	6	7	8	9	10	11	2		4								
12	23	Southend United	2-1	Pease, Lockett	9000			3	6	5		7	8	9	10	11	2		4	1							
13	30	SOUTHEND UNITED	1-0	Lockett	9000				3	5	6	7	8	9	10	11	2		4	1							
14	Nov 6	Merthyr Town	0-1		13000				3	5	6	7	8	9	10	11	2		4	1							
15	13	MERTHYR TOWN	2-2	Whitworth, Lockett	8000	1			3	5	6	7	8	9	10	11	2		4								
16	20	Plymouth Argyle	2-0	Hewson, Pease	12000	1		3	10	5	6	7	8	9		11	2		4								
17	27	PLYMOUTH ARGYLE	1-1	Jobey	8000	1		3	10	5	6	7	8	9		11	2		4								
18	Dec 4	Exeter City	0-4		6000	1		3	10	5	6	7	8	9		11	2		4								
19	11	EXETER CITY	3-3	Pease, Whitworth, Thomas	6000	1			3	5	6	7	8	9	10	11	2		4								
20	25	Gillingham	5-2	Whitworth 2, Lockett 2, Freeman	8000	1			3	5	6	7	8	9	10	11	2		4								
21	27	GILLINGHAM	2-0	Whitworth, Lockett	13290	1			3	5	6	7	8	9	10	11	2		4								
22	Jan 1	Millwall	0-1		3000				3	5	6	7	8	9	10	11	2		4	1							
23	15	LUTON TOWN	1-0	Whitworth	7000	1			3	5	6	7	9	10			2		4		8	11					
24	22	Luton Town	1-3	Churchman	12000	1			3	5	6	7	9	10			2	11	4		8						
25	29	Newport County	1-1	Whitworth	8000	1	3			5	6	7	8	10		11	2		4				9				
26	Feb 5	NEWPORT COUNTY	0-2		8000	1	3			5	6	7	8	10		11	2		4				9				
27	12	SOUTHAMPTON	2-0	Whitworth, Burnard	7000				3	5	6	7	9	10			2		4	1				8	11		
28	26	READING	1-0	Whitworth	6000				3	5	6	7	9	10			2		4	1				8	11		
29	Mar 5	Reading	0-4		4000				3	5	6	7		10			2		4	1			9	8	11		
30	9	Southampton	1-3	Whitworth	7000				3	5	6	7	9	10			2		4	1				8	11		
31	12	BRISTOL ROVERS	1-2	Thomas	5000	1			3	5	6	7	9		8		2		4					10	11		
32	19	Bristol Rovers	2-4	Whitworth, 1 og	5000				3	5	6	7	9	10		11	2		4	1				8			
33	26	Brentford	1-1	Whitworth	8000				3	5	6	7	9	10		11	2		4	1				8			
34	28	Swindon Town	1-2	Burnard	5000				3	5		7		9	10	11	2		4	1				8		6	
35	29	SWINDON TOWN	1-2	Whitworth	10000				3	5		7	9	10			2		4	1				8	11	6	
36	Apr 2	BRENTFORD	6-2	Whitworth 4, Lockett, Burnard	6000				3	5	6	7	9	10			2		4	1				8	11		
37	9	Norwich City	3-3	Whitworth 2, Lockett	6000				3	5	6	7	9	10			2		4	1				8	11		
38	16	NORWICH CITY	1-0	Whitworth	5000				3	5		7	9	10			2		4	1				8	11	6	
39	23	Crystal Palace	1-5	Whitworth	20000				2	5		7	9	10					4	1				8	11	6	3
40	30	CRYSTAL PALACE	2-2	Pease, Whitworth	8000				3	5	6	7	9	10			2			1				8	11	4	
41	May 2	BRIGHTON & HOVE ALB	1-0	Lockett	6000				3	5	6	7	9	10			2			1				8	11	4	
42	7	Brighton & Hove Albion	2-3	Whitworth, Burnard	7000				3	5	6	7	9	10			2			1				8	11	4	
					Apps	22	5	11	40	42	37	42	40	41	21	25	38	3	32	20	2	1	3	16	13	7	1
					Goals				1	2		5	28	13	2	2					1			4			

One own goal

F.A. Cup

	Date	Opponent	Score	Scorers	Att.	Thorpe T	Sproson A	McKechnie JP	Hewison R	Jobey G	Tomkins EF	Pease WH	Whitworth GH	Lockett WC	Thomas WS	Freeman E	Watson WJ	Bellamy BW	Grendon FJW	Smith HC	Churchman E	Tysoe J	Weston CA	Burnard WT	Chambers L	Bedford SG	Hawtin LC
Q6	Dec 18	GILLINGHAM	3-1	Jobey, Whitworth 2	8000	1			3		6	7	9	10	8	11	2		4								
R1	Jan 8	SOUTHAMPTON	0-0		16000	1			3	5	6	7	9	10	8	11	2		4								
rep	12	Southampton	1-4	Whitworth	16000	1			3	5	6	7	9	10	8	11	2		4								

Played in Q6: Roe (number 5)

		P	W	D	L	F	A	W	D	L	F	A	Pts
1	Crystal Palace	42	15	4	2	45	17	9	7	5	25	17	59
2	Southampton	42	14	5	2	46	10	5	11	5	18	18	54
3	Queen's Park Rgs.	42	14	4	3	38	11	8	5	8	23	21	53
4	Swindon Town	42	14	5	2	51	17	7	5	9	22	32	52
5	Swansea Town	42	9	10	2	32	19	9	5	7	24	26	51
6	Watford	42	14	4	3	40	15	6	4	11	19	29	48
7	Millwall	42	11	5	5	25	8	7	6	8	17	22	47
8	Merthyr Town	42	13	5	3	46	20	2	10	9	14	29	45
9	Luton Town	42	14	6	1	51	15	2	6	13	10	41	44
10	Bristol Rovers	42	15	3	3	51	22	3	4	14	17	35	43
11	Plymouth Argyle	42	10	7	4	25	13	1	14	6	10	21	43
12	Portsmouth	42	10	8	3	28	14	2	7	12	18	34	39
13	Grimsby Town	42	12	5	4	32	16	3	4	14	17	43	39
14	NORTHAMPTON TOWN	42	11	4	6	32	23	4	4	13	27	52	38
15	Newport County	42	8	5	8	20	23	6	4	11	23	41	37
16	Norwich City	42	9	10	2	31	14	1	6	14	13	39	36
17	Southend United	42	13	2	6	32	20	1	6	14	12	41	36
18	Brighton & Hove A.	42	11	6	4	28	20	3	2	16	14	41	36
19	Exeter City	42	9	7	5	27	15	1	8	12	12	39	35
20	Reading	42	8	4	9	26	22	4	3	14	16	37	31
21	Brentford	42	7	9	5	27	23	2	3	16	15	44	30
22	Gillingham	42	6	9	6	19	24	2	3	16	15	50	28

1921/22   17th in Division 3(S)

No	Date	Opponent	Score	Scorers	Att	Smith HC	Watson WJ	Williams W	Bedford SG	Jobey G	Tomkins EF	Pease WH	Seabrook A	Whitworth GH	Lockett WC	Harron J	Hewison R	Ambridge FW	Hawtin LC	Davies LJ	Grendon FJW	Burnard WT	Davies AT	Chambers L	Jeffs TE	Williams JS	Johnson PR	Wood JT	Graham W	Weston CA
1	Aug 27	Millwall	0-0		22000	1	2	3	4	5	6	7	8	9	10	11														
2	Aug 29	Swindon Town	2-4	Pease, Lockett	5000	1	2	3	4	5	6	7	8	9	10	11														
3	Sep 3	MILLWALL	0-3		8000	1	2	3	4	5	6	7	8	9	10	11														
4	Sep 5	SWINDON TOWN	2-1	Whitworth, Harron	7000		2			5	6	7	8	9	10	11	4	1	3											
5	Sep 10	Reading	0-0		12000		2			5		7	8	9	10	11	4	1	3	6										
6	Sep 17	READING	2-1	Lockett 2	10000		2			5	6	7	8	9	10	11		1	3			4								
7	Sep 24	Bristol Rovers	0-2		10000	1	2			5	6	7	8	9	10	11			3			4								
8	Oct 1	BRISTOL ROVERS	2-2	Pease, Burnard	8000	1	2		4	5	6	7		9	10	11			3				8							
9	Oct 8	Brentford	0-1		16000	1	2			5	6	7	8	9	10	11			3			4								
10	Oct 15	BRENTFORD	2-0	Whitworth 2	8000	1	2	3		5	6	7		9	10		4						8	11						
11	Oct 22	ABERDARE ATHLETIC	2-0	Pease, Whitworth	10000	1	2	3	4	5		7		9	10		6						8	11						
12	Oct 29	Aberdare Athletic	2-4	Whitworth, Lockett	6000	1	2	6		5		7		9	10				3		4		8	11						
13	Nov 5	Brighton & Hove Albion	0-7		7000	1	2			5	6	7		9	10		4		3				8	11						
14	Nov 12	BRIGHTON & HOVE ALB	2-0	Whitworth 2	8000		2			5	6	7		9	10		4	1	3				8	11						
15	Nov 19	WATFORD	1-0	AT Davies	6000		2			5	6	7		9	10		4	1					8	11	3					
16	Dec 10	Charlton Athletic	2-2	Watson, Lockett	10000		2		4		6	7		9	10	11	5	1					8		3					
17	Dec 24	Southampton	0-8		10000		2		4		6	7		9	10	11	5	1							3	8				
18	Dec 26	Gillingham	2-3	Hewison 2	10000		2		4	5	6	7		9		11	10	1							3	8				
19	Dec 27	GILLINGHAM	3-1	Watson, Whitworth 2	12000		2		4	5	6	7		9	10	11	8	1							3					
20	Dec 31	Queen's Park Rangers	0-4		9000		2		4	5	6	7	8	9	10	11		1							3					
21	Jan 14	QUEEN'S PARK RANGERS	1-0	Whitworth	7000			3	4	5	6	7		9	10	11	8	1									2			
22	Jan 19	CHARLTON ATHLETIC	1-0	Whitworth	4000		2	3	4	5	6	7		9	10	11	8	1												
23	Jan 21	EXETER CITY	2-3	Lockett 2	4000		2	3	4	5	6	7		9	10		8	1						11						
24	Feb 4	SWANSEA TOWN	0-1		3000	1				5	6			9	10	11	8				4				3	7	2			
25	Feb 11	Swansea Town	2-2	Whitworth 2	8000	1	2		4	5	6	7		9	10		8							11	3					
26	Feb 18	SOUTHEND UNITED	0-2		6000	1	2		4	5	6	7		9			8					10	11		3					
27	Feb 25	Southend United	1-1	Whitworth	6000	1	2		4	5	6	7		9	10		8							11	3					
28	Mar 4	PORTSMOUTH	0-0		8000	1	2	6	4	5		7			9		10							11	3			8		
29	Mar 11	Portsmouth	1-1	Pease	6000	1	2	6	4	5		7			9		10							11	3				8	
30	Mar 18	Merthyr Town	1-2	Lockett	6000	1	2	6	4	5		7			9		10							11	3				8	
31	Mar 25	MERTHYR TOWN	2-0	Lockett 2	7000	1	2	6	4	5		7			9		10							11	3				8	
32	Apr 1	Plymouth Argyle	0-2		10000	1	2	6	4	5		7			9		10							11	3				8	
33	Apr 3	Exeter City	0-2		4000	1	2	6	4	5		7			9		10							11	3				8	
34	Apr 8	PLYMOUTH ARGYLE	1-3	Lockett	5000	1	2	6	4	5		7			9		10							11	3				8	
35	Apr 14	Watford	2-2	Lockett, Graham	8000	1	2	6		5		7			9		10							11	3				8	4
36	Apr 15	Newport County	2-2	Lockett, Graham	6000	1	2	6	4	5		7			9		10							11	3				8	
37	Apr 17	Norwich City	0-2		14000	1	2	6	4	5		7			9		10							11	3				8	
38	Apr 18	NORWICH CITY	3-0	Hewson 3	7000	1	2	6	4	5		7			9		10							11	3				8	
39	Apr 22	NEWPORT COUNTY	2-0	Lockett, Graham	3000	1	2	6	4	5		7			9		10						11		3				8	
40	Apr 24	SOUTHAMPTON	0-0		7000	1	2	6	4	5		7			9		10							11	3				8	
41	Apr 29	LUTON TOWN	2-0	Lockett 2	7000	1	2	6	4	5		7			9		10							11	3				8	
42	May 6	Luton Town	0-3		0	1	2	6	5			7			9	10						4		11	3				8	
		Apps				29	40	35	21	36	25	40	10	27	40	18	34	13	8	1	6	9	10	15	24	2	2	1	15	1
		Goals					2					4		14	16	1	5					1	1						3	

F.A. Cup

Rnd	Date	Opponent	Score	Scorers	Att	Smith HC	Watson WJ	Williams W	Bedford SG	Jobey G	Tomkins EF	Pease WH	Seabrook A	Whitworth GH	Lockett WC	Harron J	Hewison R	Ambridge FW	Hawtin LC	Davies LJ	Grendon FJW	Burnard WT	Davies AT	Chambers L	Jeffs TE	Williams JS	Johnson PR	Wood JT	Graham W	Weston CA
Q5	Dec 3	Lincoln City	2-1	Whitworth, Lockett	6800		2		4		6	7	8	9	10		5	1						11	3					
Q6	Dec 17	LANCASTER T	1-0	Jobey	12000		2			5	6	7		9	10		4	1				8	11		3					
R1	Jan 7	READING	3-0	Lockett 3	8895		2		4	5	6	7		9	10	11	8	1							3					
R2	Jan 28	STOKE	2-2	Hewison, Lockett	16532				4	5	6	7		9	10		8	1			2		11		3					
rep	Feb 2	Stoke	0-2		20000	1				5	6	7		9	10	11	8				2	4			3					

		P	W	D	L	F	A	W	D	L	F	A	Pts
1	Southampton	42	14	7	0	50	8	9	8	4	18	13	61
2	Plymouth Argyle	42	17	4	0	43	4	8	7	6	20	20	61
3	Portsmouth	42	13	5	3	38	18	5	12	4	24	21	53
4	Luton Town	42	16	2	3	47	9	6	6	9	17	26	52
5	Queen's Park Rgs.	42	13	7	1	36	12	5	6	10	17	32	49
6	Swindon Town	42	10	7	4	40	21	6	6	9	32	39	45
7	Watford	42	9	9	3	34	21	4	9	8	20	27	44
8	Aberdare Ath.	42	11	6	4	38	18	6	4	11	19	33	44
9	Brentford	42	15	2	4	41	17	1	9	11	11	26	43
10	Swansea Town	42	11	8	2	40	19	2	7	12	10	28	41
11	Merthyr Town	42	14	2	5	33	15	3	4	14	12	41	40
12	Millwall	42	6	13	2	22	10	4	5	12	16	32	38
13	Reading	42	10	5	6	28	15	4	5	12	12	32	38
14	Bristol Rovers	42	8	8	5	32	24	6	2	13	20	43	38
15	Norwich City	42	8	10	3	29	17	4	3	14	21	45	37
16	Charlton Athletic	42	10	6	5	28	19	3	5	13	15	37	37
17	NORTHAMPTON TOWN	42	13	3	5	30	17	0	8	13	17	54	37
18	Gillingham	42	11	4	6	36	20	3	4	14	11	40	36
19	Brighton & Hove A.	42	9	6	6	33	19	4	3	14	12	32	35
20	Newport County	42	8	7	6	22	18	3	5	13	22	43	34
21	Exeter City	42	7	5	9	22	29	4	7	10	16	30	34
22	Southend United	42	7	5	9	23	23	1	6	14	11	51	27

1922/23   8th in Division 3 (South)

#	Date	Opponent	Score	Scorers	Att	Smith HC	Watson WJ	Jeffs TE	Bedford SG	Newton F	Williams W	Pease WH	Seabrook A	Brown WY	Myers EC	Page LA	Graham W	Tomkins EF	Lockett WC	Civil H	Hewison R	Johnson PR	Forrest J	Page W	Wood EE	Hawtin LC
1	Aug 26	Swindon Town	0-2		10000	1	2	3	4	5	6	7	8	9	10	11										
2	28	GILLINGHAM	1-0	Graham	10000	1	2	3		5	6	7	8	9		11	10	4								
3	Sep 2	SWINDON TOWN	1-2	L Page	11000	1	2	3		5	6	7			10	11	8	4	9							
4	6	Gillingham	3-0	Seabrooke, Lockett 2	6000	1	2	3	5		7	8			10	11		4	9	6						
5	9	WATFORD	1-1	Lockett	8000	1	2	3	5		6	7	8		10	11		4	9							
6	16	Watford	0-0		10000	1	2	3	5		6	7	8		10	11		4	9							
7	23	BRENTFORD	1-1	Myers	6000	1	2	3	5		6	7			10	11	8	4	9							
8	30	Brentford	1-2	L Page	7000	1	2	3	5			7	8		10	11		4	9	6						
9	Oct 7	Norwich City	0-1		9000	1	2	3	5		6	7			10	11	8	4	9							
10	14	NORWICH CITY	1-1	Graham	8000	1	2		5		6	7			10	11	8	4	9		3					
11	21	Aberdare Athletic	2-0	Seabrooke, Lockett	7000	1	2		5		6	7	8		10		11		9		3	4				
12	28	ABERDARE ATHLETIC	3-1	Watson, Williams, Myers	7000	1	2		5		6	7	8		10		11		9		3	4				
13	Nov 4	Southend United	2-1	Myers 2	7000	1	2		5		6	7	8		10	11			9		3	4				
14	11	SOUTHEND UNITED	5-2	Bedford, Williams, L Page, Graham 2	8000	1	2		5		6	7			10	11	8		9		3		4			
15	25	EXETER CITY	3-0	Watson, Myers, Lockett	7000	1	2	3	5		6	7			10	11	8		9				4			
16	Dec 9	MERTHYR TOWN	1-1	Lockett	7000	1	2	3	5		6	7			10	11		4	9					8		
17	16	Reading	0-0		6000	1	2	3	5		6	7			10	11		4	9					8		
18	23	READING	5-0	Pease, Myers, L Page, Lockett, W Page	10000	1	2	3	5		6	7			10	11		4	9					8		
19	25	Plymouth Argyle	0-1			1	2	3	5		6	7			10	11		4	9					8		
20	26	PLYMOUTH ARGYLE	1-0	Pease	18123	1	2	3	5		6	7			10	11			9			4		8		
21	30	BRIGHTON & HOVE ALB	0-0		5000	1	2	3	5		6	7		9	10	11						4		8		
22	Jan 6	Brighton & Hove Albion	0-1		10000	1	2	3	5		6	7			10	11			9			4		8		
23	13	Exeter City	2-1	Pease, Lockett	6000	1	2	3	5		6	7			10	11			9			4		8		
24	20	Bristol Rovers	0-0		8000	1	2	3	5		6	7			10	11			9			4		8		
25	27	BRISTOL ROVERS	1-0	Myers	7000	1	2	3	5		6	7			10	11			9			4		8		
26	Feb 3	Swansea Town	0-4		15000	1	2		5		6	7			9	11	10				3	4		8		
27	10	SWANSEA TOWN	1-3	Myers	5000	1	2		5		6	7			10	11	8		9		3	4				
28	17	NEWPORT COUNTY	2-1	Lockett 2	6000	1	2	3	4	5	6	7	9		8	11			10							
29	24	Newport County	1-1	Pease	4000	1	2	3	4	5	6	7	9			11	8		10							
30	Mar 3	Bristol City	0-1		14000	1	2	3		5	6	7	9			11			10			4		8		
31	5	Merthyr Town	0-3			1	2	3		5	6	7	9			11			10			4		8		
32	10	BRISTOL CITY	2-1	Pease, Lockett	10000	1	2	3	5	4	6	7	8		10	11			9							
33	17	PORTSMOUTH	3-0	Seabrooke, L Page, Lockett	7000	1	2	3		4	6	7	8			11	10		9						5	
34	24	Portsmouth	0-0		7790	1		3		4	6	7	8			11	10		9						5	2
35	31	MILLWALL	2-1	Seabrooke, one og	7000	1	2	3		4	6	7	8			11	10		9						5	
36	Apr 2	Charlton Athletic	0-2		8000	1	2	3		4	6	7	8			11	10		9						5	
37	3	CHARLTON ATHLETIC	0-0		10000	1	2	3	4		6	7	8			11	10		9						5	
38	7	Millwall	0-2		12000	1	2	3		4	6	7	8			11	10		9						5	
39	14	LUTON TOWN	2-0	Pease, Lockett	10000	1	2	3		4	6	7			10	11	8		9						5	
40	21	Luton Town	1-2	Myers	8000	1	2	3		4	6	7			10	11	8		9						5	
41	28	QUEEN'S PARK RANGERS	4-2	Pease, Seabrooke 2, Lockett	8000	1	2	3		4	6	7	8		10	11			9						5	
42	Ma 5	Queen's Park Rangers	2-3	Myers, Wood	9000	1	2			4	6	7	8		10		11		9		3				5	
		Apps				42	40	33	29	18	39	42	23	2	32	39	21	13	38	2	14	9	2	13	10	1
		Goals					2		1		2	7	6		10	5	4		14					1	1	

One own goal

F.A. Cup

#	Date	Opponent	Score	Att	Smith HC	Watson WJ	Jeffs TE	Bedford SG	Newton F	Williams W	Pease WH	Seabrook A	Brown WY	Myers EC	Page LA	Graham W	Tomkins EF	Lockett WC	Civil H	Hewison R	Johnson PR	Forrest J	Page W	Wood EE	Hawtin LC
05	Dec 2	Charlton Athletic	0-2	5000	1	2	3	5		6	7			10	11	8		9				4			

		P	W	D	L	F	A	W	D	L	F	A	Pts
1	Bristol City	42	16	4	1	43	13	8	7	6	23	27	59
2	Plymouth Argyle	42	18	3	0	47	6	5	4	12	14	23	53
3	Swansea Town	42	13	6	2	46	14	9	3	9	32	31	53
4	Brighton & Hove A.	42	15	3	3	39	13	5	8	8	13	21	51
5	Luton Town	42	14	4	3	47	18	7	3	11	21	31	49
6	Millwall	42	9	10	2	27	13	5	8	8	18	27	46
7	Portsmouth	42	10	5	6	34	20	9	3	9	24	32	46
8	NORTHAMPTON TOWN	42	13	6	2	40	17	4	5	12	14	27	45
9	Swindon Town	42	14	4	3	41	17	3	7	11	21	39	45
10	Watford	42	10	6	5	35	23	7	4	10	22	31	44
11	Queen's Park Rgs.	42	10	4	7	34	24	6	6	9	20	25	42
12	Charlton Athletic	42	11	6	4	33	14	3	8	10	22	37	42
13	Bristol Rovers	42	7	9	5	25	19	6	7	8	10	17	42
14	Brentford	42	9	4	8	27	23	4	8	9	14	28	38
15	Southend United	42	10	6	5	35	18	2	7	12	14	36	37
16	Gillingham	42	13	4	4	38	18	2	3	16	13	41	37
17	Merthyr Town	42	10	4	7	27	17	1	10	10	12	31	36
18	Norwich City	42	8	7	6	29	26	5	3	13	22	45	36
19	Reading	42	9	8	4	24	15	1	6	14	12	40	34
20	Exeter City	42	10	4	7	27	18	3	3	15	20	66	33
21	Aberdare Ath.	42	6	8	7	25	23	3	3	15	17	47	29
22	Newport County	42	8	6	7	28	21	0	5	16	12	49	27

1923/24   8th in Division 3 (South)

#	Date	Opponent	Res	Scorers	Att	Smith HC	Watson WJ	Brett FB	Newton F	Wood EE	Williams W	Pease WH	Wood W	Lockett WC	Myers EC	Page LA	York R	Hewison R	Jeffs TE	Bedford SG	Hobbs RV	Gray GR	Seabrook A	Graham W	Facer A	Sorenson IM	Needham GW	Wright RL	Braidford L
1	Aug 25	BRIGHTON & HOVE ALB	3-0	Myers 2, Pease	14256	1	2	3	4	5	6	7	8	9	10	11													
2	27	Luton Town	1-1	Lockett		1	2	3	4	5	6	7	8	9	10	11													
3	Sep 1	Brighton & Hove Albion	0-2		8712	1	2	3	4	5	6	7	8	9	10	11													
4	3	LUTON TOWN	2-0	Myers, W Wood	9968	1	2	3	4	5	6	7	8		10	11	9												
5	8	Swansea Town	1-2	W Wood	18000	1	2	3	4	5	6	7	8			11	9	10											
6	10	BRISTOL ROVERS	0-0		10000	1			4	5	6	7	8	9						3									
7	15	SWANSEA TOWN	2-0	Myers 2	11951	1	2	3	4	5	6	7	8	9	10	11													
8	22	Newport County	1-1	Lockett	9500	1	2	3	4	5	6	7	8	9	10	11													
9	29	NEWPORT COUNTY	0-0		10000	1	2	3	4	5	6	7	8	9	10	11													
10	Oct 6	Gillingham	1-1	Myers	7000	1		3	4	5	6	7	8	9	10	11			2										
11	13	GILLINGHAM	2-0	Lockett, W Wood	10000	1	2	3	4	5	6	7	8	9	10	11													
12	20	QUEEN'S PARK RANGERS	3-0	Myers 2, Pease	8000	1	2	3	4		6	7	8	9	10	11				5									
13	27	Queen's Park Rangers	2-3	Page, W Wood	5000	1	2	3	4		6	7	8	9	10	11				5									
14	Nov 3	Plymouth Argyle	0-0		11000	1	2	3	4		6	7	8	9	10	11				5									
15	10	PLYMOUTH ARGYLE	1-0	Myers	11000	1	2	3	4		6	7	8	9	10	11				5									
16	17	MERTHYR TOWN	3-0	Lockett, Myers, Newton	7000	1	2	3	4		6	7	8	9	10	11				5									
17	24	Merthyr Town	0-0			1	2	3	4		6	7	8	9	10	11				5			3						
18	Dec 8	Bristol Rovers	1-1	W Wood	8000	1	2	3	4		6	7	8	9		11				5	10								
19	22	Charlton Athletic	0-0		10000	1	2	3	4		6	7	8	9	10	11				5									
20	26	Swindon Town	0-2		10000	1	2	3	4		6	7	8	9	10	11				5									
21	27	SWINDON TOWN	1-1	Myers	9000	1	2	3			6	7		9	10	11				5		4		8					
22	29	NORWICH CITY	1-0	Lockett	10796	1	2	3			6	7		9		11	9			5		4		8					
23	Jan 5	Norwich City	4-1	Graham, Lockett, Page 2	6000	1	2	3	4		6	7	10	9		11				5				8					
24	19	READING	3-1	Graham, Lockett, Pease	7000	1	2			5	6	7	10	9		11			3			4		8					
25	26	Reading	0-1		7000	1	2	3			6	7	10	9		11						4		8			5		
26	Feb 2	BOURNEMOUTH	3-1	Myers, Page, Pease	7663	1	2	3			6	7	8		10	11						4			9		5		
27	9	Bournemouth	1-2	Lockett	5000	1	2	3			6	7	8	9		11						4					5	10	
28	16	Millwall	3-4	Myers, Page, Pease	15000	1	2	3			6	7		9	10	11						4		8			5		
29	23	MILLWALL	2-1	Myers 2	8000	1	2	3			6	7		9	10	11						4		8			5		
30	Mar 8	Aberdare Athletic	2-2	Pease 2	8000	1	2	3			6	7	8	9		11						4		10			5		
31	13	CHARLTON ATHLETIC	1-0	Braidford	5000	1	2	3			6	7		9		11				5		4		10					8
32	15	Southend United	1-5	Lockett	9000	1	2	3			6	7		9	10	11						4					5		8
33	22	SOUTHEND UNITED	8-0	*see below	7000	1	2	3		5	6	7		9	10	11							8				4		
34	29	Exeter City	1-2	Pease	4000	1	2	3		5	6	7			10	11							8				4		9
35	Apr 5	EXETER CITY	1-0	Lockett	7000	1	2	3		5	6	7		9	10	11											4		8
36	7	ABERDARE ATHLETIC	1-2	Brett		1	2	3		5	6	7		9	10	11											4		8
37	12	Portsmouth	3-1	Lockett, Myers, W Wood	11704	1	2	3		5	6	7	8	9	10	11											4		
38	19	PORTSMOUTH	0-4		13500	1	2	3		5	6	7	8	9	10	11											4		
39	21	Watford	2-0	Lockett 2		1		3		5	6	7	8	9	10	11			2								4		
40	22	WATFORD	1-2	Lockett	8000	1		3		5	6	7	8	9	10	11			2								4		
41	26	Brentford	0-1		3000	1		3	4	5	6	7	8	9		11			2								4		
42	May 3	BRENTFORD	2-3	Graham, Lockett	6000	1		3		5	6	7	8	9		11			2							10	4		

Scorers in game 33: Lockett 3, Seabrook 3, Myers, Pease.

	Smith HC	Watson WJ	Brett FB	Newton F	Wood EE	Williams W	Pease WH	Wood W	Lockett WC	Myers EC	Page LA	York R	Hewison R	Jeffs TE	Bedford SG	Hobbs RV	Gray GR	Seabrook A	Graham W	Facer A	Sorenson IM	Needham GW	Wright RL	Braidford L
Apps	42	37	39	23	21	42	42	32	38	32	42	3	1	8	13	1	11	3	9	2	1	14	1	5
Goals		1					9	6	18	17	5								3	3				1

F.A. Cup

Rd	Date	Opponent	Res	Scorers	Att	Smith HC	Watson WJ	Brett FB	Newton F	Wood EE	Williams W	Pease WH	Wood W	Lockett WC	Myers EC	Page LA	York R	Hewison R	Jeffs TE	Bedford SG	Hobbs RV	Gray GR	Seabrook A	Graham W	Facer A	Sorenson IM	Needham GW	Wright RL	Braidford L
Q5	Dec 1	LINCOLN CITY	5-1	Bedford, Myers 2, Page, Pease	11000	1	2	3	4		6	7	8	9	10	11				5									
Q6	15	Wigan Borough	6-0	Myers, Page, Pease 2, W Wood 2	18000	1	2	3	4		6	7	8	9	10	11				5									
R1	Jan 12	HALIFAX TOWN	1-1	Lockett	11000	1	2	3	4		6	7	8	9		11				5							10		
rep	15	Halifax Town	1-1	W Wood	10000	1	2		5	4	6	7	8	9		11			3								10		
rep2	21	Halifax Town	2-4	Lockett, W Wood	7500	1	2				6	7	8	9		11	4		3				5				10		

Replay 2 at Bramall Lane, Sheffield

		P	W	D	L	F	A	W	D	L	F	A	Pts
1	Portsmouth	42	15	3	3	57	11	9	8	4	30	19	59
2	Plymouth Argyle	42	13	6	2	46	15	10	3	8	24	19	55
3	Millwall	42	17	3	1	45	11	5	7	9	19	27	54
4	Swansea Town	42	18	2	1	39	10	4	6	11	21	38	52
5	Brighton & Hove A.	42	16	4	1	56	12	5	5	11	12	25	51
6	Swindon Town	42	14	5	2	38	11	3	8	10	20	33	47
7	Luton Town	42	11	7	3	35	19	5	7	9	15	25	46
8	NORTHAMPTON TOWN	42	14	3	4	40	15	3	8	10	24	32	45
9	Bristol Rovers	42	11	7	3	34	15	4	6	11	18	31	43
10	Newport County	42	15	4	2	39	15	2	5	14	17	49	43
11	Norwich City	42	13	5	3	45	18	3	3	15	15	41	40
12	Aberdare Ath.	42	9	9	3	35	18	3	5	13	10	40	38
13	Merthyr Town	42	11	8	2	33	19	0	8	13	12	46	38
14	Charlton Athletic	42	8	7	6	26	20	3	8	10	12	25	37
15	Gillingham	42	11	6	4	27	15	1	7	13	16	43	37
16	Exeter City	42	14	3	4	33	17	1	4	16	4	35	37
17	Brentford	42	9	8	4	33	21	5	0	16	21	50	36
18	Reading	42	12	2	7	35	20	1	7	13	16	37	35
19	Southend United	42	11	7	3	35	19	1	3	17	18	65	34
20	Watford	42	8	8	5	35	18	1	7	13	10	36	33
21	Bournemouth	42	6	8	7	19	19	5	3	13	21	46	33
22	Queen's Park Rgs.	42	9	6	6	28	26	2	3	16	9	51	31

1924/25 — 9th in Division 3 (South)

#		Date	Opponent	Score	Scorers	Att	Smith HC	Watson WJ	Brett FB	Needham GW	Wood EE	Williams W	Pease WH	Cook J	Lockett WC	Myers EC	Page LA	Poyntz WI	Jeffs TE	Hewison R	Molloy W	Oxley RL	George HS	Cockle ES	Hoten RV	Hammond L	Chapman WJ	Evans CJH
							1	2	3	4	5	6	7	8	9	10	11											
1	Aug	30	Watford	0-1		5000	1	2	3	4	5	6	7	8	9	10	11											
2	Sep	1	Charlton Athletic	0-0			1	2	3	4	5	6	7	8		10	11	9										
3		4	ABERDARE ATHLETIC	5-0	Cook, Lockett 4		1	2	3	4	5	6	7	8		10	11	9										
4		6	SOUTHEND UNITED	0-1		8000	1	2	3	4	5	6	7	8		10	11	9										
5		8	CHARLTON ATHLETIC	2-1	Pease, Cook	5189	1	2	3	4	5	6	7	8		10	11	9										
6		13	Newport County	0-1		6000	1	2	3	4	5	6	7	8		10	11	9										
7		15	LUTON TOWN	1-0	Pease	5340	1	2		4	5	6	7	8	9	10	11		3									
8		20	BRISTOL ROVERS	5-0	Wood, Myers, Page	7000	1	2	3	4	5	6	7		9	10	11		8									
9		22	Luton Town	0-2		5000	1	2	3	4		5	6	7	9	10	11		8									
10		27	Exeter City	0-0		7000	1	2		5		6	7	8	9	10	11		3	4								
11	Oct	4	SWANSEA TOWN	1-3	Pease	10000	1	2		5		6	7	8	9	10	11		3	4								
12		11	Reading	1-0	Lockett	10000	1	2		5		6	7	8	9	10	11		3	4								
13		18	MERTHYR TOWN	2-0	Wood, Page	7781	1	2	3	10	5	6	7		9		11		8	4								
14		25	Gillingham	1-0	Lockett	5000	1	2			5	6	7		9		11	9										
15	Nov	1	Bournemouth	2-1	Needham, Pease	2000	1	2	3	4	5	6	7	8		10	11	9										
16		8	BRIGHTON & HOVE ALB	1-0	Hewison	9000	1	2	5	4		6	7	8	9		11		3	10								
17		15	Plymouth Argyle	1-2	Hewison	9000	1	2	5	4		6	7	8	9		11		3	10								
18		22	BRISTOL CITY	1-2	Page	8000	1	2	6	4	5		7	8	9		11		3	10								
19		29	Swindon Town	0-5		7000	1	2	3	4	5	6		8	9		11	9			10	7						
20	Dec	20	BRENTFORD	0-2		6000	1	2	3	5		6	7	8	9		11				4		10	11				
21		25	Millwall	1-3	Page	15000	1	2	3	4	5	6	7	8			11							9	10			
22		26	MILLWALL	0-2		11534		2		4		6	7	8	9		11		3						10	1	5	
23		27	WATFORD	1-1	Page	2000		2		4		6	7		9		11	8	3						10	1	5	
24	Jan	3	Southend United	1-0	Pease	6000	1	2				6	7		9		11	8	3						10		5	4
25		17	NEWPORT COUNTY	0-2		6000	1	2				6	7	8	9	10	11		3								5	4
26		24	Bristol Rovers	2-0	Pease, Poyntz	6000	1	2	5				7				11		8	3				9	10		6	4
27		31	EXETER CITY	2-1	Page, Hoten	5000	1	2	5				7				11		8	3				9	10		6	4
28	Feb	7	Swansea Town	1-2	Cockle	18000	1	2	5				7				11		8	3				9	10		6	4
29		14	READING	2-0	Page, Cockle	6000	1	2	5				7				11		8	3				9	10			4
30		21	Merthyr Town	2-0	Pease, Cockle	3500	1	2	5			6	7				11		8	3				9	10			4
31		28	Gillingham	1-0	Pease	6000	1	2	5			6	7				11		8	3				9	10			4
32	Mar	7	BOURNEMOUTH	3-0	Page 2, Evans	5000	1	2	5			6	7				11		8	3				9	10			4
33		14	Brighton & Hove Albion	1-0	Page	7000	1	2	5			6	7				11		8	3				9	10			4
34		21	PLYMOUTH ARGYLE	5-2	Pease, Page 2, Cockle, Hoten	9221	1	2	5			6	7				11		8	3				9	10			4
35		28	Bristol City	0-1		11000	1	2	5			6	7				11		8	3				9	10			4
36	Apr	4	SWINDON TOWN	0-0		8000	1	2	5			6	7				11		8	3				9	10			
37		11	Aberdare Athletic	1-1	Evans	7000	1	2	5		4	6	7				11		8	3				9	10			4
38		13	Queen's Park Rangers	0-2		8000	1	2	5			6	7				11		8	3				9	10			4
39		14	QUEEN'S PARK RANGERS	1-0	Poyntz	6000	1	2	5		4	6	7				11		8	3				9	10			
40		18	NORWICH CITY	1-1	Page	5500	1	2	5			6					11		8	3	7			9	10		1	4
41		23	Norwich City	0-4		5000		2	5			6					11		8	3	7			9	10			4
42		25	Brentford	3-1	Poyntz 2, OG	5000	1	2	5			6					11		8	3	7			9	10			4

	Smith HC	Watson WJ	Brett FB	Needham GW	Wood EE	Williams W	Pease WH	Cook J	Lockett WC	Myers EC	Page LA	Poyntz WI	Jeffs TE	Hewison R	Molloy W	Oxley RL	George HS	Cockle ES	Hoten RV	Hammond L	Chapman WJ	Evans CJH
Apps	39	42	34	21	19	37	39	20	23	8	41	29	28	10	3	1	1	18	21	3	8	17
Goals			1	2			9	2	6	2	14	4		2				4	2			2

One own goal

F.A. Cup

	Date	Opponent	Score		Att	Smith HC	Watson WJ	Brett FB	Needham GW	Wood EE	Williams W	Pease WH	Cook J	Lockett WC	Myers EC	Page LA	Poyntz WI	Jeffs TE	Hewison R	Molloy W	Oxley RL	George HS	Cockle ES	Hoten RV	Hammond L	Chapman WJ	Evans CJH
R1	Jan 10	Tottenham Hotspur	0-3		32718	1	2		4		6	7		9		11		8	3					10			5

League table

		P	W	D	L	F	A	W	D	L	F	A	Pts
1	Swansea Town	42	17	4	0	51	12	6	7	8	17	23	57
2	Plymouth Argyle	42	17	3	1	55	12	6	7	8	22	26	56
3	Bristol City	42	14	5	2	40	10	8	4	9	20	31	53
4	Swindon Town	42	17	2	2	51	13	3	9	9	15	25	51
5	Millwall	42	12	5	4	35	14	6	8	7	23	24	49
6	Newport County	42	13	6	2	35	12	7	3	11	27	30	49
7	Exeter City	42	13	4	4	37	19	6	5	10	22	29	47
8	Brighton & Hove A.	42	14	3	4	43	17	5	5	11	16	28	46
9	NORTHAMPTON TOWN	42	12	3	6	34	18	8	3	10	17	26	46
10	Southend United	42	14	1	6	34	18	5	4	12	17	43	43
11	Watford	42	12	3	6	22	20	5	6	10	16	27	43
12	Norwich City	42	10	8	3	39	18	4	5	12	14	33	41
13	Gillingham	42	11	8	2	25	11	2	6	13	10	33	40
14	Reading	42	9	6	6	28	15	5	4	12	9	23	38
15	Charlton Athletic	42	12	6	3	31	13	1	6	14	15	35	38
16	Luton Town	42	9	10	2	34	15	1	7	13	15	42	37
17	Bristol Rovers	42	10	5	6	26	13	2	8	11	16	36	37
18	Aberdare Ath.	42	13	4	4	40	21	1	5	15	14	46	37
19	Queen's Park Rgs.	42	10	6	5	28	19	4	2	15	14	44	36
20	Bournemouth	42	8	6	7	20	17	5	2	14	20	41	34
21	Brentford	42	8	7	6	28	26	1	0	20	10	65	25
22	Merthyr Town	42	8	3	10	24	27	0	2	19	11	50	21

1925/26 12th in Division 3(S)

#	Date	Opponent	Res	Scorers	Att	Allen PW	Bradshaw H	Brett FB	Cockle ES	Ferrari FW	George HS	Hoten RV	Hammond L	Jeffs TE	Lockett WC	O'Rourke P	Pease WH	Robinson LStJ	Shaw WH	Smith H	Tomkins EF	Tresadern J	Watson WJ	Williams W	Yorke AE
1	Aug 29	Brentford	4-3	Cockle 4	12317	4		5	9			10		3	11		7	8		1		6	2		
2	Sep 5	CRYSTAL PALACE	4-0	Cockle, Hoten, Robinson 2	9005	4		5	9			10	1	3	11		7	8				6	2		
3	12	Bristol City	1-1	Robinson	14954	5		3	9			10	1		11		7	8				6	2	4	
4	14	ABERDARE ATHLETIC	3-2	Cockle 2, Shaw	7339	4		5	9			10	1	3			7	8	11			6	2		
5	19	PLYMOUTH ARGYLE	2-1	Pease, Robinson	6344	4		5	9			10	1				7	8	11				2	6	3
6	21	Aberdare Athletic	0-1		4432	4		5	9			10	1				7	8	11				2	6	3
7	26	Southend United	1-6	Cockle	7332	4	11	5	9			10	1				7	8				6	2		3
8	30	Gillingham	1-1	Cockle	4347	4	11	5	9			10	1				7	8				6	2		3
9	Oct 3	NORWICH CITY	3-2	Robinson 3	10805	4		5	9		11	10	1				7	8				6	2		3
10	10	Millwall	1-4	Pease	18675	4		5	9		11	10	1				7	8				6	2		3
11	17	Merthyr Town	3-5	Cockle, Robinson, Shaw	5288	5		3	9			11	1				7	8	10			4	2	6	
12	24	NEWPORT COUNTY	2-0	Cockle 2	7987	4		5	9			11	1				7	8	10			6	2		3
13	31	Bournemouth	1-1	Hoten	6495	4		5	9			11	1				7	8	10			6	2		3
14	Nov 7	CHARLTON ATHLETIC	2-1	Pease, Robinson	6201			5	9	4	11		1	3			7	8	10				2	6	
15	14	Bristol Rovers	2-1	Cockle, Hoten	6695			5	9	4	11	10	1	3			7	8					2	6	
16	21	SWINDON TOWN	2-0	Pease, Robinson	8782			5	9		11	10	1	3			7	8				4	2	6	
17	Dec 5	READING	0-1		7494			5	9		11	10	1	3			7	8				4	2	6	
18	19	QUEEN'S PARK RANGERS	3-2	George, Pease, Robinson	5495	4		5	9		11		1				7	8	10				2	6	3
19	25	Watford	2-3	Pease, Robinson	7771	4		5	9	3	11		1				7	8	10				2	6	
20	26	WATFORD	2-2	Allen, Cockle	12335	4		5	9	3	11		1				7	8	10				2	6	
21	28	GILLINGHAM	1-2	Robinson	7075	4		5	9	3	11		1				7	8	10				2	6	
22	Jan 2	BRENTFORD	6-1	Cockle 2, Pease 2, Robinson 2	4649			5	9	6		10	1	3	11		7	8				4	2		
23	16	Crystal Palace	0-1		7113	4		5	9	3	11		1	2		10	7	8						6	
24	23	BRISTOL CITY	1-2	Cockle	5027	4		5	9	2	11		1	3			7	8	10			6			
25	30	Plymouth Argyle	4-2	Allen, George, Robinson, Shaw	10670	4		5	9		11		1	3			7	8	10			6	2		
26	Feb 6	SOUTHEND UNITED	3-3	Cockle 2, Hoten	7414	4		5	9		11	10	1	3			7	8				6	2		
27	13	Norwich City	1-2	Pease	6032	6			9	5	11		1	3			7	8	10		4		2		
28	22	Luton Town	2-3	Pease, one og	5549	6			9	5	11	10	1	3			7	8			4		2		
29	27	MERTHYR TOWN	4-1	Cockle, Robinson 3	5778	4			9	5	11		1	3			7	8	10		6		2		
30	Mar 6	Newport County	0-3		5293	4			9	5	11		1	2			7	8	10		6			3	
31	13	Bournemouth	2-4	Robinson, Williams	5376	4		3	9	5		10	1				7	8	11				2	6	
32	20	Charlton Athletic	3-3	Hoten, Pease, one og	5869	4		5	9	3		10	1				7	8	11				2	6	
33	27	BRISTOL ROVERS	2-0	Cockle, Hoten	5241	4		5	9	3		10	1				7	8	11				2	6	
34	Apr 2	Brighton & Hove Albion	2-2	Cockle, Shaw	10450	4			9	5		10	1				7	8	11				2	6	3
35	3	Swindon Town	2-1	Cockle, Robinson	6192	4			9	5		10	1				7	8	11				2	6	3
36	6	BRIGHTON & HOVE ALB	1-2	Cockle	8434	4		5	9	2		10	1				7	8						6	3
37	10	EXETER CITY	2-1	Cockle, Robinson	4717			5	9			11	1				7	8	10			4	2	6	3
38	14	Exeter City	0-1		2977			5	9			10	1				7	8	11			4	2	6	3
39	17	Reading	2-4	Cockle, Shaw	13722	4		5	9			10	1			8	7		11				2	6	3
40	24	LUTON TOWN	0-1		6697	4		5	9		11	10	1				7	8					2	6	3
41	26	MILLWALL	3-1	Hoten 2, Robinson	3155	4		5	9			11	1					8	10			7	2	6	3
42	May 1	Queen's Park Rangers	2-3	Cockle, Lockett	4586	4		5	9			10	1		11		7	8					2	6	3
		Apps				35	2	36	42	18	19	31	41	16	5	2	41	41	26	1	4	20	38	31	13
		Goals				2			27		2	8					11	23	5					1	

Two own goals

F.A. Cup

#	Date	Opponent	Res	Scorers	Att	Allen PW	Bradshaw H	Brett FB	Cockle ES	Ferrari FW	George HS	Hoten RV	Hammond L	Jeffs TE	Lockett WC	O'Rourke P	Pease WH	Robinson LStJ	Shaw WH	Smith H	Tomkins EF	Tresadern J	Watson WJ	Williams W	Yorke AE
R1	Nov 28	BARNSLEY	3-1	George 2, Robinson	14000			5	9		11	10	1	3			7	8				4	2	6	
R2	Dec 12	NEWPORT COUNTY	3-1	Robinson 3	11000			5	9		11	10	1	3			7	8				4	2	6	
R3	Jan 9	CRYSTAL PALACE	3-3	Lockett, Robinson 2	14467			5	9		11		1	3	10		7	8				4	2	6	
rep	13	Crystal Palace	1-2	Pease		4		5	9		11		1	2			7	8	10			6			3

		P	W	D	L	F	A	W	D	L	F	A	Pts
1	Reading	42	16	5	0	49	16	7	6	8	28	36	57
2	Plymouth Argyle	42	16	2	3	71	33	8	6	7	36	34	56
3	Millwall	42	14	6	1	52	12	7	5	9	21	27	53
4	Bristol City	42	14	3	4	42	15	7	6	8	30	36	51
5	Brighton & Hove A.	42	12	4	5	47	33	7	5	9	37	40	47
6	Swindon Town	42	16	2	3	48	22	4	4	13	21	42	46
7	Luton Town	42	16	4	1	60	25	2	3	16	20	50	43
8	Bournemouth	42	10	5	6	44	30	7	4	10	31	61	43
9	Aberdare Ath.	42	11	6	4	50	24	6	2	13	24	42	42
10	Gillingham	42	11	4	6	36	19	6	4	11	17	30	42
11	Southend United	42	13	2	6	50	20	6	2	13	28	53	42
12	NORTHAMPTON TOWN	42	13	3	5	47	26	4	4	13	35	54	41
13	Crystal Palace	42	16	1	4	50	21	3	2	16	25	58	41
14	Merthyr Town	42	13	3	5	51	25	1	8	12	18	50	39
15	Watford	42	12	5	4	47	26	3	4	14	26	63	39
16	Norwich City	42	11	5	5	35	26	4	4	13	23	47	39
17	Newport County	42	11	5	5	39	27	3	5	13	25	47	38
18	Brentford	42	12	4	5	44	32	4	2	15	25	62	38
19	Bristol Rovers	42	9	8	4	44	28	6	2	13	22	41	36
20	Exeter City	42	13	2	6	54	25	2	3	16	18	45	35
21	Charlton Athletic	42	9	7	5	32	23	2	6	13	16	45	35
22	Queen's Park Rgs.	42	5	7	9	23	32	1	2	18	14	52	21

1926/27
18th in Division 3(S)

League matches

#		Date	Opponent	Score	Scorers	Att
1	Aug	28	Coventry City	3-0	Robinson, Shaw, one og	16330
2	Sep	1	Plymouth Argyle	0-3		9380
3		4	BRENTFORD	2-3	Cockle, Edwards	10082
4		6	NORWICH CITY	3-0	Cockle, Hoten 2	4491
5		11	Millwall	2-4	Allen, Cockle	14271
6		13	Luton Town	0-2		8856
7		18	BRISTOL ROVERS	3-0	Edwards, Robinson, Shaw	6318
8		20	Norwich City	1-6	Tresadern	5123
9		25	Swindon Town	1-3	Cockle	8298
10	Oct	2	EXETER CITY	2-2	Shaw 2	5616
11		9	Merthyr Town	0-2		2840
12		16	Watford	0-4		8022
13		23	CRYSTAL PALACE	1-1	Shaw	5676
14		30	Queen's Park Rangers	2-4	Cockle, Oxley	10058
15	Nov	6	CHARLTON ATHLETIC	0-1		2147
16		13	Bristol City	3-4	Cockle, Hoten, Robinson	8280
17		20	BOURNEMOUTH	2-2	Hoten, Robinson	4165
18	Dec	4	NEWPORT COUNTY	1-2	Hoten	5508
19		18	GILLINGHAM	2-1	Brett 2	4979
20		25	Brighton & Hove Albion	0-2		12991
21		27	BRIGHTON & HOVE ALB	0-0		12782
22		28	LUTON TOWN	2-1	Hoten, Shaw	8700
23	Jan	1	Newport County	0-1		5006
24		8	Aberdare Athletic	1-6	Robinson	1724
25		15	COVENTRY CITY	2-1	Cockle 2	8386
26		22	Brentford	1-1	Hoten	4775
27	Feb	5	Bristol Rovers	2-5	Groome 2	3972
28		12	SWINDON TOWN	1-0	Cockle	5267
29		19	Exeter City	2-3	Groome, Wells	5483
30		26	MERTHYR TOWN	2-0	Groome, Robinson	5062
31	Mar	5	WATFORD	3-2	Cockle, Groome, Robinson	5829
32		12	Crystal Palace	0-3		11460
33		19	QUEEN'S PARK RANGERS	1-0	Allon	5369
34		26	Charlton Athletic	2-5	Hoten, Shaw	4442
35	Apr	2	BRISTOL CITY	2-0	Groome, Robinson	7191
36		7	MILLWALL	1-4	Brett	3543
37		9	Bournemouth	1-3	Robinson	3579
38		16	PLYMOUTH ARGYLE	2-1	Cockle	4680
39		18	Southend United	0-2		7809
40		19	SOUTHEND UNITED	2-1	Cockle 2	6710
41		30	ABERDARE ATHLETIC	2-1	Shaw, Walden	4608
42	May	7	Gillingham	2-1	Cockle, Wells	4128

Played in one game: GW Cockburn (game 24, at 11), S Seddon (2,7),
AG Shipley (24,9), F Wilson (18,8).

Appearances / Goals (by player)

Player	Apps	Goals
Adey TW	10	
Allen PW	9	1
Allon TG	27	1
Boyd MS	2	
Brett FB	42	3
Buckby LC	4	
Cockle ES	36	15
Edwards EJ	11	2
Fraser WC	10	
Groome JPG	13	6
Gunnell RC	11	
Hammond L	42	
Hoten RV	34	8
Jeffs TE	14	
Jennings W	3	
Jones H	5	
Maloney RJH	25	
Oxley W	3	1
Robinson LStJ	32	9
Shaw WH	31	8
Tomkins EF	3	
Tresadern J	14	
Walden FI	20	1
Watson WJ	29	
Wells TC	14	2
Williams W	3	
Yorke AE	11	

One own goal

Shirt numbers (selected, as worn in each match)

#	Match	Ham	Wel	Bre	Wal	Ade	Wil	Wat	Rob	Coc	Sha	Edw	Boy	Buc	Fra	Hot	Yor
1	Coventry City	1	2	3	4	5	6	7	8	9	10	11					
2	Plymouth Argyle	1	2	3	4	5	6		8	9	10	11					
3	Brentford	1	2	3	4	5	6	7	8	9	10	11					
4	Norwich City	1	2	7		6			8	5		9	4	3	11	10	
5	Millwall	1	2	7		6			8	5		9	4		11	10	3

(Seddon wore 7 in game 2; Wilson wore 8 in game 18; Cockburn wore 11 and Shipley wore 9 in game 24.)

F.A. Cup

	Date	Opponent	Score	Scorers	Att
R1	Nov 27	Boston	1-1	Gunnell	6000
rep	30	BOSTON	2-1	Hoten, Watson	4533
R2	Dec 11	Exeter City	0-1		11314

Division 3(S) final table

		P	W	D	L	F	A	W	D	L	F	A	Pts
1	Bristol City	42	19	1	1	71	24	8	7	6	33	30	62
2	Plymouth Argyle	42	17	4	0	52	14	8	6	7	43	47	60
3	Millwall	42	16	2	3	55	19	7	8	6	34	32	56
4	Brighton & Hove A.	42	15	4	2	61	24	6	7	8	18	26	53
5	Swindon Town	42	16	3	2	64	31	5	6	10	36	54	51
6	Crystal Palace	42	12	6	3	57	33	6	3	12	27	48	45
7	Bournemouth	42	13	2	6	49	24	5	6	10	29	42	44
8	Luton Town	42	12	9	0	48	19	3	5	13	20	47	44
9	Newport County	42	15	4	2	40	20	4	2	15	17	51	44
10	Bristol Rovers	42	12	4	5	46	28	4	5	12	32	52	41
11	Brentford	42	10	9	2	46	20	3	5	13	24	41	40
12	Exeter City	42	14	4	3	46	18	1	6	14	30	55	40
13	Charlton Athletic	42	13	5	3	44	22	3	3	15	16	39	40
14	Queen's Park Rgs.	42	9	8	4	41	27	6	1	14	24	44	39
15	Coventry City	42	11	4	6	44	33	4	3	14	27	53	37
16	Norwich City	42	10	5	6	41	25	2	6	13	18	46	35
17	Merthyr Town	42	11	5	5	42	25	2	4	15	21	55	35
18	NORTHAMPTON TOWN	42	13	4	4	36	23	2	1	18	23	64	35
19	Southend United	42	12	3	6	44	25	2	3	16	20	52	34
20	Gillingham	42	10	5	6	36	26	1	5	15	18	46	32
21	Watford	42	9	6	6	36	27	3	2	16	21	60	32
22	Aberdare Ath.	42	8	2	11	38	48	1	5	15	24	53	25

1927/28   2nd in Division 3(S)

Player columns (left→right): Aitkin JG · Allon TG · Bowen EC · Brett FB · Cave W · Cockle ES · Daley J · Fraser WC · George HS · Hammond L · Hoten RV · Jeffs TE · Loasby H · Maloney RJH · Odell GW · Price E · Russell GH · Shaw WH · Smith TG · Watson WJ · Wells TC · Wilson JR

#	Date	Opponent	Res	Scorers	Att	Ait	All	Bow	Bre	Cav	Coc	Dal	Fra	Geo	Ham	Hot	Jef	Loa	Mal	Ode	Pri	Rus	Sha	Smi	Wat	Wel	Wil
1	Aug 27	MILLWALL	5-2	Aitken, Hoten, Loasby 2, Smith	12188	11	4					7			1	10	3	9	5	6				8	2		
2	29	Brentford	0-3		7220	11	4					7			1	10	3	9	5	6				8	2		
3	Sep 3	Crystal Palace	0-1		13771	11	4					7			1	10	3	9	5	6				8	2		
4	5	BRENTFORD	3-2	Aitken, Loasby, Smith	7220	11	4					7			1	10	3	9	5	6		2		8			
5	10	EXETER CITY	5-0	Daley, Hoten, Loasby, Smith, Wilson	10249		4		2			7			1	10	3	9	5					8		11	6
6	17	Torquay United	5-1	Loasby, Wells 2, one og	4625		4		2			7			1	10	3	9	5					8		11	6
7	24	NORWICH CITY	4-2	Loasby 2, Wells 2	13921		4		2			7			1	10	3	9	5					8		11	6
8	Oct 1	Gillingham	3-1	Loasby 2, Smith	4226		4		2			7			1	10	3	9	5					8		11	6
9	8	Southend United	0-2		8768		4		2			7			1	10	3	9	5					8		11	6
10	15	BRIGHTON & HOVE ALB	1-0	one og	13214	11	4		2			7			1	10	3	9	5	6				8			
11	22	PLYMOUTH ARGYLE	2-1	Hoten, Maloney	9434		4		2			7			1	10	3	9	5	6				8		11	
12	29	Merthyr Town	3-1	Allon, Loasby 2	5000		4		2			7			1	10	3	9	5	6				8		11	
13	Nov 5	WALSALL	10-0	*see below	11340		4	5				7			1	10	3	9		6				8	2	11	
14	12	Bristol Rovers	2-2	Loasby, Smith	7846		4	5				7			1	10	3	9		6				8	2	11	
15	19	CHARLTON ATHLETIC	2-1	Loasby, O'Dell	10210		4	5				7			1	10	3	9		6				8	2	11	
16	Dec 3	QUEEN'S PARK RANGERS	1-0	Loasby	9737		4	5				7			1	10	3	9		6				8	2	11	
17	17	NEWPORT COUNTY	1-2	Maloney	8945		4	3			9	7			1	10			5	6				8	2	11	
18	24	Coventry City	4-2	O'Dell 2, Daley, Smith	9250		4	3				7			1	10			5	9				8	2	11	6
19	26	LUTON TOWN	6-5	Allon, Daley, Hoten, Maloney, Smith 2	10153		4	3				7			1	10			5	9				8	2	11	6
20	31	Millwall	0-3		26334		4	3				7			1	10			5	9				8	2	11	6
21	Jan 7	CRYSTAL PALACE	1-1	O'Dell	9860	11	4					7			1	10			5	9		3		8	2		6
22	21	Exeter City	1-1	Wells	10231		4					7			1		3		5	6	10	9		8	2	11	
23	28	TORQUAY UNITED	4-4	Allon, Price 2, Wells	4832		4							7	1		3		5	6	10	9		8	2	11	
24	Feb 4	Norwich City	4-3	Bowen 3, Wells	6760		4	9				7			1		3		5		10			8	2	11	6
25	11	GILLINGHAM	1-0	Shaw	9538		4	9				7			1		3		5				10	8	2	11	6
26	18	SOUTHEND UNITED	2-1	Allon, Wells	13133		4	9		1			7			10			5	6		3		8	2	11	
27	25	Brighton & Hove Albion	1-2	Wells	12631		4	9	3			7			1	10			5	6				8	2	11	
28	Mar 3	Plymouth Argyle	3-3	Bowen 2, Fraser	13942		4	9	3				7		1	10			5	6				8	2	11	
29	10	MERTHYR TOWN	6-0	Aitken 2, Bowen, Fraser, O'Dell	8549	11	4	9	3				7		1				5	6				8	2	10	
30	17	Walsall	1-1	Fraser	7800		4	9	3				7		1				5	6				8	2	10	
31	19	Luton Town	0-2		8194	11	4	9	3				7		1				5	6				8	2		
32	24	BRISTOL ROVERS	2-0	Bowen, Fraser	9770		4	9	3				7	11	1	10			5	6				8	2		
33	31	Charlton Athletic	2-2	Bowen, Wells	7121		4	9				7			1	10			5	6			3	8	2	11	
34	Apr 7	SWINDON TOWN	3-0	Bowen 2, Hoten	14174		4	9				7			1	10			5	6			3	8	2	11	
35	9	Bournemouth	1-1	Bowen	9099	11	4	9				7			1	10			5	6			3	8	2		
36	10	BOURNEMOUTH	1-1	Aitken	11693	11	4	9				7			1	10			5	6			3	8	2		
37	14	Queen's Park Rangers	4-0	Bowen, Hoten 2, O'Dell	8399		4	9				7			1	11			5	10			3	8	2		6
38	18	Watford	0-2		4221		4	9				7			1	11			5	10			3	8	2		6
39	21	WATFORD	5-0	Allon, Bowen, Hoten 2, Smith	6255		4	9				7			1	10			5	6			3	8	2	11	
40	25	Swindon Town	0-4		5289		4	9				7			1	10			5	6			3	8	2	11	
41	28	Newport County	1-4	Bowen	2753		4	9				7			1	10			5	6			3	8	2	11	
42	May 5	COVENTRY CITY	2-1	Bowen, Daley	7583		4	9				7			1	10			5	6			3	8	2	11	
		Apps				10	41	19	22	1	1	33	7	2	41	34	20	16	38	35	4	13	6	42	33	29	15
		Goals				5	5	15				4	4			10		18	3	6	2		2	12		13	1

Scorers in game 13: Loasby 3, Smith 3, Wells 3, Hoten

Two own goals

F.A. Cup

Rd	Date	Opponent	Res	Scorers	Att	Ait	All	Bow	Bre	Dal	Ham	Hot	Jef	Mal	Ode	Rus	Smi	Wat	Wel
R1	Nov 26	LEYTON	8-0	*See below	12043		4	5		7	1	10	3	9	6		8	2	11
R2	Dec 10	BRIGHTON & HOVE ALB.	1-0	Daley	16092		4	3		7	1	10		9	5/6	6	8	2	11
R3	Jan 14	Sunderland	3-3	Cowen, Daley, Wells	20000		4			7	1	10	3		5	6	8	2	11
rep	19	SUNDERLAND	0-3		21148		4			7	1	10	3	9	5	6	8	2	11

Scorers in R1: Daley, Hoten 2, Loasby 3, Wells, one og

Played in R3: JE Cowen (at 9)

Division 3 (South) Final Table

		P	W	D	L	F	A	W	D	L	F	A	Pts
1	Millwall	42	19	2	0	87	15	11	3	7	40	35	65
2	NORTHAMPTON TOWN	42	17	3	1	67	23	6	6	9	35	41	55
3	Plymouth Argyle	42	17	2	2	60	19	6	5	10	25	35	53
4	Brighton & Hove A.	42	14	4	3	51	24	5	6	10	30	45	48
5	Crystal Palace	42	15	3	3	46	23	3	9	9	33	49	48
6	Swindon Town	42	12	6	3	60	26	7	3	11	30	43	47
7	Southend United	42	14	2	5	48	19	6	4	11	32	45	46
8	Exeter City	42	11	6	4	49	27	6	6	9	21	33	46
9	Newport County	42	12	5	4	52	38	6	4	11	29	46	45
10	Queen's Park Rgs.	42	8	5	8	37	35	9	4	8	35	36	43
11	Charlton Athletic	42	12	5	4	34	27	3	8	10	26	43	43
12	Brentford	42	12	4	5	49	30	4	4	13	27	44	40
13	Luton Town	42	13	5	3	56	27	3	2	16	38	60	39
14	Bournemouth	42	12	6	3	44	24	1	6	14	28	55	38
15	Watford	42	10	5	6	42	34	4	5	12	26	44	38
16	Gillingham	42	10	3	8	33	26	3	8	10	29	55	37
17	Norwich City	42	9	8	4	41	26	1	8	12	25	44	36
18	Walsall	42	9	6	6	52	35	3	3	15	23	66	33
19	Bristol Rovers	42	11	3	7	41	36	3	1	17	26	57	32
20	Coventry City	42	5	8	8	40	36	6	1	14	27	60	31
21	Merthyr Town	42	7	6	8	38	40	2	7	12	15	51	31
22	Torquay United	42	4	10	7	27	36	4	4	13	26	67	30

1928/29   3rd in Division 3(S)

#	Date	Opponent	Res	Scorers	Att	Allon TG	Bowen EC	Brett FB	Cave W	Cowen JE	Eccles J	Hammond L	Harrington JW	Hicks TG	Hoten RV	Lincoln A	Loasby H	Maloney RJH	McIlvenny P	McNaughton WF	Odell GW	Russell GH	Shaw WH	Smith TG	Watson WJ	Wells TC	Weston JM	Wilson JR
1	Aug 25	CHARLTON ATHLETIC	4-1	Bowen, O'Dell, Smith, one og	15135	4	9	5				1	7	3		10					6			8	2	11		
2	30	LUTON TOWN	2-2	Bowen 2	12220	4	9	5				1	7	3		10					6			8	2	11		
3	Sep 1	Norwich City	1-1	Hoten	11120		9	5				1	7	3	10						4	2		8		11		6
4	3	Luton Town	0-4		10931		9	5			7	1		3						10	6	2		8		11		4
5	8	BRIGHTON & HOVE ALB	1-1	Bowen	11214		7	3		9		1			10			5			6			8	2	11		4
6	15	Exeter City	0-2		6282		9	3				1	7		10			5			6			8	2	11		4
7	17	PLYMOUTH ARGYLE	3-0	Bowen 2, O'Dell	7110	4	9	3			7	1			11			5			10	2		8				6
8	22	SOUTHEND UNITED	2-3	Hoten 2	10711	4	9	2				1			11			5			10	3		8			7	6
9	29	Merthyr Town	2-2		3983	4	9	3				1	7		10			5			8	2				11		6
10	Oct 6	BOURNEMOUTH	2-0	Bowen 2	8519	4	9	3				1	7		10			5			6			8	2	11		
11	13	Brentford	2-2	Allon, Bowen	9260	4	9	3				1	7		10			5			6			8	2	11		
12	20	Newport County	3-0	Bowen, McIlvenny 2	4405	4	9	3				1			10			5	7		6			8	2	11		
13	27	CRYSTAL PALACE	8-1	Bowen, Hoten 5, Smith, Wells	7299	4	9	3				1			10			5	7		6			8	2	11		
14	Nov 3	Swindon Town	1-0	Bowen	7099	4	9	3				1			10			5	7		6			8	2	11		
15	10	TORQUAY UNITED	6-1	Bowen Hoten 4, Smith	8384	4	9	3				1			10			5	7		6			8	2	11		
16	17	Gillingham	1-2	Smith	5312	4	9	3				1			10			5	7		6			8	2	11		
17	Dec 1	Fulham	1-2	Bowen	16952	4	9	3				1			10			5	7		6			8	2	11		
18	8	QUEEN'S PARK RANGERS	4-2	Bowen 2, Hoten, Wells	10124	4	9	3			7	1			10			5			6			8	2	11		
19	15	Bristol Rovers	2-1	Hoten, one og	4970	4	9	3			7	1			10			5			6	2		8			11	
20	22	WATFORD	3-0	Bowen 2, Weston	9438	4	9	3			7	1			10			5			6	2		8			11	
21	25	Walsall	3-4	Bowen, Hoten 2	8419	4	9	3			7	1			10			5			6	2		8			11	
22	26	WALSALL	4-2	Bowen 2, Hoten, Smith	15987	4	9	3			7	1			10			5			6			8	2		11	
23	29	Charlton Athletic	1-3	Bowen	12073		9	3			7	1			10			5			6			8	2		11	4
24	Jan 5	NORWICH CITY	2-0	Bowen, Hoten	7057		9	3				1			10			5	7		4		6	8	2		11	
25	19	Brighton & Hove Albion	3-0	Hoten, Loasby, Weston	7197	4		3			7	1			10		9	5		8		2	6				11	
26	26	EXETER CITY	4-0	Hoten, Loasby 2, Weston	9477	4		3				1			10		9	5	7	8		2	6				11	
27	Feb 2	Southend United	2-2	Eccles, Loasby	5944			3			7	1			10		9	5				2	6	8			11	4
28	9	MERTHYR TOWN	4-1	Bowen, Hoten 2, Weston	6372	4	9	3			7	1			10			5			6			8	2		11	
29	23	BRENTFORD	1-1	Maloney	8555	4	9	3			7	1			10			5			6			8	2		11	
30	Mar 2	NEWPORT COUNTY	7-0	Bowen 2, Hoten 3, Wells 2	8864	4	9				7	1			10			5			6	3		8	2	11		
31	9	Crystal Palace	0-1		25072	4	9				7	1		3	10			5			6	2		8		11		
32	16	SWINDON TOWN	1-1	Bowen	10070	4	9	3			7	1			10			5			6	2		8		11		
33	20	Bournemouth	0-2		3196	4	9	3				1			10			5			6		7	8	2	11		
34	23	Torquay United	1-0	Loasby	3655	4	9	3	1						10		7	5			6	2		8		11		
35	30	GILLINGHAM	1-0	Hoten	10058	4	9	3	1		7				10			5			6			8	2	11		
36	Apr 1	Coventry City	2-0	Bowen, Loasby	20227	4	9	3	1						10		7	5			6			8	2	11		
37	2	COVENTRY CITY	3-3	Bowen 2, Hoten	17152	4	9	3	1						10		7	5			6			8	2	11		
38	6	Plymouth Argyle	1-1	Bowen	11376	4	9	3	1						10		7	5			6			8	2	11		
39	13	FULHAM	3-3	Hoten, Wells 2	9436	4	9	3	1						10		7	5			6			8	2	11		
40	20	Queen's Park Rangers	1-4	Wells	21916	4	9	3				1			10			5			6			8	2	11		7
41	27	BRISTOL ROVERS	3-1	Bowen, Wells 2	9566	4	9	3				1			10		7	5			6			8	2	11		
42	May 4	Watford	1-1	Hoten	10926	4	9					1			10		7	5			6	3		8	2	11		
		Apps				35	39	39	6	1	15	36	8	5	38	2	10	38	8	2	39	15	6	40	29	28	14	9
		Goals				1	34				1				29		6	1	2		2			5		9	4	

Two own goals

F.A. Cup

	Date	Opponent	Res	Scorers	Att	Allon TG	Bowen EC	Brett FB	Cave W	Cowen JE	Eccles J	Hammond L	Harrington JW	Hicks TG	Hoten RV	Lincoln A	Loasby H	Maloney RJH	McIlvenny P	McNaughton WF	Odell GW	Russell GH	Shaw WH	Smith TG	Watson WJ	Wells TC	Weston JM	Wilson JR
R3	Jan 12	Millwall	1-1	Watson	28784		9	3			7	1			10			5			4		6	8	2	11		
rep	17	MILLWALL	2-2	Hoten 2	18261			3			7	1			10			5		9	6			8	2	11		4
rep2	21	Millwall	0-2		32391		9	3			7	1			10			5			4		6	8	2	11		

Replay a.e.t. Second replay at Highbury

		P	W	D	L	F	A	W	D	L	F	A	Pts
1	Charlton Athletic	42	14	5	2	51	22	9	3	9	35	38	54
2	Crystal Palace	42	14	2	5	40	25	9	6	6	41	42	54
3	NORTHAMPTON TOWN	42	14	6	1	68	23	6	6	9	28	34	52
4	Plymouth Argyle	42	14	6	1	51	13	6	6	9	32	38	52
5	Fulham	42	14	3	4	60	31	7	7	7	41	40	52
6	Queen's Park Rgs.	42	13	7	1	50	22	6	7	8	32	39	52
7	Luton Town	42	16	3	2	64	28	3	8	10	25	45	49
8	Watford	42	15	3	3	55	31	4	7	10	24	43	48
9	Bournemouth	42	14	4	3	54	31	5	5	11	30	46	47
10	Swindon Town	42	12	5	4	48	27	3	8	10	27	45	43
11	Coventry City	42	9	6	6	35	23	5	8	8	27	34	42
12	Southend United	42	10	7	4	44	27	5	4	12	36	48	41
13	Brentford	42	11	4	6	34	21	3	6	12	22	39	38
14	Walsall	42	11	7	3	47	25	2	5	14	26	54	38
15	Brighton & Hove A.	42	14	2	5	39	28	2	4	15	19	48	38
16	Newport County	42	8	6	7	37	28	5	3	13	32	58	35
17	Norwich City	42	12	3	6	49	29	2	3	16	20	52	34
18	Torquay United	42	10	3	8	46	36	4	3	14	20	48	34
19	Bristol Rovers	42	9	6	6	39	28	4	1	16	21	51	33
20	Merthyr Town	42	11	6	4	42	28	0	2	19	13	75	30
21	Exeter City	42	7	6	8	49	40	2	5	14	18	48	29
22	Gillingham	42	7	8	6	22	24	3	1	17	21	59	29

1929/30   4th in Division 3(S)

#	Date		Opponent	Score	Scorers	Att.	Hammond L	Anthony C	Brett FB	Allon TG	Maloney RJH	Odell GW	Sissons AE	Dawes AG	Bowen EC	Hoten RV	Weston JM	Smith TG	Berridge R	Dawes FW	Loasby H	McNaughton WF	Riches LE	Russell GH	Shaw WH	Wells TC	Young JW
1	Aug	31	BOURNEMOUTH	2-0	Bowen, Smith	14397	1	2	3	4	5	6			9	10		8				7				11	
2	Sep	2	Merthyr Town	0-1		6817	1	2	3	4	5	6			9	10		8				7				11	
3		7	Walsall	2-1	Bowen 2	10025	1	2	3	4	5	6	7		9	10		8								11	
4		9	MERTHYR TOWN	2-0	Sissons, Bowen	8215	1	2	3	4	5	6	7		9	10		8								11	
5		14	QUEEN'S PARK RANGERS	2-1	Hoten, Smith	12876	1	2	3	4	5			10	9	6		8				7				11	
6		16	Southend United	2-1	Bowen, McNaughton	8145	1	2	3	4	5			10	9	6		8				7				11	
7		21	Fulham	0-1		20406	1	2	3	4	5			10	9	6		8				7				11	
8		28	NORWICH CITY	4-0	O'Dell, Hoten 2, Wells	12302	1	2	3	4	5	6			9	10		8				7				11	
9	Oct	5	Crystal Palace	3-1	Bowen 2, Smith	17562	1	2	3	4	5	6			9	10		8				7				11	
10		12	GILLINGHAM	3-1	Bowen, Hoten 2	10663	1	2	3	4	5	6			9	10		8				7				11	
11		19	PLYMOUTH ARGYLE	1-1	Bowen	21102	1	2	3	4	5			10	9	6		8				7				11	
12		26	Swindon Town	0-2		7695	1		3	4	5		7		9	10		8						2	6	11	
13	Nov	2	BRIGHTON & HOVE ALB	1-3	Wells	4704	1		3	4	5		7		9	10		8						2	6	11	
14		9	Bristol Rovers	3-2	Wells 3	7483	1	2	3	4	5	6	7		9	10		8								11	
15		16	BRENTFORD	1-1	Sissons	6165	1	2	3	4	5	6	7		9	10		8								11	
16		23	Clapton Orient	0-0		8497	1		3	4	5	6	7		9	10		8						2		11	
17	Dec	7	Watford	2-1	Bowen, Hoten	6989	1		3	4	5	6	7		9	10		8						2		11	
18		21	Torquay United	1-0	Wells	3730	1		3	4	5	6	7		9	10		8						2		11	
19		25	Luton Town	0-1		9473	1		3	4	5	6	7		9	10		8						2		11	
20		26	LUTON TOWN	4-1	Hoten 3, Smith	19251	1		3	4	5	6			9	10		8					7	2		11	
21		31	NEWPORT COUNTY	2-0	Bowen 2	5797	1		3	4	5	6			9	10		8					7	2		11	
22	Jan	4	WALSALL	1-0	Hoten	9433	1		3	4	5	6			9	10	7	8						2		11	
23		18	Queen's Park Rangers	2-0	A Dawes, Wells	11696	1		3	4	5	6		8	9	10	7							2		11	
24	Feb	1	Norwich City	3-4	A Dawes, Hoten, Wells	11681	1		3	4	5	6	7	8	9	10								2		11	
25		8	CRYSTAL PALACE	2-0	A Dawes, Bowen	8480	1		3	4	5	6		8	9	10	7							2		11	
26		15	Gillingham	2-5	Bowen, Hoten	4665	1		3	4	5	6	7	8	9	10								2		11	
27		22	Plymouth Argyle	0-1		15376	1		3	4	5		7	8	9	6								2		11	
28		26	Bournemouth	1-3	Loadsby	3889	1		3	4	5		7	10		6	11	8			9			2			
29	Mar	1	SWINDON TOWN	3-3	Sissons, Young 2	9254	1	2	3	4	5		7	10		6		8								11	9
30		8	Brighton & Hove Albion	1-2	McNaughton	10622	1		3		5	6			9	10		4				7		2		11	8
31		13	FULHAM	3-1	Bowen, Weston, Smith	4727	1		3		5	6			9	10	7	8						2		11	
32		15	BRISTOL ROVERS	6-1	Bowen 3, Hoten, Weston 2	5402	1		3		5	6			9	10	7	8						2		11	
33		22	Brentford	0-2		16460	1		3		5	6			9	10	7	8						2		11	
34		29	CLAPTON ORIENT	3-0	Bowen 2, Wells	6763	1		3		5	6			9	10	7	8						2		11	
35	Apr	5	Coventry City	2-2	Hoten 2	13085	1		3		5	6			9	10	7	8						2		11	
36		7	COVENTRY CITY	2-2	Bowen 2	4649	1		3		5	6			9	10	7	8						2		11	
37		12	WATFORD	2-0	A Dawes, Bowen	6134	1		3	4	5	6		8	9	10	7							2		11	
38		19	Newport County	1-2	Weston	3282	1		3	4	5	6		8	9	10	7							2		11	
39		21	Exeter City	4-6	Sissons, Weston 3	8258	1	2	3	4	5	6	7	8	9	10	11										
40		22	EXETER CITY	2-2	Bowen, Hoten	7621	1	2	3	4	5	6	7		9	10	11	8									
41		26	TORQUAY UNITED	2-2	Hoten, Weston	4100	1	2		4	5	6	7	8	9	10	11			3							
42	May	3	SOUTHEND UNITED	5-1	A Dawes, Bowen 2, Hoten, Weston	3454	1		3	4	5		7	8	9	10	11			2					6		
			Apps				42	17	42	33	39	36	19	26	40	39	16	30	1	2	1	9	5	23	3	37	2
			Goals									1	4	5	26	18	9	5			1	2				9	2

F.A. Cup

#	Date		Opponent	Score	Scorers	Att.	Hammond L	Anthony C	Brett FB	Allon TG	Maloney RJH	Odell GW	Sissons AE	Dawes AG	Bowen EC	Hoten RV	Weston JM	Smith TG	Berridge R	Dawes FW	Loasby H	McNaughton WF	Riches LE	Russell GH	Shaw WH	Wells TC	Young JW
R1	Nov	30	Aldershot	1-0	Hoten	8000	1		3	4	5	6	7			10		8				9		2		11	
R2	Dec	14	MARGATE	6-0	Sissons, Bowen 2, Hoten 3	11012	1		3	4	5	6	7		9	10		8						2		11	
R3	Jan	11	Blackburn Rovers	1-4	Wells	27000	1		3		5	6		8	9	10	7							2		11	

Played in R3: JR Wilson (at 4)

	Club	P	W	D	L	F	A	W	D	L	F	A	Pts
1	Plymouth Argyle	42	18	3	0	63	12	12	5	4	35	26	68
2	Brentford	42	21	0	0	66	12	7	5	9	28	32	61
3	Queen's Park Rgs.	42	13	5	3	46	26	8	4	9	34	42	51
4	NORTHAMPTON TOWN	42	14	6	1	53	20	7	2	12	29	38	50
5	Brighton & Hove A.	42	16	2	3	54	20	5	6	10	33	43	50
6	Coventry City	42	14	3	4	54	25	5	6	10	34	48	47
7	Fulham	42	12	6	3	54	33	6	5	10	33	50	47
8	Norwich City	42	14	4	3	55	28	4	6	11	33	49	46
9	Crystal Palace	42	14	5	2	56	26	3	7	11	25	48	46
10	Bournemouth	42	11	6	4	47	24	4	7	10	25	37	43
11	Southend United	42	11	6	4	41	19	4	7	10	28	40	43
12	Clapton Orient	42	10	8	3	38	21	4	5	12	17	41	41
13	Luton Town	42	13	4	4	42	25	1	8	12	22	53	40
14	Swindon Town	42	10	7	4	42	25	3	5	13	31	58	38
15	Watford	42	10	4	7	37	30	5	4	12	23	43	38
16	Exeter City	42	10	6	5	45	29	2	5	14	22	44	35
17	Walsall	42	10	4	7	45	24	3	4	14	26	54	34
18	Newport County	42	9	9	3	48	29	3	1	17	26	56	34
19	Torquay United	42	9	6	6	50	38	1	5	15	14	56	31
20	Bristol Rovers	42	11	3	7	45	31	0	5	16	22	62	30
21	Gillingham	42	9	5	7	38	28	2	3	16	13	52	30
22	Merthyr Town	42	5	6	10	39	49	1	3	17	21	86	21

1930/31 6th in Division 3(S)

#	Date	Opponent	Score	Scorers	Att	Allon TG	Anthony C	Armitage JH	Bowen EC	Boyle TW	Cave W	Crawford GW	Davies FP	Dawes AG	Eyre FMB	Hammond L	Inglis WW	McLachlan ER	Maloney RJH	Muir Malcolm	Odell GW	Riches LE	Russell GH	Shaw WH	Taylor JW	Wells TC	Weston JM	Whyte C	Wonnacott CB
1	Aug 30	Bristol Rovers	4-1	Bowen 2, Wells, Boyle	7649	4	3		9	8				10		1		7	5	2	6					11			
2	Sep 3	Brentford	4-0	Bowen 3, Dawes	11356	4	3		9	8		5	6	10		1	2	7								11			
3	6	NEWPORT COUNTY	1-0	Dawes	13239	4	3		9	8			6	10		1	2	7	5							11			
4	8	CRYSTAL PALACE	0-0		10040	4	3		9	8			6	10		1	2	7	5							11			
5	13	Gillingham	2-0	Bowen 2	4821		3		9	8			6	10		1	2	7	5			4				11			
6	17	Crystal Palace	0-0		11253		3		9				6	10		1	2	8	5			4				11		7	
7	20	EXETER CITY	1-0	Bowen	7346		3		9				6	10		1	2	7	5			4	8			11			
8	27	Brighton & Hove Albion	1-1	Wells	10105		3		9	8			6	10		1	2	7	5			4				11			
9	Oct 4	TORQUAY UNITED	0-3		11852		3		9				8	10		1	2	7	5		6	4				11			
10	11	Coventry City	1-0	Dawes	19569		3		9				6	8		1	2		5			4				11		7	10
11	18	WALSALL	3-0	Dawes, Bowen 2	9341		3		9				6	8		1	2		5			4				11		7	10
12	25	Queen's Park Rangers	2-0	Dawes, Whyte	8362		3		9	8			6	10		1	2		5			4				11		7	
13	Nov 1	NORWICH CITY	3-1	Dawes 2, Bowen	9393		3		9	8			6	10		1	2		5			4				11		7	
14	8	Thames	1-2	McLaughlin	2168		3		9				6	10		1	2	7	5			4				11			
15	15	CLAPTON ORIENT	0-0		6820	4	3		9				10	8		1	2	7	5		6					11			
16	22	Notts County	2-2	Dawes 2	21329	4	3		9	8			6	10		1			5					2		11	7		
17	Dec 6	Bournemouth	3-1	Wells 2, Bowen	4850	4	3		9	8			6	10		1	2		5							11	7		
18	13	SWINDON TOWN	3-0	Bowen 3	7625	4	3		9	8			6	10		1	2		5			7				11			
19	20	Fulham	2-4	Bowen 2	9646	4	3		9	8				10		1	2		5			7				11	6		
20	25	Southend United	1-2	Boyle	10068	4		5	9	8			6	10		1	3					7	2			11			
21	26	SOUTHEND UNITED	4-0	Dawes 3, Riches	9976	4		5	9	8			6	10		1	2					7				11			
22	27	BRISTOL ROVERS	1-1		10863	4	3	5	9	8			6	10		1				2		7				11			
23	Jan 3	Newport County	2-5	Dawes, Bowen	2977	4	3	5	9	8			6	10		1	2					7				11			
24	15	WATFORD	2-3	Riches, Wells	3952	4	3		9	8			6	10		1			5	2		7				11			
25	17	GILLINGHAM	0-1		6452	4	3		9	8			6	10		1	2		5			7				11			
26	28	Exeter City	3-3	Wonnacott, Weston, Bowen	3595		3		9	8	1		6	4			2		5			7					11		10
27	31	BRIGHTON & HOVE ALB	2-1	Bowen, Weston	5868		3		9	8	1		6	4	10		2		5			7					11		
28	Feb 7	Torquay United	0-3		4270	4	3		9	8			6	10		1	2		5			7						11	
29	14	COVENTRY CITY	0-3		7033	4	3		9				10	8		1	2		5		6	7				11			
30	21	Walsall	6-2	Wells 2, Bowen 2, Dawes 2	6345	4	3		9	8				10		1	2		5		6	7				11			
31	28	QUEEN'S PARK RANGERS	6-0	Boyle 2, Riches 2, Wells, Bowen	5198	4	3		9	8				10		1	2		5		6	7				11			
32	Mar 7	Norwich City	1-1	Dawes	6033	4	3		9	8				10		1	2		5			7				11			
33	14	THAMES	4-1	Dawes 2, O'Dell, Boyle	5587	4	3		9	8				10		1	2		5			7				11			
34	21	Clapton Orient	2-2	Boyle, Bowen	5542	4	3		9	8		5	6	10		1	2					7				11			
35	28	NOTTS COUNTY	0-0		14284	4	3		9	8			6	10		1	2		5			7				11			
36	Apr 4	Watford	2-1	Bowen, Wells	8157	4	3		9	8			6	10		1	2		5			7				11			
37	6	Luton Town	0-4		12292	4	3		9	8			6	10		1	2		5			7				11			
38	7	LUTON TOWN	0-0		8614	4	3		9	8			6			1	2		5			7				11			10
39	11	BOURNEMOUTH	2-2	Bowen, Wells	4830	4	3		9	8			6			1	2		5			7				11			10
40	18	Swindon Town	1-5	Wonnacott	3330	4	3		9	8			6			1	2		5			7				11			10
41	25	FULHAM	4-2	Dawes 2, Boyle, Wonnacott	2753	4	3			8				10		1	2		5							11		7	9
42	May 2	BRENTFORD	1-2	Dawes	3698	4	3				1		10	9			2		5		6				8	11	7		
		Apps				30	41	4	40	34	3	2	33	42	1	39	38	11	36	3	18	24	2	2	1	39	7	5	7
		Goals							27	7				21				1			1	4				10	2	1	3

F.A. Cup

#	Date	Opponent	Score	Scorers	Att	Allon TG	Anthony C	Armitage JH	Bowen EC	Boyle TW	Cave W	Crawford GW	Davies FP	Dawes AG	Eyre FMB	Hammond L	Inglis WW	McLachlan ER	Maloney RJH	Muir Malcolm	Odell GW	Riches LE	Russell GH	Shaw WH	Taylor JW	Wells TC	Weston JM	Whyte C	Wonnacott CB
R1	Nov 29	COVENTRY CITY	1-2	Bowen	8807	4	3		9	8			6	10		1			5					2		11	7		

		P	W	D	L	F	A	W	D	L	F	A	Pts
1	Notts County	42	16	4	1	58	13	8	7	6	39	33	59
2	Crystal Palace	42	17	2	2	71	20	5	5	11	36	51	51
3	Brentford	42	14	3	4	62	30	8	3	10	28	34	50
4	Brighton & Hove A.	42	13	5	3	45	20	4	10	7	23	33	49
5	Southend United	42	16	0	5	53	26	5	5	10	23	34	49
6	NORTHAMPTON TOWN	42	10	6	5	37	20	8	6	7	40	39	48
7	Luton Town	42	15	3	3	61	17	4	5	12	15	34	46
8	Queen's Park Rgs.	42	15	0	6	57	23	5	3	13	25	52	43
9	Fulham	42	15	3	3	49	21	3	4	14	28	54	43
10	Bournemouth	42	11	7	3	39	22	4	6	11	33	51	43
11	Torquay United	42	13	5	3	56	26	4	4	13	24	58	43
12	Swindon Town	42	15	5	1	68	29	3	1	17	21	65	42
13	Exeter City	42	12	6	3	55	35	5	2	14	29	55	42
14	Coventry City	42	11	4	6	55	28	5	5	11	20	37	41
15	Bristol Rovers	42	12	3	6	49	36	4	5	12	26	56	40
16	Gillingham	42	10	6	5	40	29	4	4	13	21	47	38
17	Walsall	42	9	5	7	44	38	5	4	12	34	57	37
18	Watford	42	9	4	8	41	29	5	3	13	31	46	35
19	Clapton Orient	42	12	3	6	47	33	2	4	15	16	58	35
20	Thames	42	12	5	4	34	20	1	3	17	20	73	34
21	Newport County	42	10	5	6	45	31	1	1	19	24	80	28
22	Norwich City	42	10	7	4	37	20	0	1	20	10	56	28

1931/32 14th in Division 3(S)

#	Date	Opponent	Score	Scorers	Att	Allon TG	Anthony C	Bowen EC	Boyle TW	Cave W	Davies FP	Dawes AG	Dowsey J	Hammond L	Inglis WW	Lovatt HA	Maloney RJH	Mortimer R	Oakley JE	Odell GW	Park O	Radford B	Riches LE	Russell C	Scott J	Wells TC	Weston JM	Wonnacott CB	Dawes FW
1	Aug 29	CARDIFF CITY	1-0	Wells	13448	4	3	9	8		6	10		1	2					5					7	11			
2	31	Luton Town	0-1		11235	4	3	9	8		6	10		1	2					5					7	11			
3	Sep 5	Norwich City	0-0		12455	4	3	9			6	8		1	2					5		10			7	11			
4	7	EXETER CITY	2-1	Bowen, Dawes	7037	4		9			6	8		1	2					6		10			7		11		3
5	12	Reading	2-3	Dawes 2	6486	4	3	9			5	8		1	2					6		10			7		11		3
6	16	Exeter City	0-0		5024	4	3				6	8		1	2				9	5					7		11	10	
7	19	SOUTHEND UNITED	1-2	Wonnacott	8779	4					6	8		1	2				9	5					7		11	10	3
8	26	Fulham	3-1	Bowen, Wells, Dawes	19742	4	3	9	8		6	10		1	2					5					7	11			
9	28	LUTON TOWN	1-2	Bowen	6503	4	3	9	8		6	10		1	2					5					7	11			
10	Oct 3	THAMES	0-4		7160	4	3	9	8		6	10		1					2	5					7	11			
11	10	Brentford	0-2		12694	4			8			10		1	2				9	6	5				7	11			3
12	17	BRIGHTON & HOVE ALB	0-1		5714	4			8			9		1	2					6	5	10			7	11			3
13	24	Mansfield Town	0-2		7015	4	2		8			10		1					9	6	5				7		11		3
14	31	WATFORD	1-1	Bowen	5927		2	9			6	8		1						4	5	10			7		11		3
15	Nov 7	Crystal Palace	0-4		16119		2					6		1					9		5	10	4		7		11	8	3
16	14	BOURNEMOUTH	1-1	Bowen	6161		2	9			6	8	4	1						5		10			7		11		3
17	21	Queen's Park Rangers	2-3	Dawes, Lovatt	12117	4		9			6	11	10	1		8					2	5			7				3
18	Dec 5	Torquay United	1-4	Dawes	2547	4	2	9			6	10	5	1									8		7	11			3
19	19	Swindon Town	0-3		3919			9			6	10	4	1	2	8	5								7	11			3
20	25	Gillingham	2-3	Bowen, Mortimer	6823			9			6		4	1	2	8	5	7								11			3
21	26	GILLINGHAM	1-0	Lovatt	12491			10			6		4	1	2	9	5	7					8			11			3
22	28	BRISTOL ROVERS	6-0	Bowen 2, Lovatt 2, Wells 2	6087			9			6		4	1	2	8				2		5			7	11			3
23	Jan 2	Cardiff City	0-5		3917			9			6		4	1	2	8	5								7	11		10	3
24	16	NORWICH CITY	2-2	Bowen 2	4905		3	9	8			10	4	1		5		2	6				7			11			
25	28	READING	2-4	Lovatt, Bowen	2672			9	8			11	6	1	2	10	5	7			4								3
26	30	Southend United	1-0	Bowen	6465	4		9	8			10	6	1	2	7				5						11			
27	Feb 6	FULHAM	0-1		6239	4		9	8			10	6	1	2	7				5						11			
28	13	Thames	2-0	Boyle, Dawes	1203	4		9	8			10	6	1	2					5					7	11			
29	20	BRENTFORD	3-0	Boyle, Lovatt, Davies	6533				8		6	10	4	1	2	9		7		5						11			3
30	27	Brighton & Hove Albion	0-0		7966		2		8		6	10	4	1		9		7		5						11			3
31	Mar 5	MANSFIELD TOWN	3-0	Boyle 2, England (og)	5777		2		8		6	10	4	1		9		7		5						11			3
32	12	Watford	2-1	Wells, Mortimer	7600		2		8		6	10	4	1		9		7		5						11			3
33	19	CRYSTAL PALACE	5-0	Mortimer 2, Boyle, Wells, Lovatt	6685		2		8		6	10	4	1		9		7		5						11			3
34	26	Bournemouth	1-1	Dawes	3272		2	9	8		6	10	4	1				7		5						11			3
35	28	Coventry City	1-4	Dawes	17062		2	9	8		6	10	4	1				7		5						11			3
36	29	COVENTRY CITY	3-2	Wells, Dawes, Mortimer	7854	4			8	1		10	6		2			7		5				9		11			3
37	Apr 2	QUEEN'S PARK RANGERS	6-1	Boyle, Russell 2, Wells, Mortimer 2	6444				8	1	6	10	4		2			7		5				9		11			3
38	9	Bristol Rovers	2-3	Dowsey 2	3614		2		8		6	10	4	1				7		5				9		11			3
39	16	TORQUAY UNITED	2-0	Dawes, Russell	2882		2		8		6	10	4	1				7		5				9		11			3
40	21	CLAPTON ORIENT	4-3	Russell, Dawes, Wells, Mortimer	2883				8		6	10	4	1	2		5	7						9		11			3
41	23	Clapton Orient	2-3	Mortimer, Russell	4453				8		6	10	4	1	2			7		5		11		9					3
42	30	SWINDON TOWN	4-1	Dawes, Russell 3	5058		2		8		6	10	4	1				7		5				9		11			3

	Allon TG	Anthony C	Bowen EC	Boyle TW	Cave W	Davies FP	Dawes AG	Dowsey J	Hammond L	Inglis WW	Lovatt HA	Maloney RJH	Mortimer R	Oakley JE	Odell GW	Park O	Radford B	Riches LE	Russell C	Scott J	Wells TC	Weston JM	Wonnacott CB	Dawes FW
Apps	19	23	24	27	2	32	38	27	40	24	14	7	22	4	19	21	8	4	7	22	31	8	6	33
Goals			12	6		1	13	2			7		9						8		9		1	

One own goal

F.A. Cup

Rd	Date	Opponent	Score	Scorers	Att	Allon TG	Anthony C	Bowen EC	Boyle TW	Cave W	Davies FP	Dawes AG	Dowsey J	Hammond L	Inglis WW	Lovatt HA	Maloney RJH	Mortimer R	Oakley JE	Odell GW	Park O	Radford B	Riches LE	Russell C	Scott J	Wells TC	Weston JM	Wonnacott CB	Dawes FW
R1	Nov 28	METROPOLITAN POLICE	9-0	*See below	6000			9			6	10	4	1	2					5			8		7	11			3
R2	Dec 12	SOUTHEND UNITED	3-0	Bowen, Dawes, Lovatt	12627		3	9			6	10	4	1	2	8	5								7	11			
R3	Jan 9	Darlington	1-1	Lovatt	8792			9			6	10	4	1	2	8				5					7	11			3
rep	14	DARLINGTON	2-0	Dawes, Lovatt				9			6	10	5	1	2	8		7			4					11			3
R4	23	Bradford Park Ave.	2-4	Lovatt, Wells	20487		3	9			6	10	4	1	2	8				5		7				11			

Scorers in R1: Bowen 2, Dawes 3, Riches, Wells 2, 1 og

		P	W	D	L	F	A	W	D	L	F	A	Pts
1	Fulham	42	15	3	3	72	27	9	6	6	39	35	57
2	Reading	42	19	1	1	65	21	4	8	9	32	46	55
3	Southend United	42	12	5	4	41	18	9	6	6	36	35	53
4	Crystal Palace	42	14	7	0	48	12	6	4	11	26	51	51
5	Brentford	42	11	6	4	40	22	8	4	9	28	30	48
6	Luton Town	42	16	1	4	62	25	4	6	11	33	45	47
7	Exeter City	42	16	3	2	53	16	4	4	13	24	46	47
8	Brighton & Hove A.	42	12	4	5	42	21	5	8	8	31	37	46
9	Cardiff City	42	14	2	5	62	29	5	6	10	25	44	46
10	Norwich City	42	12	7	2	51	22	5	5	11	25	45	46
11	Watford	42	14	4	3	49	27	5	4	12	32	52	46
12	Coventry City	42	17	2	2	74	28	1	6	14	34	69	44
13	Queen's Park Rgs.	42	11	6	4	50	30	4	6	11	29	43	42
14	NORTHAMPTON TOWN	42	12	3	6	48	26	4	4	13	21	43	39
15	Bournemouth	42	8	8	5	42	32	5	4	12	28	46	38
16	Clapton Orient	42	7	8	6	41	35	5	3	13	36	55	35
17	Swindon Town	42	12	2	7	47	31	2	4	15	23	53	34
18	Bristol Rovers	42	11	6	4	46	30	2	2	17	19	62	34
19	Torquay United	42	9	6	6	49	39	3	3	15	23	67	33
20	Mansfield Town	42	11	5	5	54	45	0	5	16	21	63	32
21	Gillingham	42	8	6	7	26	26	2	2	17	14	56	28
22	Thames	42	6	7	8	35	35	1	2	18	18	74	23

1932/33   8th in Division 3(S)

No	Date		Match	Score	Scorers	Att	Allan CE	Boyle TW	Cave W	Conway T	Davies FP	Dawes AG	Dawes FW	Dowsey J	Fairhurst WS	Forbes FJ	Hammond L	Henson GH	Kavanagh PJ	McFarlane J	McGuire JP	Mortimer R	Oakley JE	Park O	Riches LE	Strang R	Wallbank J	Wells TC
1	Aug	27	Luton Town	1-2	A Dawes	11414		8		4	6	9	3			10	1					7	2	5				11
2		29	EXETER CITY	5-3	Boyle, A Dawes 2, Mortimer 2	7330		8			6	9	3	4		10	1					7	2	5				11
3	Sep	3	NEWPORT COUNTY	8-0	Boyle 2, A Dawes 4, F Dawes, Mortimer	8920		8			6	9	3	4		10	1					7	2	5				11
4		7	Exeter City	1-3	Mortimer	6180		8			6	9	3	4		10	1					7	2	5				11
5		10	Bournemouth	1-1	Mortimer	6623		8			6	9	3	4	2	10	1					7		5				11
6		17	SWINDON TOWN	6-0	Boyle, A Dawes 4, Forbes	7955		8			6	9	3	4	2	10	1					7		5				11
7		22	BRIGHTON & HOVE ALB	0-0		3784		8			6	9	3	4	2	10	1					7		5				11
8		24	Clapton Orient	2-2	A Dawes, Mortimer	8981		8			6	9	3	4	2	10	1					7		5				11
9	Oct	8	BRISTOL CITY	2-1	A Dawes, Forbes	9033		8			6	9	3	4	2	10	1					7		5				11
10		15	Coventry City	1-3	Boyle	14552		8			6	9	3	4	2	10	1					7		5				11
11		22	Bristol Rovers	3-4	A Dawes 2, Mortimer	8461		8			6	9	3	4	2	10	1					7		5				11
12		29	ALDERSHOT	5-2	Boyle, A Dawes 2, Dowsey, Mortimer	6673		8			6	9	3	4	2	10	1					7		5				11
13	Nov	5	Queen's Park Rangers	1-1	Wells	8895		8			6	9	3	4	2	10	1					7		5				11
14		12	SOUTHEND UNITED	0-0		6474		8			6	9	3	4	2	10	1					7		5				11
15		19	Crystal Palace	0-2		6483					6		3	4	2	10	1	9				7		5	8			11
16	Dec	3	Watford	0-4		7571		8			6	9	3	4	2	10	1					7		5				11
17		17	Reading	0-4		7544		8	1		6	9	3	4	2	10					5	7						11
18		24	NORWICH CITY	2-2	A Dawes 2	6237	2		1		6	9	3	4		10						7		5	8			11
19		26	BRENTFORD	1-0	A Dawes	14210			1		6	9	3	4		10						7	2	5	8			11
20		27	Brentford	0-1		18747		10	1		6	9	3	4		10				11		7	2	5	8			
21		31	LUTON TOWN	1-0	Wells	8321		10	1		6	9	3	4		7							2	5	8			11
22	Jan	7	Newport County	3-0	Boyle 2, Wells	4217		10	1		6	9	3	4		8						7	2	5				11
23		14	GILLINGHAM	1-0	Mortimer	3289		10	1		6	9	3	4		8						7	2	5				11
24		21	BOURNEMOUTH	6-0	Boyle, Davies, A Dawes 3, Wells	5018		10	1		6	9	3	4		8						7	2	5				11
25		28	Swindon Town	1-2	Wells	2937		10	1		6	9	3	4		8						7	2	5				11
26	Feb	4	CLAPTON ORIENT	3-0	Mortimer, Riches, Wells	5039		10	1			9	3	4								7	2	5	8	6		11
27		11	Brighton & Hove Albion	1-2	Riches	6755		10	1			9	3	4								7	2	5	8	6		11
28		18	Bristol City	4-5	A Dawes, Dowsey, Forbes, Mortimer	6334			1		4	9	3	8		10						7	2	5		6		11
29		25	COVENTRY CITY	5-1	Boyle, Davies, A Dawes, Mortimer, Wells	2791		8	1		6	9	3	4		10						7	2	5				11
30	Mar	4	BRISTOL ROVERS	1-1	A Dawes	5919		8	1		6	9	3	4								7	2	5				11
31		11	Aldershot	1-0	A Dawes	5045		8	1		6	9	3	4						10		7	2	5				11
32		18	QUEEN'S PARK RANGERS	2-1	A Dawes, McFarlane	5293		8	1		6	9	3	4						10		7	2	5				11
33		25	Southend United	0-1		5670		8	1		6	9		4	3						10	7	2	5				11
34	Apr	1	CRYSTAL PALACE	1-0	A Dawes	4799	3	8	1		6	9		4		10						7	2	5				11
35		8	Gillingham	1-5	Boyle	7352	3	8	1		6	9		4		10							2	5	7			11
36		10	CARDIFF CITY	2-0	A Dawes	2304	3	8	1		6	9		4		10						7	2	5				11
37		15	WATFORD	0-0		6197		8	1		6	9		4		10						7	2			5	3	11
38		17	Torquay United	1-5	Mortimer	3553		8	1		6	9		4		10						7	2			5	3	11
39		18	TORQUAY UNITED	2-0	Boyle, A Dawes	4049		8	1	2	6	9		4		10						7		3		5		11
40		22	Cardiff City	0-6		6631		8	1	2	6	9		4		10					5	7		3				11
41		29	READING	1-0	Boyle	3543	3	8	1		6	9		4		10						7	2			5		11
42	May	6	Norwich City	0-2		7913	3	8			6	9		4			1	10				7	2			5		11
			Apps				6	38	25	3	40	41	32	41	13	35	17	2	1	3	2	40	29	36	8	7	2	41
			Goals					13			2	32	1	2		3				1		13			2			7

F.A. Cup

No	Date		Match	Score	Scorers	Att	Davies FP	Dawes AG	Dawes FW	Dowsey J	Fairhurst WS	Forbes FJ	Hammond L	McFarlane J	Mortimer R	Park O	Wells TC
R1	Nov	26	LLOYDS	8-1	A Dawes 5, Dowsey, McFarlane, Wells	6000	6	9	3	4	2	10	1	8	7	5	11
R2	Dec	10	DONCASTER ROVERS	0-1		10008	6	9	3	4	2	10	1	8	7	5	11

		P	W	D	L	F	A	W	D	L	F	A	Pts
1	Brentford	42	15	4	2	45	19	11	6	4	45	30	62
2	Exeter City	42	17	2	2	57	13	7	8	6	31	35	58
3	Norwich City	42	16	3	2	49	17	6	10	5	39	38	57
4	Reading	42	14	5	2	68	30	5	8	8	35	41	51
5	Crystal Palace	42	14	4	3	51	21	5	4	12	27	43	46
6	Coventry City	42	16	1	4	75	24	3	5	13	31	53	44
7	Gillingham	42	14	4	3	54	24	4	4	13	18	37	44
8	NORTHAMPTON TOWN	42	16	5	0	54	11	2	3	16	22	55	44
9	Bristol Rovers	42	13	5	3	38	22	2	9	10	23	34	44
10	Torquay United	42	12	7	2	51	26	4	5	12	21	41	44
11	Watford	42	11	8	2	37	22	5	4	12	29	41	44
12	Brighton & Hove A.	42	13	3	5	42	20	4	5	12	24	45	42
13	Southend United	42	11	5	5	39	27	4	6	11	26	55	41
14	Luton Town	42	12	8	1	60	32	1	5	15	18	46	39
15	Bristol City	42	11	5	5	59	37	1	8	12	24	53	37
16	Queen's Park Rgs.	42	9	8	4	48	32	4	3	14	24	55	37
17	Aldershot	42	11	6	4	37	21	2	4	15	24	51	36
18	Bournemouth	42	10	7	4	44	27	2	5	14	16	54	36
19	Cardiff City	42	12	4	5	48	30	0	3	18	21	69	31
20	Clapton Orient	42	7	8	6	39	35	1	5	15	20	58	29
21	Newport County	42	9	4	8	44	42	2	3	16	19	63	29
22	Swindon Town	42	7	9	5	36	29	2	2	17	24	76	29

1933/34   13th in Division 3(S)

#	Date		Opponent	Score	Scorers	Att.	Allan CE	Allen T	Boyle TW	Bennett J	Brown A	Cave W	Cherry J	Cochrane AF	Crilly T	Davies FP	Dawes AG	Dawes FW	Dowsey J	Fraser WC	Henson GH	McGuire JP	McAleer J	McMenemy F	Mitchell A	Park O	Partridge AE	Riches LE	Thompson WJ	Tolland D	Warren E	Wells TC	Wheeler AJ
1	Aug 26		LUTON TOWN	2-3	Tolland 2	16823			8		1		7		2	6	9	3	4							5				10		11	
2	30		Aldershot	1-1	Cherry	5444			8		1		7		2	6	9	3	4					11		5				10			
3	Sep 2		Bournemouth	0-4		7925			8	4	1				2	6	9	3								5		7		10		11	
4	4		ALDERSHOT	0-0		5499			8	4	1				2	6	9	3								5		7				11	10
5	9		Torquay United	2-3	A Dawes, Wheeler	4104			8	4	1				2	6	9	3								5		7				11	10
6	16		QUEEN'S PARK RANGERS	2-1	A Dawes, Wells	7025			10		1		7		2	6	9	3	4			5								8		11	
7	23		Newport County	0-2		4842	3		10		1		7		2	6	9		4			5								8		11	
8	30		NORWICH CITY	2-2	Cherry, Henson	7606	3		8		1		7		2	6			4		9	5										11	
9	Oct 7		Bristol City	3-2	A Dawes 2, Henson	8598	3		8		1		7		2	6	10		4		9	5										11	
10	14		CLAPTON ORIENT	3-0	Boyle, A Dawes 2	5336	3		8		1		7		2	6	10		4		9					5						11	
11	21		CHARLTON ATHLETIC	1-2	Henson	6956	3		8		1				2	6	10		4		9					5	7					11	
12	28		Watford	0-2		7027	3		8		1				2	6	10		4		9					5	7					11	
13	Nov 4		READING	2-4	Boyle, Fraser	6244	3		8		1		7		2	6	9		4	10						5						11	
14	11		Coventry City	1-3	Henson	17975	3	1	8				7		2	6	10				9	5						4				11	
15	18		SOUTHEND UNITED	2-0	A Dawes, Henson	3520	3	1	8				7		2	6	10				9	5						4				11	
16	Dec 2		CRYSTAL PALACE	4-2	A Dawes 3, Henson	5034		1	8						2	6	10	3	7		9	5						4				11	
17	16		EXETER CITY	5-3	A Dawes, Riches, Wells 3	4989		1	8							6	10	3	7		9	5				2		4				11	
18	23		Cardiff City	3-1	Boyle, Dowsey, Henson	6168		1	8							6		3	7		9	5				2		4		10		11	
19	25		BRIGHTON & HOVE ALB	1-1	Boyle	5755		1	8							6		3	7		9	5				2		4		10		11	
20	26		Brighton & Hove Albion	3-3	F Davies, McAleer, Wells	7907		1								6		3	8		9	5	7			2		4		10		11	
21	30		Luton Town	1-3	Henson	7696		1								6		3	8		9	5				2		4	7	10		11	
22	Jan 6		BOURNEMOUTH	4-1	F Davies, Henson, Tolland, Wells	11978		1	8						2	6		3			9	5						4		10		11	
23	20		TORQUAY UNITED	1-1	Tolland	6480		1	8						2	6		3			9	5						4		10		11	
24	31		Queen's Park Rangers	1-2	Wells	5368		1	8						2	6					9	5						4	3	10		11	
25	Feb 3		NEWPORT COUNTY	5-3	Boyle, Henson 2, McAleer, Wells	5048		1	8						2	6		3			9	5	7					4		10		11	
26	10		Norwich City	0-2		13174		1	8						2	6		3			9	5	7					4		10		11	
27	22		BRISTOL CITY	2-3	Boyle, Henson	3072		1	8					10	2	6		3			9	5				7		4				11	
28	24		Clapton Orient	1-5	Cochrane	8746		1	9					10	2	6		3				5	7					4				11	
29	28		Bristol Rovers	1-1	Wells	5463			8	2		1		10		6		3			9	5				7		4				11	
30	Mar 3		Charlton Athletic	1-1	Henson	11012			8	2		1		10		6		3			9	5				7		4				11	
31	10		WATFORD	1-0	F Davies	4756			8	2		1				6		3			9	5				7		4		10		11	
32	17		Reading	2-2	Henson, Mitchell	7297						1			2	6		3			9	5			8	7		4		10		11	
33	24		COVENTRY CITY	2-2	Henson, Mitchell	6930						1			2	6		3			9	5			8	7		4		10		11	
34	30		Swindon Town	1-1	Mitchell	10858				2		1				6		3			9	5			8	7		4		10		11	
35	31		Southend United	0-2		6513				2		1				6		3			9	5				7		4		10		11	8
36	Apr 2		SWINDON TOWN	2-2	Henson, Tolland	7059				2		1				6		3			9	5			8	7		4		10		11	
37	7		BRISTOL ROVERS	1-2	Wells	4894			8	2		1				6		3			9	5				7		4				11	
38	11		Gillingham	1-5	Tolland	3398			8	2	4	1		10				3				5		6		7				9		11	
39	14		Crystal Palace	2-1	F Davies, Henson	7984	1		8	2	4					6		3			9				7	5				10		11	
40	21		GILLINGHAM	1-0	McAleer	3702	1			2	4					6		3			9			11	7	5				10			8
41	28		Exeter City	2-0	McAleer 2	3018	1			2	4					6		3	8			5		11	7					10	4		9
42	May 5		CARDIFF CITY	2-0	McAleer, Warren	2992	1			2						6			8			9	11			5			3		4		

Played in one game: OT Davies (42, at 10), DM Lindsay (28,8), RH Hinson (42, 7).

	Allan	Allen	Boyle	Bennett	Brown	Cave	Cherry	Cochrane	Crilly	Davies FP	Dawes AG	Dawes FW	Dowsey	Fraser	Henson	McGuire	McAleer	McMenemy	Mitchell	Park	Partridge	Riches	Thompson	Tolland	Warren	Wells	Wheeler
Apps	9	19	30	12	6	23	10	9	25	39	17	31	8	3	30	21	8	10	18	18	2	27	2	27	2	38	5
Goals			6				2	1		4	11		1	1	17		6		3			1		6	1	10	1

F.A. Cup

	Date		Opponent	Score	Scorers	Att.	Allan	Allen	Boyle	Crilly	Davies FP	Dawes AG	Dawes FW	Dowsey	Henson	McGuire	Riches	Tolland	Wells
R1	Nov 25		EXETER CITY	2-0	Dowsey, Wells	8801		1	8	2	6	10	3	7	9	5	4		11
R2	Dec 9		TORQUAY UNITED	3-0	Boyle, A Dawes 2	9782		1	8	2	6	10	3	7	9	5	4		11
R3	Jan 13		Southampton	1-1	Wells	21847		1	8	2	6		3	7	9	5	4	10	11
rep	17		SOUTHAMPTON	1-0	Henson	16161		1	8	2	6		3	7	9	5	4	10	11
R4			Huddersfield Town	2-0	Boyle, Wells	28143		1	8	2	6		3	7	9	5	4	10	11
R5	Feb 17		Preston North End	0-4		40180		1	8	2	6		3	7	9	5	4	10	11

Third Division (South) Cup

	Date		Opponent	Score	Scorers	Bennett	Brown	Cave	Davies FP	Dawes FW	Henson	McGuire	Mitchell	Riches	Tolland	Warren	Wells
R2	Mar 8		Bournemouth	2-1	Henson 2	2	1		8	6	3	9	5	7	4	10	11
R3	21		Norwich City	2-3	Wells, og	2	1		8	6	3	9	5	7		10	4	11

		P	W	D	L	F	A	W	D	L	F	A	Pts
1	Norwich City	42	16	4	1	55	19	9	7	5	33	30	61
2	Coventry City	42	16	3	2	70	22	5	9	7	30	32	54
3	Reading	42	17	4	0	60	13	4	8	9	22	37	54
4	Queen's Park Rgs.	42	17	2	2	42	12	7	4	10	28	39	54
5	Charlton Athletic	42	14	5	2	53	27	8	3	10	30	29	52
6	Luton Town	42	14	3	4	55	28	7	7	7	28	33	52
7	Bristol Rovers	42	14	4	3	49	21	6	7	8	28	26	51
8	Swindon Town	42	13	5	3	42	25	4	6	11	22	43	45
9	Exeter City	42	12	5	4	43	19	4	6	11	25	38	43
10	Brighton & Hove A.	42	12	7	2	47	18	3	6	12	21	42	43
11	Clapton Orient	42	14	4	3	60	25	2	6	13	15	44	42
12	Crystal Palace	42	11	6	4	40	25	5	3	13	31	42	41
13	NORTHAMPTON TOWN	42	10	6	5	45	32	4	6	11	26	46	40
14	Aldershot	42	8	6	7	28	27	5	6	10	24	44	38
15	Watford	42	12	4	5	43	16	3	3	15	28	47	37
16	Southend United	42	9	6	6	32	27	3	4	14	19	47	34
17	Gillingham	42	8	8	5	49	41	3	3	15	26	55	33
18	Newport County	42	6	9	6	25	23	2	8	11	24	47	33
19	Bristol City	42	7	8	6	33	22	5	5	13	25	63	33
20	Torquay United	42	10	4	7	32	28	3	3	15	21	65	33
21	Bournemouth	42	7	7	7	41	37	2	2	17	19	65	27
22	Cardiff City	42	6	4	11	32	43	3	2	16	25	62	24

1934/35   7th in Division 3(S)

#	Date	Opponent	Score	Scorers	Att	Baker TW	Bell T	Bennett J	Boyle TW	Brown A	Brown AR	Cave W	Cochrane AF	Crilly T	Dawes FW	Edwards SC	Henson GH	Higgins T	Hobbs EC	Kilsby RH	Lyman CC	McGuire JP	McMenemy F	Melville J	Potter FL	Riches LE	Robson T	Tolland D	Watson WJB	Wells TC	Craven J
1	Aug 25	Coventry City	0-2		22789	1		2	8	7				3			9						6	5		4		10		11	
2	27	EXETER CITY	2-1	McMenemy, Tolland	7685	1		2	8	7				3			9						6	5		4		10		11	
3	Sep 1	CLAPTON ORIENT	3-1	R Brown, Henson 2	9301	1		2	8	7				3			9						6	5		4				11	
4	5	Exeter City	0-3		6093	1		2	8	7		10		3			9						6	5		4			11		
5	8	Gillingham	1-3	Henson	3783			2	8	7	10	1		3			9						6	5		4			11		
6	15	READING	1-3	Watson	7832			2	8	7	10	1		3			9						6	5		4			11		
7	22	Aldershot	0-2		3526			3	10	7		1		2			9					5	6			4		8		11	
8	29	Bournemouth	1-0	Boyle	3641			3	10	4	11	1	8		2		7					5	6					9			
9	Oct 6	WATFORD	1-0	Cochrane	5534			3	10	4	11	1	8		2		7					5	6					9			
10	13	Newport County	3-1	R Brown, Henson, Wells	6365			3		4	7	1	8		2		9					5	6					10		11	
11	20	SWINDON TOWN	4-2	R Brown, Cochrane, Tolland, Wells	7033			3		4	7	1	8		2		9					5	6					10		11	
12	27	Torquay United	0-2		3561			3		4	7	1	8		2		9					5	6					10		11	
13	Nov 3	BRIGHTON & HOVE ALB	4-1	Cochrane, Henson 2, McMenemy	7366			3		4	7	1	8		2		9					5	6					10		11	
14	10	Cardiff City	2-2	Edwards, Tolland	9378		9			4	7	1	8		2	3						5	6					10		11	
15	17	CHARLTON ATHLETIC	1-1	Wells	8895		9			4	7	1	8		2	3						5	6					10		11	
16	Dec 1	SOUTHEND UNITED	1-1	Tolland	5933		9			4		1	8		2	3				7		5	6					10		11	
17	15	QUEEN'S PARK RANGERS	1-0	Riches	5008		9				7	1	8	3	2							5				4	6	10		11	
18	22	Crystal Palace	0-2		9318		9			4	7	1	8	3	2							5	6					10		11	
19	25	Bristol City	1-1	Bell	11914		9			4	7	1	8	3	2							5	6					10		11	
20	26	BRISTOL CITY	2-2	Bell, R Brown	13604		9			4	7	1	8	3	2							5	6					10		11	
21	29	COVENTRY CITY	3-4	Bell, A Brown, Wells	10683		9			4	7	1	8	3	2							5						10		11	
22	Jan 5	Clapton Orient	2-3	R Brown 2	8436		9			4	7	1	8		2						7	5	6			4		10			3
23	16	Bristol Rovers	1-7	Bell	3109		9				11	1	8		2						7	5	6			4		10			
24	19	GILLINGHAM	2-1	Watson 2	3783	1				10	4		7									8	2	3				5		11	
25	30	Reading	1-3	Crilly	5196	1	9			10	4		7										5	6				6	10	11	
26	Feb 2	ALDERSHOT	0-0		3526	1	9	2	8	4	7																		11		
27	9	BOURNEMOUTH	0-1		3641	1		2		4	9		10								7	5	6			8		10			
28	16	Watford	1-1	Lyman	9442	1	9	2		4	7		8								11	5	6					10			
29	23	NEWPORT COUNTY	2-0	R Brown, Lyman	2925	1	9			10	4		7								11	5					6	10			
30	Mar 2	Swindon Town	3-5	Bell, R Brown, one og	5661	1	9			4	7		8		2						11	5	6					10			
31	9	TORQUAY UNITED	3-0	Bell, Lyman, Tolland	2853	1	9			4	7		8		2						11	5	6					10			
32	16	Brighton & Hove Albion	3-2	Bell 2, Lyman	5550	1	9	2		4	7		8								11	5	6					10			
33	23	CARDIFF CITY	3-0	R Brown, Cochrane, Lyman	3476		9	2		4	7		8								11	5	6					10			
34	30	Charlton Athletic	1-0	Bell	14926		9	2		4	7		8								11	5	6					10			
35	Apr 6	BRISTOL ROVERS	1-0	Lyman	4946		9	2		4	7		8								11	5	6					10			
36	13	Southend United	1-2	R Brown	5992		9	2		4	7		8								11	5	6					10	8		
37	19	Millwall	1-0	Bell	16140		9	2		4	7		8					6			11	5						10			
38	20	LUTON TOWN	2-1	Cochrane 2	7240		9	2		4	7		8					6			11	5						10			
39	22	MILLWALL	1-0	R Brown	8922		9	2		4	7		8					6			11	5						10			
40	23	Luton Town	2-2	Bell, Lyman	8168		9	2			8			1							7	5			6	4		10		11	
41	27	Queen's Park Rangers	1-3	Lyman	3603		9	2			8			1							7	5			6			10		11	
42	May 4	CRYSTAL PALACE	3-2	Bell 2, Potter	4629		9	3		4	7			1							11	5			10			6	8		

Played in one game: WJ Thompson (42, at 2).

	Baker TW	Bell T	Bennett J	Boyle TW	Brown A	Brown AR	Cave W	Cochrane AF	Crilly T	Dawes FW	Edwards SC	Henson GH	Higgins T	Hobbs EC	Kilsby RH	Lyman CC	McGuire JP	McMenemy F	Melville J	Potter FL	Riches LE	Robson T	Tolland D	Watson WJB	Wells TC	Craven J
Apps	13	26	27	13	32	40	29	33	21	34	3	11	3	2	1	17	36	28	7	1	11	10	35	7	20	1
Goals		13		1	1	11		6	1			6				8		2					5	3	4	

One own goal

F.A. Cup

Rnd	Date	Opponent	Score	Scorers	Att	Bell T	Brown A	Brown AR	Cave W	Cochrane AF	Crilly T	Dawes FW	Hobbs EC	McGuire JP	McMenemy F	Riches LE	Tolland D	Watson WJB	Wells TC
R1	Nov 24	Barry	1-0	Cochrane	9877	9	4	7	1	8		2		5	6		10		11
R2	Dec 8	WORKINGTON	0-0		8000	9			1	8		2		5	6	4	10	7	11
rep	13	Workington	1-0	Hobbs			4	7	1	8		2	9	5			6	10	11
R3	Jan 12	BOLTON WANDERERS	0-2		17962	9	4	7	1	8		2		5	6		10		11

Third Division (South) Cup

Rnd	Date	Opponent	Score	Scorers	Att	Baker TW	Bennett J	Boyle TW	Brown A	Brown AR	Cave W	Cochrane AF	Crilly T	Edwards SC	Henson GH	Hobbs EC	Lyman CC	McGuire JP	McMenemy F	Melville J	Riches LE	Tolland D	Wells TC
R1	Sep 24	Clapton Orient	1-1	R Brown			3	10	11	1		8	2	7				5	6			4	
rep	Oct 1	CLAPTON ORIENT	4-0	R Brown 2, Edwards, Tolland	3000		3	10	4	11	1	8	2	7				5	6			9	
R2	22	NEWPORT COUNTY	3-0	Hobbs 2, Tolland	2500		3		4	7	1	8	2		9						5	6	10	11
R3	Feb 21	BRISTOL ROVERS	0-2		1000	1	2		4	7		8			3	9	11				5	6	10

1935/36   15th in Division 3(S)

Player columns (in order): Bartram JL · Bell T · Bennett J · Brown A · Brown AR · Cave W · Dawes FW · Deacon R · Farr FE · Gormlie WJ · Hewitt JJ · Hinson RH · Hobbs EC · Little J · Lyman CC · Mackie JA · McGuire JP · McMenemy F · Melville J · O'Rourke J · Potter FL · Riches LE · Robinson TE · Robson T · Russell SEJ · Thayne W · Thompson WJ · Tolland D · Turner G

#	Date	Opponent	Score	Scorers	Att	Bartram	Bell	Bennett	BrownA	BrownAR	Cave	Dawes	Deacon	Farr	Gormlie	Hewitt	Hinson	Hobbs	Little	Lyman	Mackie	McGuire	McMenemy	Melville	O'Rourke	Potter	Riches	Robinson	Robson	Russell	Thayne	Thompson	Tolland	Turner
1	Aug 31	GILLINGHAM	0-0		15826	9		2	4	7		3		8	1					11		5	6										10	
2	Sep 2	Aldershot	0-2		3838	9		2	4	7		3			1					11		5	6										10	
3	7	Bournemouth	0-4		9547	9	8	2		7		3			1					11		5	6				4						10	
4	9	ALDERSHOT	3-0	Bartram, Robinson, one og	7210	9	8	2	4	7		3			1					11		5						10	6					
5	14	LUTON TOWN	0-0		13595	9	8	2	4	7		3			1					11		5						10	6					
6	16	CRYSTAL PALACE	3-1	Bartram, Lyman, Robinson	6319	9	8			7		3			1					11			4	5				10	6			2		
7	21	Notts County	0-3		8929	9	8			7		3			1					11			4	5				10	6			2		
8	23	Crystal Palace	1-6	Lyman	5134	8	9			7		3			1					11			4	5					6			2		
9	28	BRISTOL ROVERS	3-3	Bell, Hinson, Potter	7102		9			5		7		3	1		8			11				6		10	4					2		
10	Oct 5	Clapton Orient	0-4		8102	9	8		2	11		3			1									5			4		6				10	
11	12	SOUTHEND UNITED	2-0	Bartram, R Brown	6991	8	9	2	4	11		3	7		1									5					6					
12	19	TORQUAY UNITED	2-1	R Brown, Tolland	6075	9		2	4	7		3			1	8				11				5									10	
13	26	Millwall	1-2	Bell	10123	9		2	4	7		3			1					11				5									10	
14	Nov 2	BRISTOL CITY	0-2		6160	9		2		7		3			1	8				11				5			4		6					
15	9	Swindon Town	1-3	Lyman	7670	9		2	4	7		3			1	10	8	5		11			6											
16	16	QUEEN'S PARK RANGERS	1-4	Lyman	6472	9		2	4	7		3			1	10		5		11			6										8	
17	23	Brighton & Hove Albion	1-5	Hewitt	5886	9		2	4	7		3			1	10		5		11			6										8	
18	Dec 7	Newport County	1-5	Bell	3780		9	2		7	1	3	11			8								5			4		6					
19	14	COVENTRY CITY	2-4	Bell, R Brown	6803		9	2		7	1	3	11			10	8							5			4		6					
20	21	Watford	1-4	Tolland	4759		9	2	4		1	3	11				8							5					6				10	
21	25	READING	4-2	Bell 2, R Brown, Lyman	7003		9	2		7		3			1					11				5		10	4		6					
22	26	Reading	2-5	R Brown 2	18364		9	2		7		3			1		5			11						10	4		6					
23	28	Gillingham	3-2	Bell 3	6763		9		2			3			1					11				5		10	4		6					
24	Jan 4	BOURNEMOUTH	2-1	Bell, one og	6167		9			7		3			1					11				5		10	4		6			2		
25	11	EXETER CITY	1-1	R Brown	6054		9			7		3			1		5			11						10	4		6			2		
26	18	Luton Town	3-3	R Brown, Lyman, Potter	12781		9		4	7		3			1					11				5		10	4		6					
27	25	NOTTS COUNTY	3-1	Potter 2, Tolland	6285		9		2	11		3			1				7					5		10	4		6					
28	Feb 1	Bristol Rovers	2-5	Lyman, Potter	5958		9			7		3			1				5	11						10	4		6					
29	8	CLAPTON ORIENT	2-0	Bell, Tolland	6131		9			7		3			1				5	11	2					10	4		6					
30	22	Torquay United	3-3	Bell 2, Lyman	1977		9					3			1				5	11	2					10	4		6					
31	29	SWINDON TOWN	0-0		4226		9					7			1				3	11	2	5	6		8	10	4							
32	Mar 7	Coventry City	0-4		14647		9					7			1				2	11	3	5	6		8	10	4							
33	14	MILLWALL	2-4	R Brown, Turner	6111		9			8					1	4			2			7	6								5		10	11
34	21	Queen's Park Rangers	1-0	McMenemy	13687		9			7					1	4			3		2		6			10				5	8			11
35	28	BRIGHTON & HOVE ALB	1-0	Bell	6306		9			7					1	4			3		2		6			10				5	8			11
36	Apr 4	Exeter City	1-3	R Brown	2421		9			7					1	4			3		2		6			10				5	8			11
37	10	Cardiff City	0-0		11302		9			7					1	4			3		2	5	6			10					8			11
38	11	NEWPORT COUNTY	3-0	Hinson 3	5219		9		2	7					1	4	8		3			5	6			10								11
39	13	CARDIFF CITY	2-0	Bell, Turner	7890		9		2	7					1	4			3			5	6	10										11
40	18	Bristol City	2-3	R Brown 2	6463		9		2	7					1	4	8		3			5	6			10								11
41	22	Southend United	1-0	O'Rourke	4134		9		2	7					1	4			3				6		8					5			10	11
42	25	WATFORD	2-0	Bell, Tolland	4109		9		2	7					1	4			3				6		8					5			10	11
		Apps				12	38	17	17	39	3	30	3	2	39	17	7	7	14	29	8	11	19	13	5	19	19	5	26	3	9	6	30	10
		Goals				3	16			12						1	4			8			1		1	5								5	2

Played in one game: SC Edwards (game 10, at 7), J Craven (33,3).
Played in games 20, 23 and 30: J Billingham (at 7).

Two own goals

F.A. Cup

	Date	Opponent	Score	Scorers	Att	Bell	Bennett	BrownAR	Cave	Dawes	Deacon	Hinson	Lyman	Melville	Riches	Robson	Tolland
R1	Nov 30	BRISTOL ROVERS	0-0		9093	9	2	7	1	3		8	11	5	4	6	10
rep	Dec 4	Bristol Rovers	1-3	Deacon	8000	9	2	7	1	3	11	8		5	4	6	10

Third Division (South) Cup

	Date	Opponent	Score	Scorers	Att	Bartram	BrownA	BrownAR	Dawes	Gormlie	Hewitt	Hobbs	Little	Lyman	Mackie	McGuire	McMenemy	Melville	O'Rourke	Potter	Riches	Robinson	Robson	Tolland
R1	Oct 2	TORQUAY UNITED	4-1	Bartram, R Brown, Jones, Melville		9		11	3	1								5			4	8	6	10
R3	14	READING	4-0	Bartram 2, Lyman, Tolland	1000	9	4	7	3	1	10	5		11			6							8
SF	Feb 26	Swindon Town	0-1					7		1	4		5	11	2		6		8	10				

Bye in R2.
Played in R1: Jones (at 7). Played in R1 (at 2) and SF (at 3): J Craven.

1936/37   7th in Division 3(S)

#	Date	Opponent	Res	Scorers	Att	Allen RSL	Bell T	Cave W	Cook C	Dunkley MEF	Gornilie WJ	Hewitt JJ	Holt D	Lauderdale JH	Little J	Lyman CC	Mackie JA	Riches LE	Rawlings JSD	Robson T	Russell SEJ	Simpson WS	Thayne W	Tolland D	Turner G	Riley H
1	Aug 29	Swindon Town	0-2		11150				9		1	4	8		3		2		7			6	5		11	10
2	31	ALDERSHOT	5-3	Cook,Rawlings 2,Tolland,one og	8107				9		1	4			3		2		7			6	5	10	11	8
3	Sep 5	MILLWALL	2-2	Rawlings, Riley	10486				9		1	4			3		2		7			6	5	10	11	8
4	9	Aldershot	2-0	Cook, Tolland	3594				9		1				3		2	4	7			6	5	10	11	8
5	12	Bristol Rovers	0-2		11420				9		1				3		2	4	7			6	5	10	11	8
6	16	Southend United	0-2		6627				9		1				3		2	4	7			6	5	10	11	8
7	19	TORQUAY UNITED	3-0	Rawlings, Tolland, Turner	8260		9				1				3		2	4	7			6	5	10	11	8
8	26	BOURNEMOUTH	0-0		9764		9				1				3			4	7		2	6	5	10	11	8
9	Oct 3	Brighton & Hove Albion	2-1	J Hewitt, Rawlings	10499		9				1	8			3			4	7		2	6	5		11	10
10	10	WATFORD	0-1		8958		9				1	8			3			4	7		2	6	5		11	10
11	17	Notts County	2-3	Little, Riley	14557						1	9			3			4	7		2	6	5	8	11	10
12	24	CLAPTON ORIENT	1-1	Bell	8004		9				1				3			4	7		2	6	5	8	11	10
13	31	Walsall	2-2	Allen 2	5765	9					1				3	11	2	4	7			6	5	8		10
14	Nov 7	LUTON TOWN	3-1	Lyman, Rawlings	18885	9					1	8			3	11	2	4	7			6	5	10		
15	14	Cardiff City	1-2	Allen	18200	9					1	8			3	11	2	4	7			6	5	10		
16	21	CRYSTAL PALACE	2-0	Allem, Tolland	14163	9					1			8	3	11		4	7		2	6	5	10		
17	Dec 5	READING	2-1	Allen, Lyman	8543	9					1			8	3	11		4	7		2	6	5	10		
18	19	BRISTOL CITY	5-1	Allen 3, Rawlings, one og	7148	9					1			8	3	11		4	7		2	6	5	10		
19	25	NEWPORT COUNTY	3-2	Allen, Lauderdale, Rawlings	12371	9		1						8	3	11		4	7		2	6	5	10		
20	26	SWINDON TOWN	4-0	Allen,Lauderdale,Lyman,Tolland	16177	9					1			8	3	11		4	7		2	6	5	10		
21	28	Newport County	3-1	Allen, Dunkley, Lyman	8756	9				7	1			8	3	11		4			2	6	5	10		
22	Jan 2	Millwall	0-1		16485	9				7	1			10	3	11		4			2	6	5	8		
23	9	BRISTOL ROVERS	4-1	Allen 2, Lyman, Tolland	8926	9					1			10	3	11		4	7		2	6	5	8		
24	20	Exeter City	5-2	Allen,Lauderdale 2,Rawlings 2	2348	9					1			8	3	11		4	7		2	6	5	10		
25	23	Torquay United	0-5		2265	9					1			10	3	11		4	7		2	6	5	8		
26	Feb 6	BRIGHTON & HOVE ALB	2-0	Rawlings 2	13034	9					1			10	3	11		4	7		2	6	5	8		
27	13	Watford	1-4	J Hewitt	10430	9					1	8			3	11		4	7		2	6	5	10		
28	18	Queen's Park Rangers	2-3	Allen, Lyman	3751	9				7	1	4		10	3	11	2					6	5			
29	20	NOTTS COUNTY	1-1		18435	9					1			8	3	11		4	7		2	6	5	10		
30	27	Clapton Orient	1-3	Lyman	5095	9					1			10	3	11		4	7		2	6	5	8		
31	Mar 6	WALSALL	6-3	Allen 3, Lyman 2, Rawlings	6247	9					1			10	3	11		4	7		2	6	5	8		
32	13	Luton Town	2-3	Tolland, one og	19579	9					1			10	3	11		4	7		2	6	5	8		
33	20	CARDIFF CITY	2-0	Allen, Lyman	7334	9					1			10	3	11		4	7		2	6	5	8		
34	26	Gillingham	0-2		9426	9					1			8	3	11		4	7		2	6	5			
35	27	Crystal Palace	2-2	Allen 2	9523	9					1			8	3	11		4	7		2	6	5			
36	29	GILLINGHAM	5-0	Allen,J Hewitt 2,Lyman,Rawlings	10164	9					1	8			3	11			7	4	2	6	5			
37	Apr 3	EXETER CITY	2-1	Allen, Tolland	6349	9					1	4		10	3	11			7		2	6	5	8		
38	10	Reading	1-3	Rawlings	6291	9					1	4		10	3	11			7		2	6	5	8		
39	17	QUEEN'S PARK RANGERS	0-1		4056	9					1	4		10	3	11			7		2	6	5	8		
40	21	Bournemouth	2-3	Allen, Lauderdale	3684	9					1			10	3	11		4	7		2	6	5	8		
41	24	Bristol City	1-0	Rawlings	6729	9					1			10	3	11		4	7		2	6	5	8		
42	May 1	SOUTHEND UNITED	4-3	Allen 2, Lauderdale, Tolland	3751	9					1			8	3	11		4	7		2	6	5	10		
		Apps				30	5	1	6	3	41	18	1	25	41	30	11	34	39	1	32	42	42	35	12	13
		Goals				27	1		2	1		4		6	1	11			17					9	1	2

Three own goals

F.A. Cup

#	Date	Opponent	Res	Scorers	Att	Allen RSL	Bell T	Cave W	Cook C	Dunkley MEF	Gornilie WJ	Hewitt JJ	Holt D	Lauderdale JH	Little J	Lyman CC	Mackie JA	Riches LE	Rawlings JSD	Robson T	Russell SEJ	Simpson WS	Thayne W	Tolland D	Turner G	Riley H
R1	Nov 28	Walthamstow Avenue	1-6	J Hewitt	7568	9					1	8			3	11		4	7		2	6	5			10

Third Division (South) Cup

#	Date	Opponent	Res	Allen RSL	Bell T	Cave W	Cook C	Dunkley MEF	Gornilie WJ	Hewitt JJ	Holt D	Lauderdale JH	Little J	Lyman CC	Mackie JA	Riches LE	Rawlings JSD	Robson T	Russell SEJ	Simpson WS	Thayne W	Tolland D	Turner G	Riley H
R1	Sep 30	Torquay United	0-5						1					7		4			6	2	9	8	11	

Played at 5: E Hewitt. At 3: F Wallbanks. At 10: J O'Rourke

		P	W	D	L	F	A	W	D	L	F	A	Pts
1	Luton Town	42	19	1	1	69	16	8	3	10	34	37	58
2	Notts County	42	15	3	3	44	23	8	7	6	30	29	56
3	Brighton & Hove A.	42	15	5	1	49	16	9	0	12	25	27	53
4	Watford	42	14	4	3	53	21	5	7	9	32	39	49
5	Reading	42	14	5	2	53	23	5	6	10	23	37	49
6	Bournemouth	42	17	3	1	45	20	3	6	12	20	39	49
7	NORTHAMPTON TOWN	42	15	4	2	56	22	5	2	14	29	46	46
8	Millwall	42	12	4	5	43	24	6	6	9	21	30	46
9	Queen's Park Rgs.	42	12	2	7	51	24	6	7	8	22	28	45
10	Southend United	42	10	8	3	49	23	7	3	11	29	44	45
11	Gillingham	42	14	5	2	36	18	4	3	14	16	48	44
12	Clapton Orient	42	10	8	3	29	17	4	7	10	23	35	43
13	Swindon Town	42	12	4	5	52	24	2	7	12	23	49	39
14	Crystal Palace	42	11	7	3	45	20	2	5	14	17	41	38
15	Bristol Rovers	42	14	3	4	49	20	2	1	18	22	60	36
16	Bristol City	42	13	3	5	42	20	2	3	16	16	50	36
17	Walsall	42	11	3	7	38	34	2	7	12	25	51	36
18	Cardiff City	42	10	5	6	35	24	4	2	15	19	63	35
19	Newport County	42	7	7	7	37	28	5	3	13	30	70	34
20	Torquay United	42	9	5	7	42	32	2	5	14	15	48	32
21	Exeter City	42	9	5	7	36	37	1	7	13	23	51	32
22	Aldershot	42	5	6	10	29	29	2	3	16	21	60	23

1937/38   9th in Division 3(S)

#	Date		Opponent	Score	Scorers	Att	Allen RSL	Bell T	Blencowe AG	Blunt E	Bosse PL	Cook C	Dickinson A	Dunkley MEF	Gormlie WJ	Gunn K	Hewitt JJ	Hoult AA	King FAR	Lauderdale JH	Little J	Lyman CC	McCulloch K	O'Rourke J	Parris JE	Postlethwaite TW	Rawlings JSD	Riches LE	Riley H	Rodger C	Russell SEJ	Thayne W	Tolland D	Tilson SF
1	Aug	28	Mansfield Town	1-4	Lyman	9619	9								1	2	4					11				6	7		10		3	5	8	
2		31	Bristol Rovers	0-0		7690	9								1	2	4					11				6	7		10		3	5	8	
3	Sep	4	TORQUAY UNITED	0-3		10650	9							7	1	2	4				3	11				6			10			5	8	
4		6	BRISTOL ROVERS	2-0	Allen, J Hewitt	5596	9			4				7	1		8			10	3	11				6					2	5		
5		11	Clapton Orient	0-1		8939	9								1	2	8			10		11				6	7	4			3	5		
6		13	Cardiff City	1-4	Lauderdale	20693						9			1	2	8			10		11				6	7	4			3	5		
7		18	SOUTHEND UNITED	0-2		7680			9		4			7	1	2				8		11				6					3	5	10	
8		25	Queen's Park Rangers	1-1	Allen	13982	9		10		4			7	1	2						11				6					3	5	8	
9	Oct	2	BRIGHTON & HOVE ALB	3-1	Allen 2, Lyman	7998	9				4			7	1	2				8		11				6					3	5	10	
10		9	Bournemouth	0-0		7417	9				4			7	1	2				8		11				6					3	5	10	
11		16	Watford	3-1	Allen, Rawlings, Riley	11100	9				4				1	2				8						6	7		11		3	5	10	
12		23	GILLINGHAM	4-1	Allen 2, Riley, Tolland	7618	9				4				1	2				8						6	7		11		3	5	10	
13		30	Exeter City	1-4	Allen	5946	9						10	7	1	2	4			8						6			11		3	5		
14	Nov	6	SWINDON TOWN	1-0	Allen	7806	9				4			11	1	2				8						6	7				3	5	10	
15		13	Aldershot	2-0	Allen, Dunkley	5571	9				4			11	1	2				8						6	7				3	5	10	
16		20	MILLWALL	0-1		12726	9				4			11	1	2				8						6	7				3	5	10	
17	Dec	11	Notts County	0-5		9988	9				4		10		1	2			7	8					11	6					3	5		
18		18	NEWPORT COUNTY	2-0	Dunkley 2	4989	9				4		10	7	1	2		8							11	6					3	5		
19		27	Bristol City	0-1		20135	9				4		10	7	1	2	8								11	6					3	5		
20	Jan	1	MANSFIELD TOWN	3-0	Dickinson 2, Parris	6401					4	9	10	7	1	2	8								11	6					3	5		
21		8	Reading	3-4	Dickinson, Dunkley, Parris	8298					4	9	10	7	1	2	8								11	6					3	5		
22		15	Torquay United	2-1	Allen, J Hewitt	2321	9				4		10	7	1	2	8								11	6					3	5		
23		22	CLAPTON ORIENT	2-0	Dickinson, Parris	6769					4	9	10	7	1	2	8								11	6					3	5		
24		29	Southend United	2-4	Allen 2	5933	9				4		10	7	1	2	8								11	6					3	5		
25	Feb	3	CRYSTAL PALACE	1-1	Allen	3672	9				4		10	7	1	2	8								11	6					3	5		
26		5	QUEEN'S PARK RANGERS	0-2		9270	9				4		10	7	1	2	8								11	6					3	5		
27		12	Brighton & Hove Albion	2-1	Cook, J Hewitt	8447					4	9	10	7	1	2	8								11	6					3	5		
28		19	BOURNEMOUTH	1-3	Postlethwaite	5337					4	9	10	7	1	2	8								11	6					3	5		
29		26	WATFORD	3-2	Bosse 2, Parris	7085		8			10		9	7	1	2									11	6				4	3	5		
30	Mar	5	Gillingham	1-2	Bell	4582		8			10		9	7	1	2									11	6				4	3	5		
31		12	EXETER CITY	1-0	Dickinson	8603	8						9		1	2		7					4			6			11		3	5		10
32		19	Swindon Town	0-1		7678	5						9	8	1	2		7					4	3		6			11					10
33		26	ALDERSHOT	1-0	Tilson	5446				8			9		1	2							4	3	7	6			11			5		10
34	Apr	2	Millwall	0-3		24425					6				1	2	9						4	3	7			11				5	8	10
35		9	READING	2-2	J Hewitt, Tilson	5014									1	2	9						4		7	6		11			3	5	8	10
36		15	Walsall	1-1	Parris	3799									1	2	9						4		7	6		11			3	5	8	10
37		16	Crystal Palace	1-0	Tilson	14057					4				1	2	9								7	6		11			3	5	8	10
38		18	WALSALL	1-1	Bosse	6574				8	4				1	2	9								7	6		11			3	5		10
39		19	BRISTOL CITY	1-0	J Hewitt	8907									1	2	9		7				4			6		11			3	5	8	10
40		23	NOTTS COUNTY	2-0	Parris 2	11175									1	2	9						4		7	6		11			3	5	8	10
41		30	Newport County	0-0		4436									1		9						4	3	7	6		11			2	5	8	10
42	May	7	CARDIFF CITY			6410					4				1	2	9								7	6		11			3	5	8	10
			Apps				22	4	2	2	30	6	18	23	42	40	28	9	2	13	2	10	7	3	23	38	9	4	9	11	39	41	11	11
			Goals				14	1			3	1	5	4			5			1		2			7	1	1		2				1	3

Played in one game: AT Cotterill (26, at 6), R Platt (6, 6), T Robson (38, 6).

F.A. Cup

R	Date	Opponent	Score	Scorers	Att	Allen RSL	Bosse PL	Dunkley MEF	Gormlie WJ	Gunn K	Lauderdale JH	Lyman CC	Postlethwaite TW	Rawlings JSD	Russell SEJ	Thayne W	Tolland D
R1	Nov 27	CARDIFF CITY	1-2	Tolland	14000	9	4	11	1	2	8		6	7	3	5	10

Division Three (South) Cup

R	Date	Opponent	Score	Att	Allen RSL	Blencowe AG	Bosse PL	Dunkley MEF	Gormlie WJ	Gunn K	Lyman CC	Postlethwaite TW	Russell SEJ	Thayne W	Tolland D
R1	Sep 27	Cardiff City	0-1	3869	9	10	4	7	1	2	11	6	3	5	8

		P	W	D	L	F	A	W	D	L	F	A	Pts
1	Millwall	42	15	3	3	53	15	8	7	6	30	22	56
2	Bristol City	42	14	6	1	37	13	7	7	7	31	27	55
3	Queen's Park Rgs.	42	15	3	3	44	17	7	6	8	36	30	53
4	Watford	42	14	4	3	50	15	7	7	7	23	28	53
5	Brighton & Hove A.	42	15	3	3	40	16	6	6	9	24	28	51
6	Reading	42	17	2	2	44	21	3	9	9	27	42	51
7	Crystal Palace	42	14	4	3	45	17	4	8	9	22	30	48
8	Swindon Town	42	12	4	5	33	19	5	6	10	16	30	44
9	NORTHAMPTON TOWN	42	12	4	5	30	19	5	5	11	21	38	43
10	Cardiff City	42	13	7	1	57	22	2	5	14	10	32	42
11	Notts County	42	10	6	5	29	17	6	3	12	21	33	41
12	Southend United	42	12	5	4	43	23	3	5	13	27	45	40
13	Bournemouth	42	8	10	3	36	20	6	2	13	20	37	40
14	Mansfield Town	42	12	5	4	46	26	3	4	14	16	41	39
15	Bristol Rovers	42	10	7	4	28	20	3	6	12	18	41	39
16	Newport County	42	9	10	2	31	15	2	6	13	12	37	38
17	Exeter City	42	10	4	7	37	32	3	8	10	20	38	38
18	Aldershot	42	11	4	6	23	14	4	1	16	16	45	35
19	Clapton Orient	42	10	7	4	27	19	3	0	18	15	42	33
20	Torquay United	42	7	5	9	22	28	2	7	12	16	45	30
21	Walsall	42	10	4	7	34	37	1	3	17	18	51	29
22	Gillingham	42	9	5	7	25	25	1	1	19	11	52	26

1938/39 17th in Division 3(S)

Match-by-match appearance grid (shirt numbers). Player columns, in order:
Barratt AG, Barron W, Bosse PL, Blunt E, Clifford JC, Curtis LH, Dickinson A, Elwood RJ, Gormlie WJ, Gunn K, Haycox JH, Hewitt JJ, Hurel E, Jennings HW, Jones JT, King FAR, Lauderdale JH, McCartney JJ, McCulloch K, O'Rourke J, Parris JE, Platt R, Postlethwaite TW, Rodger C, Thayne W, Tilson SF, Russell SEJ

#	Date	Opponent	Score	Scorers	Att	Barratt AG	Barron W	Bosse PL	Blunt E	Clifford JC	Curtis LH	Dickinson A	Elwood RJ	Gormlie WJ	Gunn K	Haycox JH	Hewitt JJ	Hurel E	Jennings HW	Jones JT	King FAR	Lauderdale JH	McCartney JJ	McCulloch K	O'Rourke J	Parris JE	Platt R	Postlethwaite TW	Rodger C	Thayne W	Tilson SF	Russell SEJ
1	Aug 27	Torquay United	2-1	King, Lauderdale	4569			4						1	2	9					7	10						6	11	5	8	3
2	29	WATFORD	2-0	King, Rodgers	10784			4						1	2	9					7	10						6	11	5	8	3
3	Sep 3	CLAPTON ORIENT	3-0	Hewitt 2, Lauderdale	13298			4						1	2	9					7	10						6	11	5	8	3
4	7	Crystal Palace	0-2		14570			4						1	2	9					7	10						6	11	5	8	3
5	10	Newport County	1-1	King	11534									1	2	9					7	10		4				6	11	5	8	3
6	17	IPSWICH TOWN	2-0	King, Tilson	13428									1	2	9					7	10		4				6	11	5	8	3
7	24	NOTTS COUNTY	2-1	Hewott, Tilson	13949									1	2	9					7		10	4				6	11	5	8	3
8	Oct 1	Aldershot	0-3		7580							5		1	2	9					7		10	4				6	11		8	3
9	8	BRISTOL CITY	2-2	Gunn, McCulloch	10309									1	2						7	10	9	4				6	11	5	8	3
10	15	Reading	1-5	McCartney	11228									1	2	9					7		10	4		3		6	11	5	8	
11	22	CARDIFF CITY	2-1	Curtis, McCartney	10262						9			1	2						7		10	4				6	11	5	8	3
12	29	Brighton & Hove Albion	0-1		9204				6		9			1	2						7		10	4	11					5	8	3
13	Nov 5	BOURNEMOUTH	2-0	Lauderdale, Tilson	8645									1	2	9					7	10	11	4				6		5	8	3
14	12	Walsall	0-1		8996									1	2	9					7	10	11	4				6		5	8	3
15	19	MANSFIELD TOWN	3-4	King 2, Tilson	8774									1	2	9	6				7		10	4	11					5	8	3
16	Dec 3	SOUTHEND UNITED	2-2	Hewitt, McCartney	5568				6					1	2	9					7		10	4					11	5	8	3
17	10	Exeter City	2-3	McCartney, one og	3560				4						2	9	7			1			10					6	11	5	8	3
18	17	BRISTOL ROVERS	2-1	Barron, McCartney	5305		8		6						2	9	4			1	7		10						11	5		3
19	24	TORQUAY UNITED	4-1	Haycox 3, McCartney	3593				6						2	9	4			1	7		10						11	5	8	3
20	26	PORT VALE	2-0	Barron, Haycox	4734		11		6						2	9	4			1	7		10							5	8	3
21	27	Port Vale	2-0	McCartney, Rodgers	10717				6						2	9	4			1	7		10						11	5	8	3
22	31	Clapton Orient	0-3		6922				6						2	9	4			1	7		10						11	5	8	3
23	Jan 9	Queen's Park Rangers	0-3		3492		8		6				11		2	9	4			1	7		10							5		3
24	14	NEWPORT COUNTY	1-0	Tilson	9025				6				11		2	9				1	7		10	4						5	8	3
25	21	Ipswich Town	0-2		11168				6				11		2	9				1	7		10	4						5	8	3
26	28	Notts County	0-1		10924				6				11		2	9			7	1			10	4						5	8	3
27	Feb 4	ALDERSHOT	5-0	Elwood 2, Haycox, Rodgers 2	6476				6				10		2	9	4			1	7								11	5	8	3
28	11	Bristol City	0-0		10549								10		2	9				1	7			4				6	11	5	8	3
29	18	READING	1-1	Tilson	8427				6				10		2	9				1	7			4					11	5	8	3
30	25	Cardiff City	0-2		10282				6				10		2	9				1	7			4					11	5	8	3
31	Mar 4	BRIGHTON & HOVE ALB	1-4	Tilson	5044				6				10		2	9				1	7			4					11	5	8	3
32	11	Bournemouth	1-3	Haycox	4983				6	1			10		2	9					7			4					11	5	8	3
33	18	WALSALL	4-1	Barron, Blunt, Hurel, Jennings	5550		11		6	1			10		2			9	8		7			4						5		3
34	25	Mansfield Town	1-1	Jennings	4039		11		6	1			10		2			9	8		7			4						5		3
35	Apr 1	QUEEN'S PARK RANGERS	1-0	Hurel	7381		11		4	1			10					9	8		7						2	6		5		3
36	7	Swindon Town	0-1		14910		11		4	1			10					9	8		7						2	6		5		3
37	8	Southend United	0-2		7031	5	11		4	1			10		2			9	8		7							6				3
38	10	SWINDON TOWN	0-2		9203				4	1			9						8		7	10				2		6	11	5		3
39	15	EXETER CITY	0-0		4207		11		4	1			10		2			9	8		7				3			6		5		
40	22	Bristol Rovers	0-1		4620		11		4	1			10		2			9	8		7				3			6		5		
41	29	Watford	0-2		3465		11		4	1			10		2			9	8		7				3			6		5		
42	May 6	CRYSTAL PALACE	0-0		4056		11		4	1					2			9	8		7		10		3			6		5		
		Apps				1	12	4	26	11	2	1	19	16	34	17	20	12	10	15	40	9	22	28	6	2	2	23	24	41	30	35
		Goals					3		1		1		2		1	6	4	2	2		6	3	7	1					4		7	

One own goal

F.A. Cup

R	Date	Opponent	Score	Scorers	Att	Barron W	Blunt E	Gormlie WJ	Gunn K	Haycox JH	Hewitt JJ	King FAR	McCartney JJ	Thayne W	Tilson SF	Russell SEJ
R1	Nov 26	Watford	1-4	Tilson	9000	11	6	1	2	9	4	7	10	5	8	3

Third Division (South) Cup

R	Date	Opponent	Score	Scorers	Att	Bosse PL	Blunt E	Clifford JC	Dickinson A	Elwood RJ	Gormlie WJ	Gunn K	Haycox JH	Hurel E	Jennings HW	Jones JT	King FAR	McCartney JJ	McCulloch K	Platt R	Postlethwaite TW	Rodger C	Thayne W	Russell SEJ
R1	Sep 26	SOUTHEND	1-1	McCulloch							1	2	9					10	4		6	11	5	3
rep	Oct 5	Southend	3-2	Allen 3	1000	4	8	5			1						7	10		2	6	11		3
R2	Jan 23	IPSWICH TOWN	1-1	Dickinson	400		6		9	11		2		5	10	1	7		4					8
rep	Feb 1	Ipswich Town	0-1		2858	4	6		8	7		2	6	9		1		10		3		11		

R1 replay a.e.t.

Played in R1: Cuff (at 7), RSL Allen (at 8). In R1 replay: RSL Allen (at 9). In R2 replay: Smith (at 5).

League table — Division 3 (South)

		P	W	D	L	F	A	W	D	L	F	A	Pts
1	Newport County	42	15	4	2	37	16	7	7	7	21	29	55
2	Crystal Palace	42	15	4	2	49	18	5	8	8	22	34	52
3	Brighton & Hove A.	42	14	5	2	43	14	5	6	10	25	35	49
4	Watford	42	14	6	1	44	15	3	6	12	18	36	46
5	Reading	42	12	6	3	46	23	4	8	9	23	36	46
6	Queen's Park Rgs.	42	10	8	3	44	15	5	6	10	24	34	44
7	Ipswich Town	42	14	3	4	46	21	2	9	10	16	31	44
8	Bristol City	42	14	5	2	42	19	2	7	12	19	44	44
9	Swindon Town	42	15	4	2	53	25	3	4	14	19	52	44
10	Aldershot	42	13	6	2	31	15	3	6	12	22	51	44
11	Notts County	42	12	6	3	36	16	5	3	13	23	38	43
12	Southend United	42	14	5	2	38	13	2	4	15	23	51	41
13	Cardiff City	42	12	1	8	40	28	3	10	8	21	37	41
14	Exeter City	42	9	9	3	40	32	4	5	12	25	50	40
15	Bournemouth	42	10	8	3	38	22	3	5	13	14	36	39
16	Mansfield Town	42	10	8	3	33	19	2	7	12	11	43	39
17	NORTHAMPTON TOWN	42	13	5	3	41	20	2	3	16	10	38	38
18	Port Vale	42	10	5	6	36	23	4	4	13	16	35	37
19	Torquay United	42	9	5	7	27	28	7	4	10	27	42	37
20	Clapton Orient	42	10	9	2	40	16	1	4	16	13	39	35
21	Walsall	42	9	6	6	47	23	2	5	14	21	46	33
22	Bristol Rovers	42	8	8	5	30	17	2	5	14	25	44	33

1946/47   13th in Division 3(S)

		Date		Opponent	Score	Scorers	Att	Allen AR	Baines SN	Barron W	Blunt E	Briscoe JER	Dennison RS	Fowler T	Frost SD	Garrett ACE	Heaselgrave SE	Hughes TG	Lowery H	McKee RT	McKenna MJ	Morrall AD	Neal G	Quinney HJ	Roberts DG	Sankey J	Scott DP	Smalley T	Smith D	Strathie WJ	Thompson H	Jenkins RJ	Jennings HW	Jones JT
1	Aug	31	SWINDON TOWN	4-1	Heaselgrave 2, Morrall 2	12013			3	6			5	11		10					9			7	4		2	8					1
2	Sep	2	EXETER CITY	1-2	Morrall	9730			3	6			5	11		10					9			7	4		2	8					1
3		7	Bournemouth	1-2	Morrall	13461				6			5	11		9					10			7	4		2	8	3				1
4		9	Port Vale	1-1	Blunt	8709			6	11		5				10					9	4		7		1	2	8	3				
5		14	CARDIFF CITY	0-2		8853			3	6				11		10					9			7	5	1	4	8	2				
6		18	Exeter City	0-1		7933		3		6	10			11							9	4		7	5		2	8					1
7		21	Norwich City	3-2	Fowler 2, Smith	16215			3	6				11		10						4		7	5		2	8				9	1
8		28	NOTTS COUNTY	2-1	Garrett 2	11906			3	6		7	5	11	9	10									4		2	8					1
9	Oct	5	Walsall	0-2		12521			3	10		7	5	11	9			6							4		2	8					1
10		12	Aldershot	1-1	Fowler	5498			3	6		7	5	11	9			4			10						2	8					1
11		19	WATFORD	4-1	Garrett 2, Morrall, Smith	9776			3	6			5	11	9			4			10			7			2	8					1
12		26	Ipswich Town	2-1	Garrett 2	13280			3	6			5	11	9			4			10			7			2	8					1
13	Nov	2	LEYTON ORIENT	4-1	Garrett 2, Smith 2	10173			3	6			5	11	9			4			10			7			2	8					1
14		9	Queen's Park Rangers	0-1		17796			3	6			5	11	9	10		4									2	8		7			1
15		16	SOUTHEND UNITED	2-3	Garrett 2	11338			3	6			5	11	9			4			10			7			2	8					1
16		23	Bristol Rovers	3-0	Garrett, Morrall, Smith	7886			3	6			5	11	9			4			7						2	8		10			1
17	Dec	7	Torquay United	1-2	Garrett	5265			3	6			5	11	9						7				4		2	8		10			1
18		21	Reading	0-3		5374			3	6					9				4	7			2	11	5					10	8		1
19		25	BRISTOL CITY	2-2	Garrett, Smith	13501			3	6			5		9			4			7			11			2	8		10			1
20		26	Bristol City	3-2	Garrett, Morrall, Smith	23109			3				5	11	9					6	10			7			2	8		4			1
21		28	Swindon Town	1-3	Garrett	15456							5	11	9					6	10		3	7			2	8		4			1
22	Jan	4	BOURNEMOUTH	2-1	Garrett, Roberts	7176					7		5		9						10		3	11	4	1	2	8		6			
23		18	Cardiff City	2-6	Lowery, Smith	29426			3		7	5			9			4			10			11		1	2	8		6			
24		23	MANSFIELD TOWN	3-0	Fowler, Garrett, Jenkins	2713			3				5	11	9					6	7					1	2	4		10	8		
25		25	NORWICH CITY	1-0	Smith	6023				6			5	11	9			4			10			7	3		2	8					1
26	Feb	1	Notts County	0-1		13096				6			5	11	9			4						7	3	1	2	8		10			
27	Mar	8	Leyton Orient	1-2	Garrett	8567			3			7	5	11	9			4						6			2	8		10			1
28		15	QUEEN'S PARK RANGERS	4-4	Garrett 2, Smith 2	9907			3			7	5	11	9			6						4			2	8		10			1
29		22	Southend United	0-4		8465			3			7	5	11	9			6						4			2	8		10			1
30		29	BRISTOL ROVERS	1-2	Smalley	6846			3			7		11	9			4	1		10						2	8	5	6			
31	Apr	4	Brighton & Hove Albion	2-2	Roberts, Thompson	9152		3				7			9	10		1						11			2	4	5	6	8		
32		5	Mansfield Town	2-3	Briscoe, Garrett	5625		3		6	7				9	10		5	1					11			2	8		4			
33		7	BRIGHTON & HOVE ALB	6-1	*See below	8754		3		6					9	10		5	1		7			11			2	8		4			
34		8	WALSALL	0-8		5757		3		6					9	10			1		7			11			2	8	5	4			
35		12	TORQUAY UNITED	0-0		5808			3	6		5		7	9	10								11			2	8					1
36		19	Crystal Palace	2-2	Roberts, Smith	10920			3			5		7	9	10								11	4		2	8		6			1
37		26	READING	4-0	Heaselgrave, Roberts, Smith 2	5290			3					7	9	10		5						11	4		2	8		6			1
38	May	3	PORT VALE	1-0	Frost	6258			3	6				7	9	10		5						11	4		2	8					1
39		10	Watford	1-1	Garrett	5655				6				7	9	10		5						11	3		2	8		4			1
40		17	CRYSTAL PALACE	1-0	Smith	5690				6				7	9	10		5						11	3		2	8		4			1
41		29	ALDERSHOT	2-2	Garrett, Roberts	4240				6	7				9	10		5						11	3		2	8		4			1
42		31	IPSWICH TOWN	2-2	Garrett 2	3216				6	7				9	10	4	5						11	3		2	8					1

Scorers in game 33: Garrett, Morrall 2, Roberts, Smith 2

	Apps	5	1	28	30	13	27	25	6	35	20	1	24	5	4	24	3	3	31	23	6	41	41	6	24	4	1	31
	Goals			1	1		4	1	26	3		1				9			6			1	17		1	1		

F.A. Cup

		Date		Opponent	Score	Scorers	Att	Barron W	Blunt E	Briscoe JER	Fowler T	Garrett ACE	Lowery H	Morrall AD	Roberts DG	Sankey J	Scott DP	Smalley T	Smith D	Thompson H	Jones JT
R1	Nov	30	MANSFIELD TOWN	2-0	Blunt, Garrett	15600	3	10		5	11	9		6		7		4	2	8	1
R2	Dec	14	Peterborough Utd.	1-1	Garrett	10000	3	11		5		9	4		7			6	2	8	10	1
rep		19	PETERBOROUGH UTD.	1-1	Thompson	6800	3	11		5		9	6		7			4	2	8	10	1
rep 2		23	Peterborough Utd.	8-1	Garrett 4, Morrall 2, Roberts 2	13150	3			5		9	4		7		11	6	2	8	10	1
R3	Jan	11	PRESTON NORTH END	1-2	Roberts	16858	3		7	5		9	4		10		11	1	2	8	6

	P	W	D	L	F	A	W	D	L	F	A	Pts
1 Cardiff City	42	18	3	0	60	11	12	3	6	33	19	66
2 Queen's Park Rgs.	42	15	2	4	42	15	8	9	4	32	25	57
3 Bristol City	42	13	4	4	56	20	7	7	7	38	36	51
4 Swindon Town	42	15	4	2	56	25	4	7	10	28	48	49
5 Walsall	42	11	6	4	42	25	6	6	9	32	34	46
6 Ipswich Town	42	11	5	5	33	21	5	9	7	28	32	46
7 Bournemouth	42	12	4	5	43	20	6	4	11	29	34	44
8 Southend United	42	9	7	5	38	22	8	3	10	33	38	44
9 Reading	42	11	6	4	53	30	5	5	11	30	44	43
10 Port Vale	42	14	4	3	51	28	3	5	13	17	35	43
11 Torquay United	42	11	5	5	33	23	4	7	10	19	38	42
12 Notts County	42	11	4	6	35	19	4	6	11	28	44	40
13 NORTHAMPTON TOWN	42	11	5	5	46	33	4	5	12	26	42	40
14 Bristol Rovers	42	9	6	6	34	26	7	2	12	25	43	40
15 Exeter City	42	11	6	4	37	27	4	3	14	23	42	39
16 Watford	42	11	4	6	39	27	6	1	14	22	49	39
17 Brighton & Hove A.	42	8	7	6	31	35	5	5	11	23	37	38
18 Crystal Palace	42	9	7	5	29	19	4	4	13	20	43	37
19 Leyton Orient	42	10	5	6	40	28	2	3	16	14	47	32
20 Aldershot	42	6	7	8	25	26	4	5	12	23	52	32
21 Norwich City	42	6	3	12	38	48	4	5	12	26	52	28
22 Mansfield Town	42	8	5	8	31	38	1	5	15	17	58	28

1947/48   14th in Division 3(S)

#	Date	Opponent	Score	Scorers	Att	Ansell W	Barron W	Blunt E	Bowen DL	Briscoe JER	Coley WE	Dennison RS	English J	Fisher PM	Fowler T	Garrett ACE	Gillespie P	Heaselgrave SE	Hughes TG	Jenkins RJ	Jones JT	King FAR	Lowery H	Morrall AD	Roberts DG	Sankey J	Scott DP	Smalley T	Smith D	Stanton SH	Thompson H
1	Aug 23	Swindon Town	0-0		18138					7	6	5				9					1		4		11	3		2	8		10
2	28	TORQUAY UNITED	1-0	Garrett	10255			6		7		5				9				10	1		4		11	3		2	8		
3	30	PORT VALE	4-1	Briscoe, Jenkins 2, Thompson	9404	11		6		7		5				9				10	1		4					2			8
4	Sep 3	Torquay United	2-4	Jenkins 2	7019	11		4			6	5				9				10	1				7	3		2	8		
5	6	Queen's Park Rangers	0-2		21419					7	6	5				9				10			4		11	3	1	2	8		
6	11	ALDERSHOT	2-1	Garrett 2	7333		3	4			6	5				9							10	11			1	2	7		8
7	13	WATFORD	0-1		7861			6				5				9						4	10	11			1	2	7		8
8	17	Aldershot	1-1	Roberts	4333		3					5				9				10	1	6	7	11	4			2	8		
9	20	Brighton & Hove Albion	3-2	Garrett, Jenkins, Smith	8575		3					5				9				10	1	4	7	11	6			2	8		
10	27	NORWICH CITY	1-0	Garrett	9757		3					5				9				10	1	6	7	11	4			2	8		
11	Oct 4	Bristol Rovers	2-1	Briscoe, Morrall	15098		3			9		5								10	1	6	7	11	4			2			8
12	11	Walsall	0-2		15202		3			9	6	5									1	10	7	11		4		2			8
13	18	LEYTON ORIENT	1-1	Garrett	9419		3			9	6	5				7				10	1		4		11			2	8		
14	25	Exeter City	1-1	Garrett	10391		3				6	5			11	9		10			1		4		7			2	8		
15	Nov 1	NEWPORT COUNTY	1-1	Smith	9289		3				4				11	9		10			1				7	5		2	8		6
16	8	Southend United	1-3	Smith	10481		3				6	5			11	9		10			1				7	4		2	8		
17	15	NOTTS COUNTY	1-2	Garrett	18272		3				6	5			11	9					1		4		7			2	8		10
18	22	Swansea Town	1-5	Garrett	13826	11					6	5				9		10			1		4		7	3		2	8		
19	Dec 25	Crystal Palace	0-1		15095		3			9	6				11			10		8	1		5		7	4		2			
20	27	CRYSTAL PALACE	3-1	Briscoe, King, Morrall	9631		3	6		7					10						1	8	5	9	11	4		2			
21	Jan 3	Port Vale	0-1		12905			6		7	4				10						1	8	5	9	11	3		2			
22	24	BRISTOL CITY	0-4		7522		3				4	5	7		10						1	9	6	8	11			2			
23	31	Watford	1-1	Hughes	13834					7	4	5		6	11				9	10	1	8	3					2			
24	Feb 7	BRIGHTON & HOVE ALB	4-0	Briscoe 2, Hughes, Lowery	6661					7	4	5		6	11				9	10	1	8	3					2			
25	14	Norwich City	3-2	Briscoe, Hughes, Fowler	23470		3			9	4		7		11				6		1	8	5					2		10	
26	21	BRISTOL ROVERS	1-3	Briscoe	5149		3			9	4		7		11				6		1	8	5					2		10	
27	28	WALSALL	2-1	Hughes, King	8253		3	6		7	4				11				10	9	1	8	5					2			
28	Mar 6	Leyton Orient	0-5		14714		3	4		9	6				11			10			1	7	5					2	8		
29	13	EXETER CITY	3-1	Briscoe 2, Hughes	6136	1	3			9	4	5			11				10			8	7	6				2			
30	18	SWINDON TOWN	0-0		6241	1	3			9	6	5			11			10				8	7			4		2			
31	20	Newport County	2-1	Briscoe, Coley	8567	1	3			9	6	5			11			10					7			4		2	8		
32	26	Reading	1-1	King	16774	1	3			9	6	5			11			10				7					4	2	8		
33	27	SOUTHEND UNITED	2-0	Coley 2	9104	1	3			9	6	5			11			10				7					4	2	8		
34	29	READING	1-1	Briscoe	8855	1	3			9	6	5			11			10				7				4		2	8		
35	Apr 3	Notts County	2-3	Fowler, Smith	30903	1			6	9	4			3	11			10				7	5					2	8		
36	8	QUEEN'S PARK RANGERS	1-1	Coley	11260	1	3			6	4	5			11			9				8	10					2	7		
37	10	SWANSEA TOWN	0-1		8506	1	3			6		5			11			10				9	7			4		2	8		
38	17	Bournemouth	0-2		14818	1		4	6				8	5	11			10				9	3		7			2			
39	21	Ipswich Town	2-5	King 2	9285	1		6						5	11		3	10		9		8	7					2			4
40	24	IPSWICH TOWN	4-2	Heaselgrave, King 3	4410			4	6					3	11			10	9			8	5		7		1	2			
41	29	BOURNEMOUTH	3-6	Hughes 3	6674			4						3	11				10	6		9	5		7		1	2	8		
42	May 1	Bristol City	1-1	King	8392	1		4	6				7	3	11				9	10		8	5					2			
			Apps			12	29	14	6	23	28	28	5	8	25	16	1	22	12	14	25	23	35	10	25	19	5	42	24	2	9
			Goals							11	4				2	9		1	8	5		9	1	2	1				4		1

F.A. Cup

Rd	Date	Opponent	Score	Scorers	Att	Ansell W	Barron W	Blunt E	Bowen DL	Briscoe JER	Coley WE	Dennison RS	English J	Fisher PM	Fowler T	Garrett ACE	Gillespie P	Heaselgrave SE	Hughes TG	Jenkins RJ	Jones JT	King FAR	Lowery H	Morrall AD	Roberts DG	Sankey J	Scott DP	Smalley T	Smith D	Stanton SH	Thompson H
R1	Nov 29	Exeter City	1-1	Roberts	13143		3			9	6	5			11						1		4		7			2	8		10
rep	Dec 6	EXETER CITY	2-0	Briscoe, Jenkins	9500		3			9	6	5			11			8		10	1		4		7			2			
R2	13	TORQUAY UNITED	1-1	Heaselgrave	12000		3			9	6	5			11			8		10	1		4		7			2			
rep	20	Torquay United	0-2		7000		3			9	6	5			11			8		10	1		4		7			2			

First games of both rounds a.e.t.

	Team	P	W	D	L	F	A	W	D	L	F	A	Pts
1	Queen's Park Rgs.	42	16	3	2	44	17	10	6	5	30	20	61
2	Bournemouth	42	13	5	3	42	13	11	4	6	34	22	57
3	Walsall	42	13	5	3	37	12	8	4	9	33	28	51
4	Ipswich Town	42	16	1	4	42	18	7	2	12	25	43	49
5	Swansea Town	42	14	6	1	48	14	4	6	11	22	38	48
6	Notts County	42	12	4	5	44	27	7	4	10	24	32	46
7	Bristol City	42	11	4	6	47	26	7	3	11	30	39	43
8	Port Vale	42	14	4	3	48	18	2	7	12	15	36	43
9	Southend United	42	11	8	2	32	16	4	5	12	19	42	43
10	Reading	42	10	5	6	37	28	5	6	10	19	30	41
11	Exeter City	42	11	6	4	34	22	4	5	12	21	41	41
12	Newport County	42	9	8	4	38	28	5	5	11	23	45	41
13	Crystal Palace	42	12	5	4	32	14	1	8	12	17	35	39
14	NORTHAMPTON TOWN	42	10	5	6	35	28	4	6	11	23	44	39
15	Watford	42	6	6	9	31	37	8	4	9	26	42	38
16	Swindon Town	42	6	10	5	21	20	4	6	11	20	26	36
17	Leyton Orient	42	8	5	8	31	32	5	5	11	20	41	36
18	Torquay United	42	7	6	8	40	29	4	7	10	23	33	35
19	Aldershot	42	5	10	6	22	26	5	5	11	23	41	35
20	Bristol Rovers	42	7	3	11	39	34	6	5	10	32	41	34
21	Norwich City	42	8	3	10	33	34	5	5	11	28	42	34
22	Brighton & Hove A.	42	8	4	9	26	31	3	8	10	17	42	34

1948/49 — 20th in Division 3(S)

#	Date	Opponent	Score	Scorers	Att	Aldridge NH	Ansell W	Barron W	Blunt E	Bowen DL	Briscoe JER	Coley WE	Collins BV	English J	Fowler T	Freimanis E	Garrett ACE	Horne AT	Hughes TG	Jackson LW	James R	King FAR	Lowery H	McCoy W	Roberts DG	Smalley T	Smith D	Smith WH	Stanton SH	Thompson H	Williams E
1	Aug 21	Exeter City	1-5	Fowler	9586	3						6			11	9			10		4		5		7	2	8				1
2	25	Norwich City	1-2	Freimanis	22517	3			4			6			11	9			10		5	7					8			2	1
3	28	Bristol City	0-3		22663			3	4			6			11	9			10			7	5			2	8				1
4	Sep 2	NORWICH CITY	1-0	WH Smith	7127		1	3	4			6	5	7	11	9										2		8		10	
5	4	SWINDON TOWN	0-1		9410		1	3	4			6	5	7	11	9										2		8		10	
6	7	Southend United	1-0	Freimanis	8454		1	3	4			6	5		11	9			10			7				2		8			
7	11	Leyton Orient	3-0	Fowler, Freimanis, Hughes	12747		1	3	4			6			11	9			10			7	5			2		8			
8	16	SOUTHEND UNITED	2-2	Coley, James	8861		1	3	4			6			11	9			10		8	7	5			2					
9	18	PORT VALE	2-2	Briscoe, one og	9964		1	3			4	6		7	11	9			10				5			2	8				
10	25	Millwall	2-3	Hughes, D Smith	25690		1	3	4			6	5	7	11	9			10							2	8				
11	Oct 2	ALDERSHOT	2-0	Briscoe, D Smith	7924		1	3			4	6	5	7	11	9				2							8	10			
12	9	IPSWICH TOWN	1-1	D Smith	9589		1	3			4	6	5	7	11	9				2							8	10			
13	16	Bournemouth	2-5	D Smith 2	16803		1	3	4			6	5	7	11				10							2	8	9			
14	23	NEWPORT COUNTY	2-1	WH Smith 2	8178		1	3	4			6	5	7	11				10							2	8	9			
15	30	Bristol Rovers	0-1		15363		1	3				6		7	11				10				5			2	8	9	4		
16	Nov 6	READING	1-2	WH Smith	8365		1	3				6	5		11	9			10							2	8	7	4		
17	13	Swansea Town	0-1		23095		1	3				6			11	9			10				5			2	8	7	4		
18	20	WATFORD	1-1	D Smith	8437		1	3				6			11	9			10		4		5			2	8	7			
19	Dec 4	TORQUAY UNITED	0-0		11943		1	3						7	11		9					6		5		2	8	10	4		
20	18	EXETER CITY	4-0	English, Fowler, Garrett 2	7876		1	3						7	11	10	9					6		5		2	8		4		
21	25	NOTTS COUNTY	1-2	Garrett	17724		1	3						7	11		9					6		5		2	8	10	4		
22	27	Notts County	0-2		31171		1	3						7	11		9		10			8		5		2	4			6	
23	Jan 1	BRISTOL CITY	3-1	Fowler, Garrett, King	6901		1	3	6					7	11		9		10					5		2	4	8			
24	15	Swindon Town	2-2	King, one og	14306		1	3	6					7	11		9		10					5		2	4	8			
25	22	LEYTON ORIENT	4-1	English, Garrett, D Smith, King	8661		1	3	4			6		7	11		9					10		5		2	8				
26	29	Crystal Palace	2-2	Garrett 2	13972		1	3	4			6		7	11		9					10		5		2	8				
27	Feb 5	Port Vale	0-1		9369		1	3	4			6		7	11		9					10		5		2	8				
28	12	Walsall	0-1		8694		1	3	4			6			11		9					10		5		2	8	7			
29	19	MILLWALL	4-0	Fowler 3, WH Smith	10775		1	3	4			6			11		9					10		5		2	8	7			
30	26	Aldershot	1-3	Briscoe	5635		1	3			4	6			11		9					10		5		2	8	7			
31	Mar 5	Ipswich Town	2-4	Fowler, Garrett	10439		1	3			4	6		7	11		9					10		5		2	8				
32	12	BOURNEMOUTH	1-0	WH Smith	8473		1	3			4	6			11		9					10		5		2	8	7			
33	19	Newport County	0-2		14869		1	3			4	6			11		9					10		5		2	8	7			
34	26	BRISTOL ROVERS	0-1		7425		1	3			4	6			11		9					10		5		2	8	7			
35	Apr 2	Reading	0-1		14148		1	3			4	6		7	11		9					10		5		2	8				
36	9	SWANSEA TOWN	0-1		10194		1	3			4	6		7	11		9					10		5		2	8				
37	15	Brighton & Hove Albion	0-0		18271		1	3			4	6		7	11		9					10		5		2	8				
38	16	Watford	1-0	Coley	9609		1	3			4	6		7			9	10				11		5		2	8				
39	18	BRIGHTON & HOVE ALB	1-1	King	9184		1	3			4	6		7	11		9					10		5		2	8				
40	23	CRYSTAL PALACE	3-2	Briscoe 2, English	7717		1	3			4	6		7			9					10		5		2	8		11		
41	30	Torquay United	0-3		6526		1	3			4	6		7			9		10					5		2					11
42	May 7	Walsall	0-2		5995		1	3			4	6		7			9		10					5		2					11
				Apps		2	39	40	15	6	17	35	9	19	37	16	21	1	19	2	4	25	17	24	1	39	35	26	5	5	3
				Goals							5	2		3	8	3	8		2		1	4					7	6			

Two own goals

F.A. Cup

	Date	Opponent	Score	Scorers	Att	Ansell W	Barron W	Briscoe JER	Coley WE	English J	Fowler T	Garrett ACE	King FAR	Lowery H	Smalley T	Smith D	Smith WH	Stanton SH
R1	Nov 27	DULWICH HAMLET	2-1	D Smith, WH Smith	10300	1	3		6	7	11	9		5	2	8	10	4
R2	Dec 11	Mansfield Town	1-2	WH Smith	13501	1	3		6	7	11	9		5	2	8	10	4

Division 3(S) — Final Table

		P	W	D	L	F	A	W	D	L	F	A	Pts
1	Swansea Town	42	20	1	0	60	11	7	7	7	27	23	62
2	Reading	42	17	1	3	48	18	8	4	9	29	32	55
3	Bournemouth	42	15	2	4	42	17	7	6	8	27	31	52
4	Swindon Town	42	11	9	1	38	20	7	6	8	26	36	51
5	Bristol Rovers	42	13	5	3	42	23	6	5	10	19	28	48
6	Brighton & Hove A.	42	11	5	5	32	26	4	13	4	23	29	48
7	Ipswich Town	42	14	3	4	53	30	4	6	11	25	47	45
8	Millwall	42	12	7	2	42	23	5	4	12	21	41	45
9	Torquay United	42	12	5	4	45	26	5	6	10	20	44	45
10	Norwich City	42	11	6	4	32	10	5	6	10	35	39	44
11	Notts County	42	15	3	3	68	19	4	2	15	34	49	43
12	Exeter City	42	12	5	4	45	26	3	5	13	18	50	40
13	Port Vale	42	11	3	7	32	21	3	8	10	19	33	39
14	Walsall	42	9	5	7	34	28	6	3	12	22	36	38
15	Newport County	42	8	6	7	41	35	6	3	12	27	57	37
16	Bristol City	42	8	9	4	28	24	3	5	13	16	38	36
17	Watford	42	6	9	6	24	21	4	6	11	17	33	35
18	Southend United	42	5	10	6	18	18	4	6	11	23	28	34
19	Leyton Orient	42	9	6	6	36	29	2	6	13	22	51	34
20	NORTHAMPTON TOWN	42	9	6	6	33	20	3	3	15	18	42	33
21	Aldershot	42	6	5	10	26	29	5	6	10	22	30	33
22	Crystal Palace	42	7	8	6	27	27	1	3	17	11	49	27

1949/50   2nd in Division 3(S)

#	Date		Opponent	Score	Scorers	Att	Ansell W	Barron W	Candlin MH	Coley WE	Collins BV	Dunkley MEF	Dixon A	English J	Fowler T	Freimanis E	Garrett ACE	Hughes TG	King FAR	McCoy W	McCulloch ABR	McCulloch T	Mitchell AJ	Murphy E	Smalley T	Smith D	Southam JH
1	Aug	20	Bristol City	1-3	King	27463	1		4	6							9		7	5			11	10	2	8	3
2		25	NEWPORT COUNTY	4-3	Garrett 2, King, Smith	12718	1		4	6							9		7	5			11	10	2	8	3
3		27	Brighton & Hove Albion	1-1	Garrett	18661	1		4	6							9		7	5			11	10	2	8	3
4	Sep	1	Newport County	4-1	A McCulloch 2, Mitchell, Murphy	12536	1		4	6									7	5	9		11	10	2	8	3
5		3	Walsall	3-1	King, Mitchell, Murphy	14066	1		4	6									7	5	9		11	10	2	8	3
6		8	NOTTM. FOREST	0-0		19228	1		4	6			7							5	9		11	10	2	8	3
7		10	MILLWALL	1-0	Smith	13957	1		4	6			7							5	9		11	10	2	8	3
8		14	Nottingham Forest	1-0	Murphy	23394	1		4	6			7							5	9		11	10	2	8	3
9		17	Swindon Town	1-6	one og	15219	1		4	6			7							5	9		11	10	2	8	3
10		24	TORQUAY UNITED	3-0	A McCulloch 2, Mitchell	11781	1		4	6									7	5	9		11	10	2	8	3
11	Oct	1	Aldershot	0-0		6990	1			6								4	7	5	9		11	10	2	8	3
12		8	IPSWICH TOWN	1-2	King	13773	1		4	6						11			7	5	9			10	2	8	3
13		15	Exeter City	3-1	A McCulloch 2, Murphy	8353	1		4	6						11		8		5	9			10	2	7	3
14		22	LEYTON ORIENT	3-0	Garrett, A McCulloch, Murphy	11950	1		4	6						11		8		5	9			10	2	7	3
15		29	Reading	1-3	A McCulloch	18636	1		4							11		8	6	5	9			10	2	7	3
16	Nov	5	WATFORD	0-0		9722	1		4							11		8	6	5	9			10	2	7	3
17		12	Crystal Palace	4-0	Freimanis, A McCulloch, Mitchell 2	12486	1		4	6				8						5	9		11	10	2	7	3
18		19	BOURNEMOUTH	2-3	Murphy 2	15103	1			6				8				4		5	9		11	10	2	7	3
19	Dec	3	SOUTHEND UNITED	2-0	Mitchell, Murphy	12075	1			6			8	7						5	9		11	10	2	4	3
20		17	BRISTOL CITY	4-2	Mitchell 2, Murphy, Smith	11141	1		4	6										5	9	7	11	10	2	8	3
21		24	BRIGHTON & HOVE ALB	2-1	A McCulloch, Murphy	14958	1		4	6			8							5	9		11	10	2	7	3
22		26	Port Vale	1-3	A McCulloch	17212	1	3	4	6			10							5	9	7	11		2	8	
23		27	PORT VALE	1-1	English	19263	1	3	4				8	7						5	9		11	10	2	6	
24		31	WALSALL	2-0	Dixon 2	12349	1	3	4	6			8							5	9		11	10	2	7	
25	Jan	14	Millwall	2-0	A McCulloch, Mitchell	22109	1	3	4				8					6		5	9		11	10	2	7	
26		21	SWINDON TOWN	0-1		14633	1	3	4				8					6		5	9		11	10	2	7	
27	Feb	4	Torquay United	0-1		8732	1		4				8	7				6		5	9		11	10	2		3
28		18	ALDERSHOT	1-1	English	14451	1	3	4				8	7				6		5	9		11	10	2		
29		25	Ipswich Town	2-2	Dixon, A McCulloch	11174	1	3	4				8	7				6		5	9		11	10	2		
30	Mar	4	EXETER CITY	3-3	English, A McCulloch 2	11537	1	3	4				8	7				6		5	9		11	10	2		
31		11	Leyton Orient	0-1		9914	1	3	4	6			8	7	9					5			11	10	2		
32		18	READING	2-0	English, Mitchell	8938	1	3	4	6			8	7						5	9		11	10	2		
33		25	Watford	0-0		13630	1	3	4				8	7						5			11	10	2		
34	Apr	1	CRYSTAL PALACE	2-2	Dixon 2	10277	1	3	4	6			8	7						5	9		11	10	2		
35		8	Bournemouth	2-1	Dixon, Mitchell	12540	1	3	4	6			8	7						5	9		11	10	2		
36		10	Norwich City	1-2	Dixon	21015	1	3	4	6			8	7						5	9		11	10	2		
37		11	NORWICH CITY	3-1	Coley, Murphy 2	11167	1	3	4	6	5		8			11					9		7	10	2		
38		15	BRISTOL ROVERS	2-0	Fowler, Mitchell	9622	1	3	4	6	5		8			11					9		7	10	2		
39		22	Southend United	2-1	Garrett, Murphy	13195	1	3	4	6	5		8			11				9			7	10	2		
40		27	Notts County	0-2		31928	1	3	4	6	5		8			11				9			7	10	2		
41		29	NOTTS COUNTY	5-1	Dixon 2, Garrett, Mitchell 2	9971	1	3	4	6	5		8			11				9			7	10	2		
42	May	1	Bristol Rovers	0-0		11679	1	3	4	6	5		8			11				9			7	10	2		
			Apps				42	20	39	32	6	4	23	12	11	3	11	11	8	36	34	2	37	41	42	26	22
			Goals						1				9	4	1	1	6		4		15		14	13		3	

One own goal

F.A. Cup

Rd	Date		Opponent	Score	Scorers	Att	Ansell W	Barron W	Candlin MH	Coley WE	Collins BV	Dunkley MEF	Dixon A	English J	Fowler T	Freimanis E	Garrett ACE	Hughes TG	King FAR	McCoy W	McCulloch ABR	McCulloch T	Mitchell AJ	Murphy E	Smalley T	Smith D	Southam JH
R1	Nov	26	WALTHAMSTOW AVE.	4-1	Dixon, A McCulloch, Mitchell 2	15000	1		4	6			8							5	9		11	10	2	7	3
R2	Dec	10	TORQUAY UNITED	4-2	Dixon, Mitchell 3	16000	1		4	6			8							5	9		11	10	2	7	3
R3	Jan	7	SOUTHAMPTON	1-1	A McCulloch	23209	1	3	4				8					6		5	9		11	10	2	7	
rep		11	Southampton	3-2	Candlin, Dixon, Hughes	23406	1	3	4				8					6		5	9		11	10	2	7	
R4		28	Bournemouth	1-1	Mitchell	22260	1	3	4				8					6		5	9		11	10	2	7	
rep	Feb	2	BOURNEMOUTH	2-1	English, A McCulloch	22644	1	3	4				8	7				6		5	9		11	10	2		
R5		11	Derby County	2-4	Dixon 2	38063	1	3	4				8	7				6		5	9		11	10	2		

		P	W	D	L	F	A	W	D	L	F	A	Pts
1	Notts County	42	17	3	1	60	12	8	5	8	35	38	58
2	NORTHAMPTON TOWN	42	12	6	3	43	21	8	5	8	29	29	51
3	Southend United	42	15	4	2	43	15	4	9	8	23	33	51
4	Nottingham Forest	42	13	0	8	37	15	7	9	5	30	24	49
5	Torquay United	42	13	6	2	40	23	4	4	11	26	40	48
6	Watford	42	10	6	5	26	13	6	7	8	19	22	45
7	Crystal Palace	42	12	5	4	35	21	3	9	9	20	33	44
8	Brighton & Hove A.	42	9	8	4	32	24	7	4	10	25	45	44
9	Bristol Rovers	42	12	5	4	34	18	7	0	14	17	33	43
10	Reading	42	15	2	4	48	21	2	6	13	22	43	42
11	Norwich City	42	11	5	5	44	21	5	5	11	21	42	42
12	Bournemouth	42	11	6	4	38	19	5	4	12	19	37	42
13	Port Vale	42	12	6	3	33	13	3	5	13	14	29	41
14	Swindon Town	42	9	7	5	41	30	6	4	11	18	32	41
15	Bristol City	42	12	4	5	38	19	3	6	12	22	42	40
16	Exeter City	42	9	8	4	37	27	5	3	13	26	48	39
17	Ipswich Town	42	9	6	6	36	36	3	5	13	21	50	35
18	Leyton Orient	42	10	6	5	33	30	2	5	14	20	55	35
19	Walsall	42	8	8	5	37	25	1	8	12	24	37	34
20	Aldershot	42	10	5	6	30	16	3	3	15	18	44	34
21	Newport County	42	11	5	5	50	34	2	3	16	17	64	34
22	Millwall	42	11	1	9	39	29	3	3	15	16	34	32

1950/51 — 21st in Division 3(S)

No	Date		Opponent	Score	Scorers	Att	Ansell W	Barron W	Burn RG	Candlin MH	Coley WE	Collins BV	Davie JG	Dixon A	Docherty J	Duckhouse E	English J	Feehan I	Fowler T	Freeman NF	Garrett ACE	Hughes TG	Maxwell K	McCulloch ABR	Mitchell AJ	Mulgrew T	Murphy E	Potts HJ	Smalley T	Smith D	Smith JO	Southam JH	Woollard AJ
1	Aug	19	Ipswich Town	1-1	Smalley	15325	1	3		4			6	8		5								9	11		10		2		7		
2		23	Norwich City	0-0		27300	1	3		4			6	8		5								9	11		10		2		7		
3		26	Port Vale	3-0	Barron, A McCulloch, J Smith	21424	1	3		4			6	8		5								9	11		10		2		7		
4		31	NORWICH CITY	1-2	A McCulloch	17696	1	3		4			6	8		5								9	11		10		2		7		
5	Sep	2	NOTTM. FOREST	2-2	A McCulloch, Mitchell	17887	1	3		4			6	8		5								9	11		10	7	2				
6		7	Leyton Orient	0-1		17887	1	3		4			6	8		5								9	11		10	7	2				
7		9	Torquay United	1-1	Mitchell	9219	1	3		4			6	8		5								9	11		10		2		7		
8		14	LEYTON ORIENT	3-3	Dixon, A McCulloch, Murphy	11344	1	3		4			6	8		5								9	11		10	7	2				
9		16	ALDERSHOT	1-0	Dixon	12072	1	3		4			6	8		5								9	11		10	7	2				
10		21	Newport County	2-2	A McCulloch 2	13845	1	3		4			6	8		5								9	11		10	7	2				
11		23	Swindon Town	0-1		13708	1	3		4			6	8		5								9	11		10	7	2				
12		30	COLCHESTER UNITED	2-1	Candlin, Dixon	10160	1	3		4			6	8		5								9	11		10	7	2				
13	Oct	7	WALSALL	1-1	Dixon	12190	1	3		4			6	8		5								9	11		10	7	2				
14		14	Watford	1-0	Dixon	14409	1	3		4			6	8		5								9	11		10	7	2				
15		21	MILLWALL	1-2	Dixon	16346	1	3		4	5		6	8										9	11		10	7	2				
16		28	Bristol City	0-1		20798		3		4	5		6	8			7	1						9	11		10		2				
17	Nov	4	GILLINGHAM	4-1	Dixon, English 2, Mitchell	10785		3		4			6	8		5	7	1						9	11		10		2				
18		11	Bournemouth	0-1		13004	1	3		4			6	8		5	7							9	11		10		2				
19		18	EXETER CITY	4-1	Dixon, English 2, A McCulloch	11503	1	3		4		6		8		5	7					10		9	11				2				
20	Dec	2	READING	1-1	Mitchell	11106	1	3		4		6		8		5	7					10		9	11				2				
21		16	IPSWICH TOWN	2-1	Dixon 2	7123	1	3		4		6		8		5	7							9	11		10		2				
22		23	PORT VALE	1-1	Mitchell	8785	1	3		4			6	8		5	7							9	11		10		2				
23		25	Crystal Palace	0-0		11001	1	3		4			6	8		5	7							9	11		10		2				
24		26	CRYSTAL PALACE	2-0	A McCulloch 2	12607	1	3		4			6	8		5	7							9	11		10		2				
25	Jan	13	TORQUAY UNITED	1-0	Dixon	10976	1			4			6	8		5	7							9	11		10		2			3	
26		20	Aldershot	0-3		7875	1	3		4			6	8		5	7							9	11		10		2				
27	Feb	3	SWINDON TOWN	1-2	English	7195	1			4			6	8			7				5			9	11		10		2			3	
28		10	Southend United	0-3		9185	1			4			6	8			7					9	5		11		10		2			3	
29		17	Colchester United	1-2	Mitchell	7048				4			6	8			7	1				9	5		11		10		2				3
30		24	Walsall	0-1		11941		3		4			6	8		5	7	1				9			11		10		2				
31	Mar	3	WATFORD	6-0	*See below	9136		3		4			6	8			7	1			5	9			11		10		2				
32		10	Millwall	1-2	English	13187		3		4			6	8			7	1			5	9			11		10		2				
33		17	BRISTOL CITY	2-2	English 2	8042				4				8		5	7	1			6			9	11		10		2				3
34		23	Brighton & Hove Albion	1-5	one og	15511				4				8		5		1	10		6			9	11				2	7			3
35		24	Gillingham	1-3	Fowler	10657				4			6	8		5		1	10					9	11				2	7		3	
36		27	BRIGHTON & HOVE ALB	0-0		8966				4			6	8		5		1	10		7			9	11				2			3	
37		31	BOURNEMOUTH	0-1		6260				4	6			8		5		1	10		7			9	11				2			3	
38	Apr	5	NEWPORT COUNTY	1-4	Fowler	6425				4	6			8		5		1	10		7			9	11				2			3	
39		7	Exeter City	0-1		6141				4	6			8		5		1	10		7			9	11				2			3	
40		9	Plymouth Argyle	1-4	A McCulloch	7846				4	6			8		5		1	10		7			9	11				2			3	
41		14	SOUTHEND UNITED	1-1	A McCulloch	7342				4	6			8		5		1	10		7			9	11				2			3	
42		19	BRISTOL ROVERS	1-1	Hughes	6796				4	6			8		5		1	10			9			11	7			2			3	
43		21	Reading	0-2		13401				4	6			8		5		1	10					9	11	7			2			3	
44		25	Nottingham Forest	2-2	Fowler, Mulgrew	27244				4			6		8	5		1	10					9	11	7			2			3	
45		28	PLYMOUTH ARGYLE	1-3	A McCulloch	6342				4			6			5		1	10	8				9	11	7			2			3	
46	May	5	Bristol Rovers	1-1	A McCulloch	10739			8	4			6			5		1	10					9	11	7			2			3	
			Apps				26	37	1	30	9	3	39	43	1	41	18	19	13	1	11	22	2	41	44	5	30	10	36	2	5	14	3
			Goals					1		1			1	12			9		3		1	1		13	7	1	2				1		

Scorers in game 31: Davie, Dixon, English, Garrett, Mitchell, Murphy.

One own goal

F.A. Cup

Rnd	Date		Opponent	Score	Scorers	Att	Ansell W	Barron W	Candlin MH	Davie JG	Dixon A	Duckhouse E	English J	McCulloch ABR	Mitchell AJ	Murphy E	Smalley T	Southam JH
R3	Jan	6	BARNSLEY	3-1	Mitchell 2(1p), Murphy	16818	1	3	4	6	8	5	7	9	11	10	2	
R4		27	Arsenal	2-3	English 2	72408	1		4	6	8	5	7	9	11	10	2	3

Division 3 (South) — Final Table

		P	W	D	L	F	A	W	D	L	F	A	Pts
1	Nottingham Forest	46	16	6	1	57	17	14	4	5	53	23	70
2	Norwich City	46	16	6	1	42	14	9	8	6	40	31	64
3	Reading	46	15	6	2	57	17	6	9	8	31	36	57
4	Plymouth Argyle	46	16	5	2	54	19	8	4	11	31	36	57
5	Millwall	46	15	6	2	52	23	8	4	11	28	34	56
6	Bristol Rovers	46	15	7	1	46	18	5	8	10	18	24	55
7	Southend United	46	15	4	4	64	27	6	6	11	28	42	52
8	Ipswich Town	46	15	4	4	48	24	8	2	13	21	34	52
9	Bournemouth	46	17	5	1	49	16	5	2	16	16	41	51
10	Bristol City	46	15	4	4	41	25	5	7	11	23	34	51
11	Newport County	46	13	4	6	48	25	6	5	12	29	45	47
12	Port Vale	46	13	6	4	35	24	3	7	13	25	41	45
13	Brighton & Hove A.	46	11	8	4	51	31	2	9	12	20	48	43
14	Exeter City	46	11	4	8	33	30	7	2	14	29	55	42
15	Walsall	46	12	4	7	32	20	3	6	14	20	42	40
16	Colchester United	46	12	5	6	43	25	2	7	14	20	51	40
17	Swindon Town	46	15	4	4	38	17	3	0	20	17	50	40
18	Aldershot	46	11	8	4	37	20	4	2	17	19	68	40
19	Leyton Orient	46	13	2	8	36	28	2	6	15	17	47	38
20	Torquay United	46	13	2	8	47	39	1	7	15	17	42	37
21	NORTHAMPTON TOWN	46	8	9	6	39	30	7	4	16	16	37	36
22	Gillingham	46	10	7	6	41	30	3	2	18	28	71	35
23	Watford	46	8	5	10	29	28	1	6	16	25	60	29
24	Crystal Palace	46	6	5	12	18	39	2	6	15	15	45	27

1951/52   8th in Division 3(S)

#	Date		Opponent	Score	Scorers	Att.	Ansell W	Candlin MH	Collins BV	Connell PM	Croy J	Davie JG	Dixon A	Dodgin N	Duckhouse E	English J	Feehan I	Fowler T	French JR	Hughes TG	McCulloch ABR	O'Donnell W	Payne IEH	Pinchbeck CB	Ramscar FT	Smith JO	Southam JH	Starocsik F	Wilson JA	Wood AR	Adams DF
1	Aug 18		Aldershot	1-0	Ramscar	10047		4		2		6	8		5	7	1								10				11	3	
2	20		Newport County	0-2		10870		4		2		6	8		5	7	1								10				11	3	
3	Sep 1		BRISTOL CITY	1-2	Ramscar	14152	1	4		2		6			5	7						9	8		10				11	3	
4	6		NEWPORT COUNTY	5-0	English 2, Payne 3	10374	1	4		2		6			5	7						9	8		10				11	3	
5	8		IPSWICH TOWN	1-0	Starocsik	13917	1	4		2		6			5	7						9	8		10				11	3	
6	11		Southend United	0-2		6690	1	4		2		6			5	7		11				9	8		10					3	
7	15		Torquay United	2-1	O'Donnell 2	7627	1	4	2						5	7		11		6		9	8		10					3	
8	20		SOUTHEND UNITED	4-3	English 2, Hughes, Ramscar	10466	1	4	2						5	7		11		6		9	8		10					3	
9	22		GILLINGHAM	2-1	English, Fowler	12853	1	4	2						5	7		11		6		9	8		10					3	
10	27		PORT VALE	3-1	English, Fowler 2	8082	1	4	2						5	7		11		6		9	8		10					3	
11	29		Brighton & Hove Albion	0-2		15861	1	4	2						5	7		11		6		9	8		10					3	
12	Oct 6		Bristol Rovers	2-2	Fowler, A McCulloch	20905	1	4	2						5	7		11		6	9		8		10					3	
13	13		PLYMOUTH ARGYLE	3-1	English 2, Ramscar	14661	1	4	2						5	8		11		6	9				10			7		3	
14	20		Norwich City	1-2	Ramscar	28078	1	4	2						5	8		11		6	9				10			7		3	
15	27		EXETER CITY	3-1	English, Fowler, Ramscar	12943		4	2						5	7	1	11		6	9		8		10					3	
16	Nov 3		Colchester United	5-2	English 2, A McCulloch, Ramscar 2	10326		4	2						5	7	1	11		6	9		8		10					3	
17	10		CRYSTAL PALACE	5-2	English, A McCulloch 2, Ramscar 2	14845		4	2						5	7	1	11		6	9		8		10					3	
18	17		Swindon Town	1-1	Ramscar	11226		4	2						5	7	1	11		6	9		8		10					3	
19	Dec 1		Walsall	0-3		7676		4	2						5		1	11		6	9		8		10			7		3	
20	8		SHREWSBURY TOWN	6-0	*See below	13715		4	2						5	7	1	11		6	9		8		10					3	
21	22		Port Vale	0-0		8973		4	2						5	7	1	11		6	9		8		10					3	
22	25		Watford	4-2	English, A McCulloch 2, one og	7847		4	2						5	7	1	11		6	9		8		10					3	
23	26		WATFORD	1-4	Payne	18295		4	2						5	7	1	11		6	9		8		10					3	
24	29		Bristol City	0-2		18733		4	2	3				6	5	7	1	11				9	8		10						
25	Jan 5		Ipswich Town	2-3	Fowler, Pinchbech	10071		4	3	2				6	5	7	1	11					8	9	10						
26	12		MILLWALL	1-1	English	13329		4	3	2				6	5	7	1	11					8	9	10						
27	19		TORQUAY UNITED	2-4	English, Fowler	10535		4	3	2					5	7	1	11		6		9			10		8				
28	24		ALDERSHOT	6-2	English, Fowler, Pinchbech 2, Ramscar 2	4490		4	3	2	5					7	1	11		6				9	10		8				
29	26		Gillingham	1-2	O'Donnell	9625		4	3	2	5					7	1	11		6		9			10		8				
30	Feb 2		Reading	0-2		15932	5	4	2	3						7	1	11		6		9			10		8				
31	9		BRIGHTON & HOVE ALB	3-0	O'Donnell, Ramscar, Starocsik	13639	5	4	2							7	1			6		9	8		10			3	11		
32	16		BRISTOL ROVERS	2-0	English, Hughes	11704	5	4	2							7	1			6		9	8		10			3	11		
33	23		READING	0-3		15696	5	4	2							7	1			6		9	8		10			3	11		
34	Mar 1		Plymouth Argyle	0-2		22133	5	4	2							7				6			8		10	1		3	11		9
35	8		NORWICH CITY	1-2	Payne	14625	5	4	2							7				6			8		10	1		3	11		9
36	15		Exeter City	3-0	Starocsik, Adams 2	7908	5	4	2							7				6			8		10	1		3	11		9
37	22		COLCHESTER UNITED	2-0	Ramscar, Starocsik	10160	5	4	2							7				6			8		10	1		3	11		9
38	Apr 5		SWINDON TOWN	1-0	Starocsik	7419	5	4	2							7	1			6			8		10			3	11		9
39	12		Leyton Orient	1-2	Adams	8776	5	4	2							7	1			6			8		10			3	11		9
40	14		Bournemouth	0-3		9933	5	4	2							7	1			6			8		10			3	11		9
41	15		BOURNEMOUTH	5-3	English, O'Donnell, Ramscar 3	9524	5	4	2						8		1	11		6		9			10			3	7		
42	19		WALSALL	4-1	English, Fowler, O'Donnell 2	8311		4	2		5				8		1	11		6		9			10			3	7		
43	24		LEYTON ORIENT	4-0	English, O'Donnell, Ramscar 2	6907	5		2					4	8		1	11		6		9			10			3	7		
44	26		Shrewsbury Town	1-3	O'Donnell	9514	5		2					4	8		1	11		6		9			10			3	7		
45	30		Millwall	1-2	Ramscar	10389	5		2			6					1	11		4		9	8		10			3	7		
46	May 3		Crystal Palace	3-3	O'Donnell, Ramscar, Starocsik	7214	5		2					4	8		1	11		6		9			10			3	7		

Scorers in game 20: English, Fowler, A McCulloch, Payne, Ramscar

		Ansell W	Candlin MH	Collins BV	Connell PM	Croy J	Davie JG	Dixon A	Dodgin N	Duckhouse E	English J	Feehan I	Fowler T	French JR	Hughes TG	McCulloch ABR	O'Donnell W	Payne IEH	Pinchbeck CB	Ramscar FT	Smith JO	Southam JH	Starocsik F	Wilson JA	Wood AR	Adams DF
Apps		12	42	40	13	3	25	2	5	27	43	20	32	1	36	14	22	32	3	46	4	16	24	23	14	7
Goals											21		10		2	8	10	6	3	23			6			3

One own goal

F.A. Cup

	Date	Opponent	Score	Scorers	Att.	Candlin MH	Collins BV	Duckhouse E	English J	Feehan I	Fowler T	Hughes TG	McCulloch ABR	Payne IEH	Ramscar FT	Starocsik F	Wood AR
R1	Nov 24	Norwich City	2-3	Payne, Ramscar	27120	4	2	5		1	11	6	9	8	10	7	3

1952/53 3rd in Division 3(S)

#	Date	Opponent	Score	Scorers	Att	Adams DF	Baxter LR	Candlin MH	Collins BV	Croy J	Davie JG	Dodgin N	Edelston M	English J	Fowler T	Hughes TG	McLain T	O'Donnell W	Patterson RL	Ramscar FT	Southam JH	Starocsik F	Upton F	Wood AR	Mulgrew T
1	Aug 23	Bournemouth	1-0	English	14771			4				6		7	11		5	9	3	8	2			1	10
2	27	Exeter City	0-2		12729			5				4		7	11		6	9	3	10	2			1	8
3	30	SOUTHEND UNITED	4-3	Fowler 2, Ramscar 2	13611			5				4		7	11		6	9	3	10	2			1	8
4	Sep 4	EXETER CITY	3-1	Edelston, O'Donnell, Ramscar	11988			5				4	8	7	11		6	9	3	10	2			1	
5	6	Watford	1-2	English	21959			5				4	8	7	11		6	9	3	10	2			1	
6	11	COVENTRY CITY	3-1	Edelston, English, O'Donnell	13280			5				4	8	7	11		6	9	3	10	2			1	
7	13	BRIGHTON & HOVE ALB	5-3	Edelston 2, O'Donnell 3	14342			5				4	8	7	11		6	9	3	10	2			1	
8	15	Coventry City	1-1	Ramscar	18217			5				4	8	7	11		6	9	3	10	2			1	
9	20	Newport County	1-4	O'Donnell	10479						5	4	8	7	11		6	9	3	10	2			1	
10	25	SWINDON TOWN	3-1	Edelston 2, Fowler	8746						5	4	8	7	11		6	9	3	10	2			1	
11	27	CRYSTAL PALACE	5-1	English 2, Fowler, Edelston, Southam	12805						5	4	8	7	11		6	9	3	10	2			1	
12	Oct 1	Torquay United	0-3		4784			5					8	7	11	4	6	9	3	10	2			1	
13	4	Bristol City	3-2	English, O'Donnell, one og	21795			5					8	7	11	4	6	9	3	10	2			1	
14	11	BRISTOL ROVERS	2-2	English, McLain	19064			5					8	7	11	4	6	9	3	10	2			1	
15	18	Millwall	2-1	English, Ramscar	22948			5					8	7	11	4	6	9	3	10	2			1	
16	25	GILLINGHAM	3-1	Edelston, English, Ramscar	13689			5					8	7	11	4	6	9	3	10	2			1	
17	Nov 1	Walsall	5-1	Edelston, English, O'Donnell 2	8420			5					8	7	11	4	6	9	3	10	2			1	
18	8	SHREWSBURY TOWN	3-1	Edelston 2, English	13988			5					8	7	11	4	6	9	3	10	2			1	
19	15	Queen's Park Rangers	2-2	Edelston, O'Donnell	14661			5					8	7	11	4	6	9	3	10	2			1	
20	29	Aldershot	1-2	Fowler	3263		8	5						7	11	4	6	9	3	10	2			1	
21	Dec 13	Norwich City	2-1	English 2	21093			5					8	7	11	4	6	9	3	10	2			1	
22	20	BOURNEMOUTH	5-1	O'Donnell 2, Ramscar 3	8649			5				6	8		11	4		9	3	10	2	7		1	
23	26	READING	6-1	Edelston, English 2, O'Donnell 2, Ramscar	19242			5				6	8	7	11	4		9	3	10	2			1	
24	Jan 3	Southend United	1-3	O'Donnell	7425	10		5					8	7	11	4	6	9	3		2			1	
25	10	Leyton Orient	1-0	English	7826			5					8	7	11	4	6	9	3	10	2			1	
26	17	WATFORD	4-1	Edelston, English, O'Donnell 2	13250			5					8	7	11	4	6	9	3	10	2			1	
27	24	Brighton & Hove Albion	1-1	Starocsik	18750			5				6	8	7	11	4		9	3	10	2			1	
28	31	LEYTON ORIENT	3-1	Fowler, Ramscar 2	9868			5				6		7	11	4		9	3	10	2			1	
29	Feb 7	NEWPORT COUNTY	5-0	Edelston, English 2, Ramscar 2	11977			5				6	8	7	11	4		9	3	10	2			1	
30	14	Crystal Palace	3-4	Adams, O'Donnell 2	6409	8		5				6		7	11	4		9	3	10	2			1	
31	21	BRISTOL CITY	0-2		15291		8	5				6		7	11	4		9	3	10	2			1	
32	28	Bristol Rovers	1-1	Ramscar	31115		8	5				6		7	11	4		9	3	10	2			1	
33	Mar 7	MILLWALL	1-1	O'Donnell	13687				5			6	8	7	11	4		9	3	10	2			1	
34	14	Gillingham	1-1	Ramscar	10250				5			6	8	7	11	4		9	3	10	2			1	
35	21	WALSALL	2-1	O'Donnell, Ramscar	9717				5			6	8	7	11	4		9	3	10	2			1	
36	28	Shrewsbury Town	4-2	English, O'Donnell 2, Ramscar	7329		8	5				6		7	11		4	9	3	10	2			1	
37	Apr 4	QUEEN'S PARK RANGERS	4-2	Baxter, Dodgin, English, Fowler	12546		8	5				6		7	11		4	9	3	10	2			1	
38	6	Ipswich Town	1-1	Ramscar	12048			5				6	8	7	11		4	9	3	10	2			1	
39	7	IPSWICH TOWN	2-0	Fowler, McLain	12307			4	5				8	7	11		6	9	3	10	2			1	
40	11	Swindon Town	0-3		9564		8	4	5					7	11		6	9	3	10	2			1	
41	13	Reading	0-2		9020			4	5				8	7	11		6	9	3	10	2			1	
42	16	COLCHESTER UNITED	2-0	O'Donnell 2	7982		8	5						7	11	4	6	9	3	10	2			1	
43	18	ALDERSHOT	4-0	Hughes, O'Donnell, Ramscar 2	10040		8	5						7	11	4		9	3	10	2		6	1	
44	23	TORQUAY UNITED	3-3	English, Fowler, O'Donnell	11510		8		5					7	11	4		9	3	10	2		6	1	
45	25	Colchester United	2-1	English, Fowler	8122		8		5					7	11	4		9	3	10	2		6	1	
46	30	NORWICH CITY	3-3	Baxter, English, Fowler	9555		8		5					7	11	4		9	3	10	2		6	1	
Apps						2	11	28	19	2	11	14	30	45	46	29	32	46	46	45	46	1	4	46	3
Goals						1	2					1	15	24	11	1	2	27		22	1	1			

One own goal

F.A. Cup

	Date	Opponent	Score	Scorers	Att	Candlin MH	Edelston M	English J	Fowler T	Hughes TG	McLain T	O'Donnell W	Patterson RL	Ramscar FT	Southam JH	Wood AR
R1	Nov 22	Hendon	0-0		9000	5	8	7	11	4	6	9	3	10	2	1
rep	27	HENDON	2-0	Fowler, Ramscar	6100	5	8	7	11	4	6	9	3	10	2	1
R2	Dec 6	Swindon Town	0-2		12936	5	8	7	11	4	6	9	3	10	2	1

		P	W	D	L	F	A	W	D	L	F	A	Pts
1	Bristol Rovers	46	17	4	2	55	19	9	8	6	37	27	64
2	Millwall	46	14	7	2	46	16	10	7	6	36	28	62
3	NORTHAMPTON TOWN	46	18	4	1	75	30	8	6	9	34	40	62
4	Norwich City	46	16	6	1	56	17	9	4	10	43	38	60
5	Bristol City	46	13	8	2	62	28	9	7	7	33	33	59
6	Coventry City	46	15	5	3	52	22	4	7	12	25	40	50
7	Brighton & Hove A.	46	12	6	5	48	30	7	6	10	33	45	50
8	Southend United	46	15	5	3	41	21	3	8	12	28	53	49
9	Bournemouth	46	15	3	5	49	23	4	6	13	25	46	47
10	Watford	46	12	8	3	39	21	3	9	11	23	42	47
11	Reading	46	17	3	3	53	18	2	5	16	16	46	46
12	Torquay United	46	15	4	4	61	28	3	5	15	26	60	45
13	Crystal Palace	46	12	7	4	40	26	3	6	14	26	56	43
14	Leyton Orient	46	12	7	4	52	28	4	3	16	16	45	42
15	Newport County	46	12	4	7	43	34	4	6	13	27	48	42
16	Ipswich Town	46	10	7	6	34	28	3	8	12	26	41	41
17	Exeter City	46	11	8	4	40	24	2	6	15	21	47	40
18	Swindon Town	46	9	5	9	38	33	5	7	11	26	46	40
19	Aldershot	46	8	8	7	36	29	4	7	12	25	48	39
20	Queen's Park Rgs.	46	9	9	5	37	34	3	6	14	24	48	39
21	Gillingham	46	10	7	6	30	26	2	8	13	25	48	39
22	Colchester United	46	9	9	5	40	29	3	5	15	19	47	38
23	Shrewsbury Town	46	11	5	7	38	35	1	7	15	30	56	36
24	Walsall	46	5	9	9	35	46	2	1	20	21	72	24

1953/54   5th in Division 3(S)

#		Date	Opponent	Score	Scorers	Att.	Anderson JL	Baxter LR	Collins BV	Cross J	English J	Edelston M	Fowler T	Hughes TG	Jones B	Marston M	McLain T	O'Donnell W	Patterson RL	Ramscar FT	Southam JH	Smith JO	Starocsik F	Upton F	Walsh W	Wood AR	Yeoman RI
1	Aug	20	Crystal Palace	2-2	English 2	13935					7	8	11	4		2	6	9	3	10					5	1	
2		22	Southend United	0-2		10295					7	8	11	4		2	6	9	3	10					5	1	
3		26	Bournemouth	1-2	English	14409			8		7		11	4		2	6	9	3	10					5	1	
4		29	Brighton & Hove Albion	2-3	O'Donnell, Ramscar	16709			8		7		11	6		2		9	3	10	4				5	1	
5	Sep	3	BOURNEMOUTH	2-1	English 2	12618			8		7		11	6		2		9	3	10	4				5	1	
6		5	WATFORD	4-1	English 3, O'Donnell	13831					7	8	11	6		2		9	3	10	4				5	1	
7		7	Millwall	0-1		11909					7	8	11	6		2		9	3	10	4				5	1	
8		12	Torquay United	1-1	English	8148					7	8	11	6		2		9	3	10	4				5	1	
9		17	MILLWALL	4-2	English 3, Edelston	10131					7	8	11	6		2		9	3	10	4				5	1	
10		19	NEWPORT COUNTY	1-0	English	13138					7	8	11	6		2		9	3	10	4				5	1	
11		21	READING	1-1	Fowler	8778					7	8	11	6		2		9	3	10	4				5	1	
12		26	GILLINGHAM	1-1	English	12096					7	8	11	6		2		9	3	10	4				5	1	
13		30	Reading	0-2		8755			8		7		11	6		2		9	3		4	10			5	1	
14	Oct	3	Coventry City	0-0		17540			8		7		11	6		2		9	3	10	4				5	1	
15		10	Queen's Park Rangers	1-1	Fowler	13300			8		7		11	6		2		9	3	10	4				5	1	
16		17	SOUTHAMPTON	3-0	Fowler, O'Donnell, one og	14403	8				7		11	6		2		9	3	10	4				5	1	
17		24	Colchester United	1-1	Cross	7599	8			9	7		11	6		2			3	10	4				5	1	
18		31	CRYSTAL PALACE	6-0	Anderson, Cross, English 3, Ramscar	12450	8		5	9	7		11	6		2			3	10		4				1	
19	Nov	7	Bristol City	1-2	Smith	17380	8		5	9	7		11	6		2			3	10		4				1	
20		14	ALDERSHOT	6-2	*See below	11695	8		5		7		11	6		2		9	3	10		4				1	
21		28	WALSALL	5-1	Cross 3, Ramscar 2	12561	8		5	9	7		11	6		2			3	10		4				1	
22	Dec	5	Shrewsbury Town	4-2	Cross, Edelston, Ramscar, one og	7825			5	9	7	8	11	6					3	10	2	4				1	
23		19	SOUTHEND UNITED	5-0	English 4, McLain	9181	8		5		7		11	4		2	6	9	3	10						1	
24		25	LEYTON ORIENT	2-2	English, Hughes	13809	8		5	9	7		11	4		2	6		3	10						1	
25		26	Leyton Orient	0-2		14768			5	9	7		11	4		2	6			10	3		8			1	
26	Jan	2	BRIGHTON & HOVE ALB	4-2	Cross, Starocsik, two og	10989			5	9			11	4		2	6			10	3		8	7		1	
27		16	Watford	1-1	Cross	13134	8		5	9	7		11	4		2	6			10	3					1	
28		23	TORQUAY UNITED	3-1	Anderson, English, Marston	11162	8		5	9	7		11	4		2	6			10	3					1	
29	Feb	6	Newport County	0-2		10221			5		7		11	4		2	6	9		10	3	8				1	
30		13	Gillingham	1-2	English	9558			5		7		11	4		2	6	9		10	3	8				1	
31		20	COVENTRY CITY	0-1		10539	8		5		7		11	4		2	6	9		10	3					1	
32		27	QUEEN'S PARK RANGERS	2-1	English 2	8259			5		7		11	4		2	6			10	3	8			9	1	
33	Mar	6	Southampton	0-1		14196			5		7		11	4		2	6			10	3	8			9	1	
34		13	SWINDON TOWN	2-0	McLain, Ramscar	6821			5		7		11	4		2	8	9		10	3			6		1	
35		20	Walsall	1-0	Ramscar	10032			5		7		11	4		2	8	9		10	3			6		1	
36		25	IPSWICH TOWN	1-0	McLain	5968			5		7		11	4		2	8	9		10	3			6		1	
37		27	BRISTOL CITY	3-0	English, McLain, O'Donnell	8283			5		7		11	4		2	8	9		10	3			6		1	
38	Apr	3	Aldershot	1-3	Englsih	5728			5		7		11	4		2	8	9		10	3			6		1	
39		8	EXETER CITY	2-2	English, Ramscar	5597			5		7		11	4		2	8	9		10	3			6		1	
40		10	SHREWSBURY TOWN	1-0	O'Donnell	8088			5		7		11			2	8	9		10	3	4		6		1	
41		17	Exeter City	0-1		8844			5		7		11	4		2		9		10	3	8		6		1	
42		19	Norwich City	1-4	O'Donnell	22961			5		7		11	4		2	8	9		10	3			6		1	
43		20	NORWICH CITY	2-0	Ramscar, Upton	8906			5		7		11	4		2		9		10	3	8		6		1	
44		24	COLCHESTER UNITED	3-0	Anderson, English, Fowler	7344	8		5		7		11	4		2		9		10	3			6		1	
45		28	Swindon Town	0-0		5195	10		5		7		11	4		2		9			3	8		6		1	
46	Ma	1	Ipswich Town	1-2	one og	22133			5		7		11		10	2		9		8	3			6		1	4

Scorers in game 20: Anderson 2, English, Fowler, O'Donnell, Ramscar.

	Anderson JL	Baxter LR	Collins BV	Cross J	English J	Edelston M	Fowler T	Hughes TG	Jones B	Marston M	McLain T	O'Donnell W	Patterson RL	Ramscar FT	Southam JH	Smith JO	Starocsik F	Upton F	Walsh W	Wood AR	Yeoman RI
Apps	14	6	29	10	45	10	46	44	1	42	24	37	24	44	26	23	2	13	19	46	1
Goals	5			8	31	2	5	1		1	4	7		10		1	1	1			

Five own goals

F.A. Cup

		Date	Opponent	Score	Scorers	Att.	Anderson JL	Baxter LR	Collins BV	Cross J	English J	Edelston M	Fowler T	Hughes TG	Jones B	Marston M	McLain T	O'Donnell W	Patterson RL	Ramscar FT	Southam JH	Smith JO	Starocsik F	Upton F	Walsh W	Wood AR	Yeoman RI
R1	Nov	21	LLANELLY	3-0	Cross, Fowler, Ramscar	16302	8		5	9	7		11	6		2			3	10		4				1	
R2	Dec	12	HARTLEPOOLS UNITED	1-1	Ramscar	18772			5	9	7	8	11	6		2				10	3	4				1	
rep		16	Hartlepools United	0-1		12169			5		7	8	11	4		2	6	9	3	10						1	

	P	W	D	L	F	A	W	D	L	F	A	Pts
1 Ipswich Town	46	15	5	3	47	19	12	5	6	35	32	64
2 Brighton & Hove A.	46	17	3	3	57	31	9	6	8	29	30	61
3 Bristol City	46	18	3	2	59	18	7	3	13	29	48	56
4 Watford	46	16	3	4	52	23	5	7	11	33	46	52
5 NORTHAMPTON TOWN	46	18	4	1	63	18	2	7	14	19	37	51
6 Southampton	46	17	5	1	51	22	5	2	16	25	41	51
7 Norwich City	46	13	5	5	43	28	7	6	10	30	38	51
8 Reading	46	14	3	6	57	33	6	6	11	29	40	49
9 Exeter City	46	12	2	9	39	22	8	6	9	29	36	48
10 Gillingham	46	14	3	6	37	22	5	7	11	24	44	48
11 Leyton Orient	46	14	5	4	48	26	4	6	13	31	47	47
12 Millwall	46	15	3	5	44	24	4	6	13	30	53	47
13 Torquay United	46	10	10	3	48	33	7	2	14	33	55	46
14 Coventry City	46	14	5	4	36	15	4	4	15	25	41	45
15 Newport County	46	14	4	5	42	28	5	2	16	19	53	44
16 Southend United	46	15	2	6	46	22	3	5	15	23	49	43
17 Aldershot	46	11	5	7	45	31	6	4	13	29	55	43
18 Queen's Park Rgs.	46	10	5	8	32	25	6	5	12	28	43	42
19 Bournemouth	46	12	5	6	47	27	4	3	16	20	43	40
19 Swindon Town	46	13	5	5	48	21	2	5	16	19	49	40
21 Shrewsbury Town	46	12	8	3	48	34	2	4	17	17	42	40
22 Crystal Palace	46	11	7	5	41	30	3	5	15	19	56	40
23 Colchester United	46	7	7	9	35	29	3	3	17	15	49	30
24 Walsall	46	8	5	10	22	27	1	3	19	18	60	26

1954/55 — 13th in Division 3(S)

No	Date		Opponent	Score	Scorers	Att	Adams DF	Collins BV	Croy J	Danks PD	Dawson W	English J	Fowler T	Hazeldine D	Huffer P	Hughes TG	Jones B	McLain T	Marston M	Mills RWG	Newman R	Ramscar FT	Smith EWA	Smith JO	Southam JH	Starocsik F	Webber GM	Wood AR	Yeoman RI	Patterson RL	Oakley K
1	Aug	21	Newport County	1-0	English	12709		5				7	11	8		4		6	2			10			3			1			9
2		26	CRYSTAL PALACE	1-1	English	11735		5				7	11	8		4		6	2			10			3			1			9
3		28	EXETER CITY	2-0	Fowler, Oakley	9764		5				7	11	8		4		6	2			10			3			1			9
4	Sep	1	Crystal Palace	1-3	English	11626		5				7	11	8		4		6	2			10			3			1			9
5		4	Colchester United	1-4	Haseldine	7468		5				9	11	8		6	10		2	7					3		1		4		
6		9	MILLWALL	0-1		8108		5				9	11	8		6	10		2	7							1		4	3	
7		11	NORWICH CITY	1-1	Oakley	9560		5				7	11	8		6	10		2								1		4	3	9
8		13	Millwall	0-1		9558		5				7	11	8		6	10		2								1		4	3	9
9		18	Southend United	1-4	McLain	10519		5				7	11	8		6	10		2								1		4	3	
10		21	Watford	1-1	McLain	10692		5				7	11	8		6	10	9	2						3		1		4		
11		25	ALDERSHOT	2-1	Haseldine, Jones	8235		5				7	11	8		6	10	9	2						3		1		4		
12		30	WATFORD	0-1		4128			5				11	8		6	10	9	2	7							1		4	3	
13	Oct	2	Swindon Town	1-0	Jones	8899			5				11	8		6	10	9	2	7							1		4	3	
14		9	GILLINGHAM	4-1	Fowler, Haseldine 2, McLain	7827			5				11	8		6	10	9	2	7							1		4	3	
15		16	Reading	1-0	Starocsik	9864			5				11	8		6	10	9	2							7	1		4	3	
16		23	SHREWSBURY TOWN	3-1	Jones, Starocsik 2	8468			5				11	8		6	10	9	2							7	1		4	3	
17		30	Southampton	0-4		16039			5				11	8		6	10	9	2							7	1		4	3	
18	Nov	6	BRISTOL CITY	2-0	Starocsik 2	11608			5				11	8		6	10	9	2							7		1	4	3	
19		13	Torquay United	2-5	McLain, J Smith	7264			5				11	8		6	10	9	2					4		7		1		3	
20		27	Brentford	3-1	English 2, McLain	10029						8	11			6	10	9	2							7		1	4	3	
21	Dec	4	COVENTRY CITY	1-0	Starocsik	11008		2	5			8	11			6	10	9								7		1	4	3	
22		11	SWINDON TOWN	1-0	Starocsik	6609		2	5			8	11			6	10	9								7		1	4	3	
23		18	NEWPORT COUNTY	2-2	English, Starocsik	6947		2	5			8	11	10		6										7		1	4	3	9
24		25	Queen's Park Rangers	0-1		8718		2	5			8	11			6	10									7		1	4	3	9
25		27	QUEEN'S PARK RANGERS	1-3	Brown (og)	12623		2	5			8	11			6	10									7		1	4	3	9
26	Jan	1	Exeter City	1-3	Douglas (og)	7040	9	2	5			7	11	8		6	10											1	4	3	
27		8	LEYTON ORIENT	2-2	Adams, Yeoman	8864	9	2	5			7	11			4	10	6										1	8	3	
28		22	Norwich City	2-3	English 2	11159	9		5			7	11			4	10	6	2									1	8	3	
29		29	Leyton Orient	1-2	Jones	17969	9		5			7	11				10	6	2				8	4				1		3	
30	Feb	5	SOUTHEND UNITED	6-2	Jones 2, E Smith 2, Oakley 2	7709			5				11			4	10	6	2	7			8					1		3	9
31		12	Aldershot	4-3	Jones 3, E Smith	5237			5				11			4	10	6	2	7			8					1		3	9
32		19	Gillingham	2-2	Jones 2	8523			5				11			4	10	6	2	7			8					1		3	
33	Mar	5	READING	2-6	Oakley 2	7191		2	5				11			4	10	6		7			8					1		3	9
34		12	Shrewsbury Town	0-4		7778	9	2	5				11			4	10	6		7			8					1		3	
35		19	SOUTHAMPTON	2-1	Fowler, Ellerington (og)	6855	9		5				11			4	10	6	2	7			8					1		3	
36		26	Bristol City	1-5	Patterson	20955	9		5				11			4	10	6	2	7			8					1		3	
37	Apr	2	TORQUAY UNITED	1-0	Adams	5361	9					7	11			10	5	6	2				8	4				1		3	
38		4	Walsall	1-6	English	5159	9					7	11		5		10	6	2				8	4				1		3	
39		9	Brighton & Hove Albion	1-0	Starocsik	13120	9						11				10	6	2				8	4		7		1		3	
40		11	Bournemouth	1-0	Newman	8759	9		5	10		7	11					6	2		8			4	3			1			
41		12	BOURNEMOUTH	5-0	Jones 4, Starocsik	6618		5			9		11				10	6	2				8	4		7		1		3	
42		16	BRENTFORD	1-2	Dawson	6980		5			9		11				10	6	2				8	4	3	7		1			
43		18	COLCHESTER UNITED	6-1	Dawson 3, E Smith, Starocsik, Harris (og)	3198		5			9		11				10	6	2				8	4		7		1		3	
44		23	Coventry City	0-0		11631		5			9		11				10	6	2				8	4		7		1		3	
45		27	BRIGHTON & HOVE ALB	1-0	Wilson (og)	4349		5			9	8	11				10	6	2					4		7		1		3	
46		30	WALSALL	1-1	Dawson	6842		5			9	8	11				10	6	2					4		7		1		3	
			Apps				11	27	20	1	6	26	46	22	1	41	34	38	26	9	2	4	15	15	21	22	13	33	23	37	13
			Goals				2				5	9	3	4			15	5			1		4	1		11			1	1	6

Five own goals

F.A. Cup

No	Date		Opponent	Score	Scorers	Att	Adams DF	Collins BV	Croy J	Danks PD	Dawson W	English J	Fowler T	Hazeldine D	Huffer P	Hughes TG	Jones B	McLain T	Marston M	Mills RWG	Newman R	Ramscar FT	Smith EWA	Smith JO	Southam JH	Starocsik F	Webber GM	Wood AR	Yeoman RI	Patterson RL	Oakley K
R1	Nov	20	COVENTRY CITY	0-1		14667			5				11	8		6	10	9	2							7		1	4	3	

Division 3(S) Final Table

		P	W	D	L	F	A	W	D	L	F	A	Pts
1	Bristol City	46	17	4	2	62	22	13	6	4	39	25	70
2	Leyton Orient	46	16	2	5	48	20	10	7	6	41	27	61
3	Southampton	46	16	6	1	49	19	8	5	10	26	32	59
4	Gillingham	46	12	8	3	41	28	8	7	8	36	38	55
5	Millwall	46	14	6	3	44	25	6	5	12	28	43	51
6	Brighton & Hove A.	46	14	4	5	47	27	6	6	11	29	36	50
7	Watford	46	11	9	3	45	26	7	5	11	26	36	50
8	Torquay United	46	12	6	5	51	39	6	6	11	31	43	48
9	Coventry City	46	15	5	3	50	26	3	6	14	17	33	47
10	Southend United	46	13	5	5	48	28	4	7	12	35	52	46
11	Brentford	46	11	6	6	44	36	5	8	10	38	46	46
11	Norwich City	46	13	5	5	40	23	5	5	13	20	37	46
13	NORTHAMPTON TOWN	46	13	5	5	47	27	6	3	14	26	54	46
14	Aldershot	46	12	6	5	44	23	4	7	12	31	48	45
15	Queen's Park Rgs.	46	13	7	3	46	25	2	7	14	23	50	44
16	Shrewsbury Town	46	14	5	4	49	24	2	5	16	21	54	42
17	Bournemouth	46	7	8	8	32	29	5	10	8	25	36	42
18	Reading	46	7	10	6	32	26	6	5	12	33	47	41
19	Newport County	46	8	8	7	32	29	3	8	12	28	44	38
20	Crystal Palace	46	9	11	3	32	24	2	5	16	20	56	38
21	Swindon Town	46	10	8	5	30	19	1	7	15	16	45	37
22	Exeter City	46	9	7	7	30	31	2	9	13	17	42	37
23	Walsall	46	9	6	8	49	36	1	8	14	26	50	34
24	Colchester United	46	7	6	10	33	40	2	7	14	20	51	31

1955/56 11th in Division 3(S)

#	Date		Opponent	Score	Scorers	Att	Adams DF	Coleman GJ	Collins BV	Dawson W	Draper RW	Dutton CA	English J	Fowler T	Gale CM	Hughes TG	Jones B	Leek K	McLain T	Mills RWG	Marston M	Newman R	Patterson RL	Pickering PB	Smith EWA	Smith JO	Wallace J	Williams DR	Yeoman RI
1	Aug	20	Crystal Palace	3-2	Dawson, English 2	13841			5	9			7	11			8				2		3	1	10	6			4
2		24	Swindon Town	1-0	English	8642			5	9			7	11							2	8	3	1	10	6			4
3		27	BRIGHTON & HOVE ALB	3-0	English, Fowler, Yeoman	10694			5	9			7	11							2	8	3	1	10	6			4
4	Sep	1	SWINDON TOWN	2-1	Fowler, E Smith	11102			5	9			7	11							2	8	3	1	10	6			4
5		3	Southampton	3-2	English, Newman, E Smith	12373			5	9			7	11							2	8	3	1	10	6			4
6		5	ALDERSHOT	3-2	Dawson, English, E Smith	12534			5	9			7	11							2	8	3	1	10	6			4
7		10	SHREWSBURY TOWN	1-0	Fowler	13144				9			7	11							2	8	3	1	10	6	5		4
8		14	Aldershot	0-2		5811			5	9			7	11							2	8	3	1	10	6			4
9		17	Ipswich Town	0-1		17629			5		9			11	10						2	8	3	1		6			4
10		19	QUEEN'S PARK RANGERS	5-2	Draper, Fowler, Newman 2, J Smith	9735					9			11		5				7	2	8	3	1	10	6			4
11		24	WALSALL	3-1	Mills, E Smith 2	14247					9			11		5				7	2	8	3	1	10	6			4
12		29	Newport County	1-0	Newman	8076			5		9			11						7	2	8	3	1	10	6			4
13	Oct	1	Torquay United	1-3	Draper	9686			5		9			11						7	2	8	3	1	10	6			4
14		8	COVENTRY CITY	2-1	Draper 2	20370			5		9			11						7	2	8	3	1	10	6			4
15		15	Southend United	0-2		17009			5		9			11						7	2	8	3	1	10	6			4
16		22	EXETER CITY	3-0	Draper, E Smith, Yeoman	10804			5		9			11			8			7	2		3	1	10	6			4
17		29	Leyton Orient	1-1	Draper	24030			5		9			11			10			7	2	8	3	1		6			4
18	Nov	5	COLCHESTER UNITED	0-2		14091			5		9			11			8			7	2		3	1	10	6			4
19		12	Norwich City	1-4	Fowler	21845			5		9		8	11						7	2		3	1	10	6			4
20		26	Gillingham	2-0	Draper, Fowler	8429			5		9		7	11							2	8	3	1	10	6			4
21	Dec	3	MILLWALL	4-0	Draper, English 2, Jones	10759			5		9		7	11			10				2	8	3	1		6			4
22		17	CRYSTAL PALACE	1-1	English	9302					9		7	11		5					2	8	3	1	10	6			4
23		24	Brighton & Hove Albion	0-4		11004			5		9		7	11							2	8	3	1	10	6			4
24		26	Watford	2-2	Adams, English	7041	10		5		9		7	11							2	8	3	1		6			4
25		27	WATFORD	1-3	English	13778	10		5		9		7	11							2	8	3	1		6			4
26		31	SOUTHAMPTON	3-1	Draper, English, E Smith	11035					9		7	11		5					2	8	3	1	10	6			4
27	Jan	14	Shrewsbury Town	1-1	Fowler	7974			5		9		7	11	6						2	8	3	1	10				4
28		21	IPSWICH TOWN	0-5		13103			5		9		7	11							2	8	3	1	10	6			4
29		28	Reading	1-4	Mills	6807			5		9		7	11						8	2		3	1		6		10	4
30	Feb	11	TORQUAY UNITED	2-0	Draper, E Smith	5656			3		9		7	11		5					2	8		1	10	6			4
31		18	Coventry City	1-0	English	19366			3		9		7	11		5					2	8		1	10	6			4
32		25	SOUTHEND UNITED	1-1	English	9535			3		9		7	11		5					2	8		1	10	6			4
33	Mar	3	Exeter City	1-3	Doyle (og)	6996	9		3				7	11		5					2	8		1	10	6			4
34		10	LEYTON ORIENT	0-1		13544			5		9		7	11							2	8	3	1	10	6			4
35		17	Colchester United	0-2		8333			2		9		7	11	5								3	1	10	6		8	4
36		24	NORWICH CITY	1-1	Marston	9387			2		9		7	11	5					10			3	1		6		8	4
37		31	Bournemouth	0-0		9010			2		9		7	11	5					10			3	1		6		8	4
38	Apr	2	Brentford	1-2	Dutton	9527			2		9	8		11	5					7			3	1	10	6			4
39		3	BRENTFORD	1-0	J Smith	8248			2		9		7	11	5								3	1	10	6		8	4
40		7	GILLINGHAM	0-2		6553			2		9		7	11	5								3	1	10	6		8	4
41		12	BOURNEMOUTH	2-1	Draper 2	4179			2		10			11	5					7			3	1		6		8	4
42		14	Millwall	1-4	Dutton	3682			2		9			11	5			10		7			3	1		6		8	4
43		16	Walsall	0-2		11934			3		9		10	11	5					7	2			1		6		8	4
44		21	READING	1-2	Leek	5612			2		9		7	11	5			10					3	1		6		8	4
45		26	NEWPORT COUNTY	5-0	Draper 3, Leek 2	3536					9			11	5			10		7	2		3	1		6		8	4
46		28	Queen's Rangers	2-3	Leek, Mills	7157		2			9			11	5			10		7			3	1		6		8	4
			Apps				3	1	38	8	32	9	30	46	12	10	8	7	2	24	42	16	36	46	38	44	1	7	46
			Goals				1			2	15	2	14	7			1	4		3	1	4			8	2			2

One own goal

F.A. Cup

#	Date		Opponent	Score	Scorers	Att	Collins BV	Draper RW	English J	Fowler T	Hughes TG	Newman R	Marston M	Patterson RL	Pickering PB	Smith EWA	Smith JO	Yeoman RI
R1	Nov	19	MILLWALL	4-1	English 3, Hurley(og)	12878	5	9	7	11		8	2	3	1	10	6	4
R2	Dec	10	HASTINGS	4-1	Draper 2, English, E Smith	15534	5	9	7	11		8	2	3	1	10	6	4
R3	Jan	7	BLACKBURN ROVERS	1-2	English	14087		9	7	11	5	8	2	3	1	10	6	4

		P	W	D	L	F		W	D	L	F	A	Pts
1	Leyton Orient	46	18	3	2	76	20	11	5	7	30	29	66
2	Brighton & Hove A.	46	20	2	1	73	16	9	5	9	39	34	65
3	Ipswich Town	46	16	6	1	59	28	9	8	6	47	32	64
4	Southend United	46	16	4	3	58	25	5	7	11	30	55	53
5	Torquay United	46	11	10	2	48	21	9	2	12	38	42	52
6	Brentford	46	11	8	4	40	30	8	6	9	29	36	52
7	Norwich City	46	15	4	4	56	31	4	9	10	30	51	51
8	Coventry City	46	16	4	3	54	20	4	5	14	19	40	49
9	Bournemouth	46	13	6	4	39	14	6	4	13	24	37	48
10	Gillingham	46	12	3	8	38	28	7	7	9	31	43	48
11	NORTHAMPTON TOWN	46	14	3	6	44	27	6	4	13	23	44	47
12	Colchester United	46	14	4	5	56	37	4	7	12	20	44	47
13	Shrewsbury Town	46	12	9	2	47	21	5	3	15	22	45	46
14	Southampton	46	13	6	4	60	30	5	2	16	31	51	44
15	Aldershot	46	9	9	5	36	33	3	7	13	34	57	40
16	Exeter City	46	10	6	7	39	30	5	4	14	19	47	40
17	Reading	46	10	2	11	40	37	5	7	11	30	42	39
18	Queen's Park Rgs.	46	10	7	6	44	32	4	4	15	20	54	39
19	Newport County	46	12	2	9	32	26	3	7	13	26	53	39
20	Walsall	46	13	5	5	43	28	2	3	18	25	56	38
21	Watford	46	8	5	10	31	39	5	6	12	21	46	37
22	Millwall	46	13	4	6	56	31	2	2	19	27	69	36
23	Crystal Palace	46	7	3	13	27	32	5	7	11	27	51	34
24	Swindon Town	46	4	10	9	18	22	4	4	15	16	56	30

1956/57 14th in Division 3(S)

#	Date	Opponent	Res	Scorers	Att	Asher SJ	Bright G	Canning L	Claypole AW	Coleman GJ	Collins BV	Draper RW	Dutton CA	Elvy R	English J	Fowler T	Gale CM	Leek K	Marston M	Miller RL	Mills RWG	Morrow HJE	Patterson RL	Pickering PB	Poole KJ	Smith JO	Tebbutt RS	Williams DR	Woan AE	Yeoman RI
1	Aug 18	Newport County	0-3		11371					3		9				11	5	10	2		7			1		6		8		4
2	23	READING	3-0	Leek, J Smith, Davies(og)	8914						3	9				11	5	10	2		7			1		4		8		6
3	25	COLCHESTER UNITED	1-0	Draper	9269						2	9				11	5	10	3		7			1		6		8		4
4	29	Reading	1-1	Woan	11698						2		9			11	5	10	3		7			1		6			8	4
5	Sep 1	Norwich City	1-2	Draper	15246						2	9				11	5	10	3		7			1		6			8	4
6	6	QUEEN'S PARK RANGERS	3-0	Leek, J Smith, Woan	7591						2	9				11	5	10	3		7			1		6			8	4
7	8	COVENTRY CITY	4-0	Draper 2, Morrow 2	15291						2	9				11	5		3		8	7		1		6			10	4
8	10	Queen's Park Rangers	0-1		10785						2	9				11	5		3		8	7		1		6			10	4
9	15	Southampton	0-2		16018						2	9				11	5	8	3			7		1		6			10	4
10	17	PLYMOUTH ARGYLE	2-0	English, Mills	7736						2	9			7	11	5		3		8			1		6			10	4
11	22	EXETER CITY	1-1	Draper	9421						2	9			7	11	5		3		8			1		6			10	4
12	24	Plymouth Argyle	3-4	English, Mills, Woan	13727							8			7	11	5	3	2		9			1		6			10	4
13	29	Crystal Palace	1-1	Woan	13904						2				7	11	5	3			9			1		6		8	10	4
14	Oct 6	Brentford	1-2	English	10730						2	9			7	11	5	3						1		6		8	10	4
15	13	ALDERSHOT	4-2	English, Fowler, Mills, J Smith	8825						2				7	11	5	3			9			1		6		8	10	4
16	20	Watford	1-2	English	9906			4			2				7	11	5	3			9			1		6		8	10	
17	27	SHREWSBURY TOWN	1-1	Woan	8951			4			2	9		1	7	11	5	3								6		8	10	
18	Nov 3	Walsall	2-2	English, Leek	9842	9								1	7	11	5	10	2		8		3			6				4
19	10	IPSWICH TOWN	2-1	Fowler	9655	9								1	8	11	5	10	2		7		3			6				4
20	24	TORQUAY UNITED	3-0	Fowler, Leek 2	8524	8						9		1		11	5	10	2		7		3			6				4
21	Dec 1	Millwall	0-1		10940	9								1		11	5	10	2		8	7	3			6				4
22	15	NEWPORT COUNTY	0-3		6289	9								1		11	5	10	2			7	3			6			8	4
23	22	Colchester United	1-5	Leek	5899									1	8	11	5	9	2			7	3			6			10	4
24	25	SOUTHEND UNITED	2-2	Mills 2	5165						2			1	10	11	5	9			8	7	3			6				4
25	26	Southend United	1-0	J Smith	8696									1	7	11	5	9	2		8		3			6			10	4
26	29	NORWICH CITY	1-1	Asher	7603	8								1		11	5	10	2		9	7	3			6				4
27	Jan 5	GILLINGHAM	4-1	Asher 2, Fowler, Morrow	6601	9								1		11	5	10	2		8	7	3			6				4
28	12	Coventry City	1-3	Leek	15371	9								1		11	5	10	2		8	7	3			6				4
29	19	SOUTHAMPTON	2-1	Asher, Fowler	8923	9								1		11	5	10	2		8	7	3		6					4
30	26	Gillingham	2-1	Asher 2	5724	9								1		11	5	10	2		8	7	3		6					4
31	Feb 2	Exeter City	0-0		5931	9										11	5	10	2		8	7	3	1	6					4
32	9	CRYSTAL PALACE	1-0	Woan	8651	9										11	5	6	2		8	7	3	1					10	4
33	16	BRENTFORD	5-1	Asher 2, Woan 2, Bragg(og)	9306	9										11	5	6	2		8	7	3	1					10	4
34	Mar 2	WATFORD	1-2	Asher	9309	9										11	5	6	2		8	7	3	1					10	4
35	9	Brighton & Hove Albion	0-5		11922	9										11	5		2		8	7	3	1	6				10	4
36	16	WALSALL	2-3	Asher, Leek	9177	9									7	11	5	10	2				3	1		6			8	4
37	23	Ipswich Town	1-0	Asher	17144	9									7	11	5		2		8		3	1		6			10	4
38	30	BOURNEMOUTH	2-2	Mills, Woan	7549	9									7	11	5		2		8		3	1		6			10	4
39	Apr 6	Torquay United	0-2		7612	9					2				7	11	5				8		3	1		6			10	4
40	10	Aldershot	0-4		2677	9					2					11	5	10			8	7	3	1		6				4
41	13	MILLWALL	2-1	Mills, Woan	5465						2	9				11	5				8	7	3	1		6			10	4
42	20	Shrewsbury Town	0-2		7214						2	9				11	5	6			8	7	3	1					10	4
43	22	Swindon Town	0-4		7523						2	9				11	5	6			8	7	3	1		4			10	
44	23	SWINDON TOWN	2-0	English. Miller	4950										7	11	5	6	2	8	9		3	1		4			10	
45	27	Bournemouth	1-4	English	8392										7	11	5	6	2	8	9		3	1		4			10	
46	30	BRIGHTON & HOVE ALB	1-0	Fowler	4463		9		2						7	11	5	6			8		3	1		4			10	
		Apps				21	1	2	1	16	8	17	1	14	20	45	43	32	39	2	31	30	30	32	4	38	2	8	29	40
		Goals				11						5			8	6		9		1	7	3				4			10	

Two own goals

F.A. Cup

R	Date	Opponent	Res	Scorers	Att	Asher SJ	Elvy R	English J	Fowler T	Gale CM	Leek K	Marston M	Patterson RL	Smith JO	Woan AE	Yeoman RI
R1	Nov 17	Southampton	0-2		16757	9	1	7	11	5	10	2	3	6	8	4

		P	W	D	L	F	A	W	D	L	F	A	Pts
1	Ipswich Town	46	18	3	2	72	20	7	6	10	29	34	59
2	Torquay United	46	19	4	0	71	18	5	7	11	18	46	59
3	Colchester United	46	15	8	0	49	19	7	6	10	35	37	58
4	Southampton	46	15	4	4	48	20	7	6	10	28	32	54
5	Bournemouth	46	15	7	1	57	20	4	7	12	31	42	52
6	Brighton & Hove A.	46	15	6	2	59	26	4	8	11	27	39	52
7	Southend United	46	14	3	6	42	20	4	9	10	31	45	48
8	Brentford	46	12	9	2	55	29	4	7	12	23	47	48
9	Shrewsbury Town	46	11	9	3	45	24	4	9	10	27	55	48
10	Queen's Park Rgs.	46	12	7	4	42	21	6	4	13	19	39	47
11	Watford	46	11	6	6	44	32	7	4	12	28	43	46
12	Newport County	46	15	6	2	51	18	1	7	15	14	44	45
13	Reading	46	13	4	6	44	30	5	5	13	36	51	45
14	NORTHAMPTON TOWN	46	15	5	3	49	22	3	4	16	17	51	45
15	Walsall	46	11	7	5	49	25	5	5	13	31	49	44
16	Coventry City	46	12	5	6	52	36	4	7	12	22	48	44
17	Millwall	46	13	7	3	46	29	3	5	15	18	55	44
18	Plymouth Argyle	46	10	8	5	38	31	6	3	14	30	42	43
19	Aldershot	46	11	5	7	43	35	4	7	12	36	57	42
20	Crystal Palace	46	7	10	6	31	28	4	8	11	31	47	40
21	Exeter City	46	8	8	7	37	29	4	5	14	24	50	37
22	Gillingham	46	7	8	8	29	29	5	5	13	25	56	37
23	Swindon Town	46	12	3	8	43	33	3	3	17	23	63	36
24	Norwich City	46	7	5	11	33	37	1	10	12	28	57	31

1957/58   13th in Division 3(S)

#	Date	Opponent	Res	Scorers	Att	Bright G	Claypole AW	Collins BV	Corbett R	Elvy R	English J	Fowler T	Gale CM	Hawkings B	Leek K	Mills RWG	O'Neil J	Patterson RL	Peacock RJ	Pickering PB	Robinson M	Robinson TH	Smith JO	Tebbutt RS	Woan AE	Yeoman RI
1	Aug 24	Walsall	1-2	Woan	13059	9							5	8	6	7		3		1	11	2			10	4
2	29	ALDERSHOT	0-0		7907						7		5	9	6	8		3		1	11	2			10	4
3	31	COVENTRY CITY	4-0	M Robinson 2, Woan, Kirk(og)	12037							11	5	9	10			3		1	7	2	6		8	4
4	Sep 4	Aldershot	0-0		4188				3			11	5	9	10					1	7	2	6		8	4
5	7	Shrewsbury Town	1-3	Woan	9542				3			11	5	9	10					1	7	2	6		8	4
6	10	Brentford	1-7	Woan	10697				3			11	5	9	10					1	7	2	6		8	4
7	14	READING	1-2	Leek	6986				2	1		11	5	9	10	7		3					6		8	4
8	16	BRENTFORD	3-1	English 2, Leek	4528	9				1	7	11	5		10			3				2	6		8	4
9	21	Swindon Town	1-5	Leek	9967	9				1	7	11	5		10	6		3				2			8	4
10	26	COLCHESTER UNITED	4-1	Corbett, Hawkings, Leek, Mills	3454				2	1		11	5	7	8	9		3					6		10	4
11	28	Watford	2-0	Hawkings, Woan	11579				2	1		11	5	7	8	9		3					6		10	4
12	30	Colchester United	0-1		4391				2	1		11	5	7	10	9		3					6		8	4
13	Oct 5	CRYSTAL PALACE	1-2	Patterson	7594			2		1		11	5	7	10		9	3					6		8	4
14	9	Norwich City	2-2	Leek 2	22850			2		1		11	5	7	10		9	3					6		8	4
15	12	PLYMOUTH ARGYLE	5-0	Hawkings, Leek, O'Neil 2, Woan	9692			2		1			5	7	8		9	3			11		6		10	4
16	19	Port Vale	0-3		12443			2		1			5	7	8		9	3			11	6			10	4
17	26	NEWPORT COUNTY	0-3		7953			2		1			5	7	6		9				11	3		10	8	4
18	Nov 2	Southampton	1-2	English	13469			2	3	1	7		9	8					6		11	5		10		4
19	9	BRIGHTON & HOVE ALB	2-4	Hawkings, Leek	7088			2		1	7	11	5	9	10			3				6		8		4
20	23	QUEEN'S PARK RANGERS	1-5	Woan	7525			2					9	7	10	6		3	4	1	11	5			8	
21	30	Exeter City	1-0	Leek	7933			2			7	11	5	9	10	6		3		1					8	4
22	Dec 14	Millwall	0-0		6761			2		1	7	11	5	9	10	6		3						8		4
23	21	WALSALL	3-0	Hawkings, Tebbutt 2	7058			2		1	7	11	5	9	10	6		3						8		4
24	26	NORWICH CITY	0-1		11125			2		1	7	11	5	9	10	6		3						8		4
25	28	Coventry City	1-1	Leek	20375			2		1	7	11	5	9	10	6		3						8		4
26	Jan 11	SHREWSBURY TOWN	2-0	Hawkings, Leek	8391			2		1	7	11	5	9	10	6		3						8		4
27	18	Reading	2-5	Hawkings, Tebbutt	10846			2		1	7	11	5	9	10	6		3						8		4
28	Feb 1	SWINDON TOWN	3-0	Fowler, Hawkings, Leek	9845			2		1	7	11	5	9	10	6		3						8		4
29	8	WATFORD	2-3	Leek 2	8400			2		1	7	11	5	9	10	6		3						8		4
30	15	Crystal Palace	3-1	Hawkings 2, Tebbutt	16245			2		1		11	5	9	10	6		3					7	8		4
31	22	Plymouth Argyle	0-3		16667			2		1		11	5	9	10	6		3					7	8		4
32	Mar 1	PORT VALE	3-2	Hawkings 2, O'Neil	8711			2		1		11	5	9		6	10	3					7	8		4
33	8	Newport County	1-0	Hawkings	7011			2		1		11	5	9		6	8	3					7			4
34	15	SOUTHAMPTON	1-3	Patterson	9374			2		1		11	5	9	10	6	8	3					7			4
35	22	Queen's Park Rangers	0-1		7531			2		1		11	5	9	10	6		3					7	8		4
36	27	GILLINGHAM	3-1	English, Fowler, Woan	2412			2		1	7	11	5	9		6		3						8	10	4
37	29	MILLWALL	7-2	English, Hawkings 2, Tebbutt, Woan 3	6393		2			1	7	11	5	9		6		3						8	10	4
38	Apr 4	Bournemouth	1-1	Yeoman	15196		2			1	7	11	5	9		6		3						8	10	4
39	5	Brighton & Hove Albion	4-1	Mills, Patterson, Woan 2	20066		2			1	7	11	5	9		6		3						8	10	4
40	8	BOURNEMOUTH	4-0	Hawkings, Patterson, Tebbutt, Woan	9888		2			1	7	11	5	9		6		3						8	10	4
41	12	EXETER CITY	9-0	Hawkings, Mills 2, Tebbutt 3, Woan 3	9465		2			1	7	11	5	9		6		3						8	10	4
42	16	Torquay United	0-1		6598		2			1	7	11	5	9		6		3						8	10	4
43	19	Gillingham	2-1	Hawkings, Woan	5721		2			1	7	11	5	9		6		3						8	10	4
44	24	TORQUAY UNITED	1-0	Woan	10123		2			1	7	11	5	9		6		3						8	10	4
45	26	SOUTHEND UNITED	1-3	Hawkings	10975		2			1	7	11	5	9		6		3						8	10	4
46	May 2	Southend United	3-6	Hawkings, Tebbutt, Woan	9391		3	2		1	7	11	5	9		6								4	8	10
		Apps				3	10	24	8	38	20	39	46	44	32	37	6	40	2	8	11	13	23	26	34	42
		Goals							1		5	2		20	14	4	3	4		2				10	20	1

One own goal

F.A. Cup

#	Date	Opponent	Res	Scorers	Att	Collins BV	Elvy R	English J	Fowler T	Gale CM	Hawkings B	Leek K	Mills RWG	Patterson RL	Peacock RJ	Pickering PB	Robinson M	Robinson TH	Tebbutt RS	Woan AE	Yeoman RI
R1	Nov 10	NEWPORT COUNTY	3-0	Gale, Mills, Pickering	9345	2				9	7	10	6	3	4	1	11	5	8		
R2	Dec 7	BOURNEMOUTH	4-1	Leek, Woan, Hughes(og), Norris(og)	12691	2		7	11	5	9	10	6	3		1			8		4
R3	Jan 4	ARSENAL	3-1	Hawkings, Leek, Tebbutt	21344	2	1	7	11	5	9	10	6	3					8		4
R4	25	Liverpool	1-3	Hawkings	56939	2	1	7	11	5	9	10	6	3					8		4

		P	W	D	L	F	A	W	D	L	F	A	Pts
1	Brighton & Hove A.	46	13	6	4	52	30	11	6	6	36	34	60
2	Brentford	46	15	5	3	52	24	9	5	9	30	32	58
3	Plymouth Argyle	46	17	4	2	43	17	8	4	11	24	31	58
4	Swindon Town	46	14	7	2	47	16	7	8	8	32	34	57
5	Reading	46	14	5	4	52	23	7	8	8	27	28	55
6	Southampton	46	16	3	4	78	31	6	7	10	34	41	54
7	Southend United	46	14	5	4	56	26	7	7	9	34	32	54
8	Norwich City	46	11	9	3	41	28	8	6	9	34	42	53
9	Bournemouth	46	16	5	2	54	24	5	4	14	27	50	51
10	Queen's Park Rgs.	46	15	6	2	40	14	3	8	12	24	51	50
11	Newport County	46	12	6	5	40	24	5	8	10	33	43	48
12	Colchester United	46	13	5	5	45	27	4	8	11	32	52	47
13	NORTHAMPTON TOWN	46	13	1	9	60	33	6	5	12	27	46	44
14	Crystal Palace	46	12	5	6	46	30	3	8	12	24	42	43
15	Port Vale	46	12	6	5	49	24	4	4	15	18	34	42
16	Watford	46	9	8	6	34	27	4	8	11	25	50	42
17	Shrewsbury Town	46	10	6	7	29	25	4	14	20	46	40	
18	Aldershot	46	7	9	7	31	34	5	7	11	28	55	40
19	Coventry City	46	10	9	4	41	24	3	4	16	20	57	39
20	Walsall	46	10	7	6	37	24	4	2	17	24	51	37
21	Torquay United	46	9	7	7	33	34	2	6	15	16	40	35
22	Gillingham	46	12	5	6	33	24	1	4	18	19	57	35
23	Millwall	46	6	6	11	37	36	5	3	15	26	55	31
24	Exeter City	46	10	4	9	37	35	1	5	17	20	64	31

1958/59 8th in Division 4

Match results

#	Date	Opponent	Score	Scorers	Att
1	Aug 23	Port Vale	4-1	Hawkings, Kirkup, Woan 2	15018
2	28	CREWE ALEXANDRA	3-0	Hawkings, Kirkup, Woan	11916
3	30	CRYSTAL PALACE	3-0	Fowler, Kirkup, Woan	11288
4	Sep 1	Crewe Alexandra	2-1	Woan 2	7016
5	6	Chester	3-2	Fowler, Mills, Woan	9723
6	9	Carlisle United	1-2	Woan	11238
7	13	WATFORD	2-1	Hawkings, Mills	11106
8	20	Hartlepools United	0-3		7463
9	25	WORKINGTON	1-1	Baron	6487
10	27	SOUTHPORT	3-1	Fowler, Woan 2	10999
11	Oct 1	Workington	3-3	Fowler, Mills, Woan	6613
12	4	Torquay United	2-4	Baron, Norris	5399
13	9	York City	1-2		5826
14	11	EXETER CITY	1-1	Woan	10077
15	18	Coventry City	0-2		22305
16	25	SHREWSBURY TOWN	3-3	Tebbutt 2, Woan	9897
17	Nov 1	Darlington	2-2	Fowler, Hawkings	5579
18	8	WALSALL	3-2	Tebbutt, Woan, Gutteridge(og)	11858
19	22	ALDERSHOT	1-0	Kirkup	7598
20	29	Gateshead	1-4	Kirkup	2870
21	Dec 13	Barrow	2-2	Mills, Tebbutt	4209
22	20	PORT VALE	2-4	Fowler 2	6907
23	26	Gillingham	1-4	Mills	6947
24	27	GILLINGHAM	4-2	Fowler 3, Woan	9538
25	Jan 3	Crystal Palace	1-1	Hawkings	17162
26	10	Millwall	0-3		11388
27	24	OLDHAM ATHLETIC	2-1	Claypole, Woan	7168
28	31	Watford	1-3	Woan	6200
29	Feb 7	HARTLEPOOLS UNITED	2-1	Baron, Woan	6055
30	14	Southport	2-1	Woan 2	3630
31	21	TORQUAY UNITED	1-1		6329
32	28	Exeter City	4-3	English, Fowler, Leek, Woan	9870
33	Mar 7	COVENTRY CITY	4-0	Fowler, Leek 2, Woan	14365
34	14	Shrewsbury Town	0-4		7227
35	21	DARLINGTON	1-3	Woan	6399
36	27	Bradford Park Avenue	2-1	O'Neil, Woan	5988
37	28	Walsall	1-2	English	5991
38	31	BRADFORD PARK AVE.	4-1	English, Fowler, Leek, Woan	7544
39	Apr 4	MILLWALL	0-1		7284
40	6	CARLISLE UNITED	0-0		3450
41	11	Aldershot	3-1	Leek, Phillips, Woan	2567
42	13	CHESTER	4-0	Fowler, Woan 3	3865
43	18	GATESHEAD	1-0	Mills	5799
44	20	York City	1-2	Woan	9123
45	25	Oldham Athletic	1-2	Fowler	2671
46	30	BARROW	2-0	English, Woan	4324

Player appearances (shirt numbers)

Column key: Bar = Baron KP, Ban = Bannister JH, Bre = Brewer AP, Cla = Claypole AW, Cole = Coleman GJ, Coll = Collins BV, Eng = English J, Fow = Fowler T, Gal = Gale CM, Elv = Elvy R, Haw = Hawkings B, Kir = Kirkup BA, Leck = Leck DA, Loa = Loasby AA, Mlr = Miller RL, Mls = Mills RWG, Nor = Norris OP, ONe = O'Neil J, Olf = Olfa B, Pat = Patterson RL, Phi = Phillips R, Smi = Smith JO, Yeo = Yeoman RI, Teb = Tebbutt RS, Woa = Woan AE

#	Bar	Ban	Bre	Cla	Cole	Coll	Eng	Fow	Gal	Elv	Haw	Kir	Leck	Loa	Mlr	Mls	Nor	ONe	Olf	Pat	Phi	Smi	Yeo	Teb	Woa
1		2						11	5	1	9	8				7		6		3			4		10
2		2	1					11	5		9	8				7		6		3			4		10
3		2	1					11	5		9	8				7		6		3			4		10
4		2	1					11	5		9	8				7		6		3			4		10
5		2	1					11	5		9	8				7		6		3			4		10
6		2	1					11	5		9	8				7		6		3			4		10
7		2	1					11	5		9	8				7		6		3			4		10
8		2	1					11	5		9	8				7		6		3			4	10	
9	8	2	1					11	5							7	9	6		3			4		10
10	8	2						11	5	1	9					7		6		3			4		10
11	8	2						11	5	1	9					7		6		3			4		10
12	8	2						11	5	1						7	9	6		3			4		10
13	8	2						11	5	1						7	9	6		3			4		10
14	8	2				5		11		1	7					6	9			3			4		10
15	8	2				5		11		1	9					6	7			3			4		10
16		2		3			7	11	5	1	9					6							4	8	10
17			2				7	11	5	1	9					6				3			4	8	10
18	10		2					11	5	1	9					6				3		4		8	7
19	10		2					11	5	1		9				6				3		4		8	7
20			2					11	5	1		9				6	8	4		3					7
21	10				2	5		11		1	7					9	6	4		3				8	
22	10			2		5		11		1	7					9	6	4		3				8	
23	10			2		5		11		1						9	4			6	7		3		8
24	7		1	2		5		11								9	4	10	6	3					8
25	7		1	2		5		11			9						4	10		3			6		8
26	7		1	2		5		11			9						4	10		3			6		8
27	7		1	2		5		11			9						4	10		3			6		8
28	10		1	2		5		11			9							7		4			3	6	8
29	8	2	1					11	5							4	9		7			3	6		10
30	7	2	1					11	5							4	9					3	6	8	10
31	7	2	1	3				11	5		9					4							6	8	10
32	8	2	1	3			7	11	5				9			4							6		10
33	8	2	1	3			7	11	5				9			4							6		10
34	8	2	1	3			7	11	5				9			4							6		10
35	8	2	1	3			7	11	5				9			4		8					6		10
36			1	2			7	11	5				9			4		8		3			6		10
37			1	2			7	11	5							4		8		3	6			9	10
38			1	2			7	11	5				9			4		8		3			6		10
39			1	2			7	11	5				9			4		8		3			6		10
40			1				7		5				9	11		4				3	2		6		
41			1	2				11	5				9		7	8				3	4		6		10
42			1	2				11	5				9		7	8				3	4		6		10
43			1	2				11	5				9		7	8				3	4		6		10
44			1	2				11	5				7			9	8			3	4		6		10
45			1	2			7	11	5				9							3	4		6	8	10
46			1	2			7	11	5				9							3	4		6	8	10
Apps	25	24	31	26	1	10	13	45	36	15	21	17	14	2	2	42	14	22	2	38	10	23	17	14	42
Goals	4			1			4	15			5	5	5			6	1	1			1			4	32

One own goal

F.A. Cup

Rd	Date	Opponent	Score	Scorers	Att	Bar	Ban	Cla	Eng	Coll	Fow	Gal	Elv	Haw	Kir	Mls	ONe	Pat	Smi	Woa
R1	Nov 15	WYCOMBE WANDERERS	2-0	Fowler, Kirkup	12934	10		2			11	5	1	9	8	6		3	4	7
R2	Dec 6	Tooting & Mitcham	1-2	Kirkup	10203	10	2		5	7	11		1	9		6	4	3		8

Division 4 table

		P	W	D	L	F	A	W	D	L	F	A	Pts
1	Port Vale	46	14	6	3	62	30	12	6	5	48	28	64
2	Coventry City	46	18	4	1	50	11	6	8	9	34	36	60
3	York City	46	12	10	1	37	17	9	8	6	36	35	60
4	Shrewsbury Town	46	15	5	3	59	24	9	5	9	42	39	58
5	Exeter City	46	16	4	3	55	24	7	7	9	32	37	57
6	Walsall	46	13	5	5	56	25	8	5	10	39	39	52
7	Crystal Palace	46	12	8	3	54	27	8	4	11	36	44	52
8	NORTHAMPTON TOWN	46	14	5	4	48	25	7	4	12	37	53	51
9	Millwall	46	13	6	4	46	23	7	4	12	30	46	50
10	Carlisle United	46	11	6	6	37	30	8	6	9	25	35	50
11	Gillingham	46	14	6	3	53	27	6	3	14	29	50	49
12	Torquay United	46	11	5	7	45	32	5	7	11	33	45	44
13	Chester	46	10	5	8	39	33	6	7	10	33	51	44
14	Bradford Park Ave.	46	15	1	7	51	29	3	6	14	24	48	43
15	Watford	46	10	6	7	46	36	6	4	13	35	43	42
16	Darlington	46	7	8	8	37	36	6	8	9	29	32	42
17	Workington	46	9	10	4	40	32	3	7	13	23	46	41
18	Crewe Alexandra	46	11	5	7	52	32	4	5	14	18	50	40
19	Hartlepools United	46	11	4	8	50	41	4	6	13	24	47	40
20	Gateshead	46	11	3	9	33	30	5	5	13	23	55	40
21	Oldham Athletic	46	10	5	8	39	29	1	4	18	20	55	36
22	Aldershot	46	8	4	11	37	45	6	3	14	26	52	35
23	Barrow	46	6	6	11	34	45	3	4	16	17	59	28
24	Southport	46	7	8	8	26	25	0	4	19	15	61	26

1959/60   6th in Division 4

League matches

No	Date	Opponent	Score	Scorers	Att	Bowen DL	Brewer AP	Claypole AW	Cooke BA	Deakin MRF	English J	Fotheringham JG	Fowler T	Gale CM	Griffin FA	Haskins AJ	Isaac WH	Kane P	Kirkup BA	Leck DA	Mills RWG	Olha B	Patterson RL	Phillips R	Smith JO	Tebbutt RS	Tucker KJ	Vickers P	Ward JR	Woan AE	Wright ME
1	Aug 22	Exeter City	1-1	Leck	9678	6	1	2					11	5	7					9	4		3							8	10
2	27	TORQUAY UNITED	3-0	Leck 2, Tebbutt	12974	6	1	2					11	5	7				10	9	4		3			8					
3	29	Doncaster Rovers	2-3	Leck, Woan	7033		1	2					11	5	7				8	9	4		3		6					10	
4	Sep 2	Torquay United	3-5	Kirkup 2, Leck	7447		1	2					11	5	7	3			8	9	4				6					10	
5	5	WORKINGTON	0-0		11298	6	1	2					11	5	7				8	9	4		3							10	
6	10	GILLINGHAM	2-1	Mills, Woan	9622	6	1						11	5	7				8	9	4		3	2						10	
7	12	Rochdale	2-2	Leck 2	5686	6	1						11	5	7				10	9	4		3	2		8					
8	16	Gillingham	1-2	Woan	5970	6	1						11	5	7				8	9	4		3	2						10	
9	19	GATESHEAD	2-0	Leck 2	9426	6							11	5	7		1		8	9	4		3	2						10	
10	21	MILLWALL	0-3		8675								11	5	7		1		8	9	4		3	2	6					10	
11	26	Darlington	2-3	English 2	7199						7		11	5			1			9	4		3	2	6	8				10	
12	28	Millwall	1-2	English	18950	6					7		11	5		3	1			9	4			2		8				10	
13	Oct 3	ALDERSHOT	2-0	Leck, Woan	8316						7		11	5		3	1			9	4			2	6	8				10	
14	10	Oldham Athletic	1-0	Ferguson (og)	5419						7		11	5		3	1			9	4			2	6	8				10	
15	17	CARLISLE UNITED	2-2	Fowler, Woan	8789						7		11	5		3	1			9	4			2	6	8				10	
16	24	Notts County	1-2	Woan	14867						7		11	5		3	1			9	4			2	6	8				10	
17	31	Walsall	0-1		13041	6	1			9		7	11	5		3					4	10	8	2							
18	Nov 7	Hartlepools United	4-1	Deakin 2, Kane, Leck	1953	6	1			9		7	11	5				8		10	4		3	2							
19	21	Chester	1-1	Deakin	7283	6				9		7	11	5			1	8		10	4		3	2							
20	28	CRYSTAL PALACE	0-2		8121	6	1			10		7	11	5				8		9	4		3	2							
21	Dec 12	STOCKPORT COUNTY	1-1	Olha	6383	6	1		4				11	5				8		9		7	3	2					10		
22	19	EXETER CITY	1-1	Kane	4709	6	1	2	4				11	5				8		9		7	3						10		
23	28	WATFORD	1-2	Tebbutt	8369		1		4				11	5				8		9	6	7	3	2		10					
24	Jan 2	DONCASTER ROVERS	3-1	Fowler, Mills, Tebbutt	6253		1		4				11	5				10		9	6	7	3	2		8					
25	16	Workington	1-5	Bowen	3788	6	1		4				11	5						9		7	3	2		8			10		
26	23	ROCHDALE	3-1	Deakin, Olha, Kane	5355	6	1		4	10			11	5				8		9		7	3	2							
27	Feb 6	Gateshead	3-1	Leck 2, Mills	3164	6	1		4	10			11	5				8		9		7	3	2							
28	13	DARLINGTON	3-1	Kane, Olha 2	3477	6	1		4	9			11	5				8				7	3	2				10			
29	20	Aldershot	0-3		4197	6	1		4	9			11	5				8				7	3	2				10			
30	27	OLDHAM ATHLETIC	8-1	*See below	6746		1		4	9			11	5				8			6	7	3	2		10					
31	Mar 1	Watford	1-3	Kane	13024		1		4	9			11	5				8			6	7	3	2					10		
32	5	Carlisle United	2-0	Deakin, Mills	3503		1		4	9			11	5				8		10	6	7	3	2							
33	12	NOTTS COUNTY	4-2	Deakin 2, Kane, Tebbutt	8902		1		4	9			11	5				8			6	7	3	2		10					
34	19	Walsall	2-1	Deakin 2	9852		1		4	9			11	5				8			6	7	3	2		10					
35	26	HARTLEPOOLS UNITED	3-0	Deakin, Kane, Wright	5954		1		4	9			11	5				8			6	7	3	2							10
36	Apr 2	Crewe Alexandra	1-0	Deakin	5901		1		4	9			11	5				8		10	6	7	3	2							
37	7	Bradford Park Avenue	0-3		4916		1		4	9			11	5				8			6	7	3	2					10		
38	9	CHESTER	1-0	Deakin	7037		1	2	4	9			11	5				8			6	7	3						10		
39	11	BARROW	6-0	Deakin 4, Kane 2	5710		1	2	4	9			11	5				8		10	6	7	3								
40	15	Southport	4-0	Kane 3, Olha	3612		1	2	4	9			11	5				8		10	6	7	3								
41	16	Crystal Palace	1-0	Deakin	15943		1	2	4	9				5				8		10	6	7	3				11				
42	19	SOUTHPORT	2-2	Leck 2	12373		1	2	4	9				5				8		10	6	7	3				11				
43	23	BRADFORD PARK AVE.	3-1	Deakin, Fowler 2	8667		1	2	4	9			11	5				8		10	6	7	3								
44	25	Barrow	1-0	Leck	5400		1	2	4	9			11	5				8		10	6	7	3								
45	28	CREWE ALEXANDRA	0-0		10847	6	1	2		9			11	5				8		10	4	7	3								
46	30	Stockport County	0-3		3853		1	2	4	9				5				8		10	6	7	3				11				
		Apps				22	38	15	25	25	6	11	41	35	16	7	8	28	9	30	41	26	39	31	11	15	3	2	6	14	2
		Goals				1				20	3		4					16	2	14	4	5				7				6	1

Scorers in game 30: Deakin 2, Kane 2, Tebbutt 3, Ferguson (og).

Two own goals

F.A. Cup

Round	Date	Opponent	Score	Scorers	Att	Bowen DL	Brewer AP	Deakin MRF	Fowler T	Gale CM	Griffin FA	Kane P	Leck DA	Mills RWG	Patterson RL	Phillips R
R1	Nov 14	Torquay United	1-7	Kane	5661	6	1	10	11	5	7	8	9	4	3	2

Final table

		P	W	D	L	F	A	W	D	L	F	A	Pts
1	Walsall	46	14	5	4	57	33	14	4	5	45	27	65
2	Notts County	46	19	1	3	66	27	7	7	9	41	42	60
3	Torquay United	46	17	3	3	56	27	9	5	9	28	31	60
4	Watford	46	17	2	4	62	28	7	7	9	30	39	57
5	Millwall	46	12	8	3	54	28	6	9	8	30	33	53
6	NORTHAMPTON TOWN	46	13	6	4	50	22	9	3	11	35	41	53
7	Gillingham	46	17	4	2	47	21	4	6	13	27	48	52
8	Crystal Palace	46	12	6	5	61	27	7	6	10	23	37	50
9	Exeter City	46	13	7	3	50	30	6	4	13	30	40	49
10	Stockport County	46	15	6	2	35	10	4	5	14	23	44	49
11	Bradford Park Ave.	46	12	10	1	48	25	5	5	13	22	43	49
12	Rochdale	46	15	4	4	46	19	3	6	14	19	41	46
13	Aldershot	46	14	5	4	50	22	4	4	15	27	52	45
14	Crewe Alexandra	46	14	3	6	51	31	4	6	13	28	57	45
15	Darlington	46	11	6	6	40	30	6	3	14	23	43	43
16	Workington	46	10	8	5	41	20	4	6	13	27	40	42
17	Doncaster Rovers	46	13	3	7	40	23	3	7	13	29	53	42
18	Barrow	46	11	8	4	52	29	4	3	16	25	58	41
19	Carlisle United	46	8	8	5	28	28	6	5	12	23	38	41
20	Chester	46	10	8	5	37	26	4	4	15	22	51	40
21	Southport	46	9	7	7	30	32	1	7	15	18	60	34
22	Gateshead	46	12	3	8	37	27	0	6	17	21	59	33
23	Oldham Athletic	46	5	7	11	20	30	3	5	15	21	53	28
24	Hartlepools United	46	9	2	12	40	41	1	5	17	19	68	27

1960/61 3rd in Division 4

No	Date	Opponent	Score	Scorers	Att	Branston TG	Brewer AP	Brown L	Carson AM	Claypole AW	Coe NC	Cooke BA	Deakin MRF	Edwards RH	Everitt MD	Fowler T	Gale CM	Laird DS	Leck DA	Lines B	Moran J	Mills RWG	Olha B	Patterson RL	Phillips R	Spelman RE	Tucker KJ	Wright ME
1	Aug 20	Oldham Athletic	2-1	Deakin 2	8929		1			2		4	8			11	5		9			6		3			7	10
2	24	Workington	0-3		3439		1			2		4	8			11	5					6						10
3	27	ALDERSHOT	2-1	Deakin, Leck	8092		1			2		4	8			11	5	7	9			6		3				10
4	29	WORKINGTON	3-2	Leck 2, Wright	6835		1			2		4	8			11	5		9			6	7	3				10
5	Sep 3	STOCKPORT COUNTY	4-2	Deakin 2, Wright 2	8661		1			2		4	9			11	5		8			6	7	3				10
6	7	Crewe Alexandra	2-0	Deakin, Leck	8499		1			2		4	9			11	5		8			6	7	3				10
7	10	Bradford Park Avenue	3-1	Deakin, Mills, Wright	7616		1			2		4	9			11	5		8			6	7	3				10
8	13	CREWE ALEXANDRA	4-1	Deakin, Fowler, Leck, one og	9034		1			2		4	9			11	5		8			6	7	3				10
9	17	GILLINGHAM	3-1	Olha, Wright 2	9575		1			2		4	9			11	5		8			6	7	3				10
10	19	CHESTER	3-2	Fowler, Olha, Leck	9320		1			2		4	9			11	5		8			6	7	3				10
11	24	Barrow	0-1		5583		1			2		4				11	5	9	8			6	7	3				10
12	Oct 1	MILLWALL	2-2	Brown, Leck	11558		1	9		2		4				11	5		8			6	7	3				10
13	3	Accrington Stanley	2-3	Brown, Leck	4603		1	9		2		4				11	5		8			6	7	3				10
14	8	Peterborough United	3-3	Deakin, Fowler, Leck	22959	6	1			2		4	9			11	5		8				7	3				10
15	15	SOUTHPORT	3-1	Olha, Tucker 2	11014		1			2		4	9				5		8			6	7	3			11	10
16	22	Darlington	1-1	Brown	8858		1	6		2		4	9				5					7	8	3			11	10
17	29	CRYSTAL PALACE	1-2	Tucker	13943		1	6		2		4	9				5		8			7		3			11	10
18	Nov 12	HARTLEPOOLS UNITED	3-3	Brown 3	9484		1	9		2		4					5	10	8	11		6		3			7	
19	19	Wrexham	2-2	Brown 2	6328			9		2	1	4					5	10	8	11		6		3			7	
20	Dec 3	Rochdale	1-1	Lines	2173			9		3	1	4					5	10	8	11		6			2	7		
21	10	MANSFIELD TOWN	1-0	Laird	8129			9		3	1	4					5	10	8	11		6			2	7		
22	17	OLDHAM ATHLETIC	1-0	Spelman	9710			9		3	1	4					5	10	8	11		6			2	7		
23	26	York City	1-0	one og	7291			9		3	1	4					5	10	8	11		6			2	7		
24	27	YORK CITY	3-0	Brown 2, Lines	18384			9		3	1	4					5	10	8	11		6			2	7		
25	31	Aldershot	2-2	Brown, Deakin	7117			9		3	1	4					5		8	11		6			2	7		
26	Jan 21	BRADFORD PARK AVE.	0-1		9749			8		3	1	4	9				5	10		11		6			2	7		
27	28	Doncaster Rovers	2-0	Brown, Deakin	3028			9		3	1	4	10			11	5			8		6			2	7		
28	Feb 11	BARROW	3-0	Brown 2, Moran	9255	4		9		3	1		8			11	5				10	6			2	7		
29	18	Millwall	1-3	Cooke	11707			8		3	1	4	9			11	5				10	6			2	7		
30	25	PETERBOROUGH UTD.	0-3		21000			8		3	1	4		9		11	5				10	6			2	7		
31	Mar 4	Southport	0-2		4693			9		3	1	4			8	11	5				10	6			2		7	
32	8	Chester	2-0	Everitt, Leck	5455	4		9		3	1				7		5		8	11		6			2			10
33	11	DARLINGTON	1-1	Brown	10124	4		9		3	1				7		5		8	11		6			2			10
34	18	Crystal Palace	3-2	Edwards 2, Leck	20668	4				3	1			9	7		5		8	11		6			2			10
35	21	CARLISLE UNITED	0-0		11593	4				3	1			9	7		5		8	11		6			2			10
36	25	DONCASTER ROVERS	3-0	Edwards, Leck 2	8604	4				3	1			9	7		5		8	11	10	6			2			
37	Apr 1	Hartlepools United	2-4	Edwards 2	3460	4				3	1			8	7		5	10	9	11		6			2			
38	3	Exeter City	3-1	Edwards, Everitt, Moran	5903	4		10		3	1			9	7		5			11	8	6			2			
39	4	EXETER CITY	3-1	Brown 3	12402	4		10		3	1			9	7		5			11	8	6			2			
40	8	WREXHAM	3-0	Brown, Everitt, Lines	11507	4		8		3	1			9	7		5			11	10	6			2			
41	12	Gillingham	1-0	Lines	4831	4				3	1			9	8		5			11	10	6			2			7
42	15	Carlisle United	1-2	Mills	3985	4				3	1			9	8		5			11	10	6			2			7
43	17	Stockport County	1-1	Edwards	4307			8	6	3	1	4		9			5			11	10				2	7		
44	22	ROCHDALE	5-1	Brown 2, Moran 3	9535	4		9		3	1			8	7		5			11	10	6			2			
45	25	ACCRINGTON STANLEY	2-1	Brown, Lines	8167	4		8		3	1			9	7		5			11	10	6			2			
46	29	Mansfield Town	2-4	Edwards, Everitt	4872	4		8		3	1			9	7		5			11	10	6			2			
Apps						17	18	33	1	42	28	31	19	13	16	19	39	12	29	24	15	45	14	8	42	11	7	23
Goals								22				1	11	8	4	3	1		13	5	5	2	3			1	3	6

F.A. Cup

Two own goals

Rd	Date	Opponent	Score	Scorers	Att	Branston TG	Brewer AP	Brown L	Carson AM	Claypole AW	Coe NC	Cooke BA	Deakin MRF	Edwards RH	Everitt MD	Fowler T	Gale CM	Laird DS	Leck DA	Lines B	Moran J	Mills RWG	Olha B	Patterson RL	Phillips R	Spelman RE	Tucker KJ	Wright ME
R1	Nov 5	HASTINGS	2-1	Brown, Wilson	11141		1	9		2		4					5		8			6	7	3			11	
R2	26	Romford	5-1	Brown 2, Leck 3	11073			9		3	1	4					5	10	8	11		6			2	7		
R3	Jan 7	Luton Town	0-4		26220			9		3	1	4	10				5		8	11		6			2	7		

Played in R1: Wilson (10)

F.L. Cup

Rd	Date	Opponent	Score	Scorers	Att	Branston TG	Brewer AP	Brown L	Carson AM	Claypole AW	Coe NC	Cooke BA	Deakin MRF	Edwards RH	Everitt MD	Fowler T	Gale CM	Laird DS	Leck DA	Lines B	Moran J	Mills RWG	Olha B	Patterson RL	Phillips R	Spelman RE	Tucker KJ	Wright ME
R2	Oct 18	WREXHAM	1-1	Mills	12029		1	6		2		4	9				5		8			7		3			11	10
rep	25	Wrexham	0-2		7518			6		2	1	4	9				5		8	11		7		3				10

		P	W	D	L	F	A	W	D	L	F	A	Pts
1	Peterborough Utd.	46	18	3	2	85	30	10	7	6	49	35	66
2	Crystal Palace	46	16	4	3	64	28	13	2	8	46	41	64
3	NORTHAMPTON TOWN	46	16	4	3	53	25	9	6	8	37	37	60
4	Bradford Park Ave.	46	16	5	2	49	22	10	3	10	35	52	60
5	York City	46	17	3	3	50	14	4	6	13	30	46	51
6	Millwall	46	13	3	7	56	33	8	5	10	41	53	50
7	Darlington	46	11	7	5	41	24	7	6	10	37	46	49
8	Workington	46	14	3	6	38	28	7	4	12	36	48	49
9	Crewe Alexandra	46	11	4	8	40	29	9	5	9	21	38	49
10	Aldershot	46	16	4	3	55	19	2	5	16	24	50	45
11	Doncaster Rovers	46	15	0	8	52	33	4	7	12	24	45	45
12	Oldham Athletic	46	13	4	6	57	38	6	3	14	22	50	45
13	Stockport County	46	14	4	5	31	21	4	5	14	26	45	45
14	Southport	46	12	6	5	47	27	7	0	16	22	40	44
15	Gillingham	46	9	7	7	45	34	6	6	11	19	32	43
16	Wrexham	46	12	4	7	38	22	5	4	14	24	34	42
17	Rochdale	46	13	7	3	43	19	4	1	18	17	47	42
18	Accrington Stanley	46	12	4	7	44	32	4	4	15	30	56	40
19	Carlisle United	46	10	7	6	43	37	3	6	14	18	42	39
20	Mansfield Town	46	10	3	10	39	34	6	3	14	32	44	38
21	Exeter City	46	12	3	8	39	32	2	7	14	27	62	38
22	Barrow	46	10	6	7	33	28	3	5	15	19	51	37
23	Hartlepools United	46	10	4	9	46	40	2	4	17	25	63	32
24	Chester	46	9	7	7	38	35	2	2	19	23	69	31

1961/62   8th in Division 3

#	Date	Opponent	Score	Scorers	Att	Branston TG	Brodie CTG	Carson AM	Claypole AW	Clapton DP	Coe NC	Cooke BA	Dixon CH	Etheridge BG	Everitt MD	Fowler T	Foley TC	Haskins AJ	Holton CC	Leck DA	Lines B	Moran J	Patterson RL	Reid J	Robson TH	Spelman RE	Terry PA	Woods DE	Woollard AJ	Wright ME	Edwards RH	Mills RWG
1	Aug 19	Watford	0-0		16849	5			3		1				6		2			4	11	10				7	9			8		
2	22	Bristol City	0-1		14415	5			3		1				6		2			4	11	10				7	9		8			
3	26	Hull City	0-1		8027	5			3		1	7			6	11	2			4		10					9					8
4	29	BRISTOL CITY	0-1		12832	5			3	8	1	7			4	11	2			6		10					9					
5	Sep 2	PORT VALE	1-1	Terry	9573	5			3		1				8	11	2			6		10					9		7			4
6	6	Crystal Palace	4-1	Holton 3, Terry	25535	5			3		1				4	11	2		8	6		10					9		7			
7	9	LINCOLN CITY	2-2	Dixon 2	11850	5			3		1		7		4	11	2		8	6							9				10	
8	16	Torquay United	2-1	Holton, Terry	5707	5			3		1		7		4		2		8	6	11						9				10	
9	18	BOURNEMOUTH	0-3		14350	5			3		1		7		4		2		8	6	11						9				10	
10	23	SWINDON TOWN	1-2	Holton	9263	5			3		1		7		4		2		8	6	11						9					10
11	27	Bournemouth	2-3	Holton 2	14112	5		4	3		1						2		8	6	11					7					9	10
12	30	Halifax Town	3-1	Leck, Lines 2	5737	5	1	4	3								2		8	6	11					7					9	10
13	Oct 3	BARNSLEY	3-1	Holton, Terry 2	11448	5	1	4	3								2		8	6	11					7	9					10
14	7	Bradford Park Avenue	2-1	Holton, Lines	10738	5	1	4	3								2		8	6	11					7	9					10
15	11	Barnsley	2-3	Holton 2	2371	5	1	4	3								2		8	6	11					7	9					10
16	14	GRIMSBY TOWN	7-0	Holton 3, Leck, Spelman, Edwards, Mills	11201	5	1		3						4		2		8	6	11					7					9	10
17	17	CRYSTAL PALACE	1-1	Holton	13827	5	1		3						4		2		8	6	11					7					9	10
18	21	Shrewsbury Town	3-1	Holton, Edwards, Mills	6872	5	1		3						4		2		8	6	11					7					9	10
19	28	PETERBOROUGH UTD.	2-2	Everitt, Holton	17324	5	1	4	3						10		2		8	6	11					7	9					
20	Nov 11	NEWPORT COUNTY	5-0	Holton 2, Lines, Reid 2	7845	5			3		1				4		2		8	6	11			10		7	9					
21	18	Southend United	3-1	Holton, Spelman, Terry	5974	5	1		3						4		2		8	6	11			10		7	9					
22	Dec 2	Coventry City	0-1		13693	5	1		3						4		2		8	6	11			10		7	9					
23	9	BRENTFORD	5-0	Holton 2, Lines 2, Terry	10059	5	1								4		2		8	6	11			10		7	9					3
24	16	WATFORD	2-0	Terry 2	12509	5	1								4		2		8	6	11			10		7	9					3
25	23	HULL CITY	2-0	Lines, Terry	10203	5	1								4		2		8	6	11			10		7	9					3
26	26	Portsmouth	1-4	Lines	17428	5	1								4		2		8	6	11			10		7	9					3
27	Jan 13	Port Vale	1-1	Holton	8229	5	1								4		2		8	6	11			10		7	9					3
28	20	Lincoln City	0-0		5720	5	1								4		2		8	6	11			10		7	9					3
29	27	NOTTS COUNTY	1-2	Lines	11813	5	1								4		2		8	6	11			10		7	9					3
30	Feb 3	TORQUAY UNITED	1-2	Lines	8910	5	1								4		2		8	6	11			10		7					9	3
31	10	Swindon Town	2-2	Everitt, Holton	8985	5	1								7		2	3	8	6	11	9		10								4
32	17	HALIFAX TOWN	3-1	Holton, Lines, Moran	7900	5	1								7		2		8	4	11	9	3	10								6
33	24	BRADFORD PARK AVE.	2-0	Holton, Reid	7563	5	1								7		2		8	4	11	9	3	10								6
34	Mar 3	Grimsby Town	2-3	Holton 2	9318	5	1							7			2		8	4	11			10					3		9	6
35	10	SHREWSBURY TOWN	3-1	Dixon, Lines, one og	8173	5	1						7		9		2		8	4	11			10					3			6
36	17	Peterborough United	2-0	Everitt, Robson	17009	5	1						7		9		2		8	4				10	11				3			6
37	20	PORTSMOUTH	2-2	Dixon, Everitt	13622	5	1						7		9		2		8	4				10	11				3			6
38	24	READING	1-0	Holton	9746	5	1						7		9		2		8	4				10	11				3			6
39	31	Newport County	0-0		2568	5	1						7		9		2		8	4	11			10					3			6
40	Apr 7	SOUTHEND UNITED	3-1	Everitt, Holton, Lines	7657	5	1						7		9		2		8	4	11			10					3			6
41	11	Reading	0-2		5586	5					1						2		8	4				10	11	7		3			9	6
42	14	Notts County	4-1	Holton 3, Woods	5974	5					1				9		2		8	4	11			10		7		3				6
43	21	COVENTRY CITY	4-1	Holton 2, Lines, Woods	10388	5	1								9		2		8	4	11			10		7		3				6
44	23	Queen's Park Rangers	0-2		10953	5	1								9		2		8	4	11			10		7		3				6
45	24	QUEEN'S PARK RANGERS	1-1	Holton	12533		1	5							9		2		8	4	11			10		7		3				6
46	27	Brentford	0-3		6715	5	1								9		2		8	4	11			10		7		3				6
		Apps				45	32	7	22	1	14	2	15	1	37	5	46	1	41	46	38	9	2	26	4	23	24	6	13	1	10	35
		Goals											4		5				36	2	14	1		3	1	2	10	2			2	2

One own goal

F.A. Cup

#	Date	Opponent	Score	Scorers	Att	Branston	Brodie	Carson	Claypole	Clapton	Coe	Cooke	Dixon	Etheridge	Everitt	Fowler	Foley	Haskins	Holton	Leck	Lines	Moran	Patterson	Reid	Robson	Spelman	Terry	Woods	Woollard	Wright	Edwards	Mills
R1	Nov 4	MILLWALL	2-0	Lines, Terry	11844	5	1		3						4				8	6	11					7	9				10	2
R2	25	KETTERING TOWN	3-0	Holton 3	18825	5	1		3						4		2		8	6	11					7	9					10
R3	Jan 6	Port Vale	1-3	Moran	19442	5	1								4		2		8	6	11	10				7	9					3

F.L. Cup

#	Date	Opponent	Score	Scorers	Att	Branston	Brodie	Carson	Claypole	Clapton	Coe	Cooke	Dixon	Etheridge	Everitt	Fowler	Foley	Haskins	Holton	Leck	Lines	Moran	Patterson	Reid	Robson	Spelman	Terry	Woods	Woollard	Wright	Edwards	Mills
R1	Sep 13	Luton Town	1-2	Cooke	7512	5			3			6	7		8		2			4	11						9					10

Played at no. 1: B Caine

		P	W	D	L	F	A	W	D	L	F	A	Pts
1	Portsmouth	46	15	6	2	48	23	12	5	6	39	24	65
2	Grimsby Town	46	18	3	2	49	18	10	3	10	31	38	62
3	Bournemouth	46	14	8	1	42	18	7	9	7	27	27	59
4	Queen's Park Rgs.	46	15	3	5	65	31	9	8	6	46	42	59
5	Peterborough Utd.	46	16	0	7	60	38	10	6	7	47	44	58
6	Bristol City	46	15	3	5	56	27	8	5	10	38	45	54
7	Reading	46	14	5	4	46	24	8	4	11	31	42	53
8	NORTHAMPTON TOWN	46	12	6	5	52	24	8	5	10	33	33	51
9	Swindon Town	46	11	8	4	48	26	6	7	10	30	45	49
10	Hull City	46	15	2	6	43	20	5	6	12	24	34	48
11	Bradford Park Ave.	46	13	5	5	47	27	7	2	14	33	51	47
12	Port Vale	46	12	4	7	41	23	5	7	11	24	35	45
13	Notts County	46	14	5	4	44	23	3	4	16	23	51	43
14	Coventry City	46	11	6	6	38	26	5	5	13	26	45	43
15	Crystal Palace	46	8	8	7	50	41	6	6	11	33	39	42
16	Southend United	46	10	7	6	31	26	3	9	11	26	43	42
17	Watford	46	10	4	9	37	26	4	4	15	26	48	41
18	Halifax Town	46	9	5	9	34	35	6	5	12	28	49	40
19	Shrewsbury Town	46	8	7	8	43	37	5	5	13	27	47	38
20	Barnsley	46	9	6	8	45	41	4	6	13	26	54	38
21	Torquay United	46	9	4	10	48	44	6	2	15	28	56	36
22	Lincoln City	46	4	10	9	31	43	5	7	11	26	44	35
23	Brentford	46	11	3	9	34	29	2	5	16	19	64	34
24	Newport County	46	6	5	12	29	38	1	3	19	17	64	22

1962/63   Champions of Division 3

#	Date	Opponent	Res	Scorers	Att	Ashworth A	Branston TG	Brodie CTG	Carr WG	Cockcroft VH	Everitt MD	Foley TC	Hails W	Holton CC	Kurila J	Large F	Leck DA	Llewellyn HA	Martin D	Mills RWG	Reid J	Sanders RJ	Smith HR	Robson TH	Etheridge BG	Woollard AJ	Lines B
1	Aug 21	Bristol Rovers	2-2	Holton, Lines	11649	9	5	1				2		8	6		4				10	7				3	11
2	25	Swindon Town	3-2	Ashworth, Holton, Sanders	13174	9	5	1				2		8	6		4				10	7				3	11
3	28	BRISTOL ROVERS	2-0	Ashworth 2	15661	8	5	1				2		9	6		4				10	7				3	11
4	Sep 1	PETERBOROUGH UTD.	2-3	Holton, Reid	16064	9	5	1			7	2		8	6		4				10					3	11
5	8	Barnsley	1-1	Ashworth	7674	9	5	1				2		8	6		4			7	10					3	11
6	11	WREXHAM	8-0	Ashworth 2, Holton 2, Reid, Lines 3	9555	9	5	1				2		8	6		4				10	7				3	11
7	15	Colchester United	2-2	Ashworth 2	5413	9	5	1				2		8	6		4			7	10					3	11
8	17	HALIFAX TOWN	7-1	Ashworth 2, Holton 3, Lines, Leck	13975	9	5	1				2		8	6		4			7	10					3	11
9	22	QUEEN'S PARK RANGERS	1-0	Ashworth	15469	9	5	1				2		8	6		4			7	10					3	11
10	24	Halifax Town	3-1	Holton 2, Lines	4202	9	5	1				2		8	6		4					7			10	3	11
11	29	Hull City	0-2		9536	9	5	1				2		8	6		4					7			10	3	11
12	Oct 2	CRYSTAL PALACE	3-1	Holton, Leck, Evans (og)	14204		5	1				2		8	6		4			9	10	7				3	11
13	6	BOURNEMOUTH	2-2	Holton, Lines	12199		5	1				2		8	6		4			9	10	7				3	11
14	10	Crystal Palace	2-1	Ashworth, Lines	13319	9	5	1				2		8			4			6	10	7				3	11
15	13	Coventry City	1-1	Ashworth	22163	9	5	1				2		8	6		4				10	7				3	11
16	20	BRADFORD PARK AVE.	3-1	Ashworth, Reid, Williamson (og)	12634	9	5	1		3		2		8	6		4				10	7					11
17	24	Wrexham	4-1	Ashworth 2, Holton 2	18841	9	5	1		3		2		8			4			6	10	7					11
18	27	Watford	2-4	Lines, Sanders	19015	9	5	1		3		2		8	6		4				10	7					11
19	Nov 10	Reading	1-2	Ashworth	7402	8	5	1		3	9	2					4			6		7	10				11
20	17	PORT VALE	0-0		8718	9	5	1		3		2		8			4			6	10	7					11
21	Dec 1	MILLWALL	1-1	Hails	10198	9	5	1			3	2	7	8			4			6			10				11
22	8	Southend United	1-5	Ashworth	8203	9	5	1			3	2	7	8	6		4						10				11
23	15	Carlisle United	2-1	Ashworth, Reid	3933	9	5	1			3	2	7		6		4		8		10						11
24	26	Notts County	1-2	Lines	6614	10	5	1			3	2	7		6		4		9		8						11
25	Feb 9	Queen's Park Rangers	3-1	Ashworth, Lines 2	14238	8	5	1			3	2	7		6		4	9			10						11
26	23	Bournemouth	0-3		10230	8		1	5	3		2	7		6		4			9							11
27	Mar 2	COVENTRY CITY	0-0		18717	8	5	1			3	2	7		6	9	4				10						11
28	9	Bradford Park Avenue	3-2	Large, Lines 2	6551		5	1			3	2	7		6	9	4				10		8				11
29	12	COLCHESTER UNITED	3-1	Large 3	9981		5	1			3	2	7		6	9	4				10		8				11
30	16	WATFORD	1-0	Everitt	12230		5	1			3	2	7		6	9	4				10		8				11
31	23	Bristol City	1-3	Reid	9642		5	1			3	2	7		6	9	4				10		8				11
32	26	SWINDON TOWN	1-1	Hails	16812		5	1			3	2	7		6	9	4				10		8				11
33	30	READING	5-0	Ashworth 3, Large 2	7845	8	5	1			3	2	7		6	9	4				10						11
34	Apr 2	NOTTS COUNTY	2-2	Ashworth, Lines	14606	8	5	1			3	2	7		6	9				4	10						11
35	6	Port Vale	1-3	Lines	8781		5	1			3	2	7		4	9	6				10			8			11
36	8	BRISTOL CITY	5-1	Large 2, Mills, Smith 2	12366		5	1			3	2	7		4	9				6	10		8				11
37	12	Brighton & Hove Albion	5-0	Hails, Large, Leck 2, Jennings (og)	16354		5	1			3	2	7		4	9	8			6	10						11
38	13	SHREWSBURY TOWN	1-0	Large	13350		5	1			3	2	7		4	9	8			6	10						11
39	16	BRIGHTON & HOVE ALB	3-0	Kurilla, Large, Jennings (og)	17520	8	5	1			3	2	7		4	9				6	10						11
40	20	Millwall	3-1	Hails, Reid 2	9992		5	1			3	2	7		4	9	6				10		8				11
41	23	BARNSLEY	4-2	Large 2, Reid 2	15939		5	1			3	2	7		4	9	6				10		8				11
42	27	SOUTHEND UNITED	5-3	Large 3, Reid, Smith	13498		5	1			3	2	7		4	9	6				10		8				11
43	May 1	Shrewsbury Town	0-1		6052		5	1		2	3		7		6	9	4				10		8				11
44	9	CARLISLE UNITED	2-0	Large 2	15094		5	1		2	3		7		6	9	4				10		8				11
45	11	Peterborough United	4-0	Hails, Leck, Smith, Rayner (og)	17518		5	1		2	3		7		6	9	4				10		8				11
46	24	HULL CITY	3-0	Ashworth, Foley, Reid	12110	8	5	1			3	2	7			9	4			6	10						11
		Apps				30	45	46	1	8	28	43	26	21	40	20	42	1	2	19	41	15	14	1	2	15	46
		Goals				25					1	1	5	14	1	18	5			1	11	2	4				16

Five own goals

F.A. Cup

R	Date	Opponent	Res	Scorers	Att	Ashworth A	Branston TG	Brodie CTG	Carr WG	Cockcroft VH	Everitt MD	Foley TC	Hails W	Holton CC	Kurila J	Large F	Leck DA	Llewellyn HA	Martin D	Mills RWG	Reid J	Sanders RJ	Smith HR	Robson TH	Etheridge BG	Woollard AJ	Lines B
R1	Nov 3	TORQUAY UNITED	1-2	Everitt	11844	9	5	1			2			8	6		4				10	7				3	11

F.L. Cup

R	Date	Opponent	Res	Scorers	Att	Ashworth A	Branston TG	Brodie CTG	Carr WG	Cockcroft VH	Everitt MD	Foley TC	Hails W	Holton CC	Kurila J	Large F	Leck DA	Llewellyn HA	Martin D	Mills RWG	Reid J	Sanders RJ	Smith HR	Robson TH	Etheridge BG	Woollard AJ	Lines B
R2	Sep 26	COLCHESTER UTD.	2-0	Ashworth, Holton	7771	9	5	1				2		8	6		4					7			10	3	11
R3	Oct 16	PRESTON NORTH END	1-1	Lines	12418	9	5	1				2		8	6		4				10	7				3	11
rep	29	Preston North End	1-2	Reid	7040	9	5	1			3	6	2	8			4				10	7					11

League Table

		P	W	D	L	F	A	W	D	L	F	A	Pts
1	NORTHAMPTON TOWN	46	16	6	1	64	19	10	4	9	45	41	62
2	Swindon Town	46	18	2	3	60	22	4	12	7	27	34	58
3	Port Vale	46	16	4	3	47	25	7	4	12	25	33	54
4	Coventry City	46	14	6	3	54	28	4	11	8	29	41	53
5	Bournemouth	46	11	12	0	39	16	7	4	12	24	30	52
6	Peterborough Utd.	46	11	5	7	48	33	9	6	8	45	42	51
7	Notts County	46	15	3	5	46	29	4	10	9	27	45	51
8	Southend United	46	11	7	5	38	24	8	5	10	37	53	50
9	Wrexham	46	14	6	3	54	27	6	3	14	30	56	49
10	Hull City	46	12	6	5	40	22	7	4	12	34	47	48
11	Crystal Palace	46	10	7	6	38	22	7	6	10	30	36	47
12	Colchester United	46	11	6	6	41	35	7	5	11	32	58	47
13	Queen's Park Rgs.	46	9	6	8	44	36	8	5	10	41	40	45
14	Bristol City	46	10	9	4	54	38	6	4	13	46	54	45
15	Shrewsbury Town	46	13	4	6	57	41	3	8	12	26	40	44
16	Millwall	46	11	6	6	50	32	4	7	12	32	55	43
17	Watford	46	12	8	3	55	40	5	5	13	27	46	42
18	Barnsley	46	12	6	5	39	28	3	5	15	24	46	41
19	Bristol Rovers	46	11	8	4	45	29	4	3	16	25	59	41
20	Reading	46	11	4	6	51	30	3	4	16	23	48	40
21	Bradford Park Ave.	46	10	9	4	43	36	4	3	16	36	61	40
22	Brighton & Hove A.	46	7	6	10	28	38	5	6	12	30	46	36
23	Carlisle United	46	12	4	7	41	37	1	5	17	20	52	35
24	Halifax Town	46	8	3	12	41	51	1	9	13	23	55	30

1963/64   11th in Division 2

#	Date	Opponent	Score	Scorers	Att	Best WJB	Branston TG	Brodie CTG	Brown RH	Carr WG	Cockcroft VH	Coe NC	Etheridge BG	Everitt MD	Hails W	Harvey BR	Hunt RR	Jones BR	Kane P	Kieran J	Kurila J	Large F	Leck DA	Lines B	Martin D	Mills RWG	Reid J	Robson TH	Smith HR	Foley TC	Hall JL
1	Aug 27	Scunthorpe United	2-1	Large, Lines	8738		5	1						3	7					4		9	6	11			10		8	2	
2	31	Sunderland	2-0	Hails, Smith	39201		5	1						3	7					6		9	4	11			10		8	2	
3	Sep 3	SCUNTHORPE UNITED	2-0	Hails, Large	16032		5	1			2			3	7					6		9	4	11			10		8		
4	7	DERBY COUNTY	0-1		14672		5	1			2			3	7					6		9	4	11			10		8		
5	11	Norwich City	3-3	Large, Leck, Smith	19669		5	1			2			3	7					6		9	4	11			10		8		
6	13	BURY	1-2	Smith	14886		5	1			2			3	7					6		9	4	11			10		8		
7	16	NORWICH CITY	3-2	Best, Large 2	14928	7	5	1			2			3								9	4	11	6		10		8		
8	21	Manchester City	0-3		21340	7	5	1			2			3								9	4	11	6		10		8		
9	28	SWINDON TOWN	4-0	Kane 2, Large 2	18177		5	1			2			3	7				8			9	4	11	6		10				
10	Oct 1	LEEDS UNITED	0-3		15079		5				2	1		3	7				8			9	4	11	6		10				
11	5	Cardiff City	0-1		10178		5				2			3	7	1			8			9	4	11	6		10				
12	8	HUDDERSFIELD T	1-0	Large	13257		5							3	7	1			8			9	4		6		10	11		2	
13	12	Plymouth Argyle	3-0	Hails 2, Kane	13224		5							2	7	1		3	9				4		6		10	11	8		
14	19	CHARLTON ATHLETIC	1-2	Large	15221		5							2	7	1		3	8			9	4	11	6		10				
15	26	Newcastle United	3-2	Hails, Kane, Martin	25743		5							2	7	1		3	9	6				8	4		10	11			
16	Nov 2	PRESTON NORTH END	0-3		13693		5							2	7	1		3	9	6				8	4		10	11			
17	9	Leyton Orient	0-0		11532		5							2	7	1		3	9		10		4		8	6		11			
18	16	SWANSEA TOWN	2-3	Kane, Lines	10985		5							2	7	1		3	8			9	4	11	6		10				
19	23	Southampton	1-3	Martin	18025		5							2	7	1		3		6		9	4	11	8		10				
20	30	MIDDLESBROUGH	3-2	Leck, Martin 2	10346				5				8	3	7	1				6	10		4		9			11		2	
21	Dec 7	Grimsby Town	1-4	Hails	6305		5						8	3	7	1				6	10		4		9			11		2	
22	14	Leeds United	0-0		21208		5							3	7	1				10	6	9	4	11	8				2	
23	21	SUNDERLAND	5-1	Everitt, Hails, Large, Martin 2	12130		5							3	7	1				10	6	9	4	11	8				2	
24	26	ROTHERHAM UNITED	1-3	Large	15089		5							3	7	1				10	6	9	4	11	8				2	
25	28	Rotherham United	0-1		10618		5		10					3	7	1					6	9	4	11	8				2	
26	Jan 11	Derby County	0-0		10195		5		10				8	3	7	1						9	4	11	6				2	
27	18	Bury	1-1	Foley	6077		5		9					3	7	1							8	4	11	10	6		2	
28	Feb 1	MANCHESTER CITY	2-1	Kane, Martin	12330	7	5		9					3		1			10	6			4	11	8				2	
29	8	Swindon Town	3-2	Kane, Large, Lines	17455		5							3	7	1			10	6		9	4	11	8				2	
30	15	CARDIFF CITY	2-1	Hails, Kane	11871		5							3	7	1			10	6		9	4	11	8				2	
31	18	PLYMOUTH ARGYLE	0-0		9261		5							3	7	1			10	6		9	4	11	8				2	
32	Mar 7	NEWCASTLE UNITED	2-2	Hunt, Leck	11440		5							3	7	1	10		9	6			4	11	8				2	
33	21	LEYTON ORIENT	1-2	Robson	9014		5			9				3	7	1	8			6			4		10			11		2	
34	28	Charlton Athletic	1-1	Everitt	15142	7	5						8	3		1	10			6			4					11		2	9
35	30	Portsmouth	0-3		13633	7	5						8	3		1	10			6			4					11		2	9
36	31	PORTSMOUTH	2-1	Mills, Foley	10245	7	5							3		1	8			6			4		9	10		11		2	
37	Apr 4	SOUTHAMPTON	2-0	Hunt, Kurila	8047	7	5							3		1	8				6		4		9	10		11		2	
38	7	Swansea Town	1-1	Hunt	11398		5							3	7	1	10				6		4		9	8		11		2	
39	10	Middlesbrough	0-1		9220		5							3	7	1	10				6		4		9	8		11		2	
40	13	Huddersfield Town	1-0	Best	6762	7	5							3		1	8				6		4		9			11		2	10
41	18	GRIMSBY TOWN	1-2	Robson	10092		5							3	7	1	8				6		4		9			11		2	10
42	25	Preston North End	1-2	Robson	12933	7	5		10					3		1	8				6		4		9			11		2	
		Apps				9	41	9	6	1	9	1	5	42	33	32	11	7	18	19	18	27	33	25	20	22	18	17	9	26	4
		Goals				2								2	8		3		8		1	12	3	3	7	1		3	3	2	

F.A. Cup

R	Date	Opponent	Score	Att	Branston	Brown	Etheridge	Everitt	Hails	Harvey	Kieran	Large	Leck	Lines	Foley
R3	Jan 4	Sunderland	0-2	40683	5	10	8	3	7	1	6	9	4	11	2

F.L. Cup

R	Date	Opponent	Score	Scorers	Att	Branston	Brodie	Cockcroft	Everitt	Hails	Etheridge	Kane	Kieran	Leck	Lines	Martin	Mills	Reid	Robson	Smith
R2	Sep 25	Brighton & Hove Albion	1-1	Mills	5496	5	1	2	3	7				4	11	6		10		
rep	Oct 14	BRIGHTON & HOVE ALB.	3-2	Leck, Reid, Smith	5569	5	1		2	7		9		4		6		10	11	8
R3	Nov 4	Colchester United	1-4	Robson	6237	5	1				10	9	6	4			8	2	11	

Played in R2: HA Llewellyn (at 8). Played in R2 replay and R3: Sharpe (at 3).

		P	W	D	L	F	A	W	D	L	F	A	Pts
1	Leeds United	42	12	9	0	35	16	12	6	3	36	18	63
2	Sunderland	42	16	3	2	47	13	9	8	4	34	24	61
3	Preston North End	42	13	7	1	37	14	10	3	8	42	40	56
4	Charlton Athletic	42	11	4	6	44	30	8	6	7	32	40	48
5	Southampton	42	13	3	5	69	32	6	6	9	31	41	47
6	Manchester City	42	12	4	5	50	27	6	6	9	34	39	46
7	Rotherham United	42	14	3	4	52	26	5	4	12	38	52	45
8	Newcastle United	42	14	2	5	49	26	6	3	12	25	43	45
9	Portsmouth	42	9	7	5	46	34	7	4	10	33	36	43
10	Middlesbrough	42	14	4	3	47	16	1	7	13	20	36	41
11	NORTHAMPTON TOWN	42	10	2	9	35	31	6	7	8	23	29	41
12	Huddersfield Town	42	11	4	6	31	25	4	6	11	26	39	40
13	Derby County	42	10	6	5	34	27	4	5	12	22	40	39
14	Swindon Town	42	11	5	5	39	24	3	5	13	18	45	38
15	Cardiff City	42	10	7	4	31	27	4	3	14	25	54	38
16	Leyton Orient	42	8	6	7	32	32	5	4	12	22	40	36
17	Norwich City	42	9	7	5	43	30	2	6	13	21	50	35
18	Bury	42	8	5	8	35	36	5	4	12	22	37	35
19	Swansea Town	42	11	4	6	44	26	1	5	15	19	48	33
20	Plymouth Argyle	42	6	8	7	26	32	2	8	11	19	35	32
21	Grimsby Town	42	6	7	8	28	34	3	7	11	19	41	32
22	Scunthorpe United	42	8	8	5	30	25	2	2	17	22	57	30

1964/65 2nd in Division 2: Promoted

						Best WJB	Branston TG	Brown RH	Carr WG	Cockcroft VH	Etheridge BG	Everitt MD	Foley TC	Hall JL	Harvey BR	Hunt RR	Kiernan J	Kurila J	Leck DA	Leek K	Lines B	Livesey CE	Martin D	Robson TH	Walden HB	Walton RP
1	Aug 24	Middlesbrough	0-1		27122		5					3	2		1	8	6		4		11	9	10		7	
2	29	Manchester City	2-0	Foley, Hunt	20935		5					3	2		1	8	6		4		11	9	10		7	
3	Sep 1	MIDDLESBROUGH	1-1	Martin	17028		5					3	2		1	8	6		4		11	9	10		7	
4	5	Southampton	0-2		13989		5					3	2		1	8	6		4		11	9	10		7	
5	8	NEWCASTLE UNITED	1-0	Etheridge	15977	8	5				10	3	2		1		6		4		11	9			7	
6	11	HUDDERSFIELD T	3-2	Livesey, Robson 2	12984	8	5				10	3	2		1		6		4			9		11	7	
7	15	Ipswich Town	0-0		13520	8	5				10	3	2		1		6		4			9		11	7	
8	19	Coventry City	1-0	Robson	30113		5				10	3	2		1	8	6		4			9		11	7	
9	26	CARDIFF CITY	1-0	Everitt	12328		5				10	3	2		1	8	6		4			9		11	7	
10	29	IPSWICH TOWN	3-2	Hunt 3	14886		5				10	3	2		1	8	6		4			9		11	7	
11	Oct 3	Preston North End	2-2	Robson, Walden	15953		5				10	3	2		1	8	6		4			9		11	7	
12	7	Portsmouth	3-3	Branston, Livesey, Robson	12262		5				10	3	2		1	8	6		4			9		11	7	
13	10	CHARLTON ATHLETIC	1-0	Robson	13552		5			3	10		2		1	8	6		4			9		11	7	
14	17	Leyton Orient	2-2	Hall, Martin	8390		5					3	2	10	1		6		4			9	8	11	7	
15	24	BURY	2-0	Foley, Martin	11324		5					3	2	10	1		6		4			9	8	11	7	
16	31	Crystal Palace	2-1	Livesey, Robson	21331		5					3	2		1	8	6		4			9	10	11	7	
17	Nov 7	NORWICH CITY	0-0		16774		5					3	2		1	8	6		4			9	10	11	7	
18	14	Rotherham United	1-1	Leck	11273	7	5					3	2		1		6		4		10	9	8	11		
19	21	SWANSEA TOWN	2-1	Martin, Robson	13427		5					3	2		1		6		4		10	9	8	11	7	
20	28	Derby County	2-2	Brown, Martin	17367		5	10		3			2		1		6		4			9	8	11	7	
21	Dec 5	SWINDON TOWN	2-1	Brown, Walden	9586		5	8		3			2		1		6		4			9	10	11	7	
22	12	Newcastle United	0-5		40376		5	8				3	2		1		6		4			9	10	11	7	
23	19	MANCHESTER CITY	2-0	Everitt, Leck	12665		5			3		8	2		1		6		4	10	11	9			7	
24	26	Bolton Wanderers	0-0		24487		5			3		8	2		1		6		4	10		9		11	7	
25	Jan 2	SOUTHAMPTON	2-2	Branston, Leek	15245		5			3		8	2		1		6		4	10		9		11	7	
26	16	Huddersfield Town	0-2		7359		5	9				3	2		1		6		4	10			8	11		7
27	23	COVENTRY CITY	1-1	Leek	18741		5	9				3	2		1		6		4	10	7		8	11		
28	Feb 6	Cardiff City	2-0	Brown 2	7427		5	9				3	2		1		6		4	10			8	11	7	
29	13	PRESTON NORTH END	2-1	Brown, Robson	14010		5	9				3	2		1			6	4	10			8	11	7	
30	20	Charlton Athletic	1-1	Robson	8958		5	9				3	2		1		6		4	10			8	11	7	
31	27	LEYTON ORIENT	2-0	Leek, Robson	13517		5	9				3	2		1		6		4	10			8	11	7	
32	Mar 2	BOLTON WANDERERS	4-0	Foley, Leck, Martin 2	15515		5	9				3	2		1		6		4	10			8	11	7	
33	13	CRYSTAL PALACE	1-1	Brown	17350		5	9				3	2		1		6		4	10			8	11	7	
34	20	Norwich City	1-1	Robson	25199		5	9				3	2		1		6		4	10			8	11	7	
35	23	Swindon Town	2-4	Brown 2	17886			9	5			3	2	10	1		6		4				8	11	7	
36	27	ROTHERHAM UNITED	1-0	Brown	19488			9	5			3	2	10	1		6		4				8	11	7	
37	Apr 3	Swansea Town	2-1	Brown, Martin	10516			9	5			3	2	10	1		6		4				8	11	7	
38	10	DERBY COUNTY	2-2	Brown, Martin	17917			9	5			3	2	10	1		6		4				8	11	7	
39	17	Bury	4-1	Brown, Kiernan, Martin 2	6800			9	5			3	2		1	10	6		4				8	11	7	
40	19	Plymouth Argyle	2-5	Kiernan, Martin	10547			9	5			3	2		1	10	6		4				8	11	7	
41	20	PLYMOUTH ARGYLE	3-1	Brown, Martin, one og	19718			9	5			3	2		1	10	6		4				8	11	7	
42	24	PORTSMOUTH	1-1	one og	20660			9	5			3	2		1	10	6		4				8	11	7	
					Apps	4	34	20	8	6	9	39	42	6	42	16	41	1	42	12	9	25	30	36	39	1
					Goals		2	13			1	2	3	1		4	2		3	3		3	13	13	1	

Two own goals

F.A. Cup

						Best WJB	Branston TG	Brown RH	Carr WG	Cockcroft VH	Etheridge BG	Everitt MD	Foley TC	Hall JL	Harvey BR	Hunt RR	Kiernan J	Kurila J	Leck DA	Leek K	Lines B	Livesey CE	Martin D	Robson TH	Walden HB	Walton RP
R3	Jan 9	Chelsea	1-4	Foley	44335		5			3		8	2		1		6		4	10		9		11	7	

F.L. Cup

						Best WJB	Branston TG	Brown RH	Carr WG	Cockcroft VH	Etheridge BG	Everitt MD	Foley TC	Hall JL	Harvey BR	Hunt RR	Kiernan J	Kurila J	Leck DA	Leek K	Lines B	Livesey CE	Martin D	Robson TH	Walden HB	Walton RP
R2	Sep 23	Bournemouth	2-0	Hunt. Livesey	8807		5				10	3	2		1	8	6		4			9		11	7	
R3	Oct 20	PORTSMOUTH	2-1	Livesey, Martin	7380		5					3	2	10	1		6		4			9	8	11	7	
R4	Nov 4	CHESTERFIELD	4-1	Foley, Hunt, Martin 2	6695		5					3	2		1	8	6		4			9	10	11	7	
R5	25	Plymouth Argyle	0-1		21698		5	8		3			2	10	1		6	4			11	9			7	

		P	W	D	L	F	A	W	D	L	F	A	Pts
1	Newcastle United	42	16	4	1	50	16	8	5	8	31	29	57
2	NORTHAMPTON TOWN	42	14	7	0	37	16	6	9	6	29	34	56
3	Bolton Wanderers	42	13	6	2	46	17	7	4	10	34	41	50
4	Southampton	42	12	6	3	49	25	5	8	8	34	38	48
5	Ipswich Town	42	11	7	3	48	30	4	10	7	26	37	47
6	Norwich City	42	15	4	2	47	21	5	3	13	14	36	47
7	Crystal Palace	42	11	6	4	37	24	5	7	9	18	27	45
8	Huddersfield Town	42	12	4	5	28	15	5	6	10	25	36	44
9	Derby County	42	11	5	5	48	35	5	6	10	36	44	43
10	Coventry City	42	10	5	6	41	29	7	4	10	31	41	43
11	Manchester City	42	12	3	6	40	24	4	6	11	23	38	41
12	Preston North End	42	11	8	2	46	29	3	5	13	30	52	41
13	Cardiff City	42	10	7	4	43	25	3	7	11	21	32	40
14	Rotherham United	42	10	7	4	39	25	4	5	12	31	44	40
15	Plymouth Argyle	42	10	7	4	36	28	6	1	14	27	51	40
16	Bury	42	9	4	8	36	30	5	6	10	24	36	38
17	Middlesbrough	42	8	5	8	40	31	5	4	12	30	45	35
18	Charlton Athletic	42	8	5	8	35	34	5	4	12	29	41	35
19	Leyton Orient	42	10	4	7	36	34	2	7	12	14	38	35
20	Portsmouth	42	11	4	6	36	22	1	6	14	20	55	34
21	Swindon Town	42	12	3	6	43	30	2	2	17	20	51	33
22	Swansea Town	42	9	7	5	40	29	2	3	16	22	55	32

1965/66 21st in Division 1: Relegated

#	Date	Opponent	Score	Scorers	Att	Best WJB	Branston TG	Broadfoot J	Brown RH	Carr WG	Cockcroft VH	Coe NC	Everitt MD	Foley TC	Hall JL	Harvey BR	Hudson GA	Hunt RR	Kiernan J	Kurila J	Leck DA	Leek K	Lines B	Livesey CE	Mackin J	Martin D	Moore G	Walden HB	Robson TH
1	Aug 21	Everton	2-5	Brown, Hunt	48489	5			9				3	2		1		8	6		4		10					7	11
2	25	ARSENAL	1-1	Brown	17352				9	5	12		3	2		1		8	6		4		10					7	11
3	28	MANCHESTER UNITED	1-1	Hunt	21245				9	5	3			2		1		8	6		4		10					7	11
4	Sep 4	Newcastle United	0-2		28051				9	5	3			2		1		8	6		4		10					7	11
5	7	Burnley	1-4	Livesey	14792				9	5	3		12	2		1		8	6		4		11	10				7	
6	10	WEST BROMWICH ALB.	3-4	Lines, Robson 2	18528	7	5		9				3	2		1			6		4		10	8					11
7	15	BURNLEY	1-2	Robson	19336	7			9	5			3	2		1			6		4		10	8					11
8	18	Nottingham Forest	1-1	Cockcroft	19669				9	5	3		7	2	8	1			6		4		10						11
9	25	SHEFFIELD WEDNESDAY	0-0		16299				9	5	3		7	2		1			6		4		10			8			11
10	28	Arsenal	1-1	Hall	33240					5			3	2	9	1			6		4		10			8		7	11
11	Oct 2	Leicester City	1-1	Foley	27484	12				5			3	2	9	1			6		4		10			8		7	11
12	9	SHEFFIELD UNITED	0-1		17300	5				4			3	2	9	1			6				10			8		7	11
13	16	Leeds United	1-6	Best	33748	7				5			3	2		1		9	6		4		10			8			11
14	23	WEST HAM UNITED	2-1	Foley, Leek	15367					5	3			2		1		9	6		4	8	10						11
15	30	Sunderland	0-3		32216					5	3			2		1		9	6		4	8	10					7	11
16	Nov 6	ASTON VILLA	2-1	Hall 2	18836					5	3	1		2	9			8	6		4		11			10		7	12
17	13	Liverpool	0-5		41904		4			5	3	1		2	9			8	6			10	11					7	
18	20	TOTTENHAM HOTSPUR	0-2		17611		4	7	9	5	3	1		2	10				6				11			8			
19	27	Fulham	4-1	Brown 3, Hunt	11389		5	7	9	4	3	1		2	10			8	6										11
20	Dec 4	BLACKPOOL	2-1	Broadfoot, Lines	14504		5	7	9	4	3	1		2	10			8	6				11						
21	11	Blackburn Rovers	1-6	Lines	10685		5	7	9	4	3	1		2	10			8	6				11						
22	27	CHELSEA	2-3	Brown, Moore	23325		5	7	9	4	3	1		2	10				6				11				8		
23	28	Chelsea	0-1		17635		5	7	9	4		1	3	2					6				11			10	8		
24	Jan 1	Sheffield United	2-2	Lines, Martin	16143		5	7	9	4	2	1	3						6				11			10	8		
25	8	BLACKBURN ROVERS	2-1	Brown, Kiernan	15820		5	7	9	4		1	3	2					6				11			10	8		
26	15	West Ham United	1-1	Brown	20745		5	7	9	4		1	3	2	10				6				11				8		
27	29	EVERTON	0-2		16309		5	7		4	2	1	3		10				6				11			9	8		
28	Feb 5	Manchester United	2-6	Martin, Moore	35273			7		5			3	2	9				6	4			11			10	8		
29	12	Stoke City	2-6	Brown, Moore	16522			7	9	5	3	1		2					6	4			11			10	8		
30	19	NEWCASTLE UNITED	3-1	Martin 2, Moore	14541		5	7	9				3	2		1			6	4			11			10	8		
31	26	West Bromwich Albion	1-1	Martin	18923		5	7	9				3	2		1			6	4			11			10	8		
32	Mar 5	LEEDS UNITED	2-1	Hudson, Lines	21548		5	7					3	2		1	9		6	4			11			10	8		
33	12	NOTTM. FOREST	3-3	Kurila, Martin, Moore	18670		5	7					3	2		1	9		6	4			11			10	8		
34	19	Sheffield Wednesday	1-3	Hudson	16283		5	7					3	2		1	9		6	4			11		12	10	8		
35	26	LEICESTER CITY	2-2	Hudson, Moore	21564		5						3	2		1	9		6	4			11		12	10	8	7	
36	Apr 2	Aston Villa	2-1	Mackin, Moore	10438		5						3			1	9		6	4			11		2	10	8	7	
37	9	LIVERPOOL	0-0		20029		5						3			1	9		6	4			11		2	10	8	7	
38	12	STOKE CITY	1-0	Martin	20680		5						3			1	9		6	4			11		2	10	8	7	
39	16	Tottenham Hotspur	1-1	Hudson	29749		5						3		12	1	9		6	4			11		2	8	10	7	
40	23	FULHAM	2-4	Hudson, Kiernan	24523		5					1	3				9		6	4			11		2	8	10	7	
41	25	SUNDERLAND	2-1	Everitt, Hudson	17921		5						3			1	9		6	4			11		2	8	10	7	
42	30	Blackpool	0-3		15295		5						3			1	9		6	4			11		2	8	10	7	
Apps						4	28	17	21	27	18	15	32	31	15	27	11	13	42	20	10	4	40	3	9	26	21	19	16
Goals						1		1	9		1		1	2	3		6	3	2	1			5	1	1	7	7		3

F.A. Cup

Round	Date	Opponent	Score	Scorers	Att	Best WJB	Branston TG	Broadfoot J	Brown RH	Carr WG	Cockcroft VH	Coe NC	Everitt MD	Foley TC	Hall JL	Harvey BR	Hudson GA	Hunt RR	Kiernan J	Kurila J	Leck DA	Leek K	Lines B	Livesey CE	Mackin J	Martin D	Moore G	Walden HB	Robson TH
R3	Jan 22	NOTTM. FOREST	1-2	Brown	17873		5	7	9	4		1	3	2	10				6				11			8			

F.L. Cup

Round	Date	Opponent	Score	Scorers	Att	Best WJB	Branston TG	Broadfoot J	Brown RH	Carr WG	Cockcroft VH	Coe NC	Everitt MD	Foley TC	Hall JL	Harvey BR	Hudson GA	Hunt RR	Kiernan J	Kurila J	Leck DA	Leek K	Lines B	Livesey CE	Mackin J	Martin D	Moore G	Walden HB	Robson TH
R2	Sep 21	Blackburn Rovers	1-0	Everitt	8814				9	5	3		7	2		1			6		4		10			8			11
R3	Oct 13	Fulham	0-5		7835		5		9	4			3	2		1			6						10			7	11

Played in R3: BG Etheridge (at 8).

		P	W	D	L	F	A	W	D	L	F	A	Pts
1	Liverpool	42	17	2	2	52	15	9	7	5	27	19	61
2	Leeds United	42	14	4	3	49	15	9	5	7	30	23	55
3	Burnley	42	15	3	3	45	20	9	4	8	34	27	55
4	Manchester United	42	12	8	1	50	20	6	7	8	34	39	51
5	Chelsea	42	11	4	6	30	21	11	3	7	35	32	51
6	West Bromwich Alb.	42	11	6	4	58	34	8	6	7	33	35	50
7	Leicester City	42	12	4	5	40	28	9	3	9	40	37	49
8	Tottenham Hotspur	42	11	6	4	55	37	5	6	10	20	29	44
9	Sheffield United	42	11	6	4	37	25	5	5	11	19	34	43
10	Stoke City	42	12	6	3	42	22	3	6	12	23	42	42
11	Everton	42	12	6	3	39	19	3	5	13	17	43	41
12	West Ham United	42	12	5	4	46	33	3	4	14	24	50	39
13	Blackpool	42	9	5	7	36	29	5	4	12	19	36	37
14	Arsenal	42	8	8	5	36	31	4	5	12	26	44	37
15	Newcastle United	42	10	5	6	26	20	4	4	13	24	43	37
16	Aston Villa	42	10	3	8	39	34	5	3	13	30	46	36
17	Sheffield Wed.	42	11	6	4	35	18	3	2	16	21	48	36
18	Nottingham Forest	42	11	3	7	31	26	3	5	13	25	46	36
19	Sunderland	42	13	2	6	36	28	1	6	14	15	44	36
20	Fulham	42	9	4	8	34	37	5	3	13	33	48	35
21	NORTHAMPTON TOWN	42	8	6	7	31	32	2	7	12	24	60	33
22	Blackburn Rovers	42	6	1	14	30	36	2	3	16	27	52	20

1966/67 21st in Division 2: Relegated

#		Date	Opponent	Score	Scorers	Att	Best WJB	Branston TG	Brown DJ	Brown RH	Brown WDF	Carr WG	Clarke JL	Cockcroft VH	Everitt MD	Foley TC	Felton GM	Hall JL	Harvey BR	Hudson GA	Jones RS	Jordon G	Kiernan J	Kurila J	Large F	Lines B	Mackin J	Martin D	Moore G	Perryman G	Price RJ	Walden HB	Walker DCA
1	Aug	20	Preston North End	1-2	Best	12192	7	5							3				1		9		6	4		11	2	8	10				
2		27	ROTHERHAM UNITED	3-1	Best 2, Martin	13954	7	5							3				1		9		6	4		11	2	8	10				
3		30	BURY	0-0		10025	7	5							3				1		9		6	4		11	2	8	10				
4	Sep	3	Millwall	0-1		11121	7	5				3						9	1				6	4		11	2	8	10				
5		6	NORWICH CITY	1-2	Martin	14767	7	5				3						9	1				6	4		11	2	8			7		
6		10	DERBY COUNTY	0-2		10975	7	5				3						8	1		9		6	4		11	2		10			7	
7		17	PLYMOUTH ARGYLE	2-1	Lines, Walden	9802	10	5		9		3			2				1				6			11		4	8			7	
8		20	Bury	2-1	Best, Mackin	8580	10	5		9		3							1							11	2	4	8			7	
9		23	Hull City	1-6	Lines	29122	10	5		9		3							1						12	11	2	4	8			7	
10	Oct	1	PORTSMOUTH	2-4	Kiernan, Martin	10364		5				3	4		2				1		10	7	6			11	12	8	9				
11		8	Crystal Palace	1-5	Martin	18507	10	5				4						9	1			7	6			11	2	8					3
12		15	HUDDERSFIELD T	0-1		13355		5			1				2			9		8		7	6	4		11	10						3
13		29	WOLVERHAMPTON W.	0-4		16761		5			1				2					8	9		6	5			4	10					3
14	Nov	5	Ipswich Town	1-6	Best	12820	10	5			1				2		7						6	4		11		8	9				3
15		12	BRISTOL CITY	2-1	Jones, Kurila	10004	10	5			1									7			6	4		11	2	8	9				3
16		19	Carlisle United	0-2		11946	10	5			1						7						6	4		11	2	8	9				3
17		26	BLACKBURN ROVERS	2-1	Martin, Moore	9470		5			1						10						6	4		11	2	8	9			7	3
18	Dec	3	Bolton Wanderers	2-1	Mackin, Martin	10352		5			1						10						7	6		11	2	8	9				3
19		14	Cardiff City	2-4	Mackin, Martin	7954		5			1						10						7	6		11	2	8	9				3
20		17	PRESTON NORTH END	1-5	Martin	10050		5			1						10						7	6		11	2	8	9				3
21		26	Birmingham City	0-3		24302		5			1					7	11						10	6	4	9		2	8				3
22		27	BIRMINGHAM CITY	2-1	Large, Martin	15433					1	5				7							10	6	4	9	11	2	8				
23		31	Rotherham United	2-1	Large, Martin	9497		12			1	5				7							10	6	4	9	11	2	8				
24	Jan	7	MILLWALL	1-2	Kiernan	11343					1	5				7							8	6	4	9	11	2	10				
25		14	Derby County	3-4	Kiernan, Large, Martin	14533					1	5				7							10	6	4	9	11	2	8				3
26		17	CHARLTON ATHLETIC	1-1	Martin	11578					1	5		3		2	7						10	6	4	9	11		8				
27		21	Plymouth Argyle	0-1		12830					1					2							6	4	9	11	3	8	10			7	
28	Feb	4	HULL CITY	2-2	Best, Moore	12396	8	5			1				4	2	7				10		6	9			3		11				
29		11	Portsmouth	2-3	D Brown, Moore	18979		5	10						4	2			1				6	9	11	3		8			7		
30		25	CRYSTAL PALACE	1-0	D Brown	13081		5	8						3	2	7		1				4	9		6			10		11		
31	Mar	4	Wolverhampton Wan.	0-1		25672		5	8						3	2			1				4	9	11	6			10		7		
32		11	COVENTRY CITY	0-0		20100		5	8						3	2			1				6	9	11	4			10		7		
33		18	CARDIFF CITY	2-0	D Brown, Large	11787	8	5	10							2			1				6	9	11	12		4			7		3
34		25	Huddersfield Town	2-0	Large 2	18214		5	8							2			1				6	9	11	4			10		7		3
35			Coventry City	0-2		38566		5	8							2			1				6	9	11	4			10		7		3
36	Apr	1	IPSWICH TOWN	1-1	Hall	13129		5	8							2	9	1					6		11	4			10		7		3
37		7	Bristol City	0-1		23750		5								2	7	10	1				6	9		4			8		11		3
38		15	CARLISLE UNITED	3-3	Large, Walden, Mackin	10752		5								2		1					6	9	11	4	10	8			7		3
39		22	Blackburn Rovers	0-3		9883		5								2		1					6	9	11	4	8	10			7		3
40		29	BOLTON WANDERERS	2-1	Large, Martin	9387		5						3		2	7	1					6	9	11	4	8	10					
41	May	6	Charlton Athletic	0-3		15098		5						3		2	7	1					6	9	11	4	8	10					
42		13	Norwich City	0-1		13544						4	5			7		1				3	6	9	11		8		2	10			
				Apps			15	36	8	3	17	11	2	6	13	16	13	13	25	7	17	1	26	37	21	38	36	31	32	1	1	18	22
				Goals			6		3								1	1					3	1	8	2	4	13	3			2	

F.A. Cup

		Date	Opponent	Score	Scorers	Att	Best WJB	Branston TG	Brown WDF	Everitt MD	Foley TC	Felton GM	Hall JL	Kiernan J	Kurila J	Mackin J	Martin D
R3	Jan	25	WEST BROMWICH ALB.	1-3	Foley	16899	9	5	1	10	2	7	11	6	4	3	8

F.L. Cup

		Date	Opponent	Score	Scorers	Att	Best WJB	Branston TG	Brown RH	Brown WDF	Carr WG	Clarke JL	Cockcroft VH	Everitt MD	Foley TC	Felton GM	Hall JL	Harvey BR	Hudson GA	Jones RS	Kiernan J	Kurila J	Large F	Lines B	Mackin J	Martin D	Moore G	Walden HB	Walker DCA
R2	Sep	14	PETERBOROUGH UTD.	2-2	Best, R Brown	5778	8	5	9		4		3					1			6		12	11	2		10	7	
rep		26	Peterborough Utd.	2-0	Best, Martin	9484	7	5			4	2	3					1		9	6			11		8	10		
R3	Oct	5	ROTHERHAM UNITED	2-1	Hall, Mackin	5631	8	5			4						9	1			6			11	3		10	7	
R4		26	Brighton & Hove Alb.	1-1	Best	17235	8			1				2			9				6	5		11	4		10	7	3
rep	Nov	1	BRIGHTON & HOVE ALB.	8-0	Best, Martin 4, Moore 2, 1 og	6889	7	5		1				2		7					6	4		11			10	9	3
R5	Dec	7	WEST BROMWICH ALB.	1-3	Hall	14706	7	5		1				2			10				6	4	9	11	2	8			3

Played in R3; Linnell (at 2).

		P	W	D	L	F	A	W	D	L	F	A	Pts
1	Coventry City	42	17	3	1	46	16	6	10	5	28	27	59
2	Wolverhampton Wan.	42	15	4	2	53	20	10	4	7	35	28	58
3	Carlisle United	42	15	3	3	42	16	8	3	10	29	38	52
4	Blackburn Rovers	42	13	6	2	33	11	6	7	8	23	35	51
5	Ipswich Town	42	11	8	2	45	25	6	8	7	25	29	50
6	Huddersfield Town	42	14	3	4	36	17	6	6	9	22	29	49
7	Crystal Palace	42	14	4	3	42	23	5	6	10	19	32	48
8	Millwall	42	14	5	2	33	17	4	4	13	16	41	45
9	Bolton Wanderers	42	10	7	4	36	19	4	7	10	28	39	42
10	Birmingham City	42	11	5	5	42	23	5	3	13	28	43	40
11	Norwich City	42	10	7	4	31	21	3	7	11	18	34	40
12	Hull City	42	11	5	5	46	25	5	2	14	31	47	39
13	Preston North End	42	14	3	4	44	23	2	4	15	21	44	39
14	Portsmouth	42	7	5	9	34	37	6	8	7	25	33	39
15	Bristol City	42	10	8	3	38	22	2	6	13	18	40	38
16	Plymouth Argyle	42	12	4	5	42	21	2	5	14	17	40	37
17	Derby County	42	8	6	7	40	32	4	6	11	28	40	36
18	Rotherham United	42	10	5	6	39	28	3	5	13	22	42	36
19	Charlton Athletic	42	11	4	6	34	16	2	5	14	15	37	35
20	Cardiff City	42	9	7	5	43	28	3	2	16	18	59	33
21	NORTHAMPTON TOWN	42	8	6	7	28	33	4	0	17	19	51	30
22	Bury	42	9	3	9	31	30	2	3	16	18	53	28

1967/68   18th in Division 3

#	Date	Opponent	Score	Scorers	Att	Harvey BR	Mackin J	Walker DCA	Kurila J	Flowers R	Kiernan J	Best WJB	Martin D	Large F	Carr WG	Hall JL	Faulkes BK	Felton GM	Lines B	Roberts JG	Barron RW	Weaver E	Byrne J	Fairbrother J	Brown DJ	Knox T	Price RJ	Johnson WJ	Clarke JL	Brookes JT
1	Aug 19	Gillingham	0-2		7890	1	2	3	4		6	8		9	5	10	7		11											
2	26	GRIMSBY TOWN	3-0	Martin 2, Large	10206	1	2		4		6		8	9	5	10	7	3	11											
3	Sep 2	Torquay United	0-0		9449	1	2		4	5	6		8	9	10		7	3	11											
4	5	MANSFIELD TOWN	1-1	Mackin	12205	1	2		6	5	10		8	9	4		7	3	11											
5	9	READING	1-2	Large	12625	1	2		6	5			8	9	4	10	7	3	11											
6	16	Swindon Town	0-4		13457	1	2		4	5	6		8	9	7	10	12	3	11											
7	23	SHREWSBURY TOWN	2-2	Martin 2	8922	1	2		6	5			8	9	4	10	7	3	11											
8	25	Mansfield Town	2-3	Large, Hall	5506	1	2		4	5	6		8	9	10	11	7	3												
9	30	Brighton & Hove Albion	2-0	Mackin, Martin	13546	1	2		4	5	6		8	9	10	11	7	3												
10	Oct 3	ORIENT	2-1	Faulkes 2	8079	1	2		4	5	6		8	9	10	11	7	3												
11	7	Southport	3-1	Martin 2, Hall	6052	1	2		4	5	6		8	9	10	11	7	3												
12	14	SCUNTHORPE UNITED	1-0	Flowers	10097	1	2		4	5	6		8	9	10	11	7	3										12		
13	21	Oldham Athletic	0-2		5019	1	2		4	5	6	7	8	9	10	11		3												
14	24	Orient	3-1	Best 2, Large	4708	1	2	3	4	5	6	7	8	9	10	11														
15	28	BRISTOL ROVERS	4-5	Mackin, Large 3	9126	1	2	3	4	5	6	7	8	9	10	11	12													
16	Nov 4	Barrow	0-4		5851	1	2	3	4	5	6	7	8	9	10	11														
17	11	OXFORD UNITED	1-1	Martin	11318	1	11	3	4	5	6		8		10		2	7									9			
18	14	TORQUAY UNITED	1-0	Martin	8475	1	11	3	4	5	6		8		10		2	7									9			
19	18	Bury	1-3	Kiernan	6642	1	11	3	4	5	6	9	8		10		2	7												
20	25	BOURNEMOUTH	1-0	Roberts	9042	1		3	4	5	6	11	8		10		2	7		9										
21	Dec 2	Colchester United	1-2	Martin	3505	1	11	3	4	5	6	8	7		10		2			9										
22	16	GILLINGHAM	1-1	Martin	7411	1	4	3			6		8		5	11	2	7		9						10				
23	23	Grimsby Town	0-0		3595	1		3			6		10		4	9	2	7		5						11	8			
24	26	TRANMERE ROVERS	0-1		12367	1	12	3					10		4	9	2			5		7				11	8			
25	30	Tranmere Rovers	2-2	Weaver, one og	7011	1	2	3			6	7	10		4					5		8	9			11				
26	Jan 20	SWINDON TOWN	2-0	Kiernan, Martin	10339	1		3			6	10	9		4		2			5		7	8			11				
27	Feb 3	Shrewsbury Town	0-2		5382	1		2			6	10			4	3	7			5		8	9			11				
28	10	BRIGHTON & HOVE ALB	2-2	Weaver, Byrne	7882	1		3			6	10	9		4		2			5		7	8			11				
29	14	Reading	0-0		8093	1		3			6	10	9		4		2			5		7	8			11				
30	17	Stockport County	0-4		7121	1	3				6	10			4		2			5		7	8	9		11				
31	24	SOUTHPORT	1-1	Byrne	6387	1		3			6	10			4		2			5		7	8	9		11				
32	Mar 2	Scunthorpe United	1-1	Brown	2745	1			4		6						2			5		7	8	9	10	11				
33	9	WALSALL	3-0	Roberts, Fairbrother, Brown	8536	1		3	12	4	6						2	11		5		7	8	9	10					
34	16	OLDHAM ATHLETIC	1-2	Weaver	7558	1		3		4	6						2	11		5		7	8	9	10					
35	19	STOCKPORT COUNTY	4-1	Felton, Roberts, Fairbrother, Brown	6536			3		4	6						2	11		5	1	7	8	9	10					
36	23	Bristol Rovers	0-2		5413			3	12		6						2	11		5	1	7	8		10		9		4	
37	30	BARROW	3-0	Mackin, Roberts, Fairbrother	8283			3	12	4	6						2			5	1	7	8	9	10	11				
38	Apr 2	Walsall	0-4		5552			3		4	6						2			5	1	7	8	9	10	11				
39	6	Oxford United	0-1		10150	1		3		4	6						2			5		7	8	9	10	11				
40	12	Watford	1-5	Mackin	7917			3		4	6				12		2			5	1	7	8	9	10	11				
41	13	BURY	0-1		7622		2	3		4	6									5	1	7	8	9	10	11				
42	16	WATFORD	1-1	Mackin	6732	1	11	3	6	4						5	2			10		7	8	9						1
43	20	Bournemouth	2-0	Fairbrother, Brown	6148	1	11	3	6	4						5	2			10		7	8	9	12					
44	23	PETERBOROUGH UTD.	3-1	Weaver 2, Fairbrother	8934	1		3	6	4						5	2					7	8	9	10					
45	27	COLCHESTER UNITED	2-2	Flowers, Byrne	6859	1	11	3	6	4	12					5	2					7	8	9	10					
46	May 4	Peterborough United	0-4		6658	1	2	3	6	4						5						7	8	9	10	11				
		Apps				39	39	24	32	40	37	8	27	16	37	17	40	18	12	24	6	23	22	16	14	16	6	1	1	1
		Goals					6			2	2	2	12	7		2	2	1		4		5	3	5	4					

One own goal

F.A. Cup

#	Date	Opponent	Score	Scorers	Att	Harvey BR	Mackin J	Walker DCA	Kurila J	Flowers R	Kiernan J	Best WJB	Martin D	Large F	Carr WG	Hall JL	Faulkes BK	Roberts JG
R1	Dec 9	Bournemouth	0-2		4998	1	11	3	4	5	12	8	7		10	6	2	9

F.L. Cup

#	Date	Opponent	Score	Scorers	Att	Harvey BR	Mackin J	Walker DCA	Kurila J	Flowers R	Kiernan J	Best WJB	Martin D	Large F	Carr WG	Hall JL	Faulkes BK	Felton GM	Lines B
R1	Aug 23	Peterborough Utd.	3-2	Kiernan, Martin, Large	8157	1	2		4		6		8	9	5	10	7	3	11
R2	Sep 13	ASTON VILLA	3-1	Mackin, Large, Hall	11832	1	2		4		6		8	9	5	10	7	3	11
R3	Oct 11	MILLWALL	0-0		12282	1	2		4	5	6		8	9	10	11	7	3	
rep	16	Millwall	1-5	Best	10167	1	11	3	4	5	6	7	8	9	10		2		

Division 3 Table

		P	W	D	L	F	A	W	D	L	F	A	Pts
1	Oxford United	46	18	3	2	49	20	4	10	9	20	27	57
2	Bury	46	19	3	1	64	24	5	5	13	27	42	56
3	Shrewsbury Town	46	14	6	3	42	17	6	9	8	19	32	55
4	Torquay United	46	15	6	2	40	17	6	5	12	20	39	53
5	Reading	46	15	5	3	43	17	6	4	13	27	43	51
6	Watford	46	15	3	5	59	20	6	5	12	15	30	50
7	Walsall	46	12	7	4	47	22	7	5	11	27	39	50
8	Barrow	46	14	6	3	43	13	7	2	14	22	41	50
9	Peterborough Utd.	46	14	4	5	46	23	6	6	11	33	44	50
10	Swindon Town	46	13	8	2	51	16	3	9	11	23	35	49
11	Brighton & Hove A.	46	11	8	4	31	14	5	8	10	26	41	48
12	Gillingham	46	13	6	4	35	19	5	6	12	24	44	48
13	Bournemouth	46	13	7	3	39	17	3	8	12	17	34	47
14	Stockport County	46	16	5	2	49	22	3	4	16	21	53	47
15	Southport	46	13	6	4	35	22	4	6	13	30	43	46
16	Bristol Rovers	46	14	3	6	42	25	3	6	14	30	53	43
17	Oldham Athletic	46	11	3	9	37	32	7	4	12	23	33	43
18	NORTHAMPTON TOWN	46	10	8	5	40	25	4	5	14	18	47	41
19	Orient	46	10	6	7	27	24	2	11	10	19	38	41
20	Tranmere Rovers	46	10	7	6	39	28	4	5	14	23	46	40
21	Mansfield Town	46	8	7	8	32	31	4	6	13	19	36	37
22	Grimsby Town	46	10	7	6	33	21	4	2	17	19	48	37
23	Colchester United	46	6	8	9	29	40	3	7	13	21	47	33
24	Scunthorpe United	46	8	9	6	36	34	2	3	18	20	53	32

1968/69 — 21st in Division 3: Relegated

#	Date	Opponent	Score	Scorers	Att	Morritt GR	Fairfax RJ	Walker DCA	Clarke JL	Rankmore FEJ	Flowers R	Weaver E	Byrne J	Fairbrother J	Brown DJ	Knox T	Felton GM	Roberts JG	Lines B	Neal PG	Mackin J	Kiernan J	Faulkes BK	Hatton RJ	Townsend NR	Hawkins PM	Barron RW	Skeet SC
1	Aug 16	Reading	0-1		7515	1	2	3	4	5	6	7	8	9	10	11												
2	27	STOCKPORT COUNTY	1-1	one og	9622	1	2				6		8		10	11	7	9										
3	31	Walsall	1-0	Lines	7768	1	2	3	4	5			8		10		7	9	11	6								
4	Sep 7	BOURNEMOUTH	1-3	Fairbrother	7812	1	2	3		5	6		8	9		11	7	4	10									
5	10	WATFORD	2-0	Roberts 2	6824	1	2	3		5	6	7	8	9			12	10	11	4								
6	14	Crewe Alexandra	2-2	Flowers, Fairbrother	5386	1	2	3		5	6	7	8	9				11	4	10								
7	17	BRISTOL ROVERS	2-2	Fairbrother, Lines	8002	1	2	3		5	6	7	8	9			12	11	4	10								
8	21	HARTLEPOOL	0-0		6749	1	2	3		5	6		8	9				10	11		7	4						
9	28	Plymouth Argyle	1-0	Lines	10505	1	2		4		6	7	8	9			5	11			10		3					
10	Oct 5	ROTHERHAM UNITED	1-0	Fairbrother	8602	1	2		4		6	7	8	9			5	11			10		3					
11	7	Stockport County	0-1		7979	1	2	3	4		6	7	8	9			5	11			10							
12	19	TRANMERE ROVERS	2-1	Hatton 2	7359	1		3		5	6	7	8	10				4	11					2	9			
13	26	Luton Town	1-2	Fairbrother	17818	1		3		5	6	7	8	10				4		11				2	9			
14	Nov 2	TORQUAY UNITED	1-1	Fairbrother	7279	1		3		5	6	7	8	10		11		4						2	9			
15	5	GILLINGHAM	0-1		5545	1		3		5	6	7		10		11		4	8					2	9			
16	9	Mansfield Town	2-0	Fairbrother, Byrne	4635	1				5		7	8	12				10	11		6			2	9	4		
17	23	Brighton & Hove Albion	1-1	Rankmore	6813	1	2			5		4	11	10	7		8						3	9	6			
18	26	SWINDON TOWN	2-6	Roberts, Hatton	6827	1		3		5	6	7			12			10	11				8	2	9	4		
19	30	BARNSLEY	3-1	Rankmore, Flowers, Fairbrother	6195	1		3		5	6	7		8			10		11		4			2	9			
20	Dec 9	Orient	0-0		3240	1		3		5			7	8	12			6	11		10			2	9	4		
21	14	ORIENT	4-1	Walker, Rankmore, Fairbrother, Felton	5405	1	2	3		5				8			7	10	11		6			9	4	12		
22	20	Tranmere Rovers	1-2	Rankmore	4502	1	2	3		5				8			7	10	11		6			9	4			
23	28	LUTON TOWN	0-2		15161	1	2	3		5				8			7	10			6			9	4	11		
24	Jan 11	Torquay United	0-2		7570	1	2	3	4	5				8			11				6	7	10	9				
25	18	MANSFIELD TOWN	0-0		5840	1	2	3	4	5		7		8	12		11	10			6			9				
26	21	Rotherham United	1-0	Weaver	8483	1	2	3	4	5		7		8			11	10			6			9				
27	25	Gillingham	0-2		4532	1	2	3	4	5		7		8			11	10			6			9				
28	28	BARROW	4-0	Weaver, Brown, Hatton, Hawkins	5375	1	2	3	4	5		7			10			11		6	12			9	8			
29	Feb 22	OLDHAM ATHLETIC	1-1	Hatton	5419	1		3	4	5		7		8			11	12			6	2		9	10			
30	25	BRIGHTON & HOVE ALB	1-1	Weaver	4554	1		3	4	5		7		8			10	11			6	2		9	12			
31	Mar 1	Swindon Town	0-1		17281	1		3	4	5		7	12	8			10	11			6	2		9				
32	3	Barrow	2-0	Brown, Hatton	2919	1	2	3	4						11		8	7	5		6		10	9	12			
33	8	READING	4-2	Fairbrother 3, Roberts	6072		2	3	4						11		8	7	5		6		10	9			1	
34	11	SOUTHPORT	1-0	Neal	5534		2	3	4						11		8	7	5		6		10	9			1	
35	14	Watford	0-3		16549		2	3	4						11		8	7	5		6	12	10	9			1	
36	22	WALSALL	3-1	Brown, Roberts, Neal	5763		2	3	4								8	7	9	6	11		10	12	5		1	
37	26	Southport	0-2		3248		2	3	4								8	7	9	6	11		10	12	5		1	
38	29	Bournemouth	2-3	Neal, Hatton	5089			3	4								8	7	10	6	2		11	9	5		1	
39	Apr 4	Bristol Rovers	1-2	Weaver	9424			3		2	5				11		8	7	10		6			9	4		1	
40	5	PLYMOUTH ARGYLE	1-1	Roberts	6306			3		2	5				12		8	7	9		6		10		4	11	1	
41	8	SHREWSBURY TOWN	3-4	Rankmore, Roberts, Neal	5521			3		2	5	6			12	11		10			8	7		9	4			1
42	11	Hartlepool	0-3		3729			3		2	5	6				11		7	10		8			9	4		1	
43	16	Shrewsbury Town	0-1		6770			3		2	5	6				11		7	10		8			4	9		1	
44	19	CREWE ALEXANDRA	0-1		4406			3		2							8	11	7	5	12			9	4	10	1	
45	25	Barnsley	1-2	Fairbrother	7640	1		3		2	6		8		10			9			7	5		11	12	4		
46	29	Oldham Athletic	1-1	one og	2073	1		3		2	6		8		11			9	7			5	10		12	4		
		Apps				34	43	26	29	33	22	24	18	32	24	14	24	38	22	21	17	21	12	33	20	7	11	1
		Goals					1			5	2	4	1	13	3		1	7	3	4				7		1		

Two own goals

F.A. Cup

#	Date	Opponent	Score	Scorers	Att	Morritt GR	Fairfax RJ	Walker DCA	Clarke JL	Rankmore FEJ	Flowers R	Weaver E	Byrne J	Fairbrother J	Brown DJ	Knox T	Felton GM	Roberts JG	Lines B	Neal PG	Mackin J	Kiernan J	Faulkes BK	Hatton RJ	Townsend NR	Hawkins PM	Barron RW	Skeet SC
R1	Nov 16	MARGATE	3-1	Fairbrother, Roberts 2	7672	1		3		5		7	6	8			11	10			4			2	9			
R2	Dec 7	Brighton & Hove Alb.	2-1	Hatton, Townsend	8839	1		3		5	4		7	12				10	11	8				2	9	6		
R3	Jan 4	Bolton Wanderers	1-2	Knox	12632	1	2	3	4	5				8			11				6	7	10	9				

F.L. Cup

#	Date	Opponent	Score	Scorers	Att	Morritt GR	Fairfax RJ	Walker DCA	Clarke JL	Rankmore FEJ	Flowers R	Weaver E	Byrne J	Fairbrother J	Brown DJ	Knox T	Felton GM	Roberts JG	Lines B	Neal PG	Mackin J	Kiernan J	Faulkes BK	Hatton RJ	Townsend NR	Hawkins PM	Barron RW	Skeet SC
R1	Aug 14	Crewe Alexandra	1-1	Brown	5105		2	3	4	5	6	7	8	9	10	11												1
rep	21	Crewe Alexandra	0-1		5502		2	3	4	5		7	8	9	10	11					6	12						1

Both games at Crewe.

		P	W	D	L	F	A	W	D	L	F	A	Pts
1	Watford	46	16	5	2	35	7	11	5	7	39	27	64
2	Swindon Town	46	18	4	1	38	7	9	6	8	33	28	64
3	Luton Town	46	20	3	0	57	14	5	8	10	17	24	61
4	Bournemouth	46	16	2	5	41	17	5	7	11	19	28	51
5	Plymouth Argyle	46	10	8	5	34	25	7	7	9	19	24	49
6	Torquay United	46	13	4	6	35	18	5	8	10	19	28	48
7	Tranmere Rovers	46	12	3	8	36	31	7	7	9	34	37	48
8	Southport	46	14	8	1	52	20	3	5	15	19	44	47
9	Stockport County	46	14	5	4	49	25	2	9	12	18	43	46
10	Barnsley	46	13	6	4	37	21	3	8	12	21	42	46
11	Rotherham United	46	12	6	5	40	21	4	7	12	16	29	45
12	Brighton & Hove A.	46	12	7	4	49	21	4	6	13	23	44	45
13	Walsall	46	10	9	4	34	18	4	7	12	16	31	44
14	Reading	46	13	3	7	41	25	2	10	11	26	41	43
15	Mansfield Town	46	14	5	4	37	18	2	6	15	21	44	43
16	Bristol Rovers	46	12	6	5	44	21	5	4	14	22	44	43
17	Shrewsbury Town	46	11	8	4	28	17	5	3	15	23	50	43
18	Orient	46	10	8	5	31	19	4	6	13	20	39	42
19	Barrow	46	11	6	6	30	23	6	2	15	26	52	42
20	Gillingham	46	10	10	3	35	20	3	5	15	19	43	41
21	NORTHAMPTON TOWN	46	9	8	6	37	30	5	4	14	17	31	40
22	Hartlepool	46	6	12	5	25	29	4	7	12	15	41	39
23	Crewe Alexandra	46	11	4	8	40	31	2	5	16	12	45	35
24	Oldham Athletic	46	9	6	8	33	27	4	3	16	17	56	35

1969/70   14th in Division 4

League (Division 4)

#	Date	Opponent	Score	Scorers	Att	Book K	Brookes E	Clarke JL	Fagan B	Fairbrother J	Fairfax RJ	Felton GM	Hawkins PM	Kiernan J	Knight BM	Large F	Lines B	Morritt GR	McNeil R	McPartland D	Neal PG	Rankmore FEJ	Ross WE	Townsend NR	Weaver E
1	Aug 9	Crewe Alexandra	0-2		3813		3	4		9	2	7	8	6			12	1	10			5			11
2	23	Port Vale	1-4	Felton	4809		3			10	2	7		6		9	11	1			12	5			8
3	26	OLDHAM ATHLETIC	0-0		6357		3			10	2	7		6		9	12			1	4	5	8		11
4	30	LINCOLN CITY	1-1	Neal	6026		3			10	2	7		6		9	12			1	4	5	8		11
5	Sep 6	Hartlepool	1-1	Fairbrother	3090		3		6	10	2		11			9				1	4	5	8		7
6	13	DARLINGTON	1-1	Hawkins	4922		3		6	10	2	12	11			9				1	4	5	8		7
7	17	Peterborough United	0-1		8557		3		6	9	2	10	11							1	4	5	8		7
8	20	Swansea Town	2-3	Hawkins, Townsend	6660		3		6	7		10	11			9				1	4	5	8	2	
9	27	NEWPORT COUNTY	4-1	Fairbrother, Felton, Large 2	4665		3	2		10		7	11	6		9		1			4	5	8		
10	30	NOTTS COUNTY	3-1	Kiernan, Large, Rankmore	6609		3	2		10		7		6		9		1			4	5	8		11
11	Oct 4	Bradford Park Avenue	2-1	Fairbrother, Large	2555		3		6	10	2	7			4	9		1				5	8		11
12	8	Workington	0-2		1738		3		6	10	2	7			4	9		1				5	8		11
13	11	WREXHAM	0-1		6994		3			10	2	7	12	6	4	9		1				5	8		11
14	16	Aldershot	2-5	Felton, Rankmore	5747		3			10	2	7		6	4	9		1			11	5	8		
15	25	SOUTHEND UNITED	2-0	Felton, Rankmore	5154	1	3	4		10	2	7	11	6		9						5	8		
16	28	WORKINGTON	3-0	Fairbrother, Large 2	6243	1	3	4		10	2	7	11	6		9						5	8		
17	Nov 1	York City	1-1	Fairbrother	4808	1	3	4		10	2	7	11	6		9						5	8		
18	6	CHESTER	0-1		5659	1	3	4		10	2	7	11	6		9						5	8		12
19	22	BRENTFORD	1-1	Fairbrother	5315	1		4		10	2	7	8	6		9						5	11		3
20	25	COLCHESTER UNITED	1-1	Kiernan	3256	1		4		10	2	7	8	6		9					12	5	11		3
21	Dec 13	Darlington	2-2	Fairbrother 2	2063	1	3	4		10	2	7	11	6		9						5	8		
22	20	HARTLEPOOL	0-1		2979	1	3	4		10	2	7		6		9			11			5	8		
23	26	PORT VALE	2-0	Rankmore 2	7522	1	3	4		10	2	7		6		9			11			5	8		
24	27	Lincoln City	0-0		7866	1	3	4		10	2	7		6		9			11			5	8		
25	Jan 17	Newport County	2-0	Fairbrother 2	2280	1	3	4		10	2	7		6		9			11			5	8		
26	31	BRADFORD PARK AVE.	3-0	Fairfax, McNeil, Rankmore	12972	1	3	4		10	2	7		6		9			11			5	8		
27	Feb 18	SCUNTHORPE UNITED	2-1	Fairbrother, Large	3635	1	3	4		10	2	7		6		9			11			5	8		
28	21	Chester	1-2	Ross	3782	1	3	4		10	2	7		6		9			11			5	8		
29	23	CREWE ALEXANDRA	1-2	Rankmore	5315	1	3	4		10	2	7		6		9			11			5	8		
30	28	ALDERSHOT	4-0	Fairbrother, Large, Ross 2	4833	1	3	4		10	2	7		6	12	9			11			5	8		
31	Mar 2	EXETER CITY	2-0	Felton, Large	4974	1	3	4		10	2	7		6		9			11			5	8		
32	7	Brentford	0-1		7292	1	3	4		10	2	7		6	12	9	11					5			
33	9	Chesterfield	1-2	McNeil	9624	1	3	4		10	2	7		6	8		11		9			5			
34	14	GRIMSBY TOWN	3-1	Fairbrother, Kiernan, McNeil	4537	1	3	4		10	2	7		6	8	9			11			5			
35	17	Scunthorpe United	0-1		3090	1	3	4		10	2	7		6	8	9			11			5	12		
36	21	Exeter City	0-1		4981	1	3	4		10	2	7		6		9			11			5	8		
37	27	Southend United	2-2	Fairbrother 2	6359	1	3	4		10	2	7		6	8	9			11			5	12		
38	28	CHESTERFIELD	0-1		5740	1	3	4		10	2		12	6	8	9			11			5	7		
39	31	YORK CITY	2-2	Brookes, Fairbrother	4128	1	3	4		10	2	7		6		9			11			5	8		
40	Apr 4	Oldham Athletic	2-0	Fairbrother 2	5774	1	3	4		10	2	7		6		9			11			5		8	
41	6	Colchester United	3-0	McNeil 3	3776	1	3	4		10	2	7		6	12	9			11			5		8	
42	10	SWANSEA TOWN	4-1	Fairbrother 2, Felton, Large	4104	1	3	4		10	2	7		6		9	12		11			5		8	
43	14	PETERBOROUGH UTD.	2-2	Fairbrother 2	6732	1	3	4		10	2	7		6		9	12				11	5		8	
44	18	Grimsby Town	1-0	Fairbrother	3445	1	3	4		10	2	7		6		9			11			5		8	12
45	24	Notts County	0-2		2456	1	3	4		10	2	7		6		9					12	5		8	11
46	27	Wrexham	0-3		9965	1	3	4		10	2	7		6		9					11	5		8	
		Apps				32	42	44	6	46	39	44	11	41	12	40	12	8	19	6	13	45	35	13	16
		Goals					1			23	1	6	2	3		10			6		1	7	3	1	

F.A. Cup

Rd	Date	Opponent	Score	Scorers	Att	Book K	Brookes E	Clarke JL	Fagan B	Fairbrother J	Fairfax RJ	Felton GM	Hawkins PM	Kiernan J	Knight BM	Large F	Lines B	Morritt GR	McNeil R	McPartland D	Neal PG	Rankmore FEJ	Ross WE	Townsend NR	Weaver E
R1	Nov 15	WEYMOUTH	0-0		5005	1	12	4	6	10	2	7				9	11					5	8		3
rep	19	Weymouth	3-1	Ramkmore 2, Fairbrother	4500	1	12	4	6	10	2	7	8			9						5	11		3
R2	Dec 6	EXETER CITY	1-1	Neal	5227	1	3	4		10	2	7		6	11	9					12	5	8		
rep	10	Exeter City	0-0		8930	1	3	4		10	2	7		6		9					12	5	8		11
rep2	15	Exeter City	2-1	Large, McNeil	2494	1	3	4		10	2	7		6		9			11		12	5	8		
R3	Jan 12	Brentwood	1-0	Fairbrother	5320	1	3	4		10	2	7		6		9			11			5	8		
R4	24	Tranmere Rovers	1-0		7590	1	3	4		10	2	7		6		9			11			5	8		
rep	27	TRANMERE ROVERS	2-1	Rankmore, Felton	16142	1	3	4		10	2	7		6		9			11			5	8		
R5	Feb 7	MANCHESTER UTD.	2-8	Large, McNeil	21771	1	3	4		10	2	7		6		9			11			5	8		

R2 replay a.e.t. R2 second replay at Swindon.

F.L. Cup

Rd	Date	Opponent	Score	Scorers	Att	Book K	Brookes E	Clarke JL	Fagan B	Fairbrother J	Fairfax RJ	Felton GM	Hawkins PM	Kiernan J	Knight BM	Large F	Lines B	Morritt GR	McNeil R	McPartland D	Neal PG	Rankmore FEJ	Ross WE	Townsend NR	Weaver E
R1	Aug 13	Oxford United	0-2		7158		3			9	2	7	12	6			11	1	10		4	5			8

Final Table

		P	W	D	L	F	A	W	D	L	F	A	Pts
1	Chesterfield	46	19	1	3	55	12	8	9	6	22	20	64
2	Wrexham	46	17	6	0	56	16	9	3	11	28	33	61
3	Swansea Town	46	14	8	1	43	14	7	10	6	23	31	60
4	Port Vale	46	13	9	1	39	10	7	10	6	22	23	59
5	Brentford	46	14	8	1	36	11	6	8	9	22	28	56
6	Aldershot	46	16	5	2	52	22	4	8	11	26	43	53
7	Notts County	46	14	4	5	44	21	8	4	11	29	41	52
8	Lincoln City	46	11	8	4	38	20	6	8	9	28	32	50
9	Peterborough Utd.	46	13	8	2	51	21	4	6	13	26	48	48
10	Colchester United	46	14	5	4	38	22	3	9	11	26	41	48
11	Chester	46	14	3	6	39	23	7	3	13	19	43	48
12	Scunthorpe United	46	11	6	6	34	23	7	4	12	33	42	46
13	York City	46	14	7	2	38	16	2	7	14	17	46	46
14	NORTHAMPTON TOWN	46	11	7	5	41	19	5	5	13	23	36	44
15	Crewe Alexandra	46	12	6	5	37	18	4	6	13	14	33	44
16	Grimsby Town	46	9	9	5	33	24	5	6	12	21	34	43
17	Southend United	46	12	8	3	40	28	3	2	18	19	57	40
18	Exeter City	46	13	5	5	48	20	1	6	16	9	39	39
19	Oldham Athletic	46	11	4	8	45	28	2	9	12	15	37	39
20	Workington	46	9	9	5	31	21	3	5	15	15	43	38
21	Newport County	46	12	3	8	39	24	1	8	14	14	50	37
22	Darlington	46	8	7	8	31	27	5	3	15	22	46	36
23	Hartlepool	46	7	7	9	31	30	3	3	17	11	52	30
24	Bradford Park Ave.	46	6	5	12	23	32	0	6	17	18	64	23

1970/71 — 7th in Division 4

#	Date	Opponent	Score	Scorers	Att	Book K	Fairfax RJ	Brookes E	Clarke JL	Rankmore FEJ	Kiernan J	McNeil R	East KMG	Large F	Gould TR	Fairbrother J	Felton GM	Neal PG	Ross WE	Hawkins PM	McGleish JJ	Townsend NR	Buchanan J	Heslop B	Oman AJ	Hill DR
1	Aug 15	Newport County	1-0	Rankmore	4518	1	2	3	4	5	6	11	8	9		10	7									
2	22	CAMBRIDGE UNITED	2-1	East, Neal	7901	1	2	3	4	5	6		8	9		10	7	11								
3	29	Colchester United	1-1	East	5220	1	2	3	4	5	6	11	8	9		10	7									
4	Sep 1	SOUTHPORT	2-1	Rankmore, East	6264	1	2	3	4	5	6	11	8	9		10	7									
5	5	YORK CITY	3-2	East, Large, Felton	7038	1	2	3	4	5	6	11	8	9		10	7		12							
6	12	Grimsby Town	2-0	Large, Fairbrother	4760	1	2	3	4	5	6	11	8	9		10	7									
7	19	BARROW	1-0	Felton	6509	1	2	3	4	5	6	11	8	9		10	7		12							
8	22	STOCKPORT COUNTY	1-1	Fairbrother	7873	1	2	3	4	5	6	11	8	9		10	7									
9	25	Southend United	0-1		9623	1	2	3	4	5	6	11	8			10			9	7	12					
10	Oct 3	BRENTFORD	1-0	Ross	6282	1	2	3	4	5	6	12	8	9		11	7		10							
11	10	Workington	0-2		2564	1	2	3	4	5	6	7	8	9		11			10	12						
12	17	NEWPORT COUNTY	1-0	McNeil	6171	1	2	3	4	5	6	7	8	9	10	11										
13	20	CHESTER	3-1	East, Large, Fairbrother	6152	1	2	3	4	5	6	7	8	9	10	11										
14	24	Darlington	0-0		2815	1	2	3	4	5	6	7	8	9	10	11										
15	31	HARTLEPOOL	2-0	McNeil, Neal	6049	1	2	3	4	5	6	7		9	10		8				11	12				
16	Nov 7	Notts County	0-1		21012	1	2	3	4	5	6	11	8	9	10		7									
17	10	PETERBOROUGH UTD.	2-0	McNeil 2	8190	1	2	3	4	5	6	11	8	9	10	12	7									
18	14	CREWE ALEXANDRA	1-1	Rankmore	5963	1	2	3	4	5	6	11	8	9	10	12	7									
19	18	Lincoln City	3-1	Kiernan, McNeil, Large	3689	1	2	3	4	5	6	11		9	10	8			7							
20	28	Scunthorpe United	2-2	Large 2	3463	1	2	3	4		6	11	8	9	10				7			5	12			
21	Dec 5	OLDHAM ATHLETIC	1-3	McNeil	6487	1	2	3	4	5	6	11	8	9	10				7							
22	12	Stockport County	1-1	Fairbrother	1846	1	2	3	4	5	6	11		9	10	8	7									
23	19	Cambridge United	2-0	Large, Felton	4814	1	2	3	4	5	6	10		9	11	7	8									
24	26	ALDERSHOT	2-0	East, Felton	6354	1	2	3	4	5	6	11	9		10	7	8									
25	Jan 9	LINCOLN CITY	2-1	Large, Fairbrother	5957	1	2	3	4	5	6	7		9	10	11										
26	16	Chester	2-2	McNeil, Fairbrother	4031	1	2	3	4	5	6	7		9	10	11										
27	23	Bournemouth	2-4	McNeil, Large	8763	1	2	3	4		6	7		9	10	11	8					5				
28	30	SCUNTHORPE UNITED	1-0	Large	4607	1	2	3	4		6	7		9	10	11	8					5				
29	Feb 6	Oldham Athletic	1-1	Large	12806	1		3	4		6	7		9	10	11	8		2			5				
30	9	Exeter City	1-1	Fairbrother	5016	1		3	4		6	7		9	10	11	8		2			5				
31	13	BOURNEMOUTH	2-3	Fairbrother 2	8854	1		3	4		6	7		9	10	11	8		2			5				
32	20	Peterborough United	0-1		8066	1	2	3	4		6	7		9	10	11	8					5				
33	27	Hartlepool	2-2	Fairbrother, Ross	1288	1	2		4		6		8	9	10	11			7			5			3	
34	Mar 5	DARLINGTON	2-0	East, Large	6040	1	2	3	4		6	7	5	9	10	11	8									
35	13	Crewe Alexandra	0-3		3242	1		3	4		6	7	5	9	10	11	8		2							
36	16	EXETER CITY	2-2	Fairbrother 2	5724	1		3	4		6	7	5	9	10	11	8		2							
37	20	NOTTS COUNTY	1-1	Large	11923	1			4		6	7	12	9	10	11	8		2			5		3		
38	27	York City	1-4	Fairbrother	7393	1			4		6	7	12	9	10	11	8		2			5		3		
39	Apr 3	COLCHESTER UNITED	2-1	McNeil 2	7909	1			4		6	7	5	9	10	11	8		2					3		
40	9	Brentford	0-3		10058	1			4		6	7	5	9	10	11	8		2					3		
41	10	Aldershot	1-1	Fairfax	4461	1	4				6	7	5		10	11	12		2	8			9	3		
42	13	GRIMSBY TOWN	0-4		6538	1	2		4		6	7		9	10	11	8					5		3		
43	17	WORKINGTON	5-0	McNeil, Large, Gould, Fairbrother 2	3337	1			4		6	7	12	9	10	11	8		2			5		3		
44	24	Barrow	1-2	McNeil	1466	1			4		6	8		9	10	11	7		2		12	5		3		
45	26	Southport	1-2	McNeil	1550	1			4			12		7	10	11		2	6	9	8	5	11	3		
46	May 1	SOUTHEND UNITED	0-2		3713				4				8		10				2	11	7	5	9	3	6	1
		Apps				45	34	38	42	25	43	44	29	41	35	42	27	18	18	6	3	15	3	10	2	1
		Goals					1			3	1	13	7	14	1	15	4	2	2							

F.A. Cup

Rnd	Date	Opponent	Score	Scorers	Att	Book K	Fairfax RJ	Brookes E	Clarke JL	Rankmore FEJ	Kiernan J	McNeil R	East KMG	Large F	Gould TR	Fairbrother J	Felton GM	Neal PG	Ross WE
R1	Nov 21	Hereford United	2-2	McNeil, Fairbrother	10401	1	2	3	4	5	6	11		9	10	7			8
rep	24	HEREFORD UNITED	1-2	Rankmore	10641	1	2	3	4	5	6	11		9	10	7	12		8

F.L. Cup

Rnd	Date	Opponent	Score	Scorers	Att	Book K	Fairfax RJ	Brookes E	Clarke JL	Rankmore FEJ	Kiernan J	McNeil R	East KMG	Large F	Gould TR	Fairbrother J	Felton GM	Neal PG	Ross WE
R1	Aug 19	Scunthorpe United	3-2	Brookes, East, Fairbrother	4470	1	2	3	4	5	6		8	9		10	7	11	
R2	Sep 9	York City	0-0		5265	1	2	3	4	5	6	11	8	9		10	7		
rep	15	YORK CITY	1-1	Brookes	7247	1	2	3	4	5	6	11	8	9		10	7		
rep2	28	York City	2-1	East, Fairbrother	2561	1	2	3	4	5	6	12	8	9		11	7		10
R3	Oct 7	ASTON VILLA	1-1	Large	15072	1	2	3	4	5	6	7	8	9		11			10
rep	13	Aston Villa	0-3		25822	1		3	4	5	6	7	8	9		11		2	10

R2 replay a.e.t. R2 replay 2 at Villa Park.

Division 4 Final Table

	Team	P	W	D	L	F	A	W	D	L	F	A	Pts
1	Notts County	46	19	4	0	59	12	11	5	7	30	24	69
2	Bournemouth	46	16	5	2	51	15	8	7	8	30	31	60
3	Oldham Athletic	46	14	6	3	57	29	10	5	8	31	34	59
4	York City	46	16	6	1	45	14	7	4	12	33	40	56
5	Chester	46	17	2	4	42	18	7	5	11	27	37	55
6	Colchester United	46	14	6	3	44	19	7	6	10	26	35	54
7	NORTHAMPTON TOWN	46	15	4	4	39	24	4	9	10	24	35	51
8	Southport	46	15	2	6	42	24	6	4	13	21	33	48
9	Exeter City	46	12	7	4	40	23	5	7	11	27	45	48
10	Workington	46	13	7	3	28	13	5	5	13	20	36	48
11	Stockport County	46	12	8	3	28	17	4	6	13	21	48	46
12	Darlington	46	15	3	5	42	22	2	8	13	16	35	45
13	Aldershot	46	8	10	5	32	23	6	7	10	34	48	45
14	Brentford	46	13	3	7	45	27	5	5	13	21	35	44
15	Crewe Alexandra	46	13	1	9	49	35	5	7	11	26	41	44
16	Peterborough Utd.	46	14	3	6	46	23	4	4	15	24	48	43
17	Scunthorpe United	46	9	7	7	36	23	6	6	11	20	38	43
18	Southend United	46	8	11	4	32	24	6	4	13	21	42	43
19	Grimsby Town	46	13	4	6	37	26	5	3	15	20	45	43
20	Cambridge United	46	9	9	5	31	27	6	4	13	20	39	43
21	Lincoln City	46	11	4	8	45	33	2	9	12	25	38	39
22	Newport County	46	8	3	12	32	36	2	5	16	23	49	28
23	Hartlepool	46	6	10	7	28	27	2	2	19	6	47	28
24	Barrow	46	5	5	13	25	38	2	3	18	26	52	22

1971/72   21st in Division 4

#	Date		Opponent	Score	Scorers	Att	AW	Neal	Folds	Clarke	Heslop	Gould	Kiernan	McNeil	Felton	Large	Fairb	Hold	Hawk	Buch	Ross	Chatt	Bailey	Bukow	Tucker	Oman	Town	Rioch	Book
1	Aug 14		Barrow	1-0	Hawkins	2690	1	2	3		4	10	6		7	5	9		11	8									
2		21	Cambridge United	1-1	Hold	5638	1	2	3		4	8	6	10	7	5	12	11		9									
3		28	EXETER CITY	1-1	McNeil	5926	1	2	3		4	9	6	8	7	5		10	11										
4		30	Southport	0-4		4370	1	2	3	9	4		6	8	7	5			11		10								
5	Sep 4		Newport County	1-1	McNeil	4146	1	2	3	6	4	12	11	8	7	9		10				5							
6		10	STOCKPORT COUNTY	2-0	McNeil 2	5851	1	2	3	6	4			11	7	9	10		8			5							
7		17	Scunthorpe United	0-0		5440	1	2	3	4	6			8	10	9			11		7	5							
8		25	COLCHESTER UNITED	1-1	Hawkins	5800	1	2	3	4	6			11	9	7		8	10		12	5							
9		29	Chester	2-3	Large, McNeil	3454	1	2	3	6	4			8		10		9	11	7		5							
10	Oct 2		Brentford	1-6	McNeil	11004	1	2	3	4	8			11		5		10	9			7							
11		9	READING	5-0	Hawkins, McNeil (p), Large, Buchanan 2	5255	1	2	3	4	6			8		10		9	11	7		5							
12		15	BARROW	2-0	Buchanan, McNeil	6182		2	3	4	7		6	10		9			11	8		5							1
13		19	ALDERSHOT	2-3	Large, Neal	5881	1	2	3	4	7		6	10		9			11	8		5							
14		22	Doncaster Rovers	1-1	Large	5988	1	6	3		5	2				10				8	11	7	4						
15		30	GRIMSBY TOWN	3-0	Large, Hold, Buchanan	6220	1	10	3	4	6	2				9		8	11	12	7	5							
16	Nov 6		Lincoln City	0-2		6529	1	8	3	5	6	2				10		9	11	12	7	4							
17		12	CREWE ALEXANDRA	4-1	McNeil, Large 2, Buchanan	5299	1	10	3	4		2	11	7		9				8		5		6					
18		27	Bury	2-4	McNeil, Large	2895	1	8	3	5	6	2	10	7		9				11		4			12				
19	Dec 4		HARTLEPOOL	2-1	McNeil 2	4507	1	8		4	6			10		9			12	11		5				3	2		
20		18	NEWPORT COUNTY	1-1	McNeil	4151	1	4			5			8	7	9			10	11		6				2	3		
21		27	Gillingham	1-4	Gould	11795	1	8			4	2	6			10				11		5					3		
22	Jan 1		SCUNTHORPE UNITED	0-2		3929	1	2		4	3	7	8	10	12			9	11			6					5		
23		8	Exeter City	3-1	Hold 2, McNeil	4485	1	2	3	4	7		8	11		9		10				6					5		
24		15	WORKINGTON	1-2	Gould	3389	1		3	4	7	2	8		12	10	9	11				6					5		
25		22	CHESTER	4-2	Chatterley, Large 3	3161	1			2	4	3	7	10	11	9	8					6		5					
26		29	Aldershot	2-0	Large, Felton	2471	1			3	4	7	2		11	9	8					6		5		10			
27	Feb 5		PETERBOROUGH UTD.	1-1	Large	5186	1	4	2	5	3	8	10		11	9	7	12				6							
28		12	DONCASTER ROVERS	1-1	Felton	3565	1	5	3		4	7	2	10		11	9	8	12					6					
29		19	Grimsby Town	2-4	Chatterley (p), Large	10035	1	4	12	10	5		2	6		11	9	7						3	8				
30		26	LINCOLN CITY	2-3	Large, Felton	4970	1	4		10	3	2	6		11	9	7		8					12			5		
31	Mar 4		Crewe Alexandra	1-0	Hold	1552	1	4	3	10		2	6		11	9	7		8								5		
32		11	Reading	1-2	Large	4078	1	4	3	10		2	6		11	9	7		8								5		
33		15	Workington	0-2		2130	1	4	3	10		2	6		11		7		8								5	9	
34		18	CAMBRIDGE UNITED	1-2	Large	3781	1	8	3	4	10	2			7	9	12		11								5	6	
35		20	Darlington	2-5	Hold, Rioch (p)	2055	1	4	3	10	6	2			11	8	7					5						9	
36		24	Stockport County	1-3	Rioch	2262	1	10		4	11	2			9			12	7							3	5	8	
37		31	Colchester United	0-2		5375	1	11			8	2	6		10		9		7							3	5	4	
38	Apr 1		GILLINGHAM	6-1	Hawkins 2, Large 2, Rioch 2 (1 p)	2625	1	7			4	6	2	10		9			11	12						3	5	8	
39		3	BRENTFORD	0-0		5314	1	7			4	6	2	10		9			11							3	5	8	
40		8	Peterborough United	0-1		5484	1	4			2	5	6		12	8			10							3	11	7	
41		11	SOUTHEND UNITED	1-1	Gould	3604	1				2	6	4	10	7	9		8	11							3		5	
42		15	BURY	2-2	Felton, Hold	3175	1				2	6	4	8	7	9		10	11							3		5	
43		17	Southend United	1-4	Felton	13642	1	11		4	12	2	6		7	9		10			6					3		5	
44		22	Hartlepool	0-2		6907	1	11			2		4	8	7	9		10			12					3	6	5	
45		25	SOUTHPORT	0-0		2747	1	11			2	3	4	8	7	9			10								6	5	
46		29	DARLINGTON	1-2	Hawkins	2658	1	11			2		4	8	7	9		12	10							3	6	5	
	Apps						45	41	30	40	40	35	38	22	27	44	4	24	25	28	4	23	1	7	1	13	19	14	1
	Goals							1				3		14	5	19		7	6	5		2						4	

F.A. Cup

R	Date		Opponent	Score	Scorers	Att	AW	Neal	Folds	Clarke	Heslop	Gould	Kiernan	McNeil	Felton	Large	Fairb	Hold	Hawk	Buch	Ross	Chatt	Bailey	Bukow	Tucker	Oman	Town	Rioch	Book
R1	Nov 20		BASINGSTOKE T	5-1	McNeil 2, Large, Buchanan 2	3400	1	8	3	4	6	2		10	7			9	12	11		5							
R2	Dec 11		Hereford United	0-0		9519	1	8		4	6	10			7			9		11		5					2	3	
rep		14	HEREFORD UNITED	2-2	Large, Hawkins	9099	1	2			6		8	7	12	9		10	11			5					4	3	
rep2		20	Hereford United	1-2	Large	8331	1	8		4	2		6	7	12	9		10	11			5						3	

Both R2 replays a.e.t. Second replay at West Bromwich.

F.L. Cup

R	Date		Opponent	Score	Scorers	Att	AW	Neal	Folds	Clarke	Heslop	Gould	Kiernan	McNeil	Felton	Large	Fairb	Hold	Hawk	Buch
R1	Aug 18		Watford	0-2		7663	1	2	3		4	10	6		7	5	9		11	8

		P	W	D	L	F	A	W	D	L	F	A	Pts
1	Grimsby Town	46	18	3	2	61	26	10	4	9	27	30	63
2	Southend United	46	18	2	3	56	26	6	10	7	25	29	60
3	Brentford	46	16	2	5	52	21	8	9	6	24	23	59
4	Scunthorpe United	46	13	8	2	34	15	9	5	9	22	22	57
5	Lincoln City	46	17	5	1	46	15	4	9	10	31	44	56
6	Workington	46	12	9	2	34	7	4	10	9	16	27	51
7	Southport	46	15	5	3	48	21	3	9	11	18	25	50
8	Peterborough Utd.	46	14	6	3	51	24	3	10	10	31	40	50
9	Bury	46	16	4	3	55	22	3	8	12	18	37	50
10	Cambridge United	46	11	8	4	38	22	6	6	11	24	38	48
11	Colchester United	46	13	6	4	38	23	6	4	13	32	46	48
12	Doncaster Rovers	46	11	8	4	35	24	5	6	12	21	39	46
13	Gillingham	46	11	5	7	33	24	5	8	10	28	43	45
14	Newport County	46	13	5	5	34	20	5	3	15	26	52	44
15	Exeter City	46	11	5	7	40	30	5	6	12	21	38	43
16	Reading	46	14	3	6	37	26	3	5	15	19	50	42
17	Aldershot	46	5	13	5	27	20	4	9	10	21	34	40
18	Hartlepool	46	14	2	7	39	25	3	4	16	19	44	40
19	Darlington	46	9	9	5	37	24	5	2	16	27	58	39
20	Chester	46	10	11	2	34	16	0	7	16	13	40	38
21	NORTHAMPTON TOWN	46	8	9	6	43	27	4	4	15	23	52	37
22	Barrow	46	8	8	7	23	26	5	3	15	17	45	37
23	Stockport County	46	7	10	6	33	32	2	4	17	22	55	32
24	Crewe Alexandra	46	9	4	10	27	25	1	5	17	16	44	29

1972/73   23rd in Division 4

#	Date	Opponent	Result	Scorers	Att	Starling AW	Clarke JL	Burt JHL	Baxter WA	Robertson SJ	Bruck DJ	Felton GM	Buchanan J	Large F	Neal PG	Hold JD	Tucker WB	Gould TR	Oman AJ	McGleish JJ	Stratford P	Roberts JT	Rogers E	Hunt RR	Hawkins PM	Riddick GG	Gregory JC	Bukowski DJ	Buck AR	Park RC	Hurrell WT
1	Aug 12	Mansfield Town	0-1		4303	1	2	3	4	5	6	7	8	9	10	11															
2	25	Gillingham	3-1	Neal 2, Buchanan	3544	1		3	5	6	4	7	11		8	10		2	9												
3	28	Peterborough United	2-1	Hold, Felton	3628	1		3	4	5	6	7	8		10	11		2	9												
4	Sep 1	CHESTER	1-0	Gould	5008	1		3	4	5	6	7	8	12	11	10		2	9												
5	9	Bradford City	1-2	Buchanan	2427	1		3	4	5	6		11	9	8	10		2	7												
6	16	READING	1-1	Neal	3752	1		2	4	5	6	7	8	12	10	11			9		3										
7	19	Bury	2-2	Buchanan, Neal	2272	1		3	4	5	6		11		8	10		2	9	7	12										
8	22	Colchester United	2-2	Neal, Robertson	3543	1		3	4	5	6	7	11		8	10		2	9												
9	26	NEWPORT COUNTY	0-1		4014	1		3	4	5	6	7	11		9	10		2	8												
10	30	CAMBRIDGE UNITED	2-2	Neal 2	3439	1		3	4	5	6		8	11	9	10		2			7										
11	Oct 6	Doncaster Rovers	0-3		2489	1		3	5	4	6		11	10	9	8		2	7												
12	11	Lincoln City	1-1	Neal	6198	1	6		5	4	2		8	11	10	9		7	3												
13	14	BARNSLEY	2-2	Baxter (p), Gould	3013	1	6	12	5			7	11	10		9		8	7		3										
14	21	Hereford United	0-2		7202	1		3	4	5	2	7		9	10		12	6	8		11										
15	24	WORKINGTON	1-0	Hold	2897	1	12		4	5		7	8	9		10		2	6	3	11										
16	28	CREWE ALEXANDRA	1-0	Stratford	3041	1	6	12	5			7	4	9	10			2	8	3	11										
17	Nov 4	Newport County	0-1		4829	1	4		5			9						6	7	10	2	8			3	11					
18	11	BURY	0-1		2654	1	4	12	5		10	11	6		8	9		2	7	3											
19	25	EXETER CITY	1-2	Oman	2263	1	6		5	4	2	9	7		8	10			3		11										
20	Dec 9	Cambridge United	1-3	Rogers	3539		6	3	5	4	2	7	12	10								1	8	9	11						
21	15	SOUTHPORT	0-1		2407		6	3	5	4	2		8									1	7		11	10					
22	23	Torquay United	1-2	Hunt	2788		6		4	5	2	10	8					12	3			1	7	11		9					
23	26	COLCHESTER UNITED	4-0	Baxter (p), Riddick, Hunt 2	3298		6		5	4	2	9	8					12	3			1	7	11		10					
24	29	Stockport County	0-0		3496		6		4	5		9	8					2	3			1			11		7	10			
25	Jan 6	GILLINGHAM	2-1	Felton, Neil	2452		6		4	5		10	9					2	3						11	7					
26	13	Workington	0-3		1444		6		4	5		8		10			12	2	3			1			11	9	7				
27	17	Aldershot	0-3		3080		6	2	4	5		10	9				11					8		1		7			3		
28	27	BRADFORD CITY	1-2	Baxter (p)	2468	1	6		4	5		10	7				9	2	3							8			11		
29	Feb 3	LINCOLN CITY	0-0		2381	1	6		4			7				10		2	3							9	5		11	8	
30	10	Reading	0-3		5443	1	6		4	5		7				10		2	3							8				9	11
31	13	STOCKPORT COUNTY	1-1	Buck	1180	1	6		4	5		7				10		2	3							9			11	8	
32	16	MANSFIELD TOWN	1-0	Buchanan	2288	1	6		4	5		7	12				11	2	3							9			10	8	
33	23	Southport	2-1	Buck, Robertson	3262	1	6		4	5		7					11	2	3							9			10	8	
34	Mar 2	DONCASTER ROVERS	0-2		4509	1	6		4	5		7	12				11	2	3							9			10	8	
35	5	Hartlepool	0-2		3822	1	6		4	5		9	12			8		2	3							10			11	7	
36	10	Barnsley	0-2		2244	1	6		5	4		7		10		8		2	3						11				9	6	
37	17	HEREFORD UNITED	0-4		4489	1	5		4			12	7	9				2	3						10	8	11			6	
38	20	DARLINGTON	2-2	Baxter, Buck	1867	1	6		4				12			8		2	3	11					9	5			10	7	
39	24	Crewe Alexandra	0-1		1577	1			4				6	12		8		2	3						9	5		11	10	7	
40	28	Chester	0-3		1469	1			4			7						2	3	9					11	10	5	8		6	
41	31	Exeter City	1-4	Riddick	3137				5		3			11			8	2		6		1			9	7	4	12		10	
42	Apr 7	ALDERSHOT	0-2		1877			3		2				10	12	6	4		8		1			11	9				7	5	
43	14	Darlington	0-0		1937			12		3	8			9		2	4				1			11	6			10	7	5	
44	21	HARTLEPOOL	3-1	Dawes (og), Hold, Hawkins	1478			3		2	8			9		6	4				1			11				10	7	5	
45	23	TORQUAY UNITED	0-2		1982					2	8	12		9		6	4	3			1			11				10	7	5	
46	28	PETERBOROUGH UTD.	1-3	Hold	2411	1				2	8			9		6	4	3						11				10	7	5	
		Apps				33	27	21	41	31	26	36	30	11	38	20	30	35	30	5	9	13	4	5	11	20	9	5	15	18	5
		Goals							4	2		2	4		9	4		2	1		1		1	3		1	2		3		

One own goal

F.A. Cup

	Date	Opponent	Result		Att	Starling			Baxter	Robertson	Bruck	Felton	Buchanan		Neal	Hold		Gould			Stratford		Rogers								
R1	Nov 16	Peterborough Utd.	0-1		7815	1			4	5	6	10	11		9	8		2			3		7								

F.L. Cup

	Date	Opponent	Result		Att	Starling	Clarke	Burt	Baxter	Robertson	Bruck	Felton		Large	Neal	Hold															
R1	Aug 16	CHARLTON ATHLETIC	0-3		4282	1	2	3	4	5	6	7		9	8	10															

Played at no. 11: Parker

		P	W	D	L	F	A	W	D	L	F	A	Pts
1	Southport	46	17	4	2	40	19	9	6	8	31	29	62
2	Hereford United	46	18	4	1	39	12	5	8	10	17	26	58
3	Cambridge United	46	15	6	2	40	23	5	11	7	27	34	57
4	Aldershot	46	14	6	3	33	14	8	6	9	27	24	56
5	Newport County	46	14	6	3	37	18	8	6	9	27	26	56
6	Mansfield Town	46	15	7	1	52	17	5	7	11	26	34	54
7	Reading	46	14	7	2	33	7	3	11	9	18	31	52
8	Exeter City	46	13	8	2	40	18	5	6	12	17	33	50
9	Gillingham	46	15	4	4	44	20	4	7	12	19	38	49
10	Lincoln City	46	12	7	4	38	27	4	9	10	26	30	48
11	Stockport County	46	14	7	2	38	18	4	5	14	15	35	48
12	Bury	46	11	7	5	37	19	3	11	9	21	32	46
13	Workington	46	15	7	1	44	20	2	5	16	15	41	46
14	Barnsley	46	9	8	6	32	24	5	8	10	26	36	44
15	Chester	46	11	6	6	40	19	3	9	11	21	33	43
16	Bradford City	46	12	6	5	42	25	4	5	14	19	40	43
17	Doncaster Rovers	46	10	8	5	28	19	5	4	14	21	39	42
18	Torquay United	46	8	10	5	23	17	4	7	12	21	30	41
19	Peterborough Utd.	46	10	8	5	42	29	4	5	14	29	47	41
20	Hartlepool	46	8	10	5	17	19	4	7	12	17	34	41
21	Crewe Alexandra	46	7	8	8	18	23	2	10	11	20	38	36
22	Colchester United	46	8	8	7	36	28	2	3	18	12	48	31
23	NORTHAMPTON TOWN	46	7	6	10	24	30	3	5	15	16	43	31
24	Darlington	46	5	9	9	28	41	2	6	15	14	44	29

1973/74   5th in Division 4

#	Date		Opponent	Score	Scorers	Att	Starling AW	Bruck DJ	Oman AJ	Gregory JC	Riddick GG	Robertson SJ	Felton GM	Neal PG	Buchanan J	Park RC	Stratford P	Clarke JL	Hawkins PM	Buck AR	Best WJB	Carlton DG	Tucker WB	Watts D	Krzywicki RL	Christie DHM	Wainwright RK	John M
1	Aug	25	ROTHERHAM UNITED	3-1	Robertson, Felton, Neal	4098	1	2	3	4	5	6	7	8	9	10	11	12										
2	Sep	1	Mansfield Town	0-2		3109	1	2	3	6	4	5		8	9	10	7	12	11									
3		7	COLCHESTER UNITED	0-0		4916	1	2	3	6	4	5	7	8	9		11			12								
4		11	NEWPORT COUNTY	1-0	Buchanan	4061	1	2	3	6	4	5	7	8	9	12	11	10										
5		14	Stockport County	2-2	Stratford, Riddick	3552	1	2	3	6	4	5	7	8	9		11	10										
6		18	Swansea City	1-1	Robertson	1301	1	2	3	6	4	5	7	8	9		11	10										
7		21	SCUNTHORPE UNITED	2-0	Stratford 2	5049	1	2	3	6	4	5	7	8	9		11	10										
8		29	Workington	0-1		970	1	2	3	6	4	5	7	8	9		11	10					12					
9	Oct	2	SWANSEA CITY	2-0	Buchanan, Robertson	5287	1	2	3	6		5	7	8	9	12	11	10			4							
10		5	TORQUAY UNITED	0-0		6640	1	2	3	6		5	7	8	9		11	4			10							
11		13	Bradford City	1-1	Stratford	3343	1	2	3	6		5	12	8	9		11	4			10	7						
12		20	EXETER CITY	1-2	Stratford	4923	1	2	3	6		5	7	8	9		11				10	4						
13		23	Newport County	1-3	Neal (p)	3592	1	2	3	6		5	9	8			11				10	7	12					
14		27	Bury	1-3	Stratford	4360	1		3	6			9	8	7		11	5			10	4	2	12				
15	Nov	3	HARTLEPOOL	1-0	Stratford	3715	1		3			5	7	4	9		11	6			10	8	2					
16		10	Darlington	3-2	Neal, Buchanan, Best	2063	1			6		5	7	8	9		11	3			10	4	2					
17		13	BARNSLEY	2-1	Oman, Clarke	4299	1		3	6		5	7		9		11	4			8	10	2					
18		17	Peterborough United	0-3		10351	1		3	6		5	7	8	12		11	9			10	4	2					
19	Dec	8	LINCOLN CITY	1-0	Best	3464	1			3		5	7	4	6		11	12			8	10	2		9			
20		22	WORKINGTON	1-0	Krzywicki	4038	1			6		5	7	3	4		11	10			8		2		9			
21		26	Gillingham	1-3	Felton	11313	1			6		5	7	3	4		11	10			8		2		9			
22		29	Colchester United	0-1		5042	1			6		5	7	3	4			11			8	10	2		9			
23	Jan	1	MANSFIELD TOWN	2-0	Neal (p), Krzywicki	6231	1			6		5	7	3	4		11	10			8		2		9			
24		5	Hartlepool	0-1		2078	1	4		6		5		3		12	11	10		9	8		2	7				
25		12	STOCKPORT COUNTY	2-0	Krzywicki, Stratford	3396	1			6		5	7	4			11	3			8	10	2		9			
26		20	Rotherham United	2-1	Buchanan 2	4609	1			6		5	7	3	12		11	4			8	10	2		9			
27		27	READING	3-3	Best 2, Stratford	7599	1			6			7	3	4		9	5			8	10	2			11		
28	Feb	2	BRENTFORD	0-0		4130	1			6		5	7	3	9		11	4			8	10	2			12		
29		10	Scunthorpe United	2-1	Buchanan, Stratford	3603	1			6		5	7	3	9		11	4			8	10	2					
30		17	BRADFORD CITY	3-0	Buchanan, Neal, Robertson	8146	1		12	6		5	7	3	9		11	4			8	10	2					
31		24	Torquay United	0-1		4186	1			6		5	7	3	9		11	4			8	10	2				12	
32	Mar	3	GILLINGHAM	0-0		8583	1			6		5	7	3	9		11	4			8	10	2					
33		9	BURY	3-1	Best, Buchanan 2	4884	1			6		5	7	3	9		11	4			8	10	2					
34		16	Exeter City	1-1	Felton	4052	1		12	5			7	3	6		11	4			8	10	2					9
35		18	Brentford	1-3	John	3686	1		3	5			7	4	6		11				8	10	2					9
36		24	DARLINGTON	5-0	John, Best, Neal (p), Stratford 2	5416	1		12	5			7	6	4		11	3			8	10	2					9
37		26	CHESTER	3-3	Neal (p), Buchanan, John	5969	1			5			7	6	4		11	3			8	10	2					9
38	Apr	3	Reading	2-1	Buchanan 2	7055	1		12	5			7	6	4		11	3			8	10	2					9
39		6	Barnsley	2-0	Neal, John	3646	1			5			7	6	4		11	3			8	10	2					9
40		13	PETERBOROUGH UTD.	0-1		11378	1			3			7	5	4		11	6			8	10	2					9
41		15	CREWE ALEXANDRA	1-1	Neal	5389	1			6			7	5	4		9	3			8	10	2					11
42		16	Crewe Alexandra	2-0	Stratford 2	1498	1			5			7	6	4		9	3			8	10	2					11
43		20	Lincoln City	1-1	Felton	2530	1		12	5			7	6	4		9	3			8	10	2					11
44		23	Doncaster Rovers	1-2	Stratford	1561	1		3	5			7	6	4		9				8	10	2				12	11
45		27	DONCASTER ROVERS	3-1	Buchanan, Best, Felton	3137	1			5			7	6	4		9	3			8	10	2					11
46	May	1	Chester	0-0		1928	1			5			7	6	4		9	3			8	10	2					11
			Apps				46	15	22	46	8	31	44	46	42	6	45	42	1	2	39	32	34	1	8	3	1	13
			Goals						1		1	4	5	9	13		15	1			7				3			4

F.A. Cup

	Date		Opponent	Score	Scorers	Att	Sta		Oma	Gre		Rob	Fel	Nea	Buc	Par	Str	Cla		Buk	Bes	Car	Tuc					
R1	Nov	24	Banbury United	0-0		4800	1		3	6		5	7		9	4	11				8	10	2					
rep		29	BANBURY UNITED	3-2	Felton, Robertson, Best	2995	1		3	6		5	7		9	4	11				8	10	2					
R2	Dec	15	BRISTOL ROVERS	1-2	Buchanan	6181	1			6		5	7	3	4		11	10		8	9		2					

F.L. Cup

	Date		Opponent	Score	Scorers	Att	Sta	Bru	Oma	Gre	Rid	Rob	Fel	Nea	Buc	Par	Str	Cla										
R1	Aug	28	Grimsby Town	1-2	Buchanan	7829	1	2	3	6	4	5	7	8	9	10	11	12										

		P	W	D	L	F	A	W	D	L	F	A	Pts
1	Peterborough Utd.	46	19	4	0	49	10	8	7	8	26	28	65
2	Gillingham	46	16	5	2	51	16	9	7	7	39	33	62
3	Colchester United	46	16	5	2	46	14	8	7	8	27	22	60
4	Bury	46	18	3	2	51	14	6	8	9	30	35	59
5	NORTHAMPTON TOWN	46	14	7	2	39	14	6	6	11	24	34	53
6	Reading	46	11	9	3	37	13	5	10	8	21	24	51
7	Chester	46	13	6	4	31	19	4	9	10	23	36	49
8	Bradford City	46	14	7	2	45	20	3	7	13	13	32	48
9	Newport County	46	13	6	4	39	23	3	8	12	17	42	45
10	Exeter City	45	12	5	6	37	20	6	3	13	21	35	44
11	Hartlepool	46	11	4	8	29	16	5	8	10	19	31	44
12	Lincoln City	46	10	8	5	40	30	6	4	13	23	37	44
13	Barnsley	46	15	5	3	42	16	2	5	16	16	48	44
14	Swansea City	46	11	6	6	28	15	5	5	13	17	31	43
15	Rotherham United	46	10	9	4	33	22	5	4	14	23	36	43
16	Torquay United	46	11	7	5	37	23	2	10	11	15	34	43
17	Mansfield Town	46	13	8	2	47	24	0	9	14	15	45	43
18	Scunthorpe United	45	12	7	3	33	17	2	5	16	14	47	42
19	Brentford	46	9	7	7	31	20	3	9	11	17	30	40
20	Darlington	46	9	8	6	29	24	4	5	14	11	38	39
21	Crewe Alexandra	46	11	7	5	28	30	3	5	15	15	41	38
22	Doncaster Rovers	46	10	7	6	32	22	2	4	17	15	58	35
23	Workington	46	10	8	5	33	26	1	5	17	10	48	35
24	Stockport County	46	4	12	7	22	25	3	8	12	22	44	34

1974/75   16th in Division 4

#	Date		Opponent	Score	Scorers	Att	Anderson GL	Best WJB	Buchanan J	Carlton DG	Cegielski W	Christie DHM	Clarke JL	Farrington JR	Felton GM	Garnham SE	Gregory JC	Hall JL	John M	Kilkelly TF	Mabee GL	Moore J	Neal PG	Oman AJ	Robertson SJ	Starling AW	Stratford P	Tucker WB	Tumbridge RA	Wainwright RK
1	Aug	17	Brentford	0-1		5147	8	11					3	7			6				12		4		5	1	9	2		10
2		24	BRADFORD CITY	1-2	Best	4408	8	11					3	7			6				12		4		5	1	9	2		10
3		31	Reading	2-3	Wagstaff (og), Stratford	5464	8	4	10				3	7							12				5	1	9	2		12
4	Sep	6	DARLINGTON	3-0	Mabee, Stratford, Carlton	4003	8	4	10					7								6	9				11	2		12
5		14	Lincoln City	2-2	Neal 2 (1p)	3113	8	4	10					7			5				9	6	3			1	11	2		
6		21	SHREWSBURY TOWN	3-3	Stratford, Best, Carlton	4001	8	4	10					7			5				9	6	3			1	11	2		12
7		24	DONCASTER ROVERS	2-0	Mabee, Buchanan	4269	8	4	10					7			5				9	6	3			1	11	2		12
8		28	Torquay United	1-0	Wainwright	3004	8	4	10								5				9	6	3			1	11	2		7
9	Oct	1	WORKINGTON	3-0	Stratford 3	4783	8	4	10		12	3									9	6	5			1	11	2		7
10		5	Rotherham United	3-1	Mabee 2, Carlton	4934	3	4	10		12										9	6	5			1	11	2		7
11		11	STOCKPORT COUNTY	4-1	Stratford, Buchanan, John, Mabee	5846	3	4	10							1		8	6		9	5					11	2		7
12		18	Newport County	1-2		2149	3		10					7				4	8		12	9	5				11	2		6
13		21	Rochdale	2-2	Wainwright, Mabee	1379	8		4					7				5			3	9	6				10	2		11
14		26	SWANSEA CITY	5-1	Stratford, Mabee 2, Farrington, Wainwright	5096	6		4					7	12			3	8		9	5					11	2		10
15		28	Mansfield Town	0-3		5310	3		6					7				4	8		9	5					10	2		11
16	Nov	1	Cambridge United	4-3	Mabee 2, Carlton, Stratford	3589	8		6					7				5		12	9	4		3			10	2		11
17		5	ROCHDALE	0-1		5695	8		6					7				4		12	9			3			10	2		11
18		9	CHESTER	2-0	Tucker (p), Wainwright	5240	8							7				4		6	9			3	5	1	11	2		10
19		15	Southport	0-0		1851	8		6					7				4		10	9			3	5	1	11	2		12
20		29	CREWE ALEXANDRA	3-0	Mabee 2, Stratford	5037	8		12					7				4		6	9			3	5	1	11	2		10
21	Dec	7	Exeter City	2-2	Wainwright, Best	3497	8		6					7				4			9			3	5	1	11	2		10
22		21	Barnsley	1-5	Stratford	2666	8		6					7	11			4		10				3	5	1	9	2		12
23		26	LINCOLN CITY	1-0	Stratford	7275	8		6					7				4			9			3	5	1	11	2		10
24	Jan	1	Hartlepool	0-2		5178	8		6					7				4		12	9			3	5	1	11	2		10
25		4	BRENTFORD	0-0		4735	8		6					7				4			9			3	5	1	11	2		10
26		11	EXETER CITY	1-1	Best	4104	8		6					7				4		12	9			3	5	1		2		10
27		18	Crewe Alexandra	1-3	Mabee	1859	8		6					7	11			4			9			3	5	1		2		10
28	Feb	1	Chester	1-4	Hall	5209	8							7	11			4			9			3	5	1		2		10
29		8	CAMBRIDGE UNITED	1-2	Farrington	4126	8							7				4	10	12	9			3	5	1	11	2		6
30		11	SCUNTHORPE UNITED	3-0	Robertson, Hall 2	3079	8		10					7				4	9	12		10		3	5	1	11	2		6
31		15	Scunthorpe United	1-2	Best	1975	8		6				12	7				4	9	10				3	5	1	11	2		12
32		22	SOUTHPORT	1-1	Hall	3320	8		6		10			7				4	9	12				3	5	1	11	2		
33		28	READING	0-3		3039	2		6		10			7				4		8		9			5	1	11			3
34	Mar	8	Doncaster Rovers	0-2		5319	2	8			6			10			7		4				9			5	1	11	2	3
35		22	Darlington	0-2		1582	11	8		6	5	10		7				4					9				1		2	3
36		25	MANSFIELD TOWN	0-2		3846	10	8			6			7				4					9			5	1	11	2	3
37		28	BARNSLEY	2-1	Best, Farrington	2594	10	8			6			7				4					9			5	1	11	2	3
38		31	Shrewsbury Town	0-6		4315	10	8			6			7				4	12				9			5	1	11	2	3
39	Apr	1	HARTLEPOOL	3-0	John 2, Best	2758	2	8			6	10		7				4	9				9			5	1	11		
40		5	Swansea City	0-1		1591	2	8			6	10		7				4	9							5	1	11		3	12
41		9	Workington	2-2	Stratford, Best	1455	2	8			6	10		7				4	9							5	1	11		
42		12	ROTHERHAM UNITED	1-1	Gregory (p)	3714	2	8			6	10		7				4	9						3	5	1	11		
43		15	TORQUAY UNITED	1-1	Oman	2658	2	8			6	10		7				4	9						3	5	1	11		12
44		18	Stockport County	0-1		1978	2	8			6	10		7					9						3	5	1	11	4	
45		23	Bradford City	1-2	John	1697	2	8		6		10		7				4	9							5	1	11	3	
46		25	NEWPORT COUNTY	3-2	Stratford, Carlton, Best	2482		8		6	5	10						4	9				12				1	11	2	3	7

	Anderson GL	Best WJB	Buchanan J	Carlton DG	Cegielski W	Christie DHM	Clarke JL	Farrington JR	Felton GM	Garnham SE	Gregory JC	Hall JL	John M	Kilkelly TF	Mabee GL	Moore J	Neal PG	Oman AJ	Robertson SJ	Starling AW	Stratford P	Tucker WB	Tumbridge RA	Wainwright RK
Apps	11	46	11	32	11	14	6	34	11	1	41	5	28	4	32	14	10	21	31	45	44	38	11	31
Goals		9	2	5			3				1	4	4		13		2	1	1		15	1		5

One own goal

F.A. Cup

	Date		Opponent	Score	Scorers	Att	Anderson GL	Best WJB	Buchanan J	Carlton DG	Cegielski W	Christie DHM	Clarke JL	Farrington JR	Felton GM	Garnham SE	Gregory JC	Hall JL	John M	Kilkelly TF	Mabee GL	Moore J	Neal PG	Oman AJ	Robertson SJ	Starling AW	Stratford P	Tucker WB	Tumbridge RA	Wainwright RK
R1	Nov	23	Torquay United	1-0	Gregory	2659	8				12			7			6				4		9		3	5	1	11	2	10
R2	Dec	14	Rotherham United	1-2	Stratford	4741	8		6		12			7				4	9					3	5	1	11	2		10

F.L. Cup

	Date		Opponent	Score	Scorers	Att	Anderson GL	Best WJB	Buchanan J	Carlton DG	Cegielski W	Christie DHM	Clarke JL	Farrington JR	Felton GM	Garnham SE	Gregory JC	Hall JL	John M	Kilkelly TF	Mabee GL	Moore J	Neal PG	Oman AJ	Robertson SJ	Starling AW	Stratford P	Tucker WB	Tumbridge RA	Wainwright RK
R1	Aug	20	PORT VALE	1-0	Robertson	5688	8	11					3	7			6				12		4		5	1	9	2		10
R2	Sep	10	BLACKBURN ROVERS	2-2	Neal, 1 og	5706	8	4	10					7			5				9	6	3			1	11	2		
rep		18	Blackburn Rovers	0-1		8566	8	4	10					7			5				9	6	3			1	11	2		

	Club	P	W	D	L	F	A	W	D	L	F	A	Pts
1	Mansfield Town	46	17	6	0	55	15	11	6	6	35	25	68
2	Shrewsbury Town	46	16	3	4	46	18	10	7	6	34	25	62
3	Rotherham United	46	13	7	3	40	19	9	8	6	31	22	59
4	Chester	46	17	5	1	48	9	6	6	11	16	29	57
5	Lincoln City	46	14	8	1	47	14	7	7	9	32	34	57
6	Cambridge United	46	15	5	3	43	16	5	9	9	19	28	54
7	Reading	46	13	6	4	38	20	8	4	11	25	27	52
8	Brentford	46	15	6	2	38	14	3	7	13	15	31	49
9	Exeter City	46	14	3	6	33	24	5	8	10	27	39	49
10	Bradford City	46	10	5	8	32	21	7	8	8	24	30	47
11	Southport	46	13	7	3	36	19	2	10	11	20	37	47
12	Newport County	46	13	5	5	43	30	6	4	13	25	45	47
13	Hartlepool	46	13	6	4	40	24	3	5	15	12	38	43
14	Torquay United	46	10	7	6	30	25	4	7	12	16	36	42
15	Barnsley	46	10	7	6	34	24	5	4	14	28	41	41
16	NORTHAMPTON TOWN	46	12	6	5	43	22	3	5	15	24	51	41
17	Doncaster Rovers	46	10	9	4	41	29	4	3	16	24	50	40
18	Crewe Alexandra	46	9	9	5	22	16	2	9	12	12	31	40
19	Rochdale	46	9	9	5	35	22	4	4	15	24	53	39
20	Stockport County	46	10	8	5	26	27	2	6	15	17	43	38
21	Darlington	46	11	4	8	38	22	2	6	15	16	40	36
22	Swansea City	46	9	4	10	25	31	6	2	15	21	42	36
23	Workington	46	7	5	11	23	29	3	6	14	13	37	31
24	Scunthorpe United	46	7	8	8	27	29	0	7	16	14	49	29

1975/76 2nd in Division 4: Promoted

#	Date		Opponent	Score	Scorers	Att	Anderson GL	Best WJB	Carlton DG	Christie DHM	Davids NG	Farrington JR	Felton GM	Gregory JC	Hall JL	Mabee GL	Martin D	Mayes AK	McGowan A	Parton JJ	Robertson SJ	Starling AW	Stratford P	Tucker WB	Phillips SE
1	Aug	16	Huddersfield Town	1-1	Tucker	3595	3	8	4	10		7		6	9	12					1	5	11	2	
2		22	Stockport County	3-1	Hall 2, Farrington	2932	3	8	7	10		4		6	9						1	5	11	2	
3		30	Barnsley	1-3	Hall	3649	3	8	4	10		7		6	9				12		1	5	11	2	
4	Sep	5	BRADFORD CITY	4-2	Christie, Gregory, Robertson, McGowan	3675		2		8	4	7		6	9				10		5	1	11	3	
5		13	Darlington	1-0	Gregory	3788		2	12	8	4	7		6	9				10		5	1	11	3	
6		19	SWANSEA CITY	0-0		5428		2		8	4	7		6	9				10		5	1	11	3	
7		23	WORKINGTON	2-1	Stratford, Best	4677		2	12	8	6	7		4	9				10		5	1	11	3	
8		27	Torquay United	1-0	Best	2087		8	4		2	7		3	9				10		5	1	11	6	
9	Oct	3	DONCASTER ROVERS	2-1	Hall, Strarford	6155		2	12	8	4	7		6	9				10		5	1	11	3	
10		10	Tranmere Rovers	0-2		4808		2		8	4	7		6	9				10		5	1	11	3	
11		18	LINCOLN CITY	1-0	Stratford	6566		2	4			7	12	6	9				10		5	1	11	3	8
12		21	BRENTFORD	3-1	Farrington, Best 2	6225		8			4	7		2	9				10		5	1	11	3	6
13		25	Scunthorpe United	2-0	Stratford 2	2112		4			6	7	12	2	9				8		5	1	11	3	10
14	Nov	1	WATFORD	3-0	Hall, Felton, Phillips	6656		4	6				7	2	9				8		5	1	11	3	10
15		3	Rochdale	2-0	Robertson, Stratford	2995		4	6				7	2	9				8		5	1	11	3	10
16		8	Cambridge United	1-0	Hall	5560		4	6				7	2	9				8		5	1	11	3	10
17		15	SOUTHPORT	1-0	Farrington	6089		4	6	12		11	7	2	9				8		5	1		3	10
18		29	Bournemouth	0-0		5891		4	6			7		2	9		11		8		5	1		3	10
19	Dec	6	CREWE ALEXANDRA	2-1	Hall, McGowan	5705		4	6			7		2	9		11		8		5	1		3	10
20		13	Exeter City	0-0		3394		4	6			7		2	9		11		8		5	1		3	10
21		20	EXETER CITY	3-1	Hall 2, Phillips	5212		4	6			7		2	9		11		8		5	1		3	10
22		26	Hartlepool	0-3		5077		4	6			11		2	7		9		10		5	1		3	8
23		27	NEWPORT COUNTY	3-0	Phillips, Robertson, Hall	8448		4	6	12		7		2	9		11		8		5	1		3	10
24	Jan	3	Reading	0-1		10360		4	6			7		2	9		11		8		5	1		3	10
25		10	BARNSLEY	5-0	Carlton, Robertson, Hall 2, Best	6132		4	6			7		2	9		11	8			5	1		3	10
26		16	Swansea City	1-1	Mayes	3656		4	6	12		7			9			2	8	11	5	1		3	10
27		24	DARLINGTON	3-2	Robertson, Hall 2	5135		4		12		7		6	9			2	8	11	5	1		3	10
28		31	Brentford	1-2	Hall	4114		4	6			7		2	9			11	8	12	5	1		3	10
29	Feb	7	ROCHDALE	1-1	Stratford	5393		4	6					2	9			7	8		5	1	11	3	10
30		14	CAMBRIDGE UNITED	4-2	Smith (og), Mayes 2, Robertson	5969		4	6			7		2				9	8	12	5	1	11	3	10
31		21	Southport	1-0	Farrington	1332		4	6			7		2				9	8	12	5	1	11	3	10
32		25	Workington	0-1		1135		4	6	12		7		2				9	8	11	5	1		3	10
33		27	SCUNTHORPE UNITED	2-1	Mayes, Martin (p)	6804		4	6			7			9		12	8	10		5	1	11	3	
34	Mar	6	Watford	1-0	Hall	7389		4				7		2	9		6	8	10		5	1	11	3	
35		9	Doncaster Rovers	4-0	Stratford 2, McGowan, Phillips	8737			12	6		7		2	9		4		10		5	1	11	3	8
36		12	TRANMERE ROVERS	1-1	Phillips	8247			12	6		7		2	9		4		10		5	1	11	3	8
37		17	Lincoln City	1-3	Stratford	13880		4				7		2	9		6		8		5	1	11	3	10
38		20	BOURNEMOUTH	6-0	Hall 3, Best 2, Stratford	6780		4		12		7		2	9		6		10		5	1	11	3	8
39		27	Crewe Alexandra	1-0	Best	2865		4	11	7				2	9		6		10		5	1		3	10
40	Apr	3	HUDDERSFIELD T	1-1	Phillips	7218		4	11	7				2	9		6		10		5	1		3	8
41		6	TORQUAY UNITED	2-2	Phillips, Gregory	6263		4	6	11			12	2	9		5		8	7		1		3	10
42		10	Bradford City	2-1	Hall 2	3175		4	6			7		2	9		5		8			1	11	3	10
43		15	READING	4-1	McGowan, Stratford 2, Martin	9584		4				7	6	2	9		5		10			1	11	3	8
44		17	HARTLEPOOL	5-2	Starling (p), Martin 3 (1p), Robertson	7555		4				12	7	2	9		6		10		5	1	11	3	8
45		20	Newport County	1-1	Martin (p)	1718		4				7		2	9		6		10		5	1	11	3	8
46		23	STOCKPORT COUNTY	4-0	Stratford 3, Martin	7680		4				7		2	9		6		10		5	1	11	3	8

| | | | | | | Apps | 3 | 44 | 34 | 19 | 9 | 38 | 10 | 45 | 43 | 1 | 29 | 10 | 42 | 3 | 44 | 43 | 30 | 46 | 34 |
| | | | | | | Goals | | 8 | 1 | 1 | | 4 | 1 | 3 | 21 | | 7 | 4 | 4 | | 7 | 1 | 16 | 1 | 7 |

One own goal

F.A. Cup

	Date	Opponent	Score		Att	And	Bes	Car	Chr	Dav	Far	Fel	Gre	Hal		Mar	May	McG	Par	Rob	Sta	Str	Tuc	Phi
R1	Nov 22	Brentford	0-2		6640		4	6	10		11	7	2	9				8		5	1		3	

F.L. Cup

	Date	Opponent	Score	Scorers	Att	And	Bes	Car	Chr	Dav	Far	Fel	Gre	Hal	Mab	Mar	May	McG	Par	Rob	Sta	Str	Tuc	Phi
R1/1	Aug 19	Watford	0-2		3368	3	8		10		4		6	9	7					1	5		11	2	
R1/2	27	WATFORD	1-1	Hall	4255	3	8	4	10		7		6	9						1	5		11	2	

		P	W	D	L	F	A	W	D	L	F	A	Pts
1	Lincoln City	46	21	2	0	71	15	11	8	4	40	24	74
2	NORTHAMPTON TOWN	46	18	5	0	62	20	11	5	7	25	20	68
3	Reading	46	19	3	1	42	9	5	9	9	28	42	60
4	Tranmere Rovers	46	18	3	2	61	16	6	7	10	28	39	58
5	Huddersfield Town	46	11	6	6	28	17	10	8	5	28	24	56
6	Bournemouth	46	15	5	3	39	16	5	7	11	18	32	52
7	Exeter City	46	13	7	3	37	17	5	7	11	19	30	50
8	Watford	46	16	4	3	38	18	6	2	15	24	44	50
9	Torquay United	46	12	6	5	31	24	6	8	9	24	39	50
10	Doncaster Rovers	46	10	6	7	42	31	6	7	10	28	38	49
11	Swansea City	46	14	8	1	51	21	2	7	14	15	36	47
12	Barnsley	46	12	8	3	34	16	2	8	13	18	32	44
13	Cambridge United	46	7	10	6	36	28	7	5	11	22	34	43
14	Hartlepool	46	10	6	7	37	29	6	4	13	25	49	42
15	Rochdale	46	7	11	5	27	23	5	7	11	13	31	42
16	Crewe Alexandra	46	10	7	6	36	21	3	8	12	22	36	41
17	Bradford City	46	9	7	7	35	26	3	10	10	28	39	41
18	Brentford	46	12	7	4	37	18	2	6	15	19	42	41
19	Scunthorpe United	46	11	3	9	31	24	3	7	13	19	35	38
20	Darlington	46	11	7	5	30	14	3	3	17	18	43	38
21	Stockport County	46	8	7	8	23	23	5	5	13	20	53	38
22	Newport County	46	8	7	8	35	33	5	2	16	22	57	35
23	Southport	46	6	6	11	27	31	2	4	17	14	46	26
24	Workington	46	5	4	14	19	43	2	3	18	11	44	21

1976/77   22nd in Division 3: Relegated

#	Date	Opponent	Res	Scorers	Att	Bowen KB	Bowker K	Carlton DG	Christie DHM	Bryant SP	Farrington JR	Best WJB	Gregory JC	Gilligan JJ	Hall JL	Haywood RJ	Malcolm AA	Martin D	McGowan A	Owen R	Phillips SE	Parton JJ	Robertson SJ	Reilly GG	Starling AW	Stratford P	Ross I	Tucker WB	Ward RA	Williams KD
1	Aug 21	Chesterfield	0-0		4052				7		12	4	2		9			6	10		8		5		1	11		3		
2	25	Sheffield Wednesday	1-2	Christie	11684			7	10		12	4	2					9	6		8		5		1	11		3		
3	28	LINCOLN CITY	1-0	Christie	6350			7	10		12	4	2					9	6		8		5		1	11		3		
4	Sep 4	Gillingham	1-1	Hall	5375			6	7			4	2		9			11	8				5		1	10		3		
5	11	READING	1-2	Robertson	6176			7	8		12	4	2		9			6	10				5		1	11		3		
6	18	Shrewsbury Town	0-3		4191			6	7			4	2		9			11	8				5		1	10		3		
7	25	WALSALL	0-1		5656			7	8			4	2		9			11	6				5		1	10		3		
8	Oct 1	WREXHAM	0-2		5114				11		7	4	2						8		6		5		1	10		3		
9	8	Port Vale	1-2	Phillips	3962	12			11		7	4	2						8		6		5	9	1			3		
10	15	PORTSMOUTH	3-1	Hall, Robertson, Reilly	4805				11		7	4	2		10				8		6		5	9	1			3		
11	23	Swindon Town	1-5	McGowan	7483				11		7	4	2		10				8		6		5	9	1	12		3		
12	26	York City	4-1	Christie 2, Farrington, Stratford	2634				11		7	4	2		10				8		6		5	9	1	12		3		
13	30	BRIGHTON & HOVE ALB	0-2		7782				10		7	4	2					12	8	9	6		5		1	11		3		
14	Nov 2	PETERBOROUGH UTD.	2-2	Stratford, og	7483				11		7		2					4	8	10	6		5	12	1	9		3		
15	6	Preston North End	0-3		7306				11		7		2					4	8	10	6		5	12	1	9		3		
16	13	OXFORD UNITED	1-0	Robertson	7021				11				2		9			4	8	10	6	1	5	3		11	7			
17	27	Chester	1-2	Phillips	3917				9		12	5	2				3		8	10	6	1	4			11	7			
18	Dec 18	Crystal Palace	1-1	McGowan	11032				7			4	2		9		3	6	8		10		5		1	11				
19	27	ROTHERHAM UNITED	1-4	Gregory	6963		9		7	3	12	4	2					11	8		6		5		1	10				
20	Jan 1	PRESTON NORTH END	0-1		5024		9		11	3	7	4	2						8				5		1	10				
21	3	Brighton & Hove Albion	0-2		22517		9		12	3	11		2						8				5		1	10			6	
22	7	TRANMERE ROVERS	3-4	Best, Martin, Stratford	4267				12	3	11	6	2					9	8				4	5	1	10			7	
23	15	SHEFFIELD WEDNESDAY	0-2		5828		9		12	3	7	6	4					10	8				5		1	11		2		
24	22	CHESTERFIELD	2-1	Best, Gilligan	3911					3	7	8	4	10				9					5	6	1	11		2		
25	29	Grimsby Town	1-0	Farrington	3909					3	7	8	4	10				9					5		1	11		2		
26	Feb 5	Lincoln City	4-5	Best 3, Robertson	5869				12	3	7	4	6	10				9	8				5		1	11		2		
27	12	GILLINGHAM	1-2	Farrington	4391				12	3	7	6	4	8				9					5	11	1	10		2		
28	15	Bury	1-1		3809				8	3	7	6	4					9					5	11	1	10		2		
29	19	Reading	4-2	Christie, McGowan 2, Stratford	5051				8	3	7	6	4	10				9	12				5			11		2	1	
30	26	SHREWSBURY TOWN	5-3	Best 2, Gregory, Martin, Stratford	5112				11	3	7	6	4					9	12				5			10		2	1	8
31	Mar 5	Walsall	3-0	Martin, Stratford 2	4806				11	3	7	6	4					9					5			10		2	1	8
32	8	MANSFIELD TOWN	0-1		7283				11	3	7	6	4					9	12				5			10		2	1	8
33	12	Wrexham	1-3	Best	6775				11	3	7	6	4			12		9					5			10		2	1	8
34	15	CRYSTAL PALACE	3-0	Gregory, Haywood, Stratford	6253				11	3	7	6	4			9			12				5			10		2	1	8
35	19	PORT VALE	3-0	Best, Stratford 2	5808				11	3	7	6	4			9							5			10		2	1	8
36	26	Portsmouth	1-2	Stratford	9195				11	3	7	6	4			9			6				5			10		2	1	8
37	Apr 1	SWINDON TOWN	1-1	Best	5609				11	3	7	6	4			9		3	12			1	5			10		2		8
38	9	BURY	3-0	Best, Stratford, og	5262				11	3	7	6	4			9			12			1	5			10		2		8
39	11	Rotherham United	0-2		7286				11	3	7	6	4			9			12			1	5			10		2		8
40	12	Peterborough United	1-3	Gregory	8944				11	3	7	6	4			9		6	12			1	5	10				2		8
41	16	YORK CITY	3-0	Best, Reilly, Williams	5427				11	3	7	6	4			12		9				1	5	10				2		8
42	19	GRIMSBY TOWN	0-0		5699				10	3	7	6	4			11		2	12			1	5	9						8
43	23	Oxford United	0-1		5075				11	3	7	6	4					2	12			1	5	9						8
44	29	CHESTER	0-0		5015				10	3	7	6	4			9		2				1	5			11				8
45	May 2	Tranmere Rovers	1-2	Haywood	2030				12	3	7	6	4			9		2	10			1	5			11				8
46	7	Mansfield Town	0-3		11314					3	7	6	4			9		2	10			1	5			12				8
Apps						1	4	6	44	28	41	40	46	5	11	13	2	38	31	5	17	12	41	22	26	42	2	37	8	17
Goals									5		4	12	4	1	2	2		3	4		2		4	2		12				1

Two own goals

F.A. Cup

Rd	Date	Opponent	Res	Scorers	Att	Christie DHM	Farrington JR	Best WJB	Gregory JC	Hall JL	McGowan A	Phillips SE	Parton JJ	Robertson SJ	Reilly GG	Stratford P	Tucker WB
R1	Nov 20	Leatherhead	0-2		3550	7	12	4	2	10	8	6	1	5	9	11	3

F.L. Cup

Rd	Date	Opponent	Res	Scorers	Att	Christie DHM	Farrington JR	Best WJB	Gregory JC	Hall JL	Martin D	McGowan A	Phillips SE	Robertson SJ	Starling AW	Stratford P	Tucker WB
R1/1	Aug 14	Swindon Town	2-3	Christie, Gregory	6353	7	12	4	2	9	6	8	10	5	1	11	3
R1/2	18	SWINDON TOWN	2-0	Martin, Stratford	7037	7		4	2	9	6	8	10	5	1	11	3
R2	31	HUDDERSFIELD T	0-1		6641	7	12	4	2	9	6	8	11	5	1	10	3

		P	W	D	L	F	A	W	D	L	F	A	Pts
1	Mansfield Town	46	17	6	0	52	13	11	2	10	26	29	64
2	Brighton & Hove A.	46	19	3	1	63	14	6	8	9	20	26	61
3	Crystal Palace	46	17	5	1	46	15	6	8	9	22	25	59
4	Rotherham United	46	11	9	3	30	15	11	6	6	39	29	59
5	Wrexham	46	15	6	2	47	22	9	4	10	33	32	58
6	Preston North End	46	15	4	4	48	21	6	8	9	16	22	54
7	Bury	46	15	2	6	41	21	8	6	9	23	38	54
8	Sheffield Wed.	46	15	4	4	39	18	7	5	11	26	37	53
9	Lincoln City	46	12	9	2	50	30	7	5	11	27	40	52
10	Shrewsbury Town	46	13	7	3	40	21	5	4	14	25	38	47
11	Swindon Town	46	12	6	5	48	33	3	9	11	20	42	45
12	Gillingham	46	11	8	4	31	21	5	4	14	24	43	44
13	Chester	46	14	3	6	28	20	4	5	14	20	38	44
14	Tranmere Rovers	46	10	7	6	31	23	3	10	10	20	30	43
15	Walsall	46	8	7	8	39	32	5	8	10	18	33	41
16	Peterborough Utd.	46	11	4	8	33	28	2	11	10	22	37	41
17	Oxford United	46	9	8	6	34	29	3	7	13	21	36	39
18	Chesterfield	46	10	6	7	30	20	4	4	15	26	44	38
19	Port Vale	46	9	7	7	29	28	2	9	12	18	43	38
20	Portsmouth	46	8	9	6	28	26	3	5	15	25	44	36
21	Reading	46	10	5	8	29	24	3	4	16	20	49	35
22	NORTHAMPTON TOWN	46	9	4	10	33	29	4	4	15	27	46	34
23	Grimsby Town	46	10	6	7	29	22	2	3	18	16	47	33
24	York City	46	7	8	8	25	34	3	4	16	25	55	32

1977/78 — 10th in Division 4

#		Date	Opponent	Score	Scorers	Att	Best WJB	Bryant SP	Christie DHM	Farrington JR	Gamham SE	Hall JL	Haywood RJ	Geidmintis AJ	Liddle DN	Litt SE	Jayes CG	Martin D	Mead PS	McGowan A	Parton JJ	Poppy APC	Reilly GG	Robertson SJ	Stratford P	Tucker WB	Williams KD	Wassall KD	Lyon DG
1	Aug	20	Brentford	0-3		5492		3	12	7	1		10		4			11		6			9	5		2	8		
2		22	Southend United	0-0		3693	6	3	11	7	1		10		4								9	5		2	8		
3		27	Halifax Town	1-0	Bryant	1869	6	3	11	7	1		10		4					12			9	5		2	8		
4	Sep	3	TORQUAY UNITED	1-0	Christie	3889	6	3	11	7	1				4					10			9	5		2	8		
5		9	Southport	1-3	Robertson	2677	6		11	7	1				4				3	10			9	5		2	8		
6		13	STOCKPORT COUNTY	2-1	Farrington, Reilly	3880	6		12	7	1				4			10	3	11			9	5		2	8		
7		17	HARTLEPOOL UNITED	5-3	Martin, Reilly 3, Robertson	3499		6	12	7	1				4			10	3	11			9	5		2	8		
8		24	Wimbledon	0-2		3236	12	6		7	1				4	5		10	3	11			9			2	8		
9		27	HUDDERSFIELD T	3-1	Best, Reilly 2	3942	8	6	11	7	1					4		10	2				9	5		3			
10	Oct	1	Scunthorpe United	2-2	Martin 2	2711	10	6	11	7	1					5		9	2				8	4		3	12		
11		4	Darlington	0-2		1729	10	6	11	7	1				12	5		9	2				8			3	4		
12		8	READING	0-2		3861	10	6	11	7						5		9	2		1		8			3	12		
13		11	ROCHDALE	3-1	Christie 2, Reilly	2965		6	11	7						5			2	10	1		9			3			
14		14	Crewe Alexandra	2-3	Best, Christie	2807	8	6	11	7						5			2	10	1		9	4		3		12	
15		22	BOURNEMOUTH	1-0	Reilly	3479	8	6	11	7						5			2	10	1		9	4		3		12	
16		29	Rochdale	1-1	Farrington	1198		6	11	7						5	8		2	10	1		9			3			4
17	Nov	5	NEWPORT COUNTY	2-4	Christie, Martin	3568		6	11	7						5	8		2	10	1		9			3			4
18		12	Doncaster Rovers	2-4	Hall, McGowan	2688		6	11	7		8			5		1		2	10			9			3			
19		19	BARNSLEY	1-1	Reilly	3131		3	11			9			4	6		7		8	1		10	5		2			
20	Dec	3	Swansea City	4-2	Christie, Farrington, Liddle, Reilly	4735		3	11	7					4	6	1	8					10	5		2	12		9
21		10	YORK CITY	1-1	Martin	3108		3	11	7					4	5		6		12	1		10			2	8		9
22		26	Watford	0-3		15056		3	11						4	6	1	8	7				9	5		2	10		
23		27	GRIMSBY TOWN	2-1	Martin, Tucker	3518		6	7	8					4	1		12	3				10	5	9	2	11		
24		31	ALDERSHOT	1-1	Farrington	3598	9	6	11	7					4	1		12	3				10	5		2	8		
25	Jan	2	Newport County	3-5	Farrington, Reilly 2	7160	4	3	11	7						6	1	12					10	5	9	2	8		
26		14	BRENTFORD	2-2	Reilly 2	4050	6	10	11	7					4	5	1	12	3				9			2	8		
27		28	Torquay United	1-2	Reilly	2443	4	9	8	10						12	1		3	7			11	6		2	5		
28	Feb	4	SOUTHPORT	1-0	Mead	2374	4	6	11	7			10				1		3				9	5		2	8		
29		25	SCUNTHORPE UNITED	1-2	Christie	2952	4		11	7				8	2	12	1		3	10			9			6			
30		28	WIMBLEDON	0-3		2643	4		11	7				8	2	3	1	12		10		6	9						5
31	Mar	4	Reading	0-0		4321	4		11	7				8	2	6	1	12	3	10			9	5					
32		6	Stockport County	2-1	Liddle, Reilly	3358	4	12	7	11				8	2	6			3	9			10	5					
33		11	CREWE ALEXANDRA	0-0		2842	6	12	11	7				9	2	4			3	8			10	5					
34		14	HALIFAX TOWN	1-2	Farrington	2278	4	6	11	7				9	2	8	1	12	3				10	5					
35		17	Bournemouth	1-1	McGowan	2221	4	6	11	7				9	2	8	1		3	12			10	5					
36		21	SOUTHEND UNITED	0-0		2431	4	6	11	7					2	8	1		3	10			9	5					
37		25	Grimsby Town	1-0	McGowan	5077	4	6	11	7					2	8	1	12	3	10			9	5					
38		28	WATFORD	0-2		8041	4	6	11	7					2	8		12	3	10	1		9	5					
39	Apr	1	Aldershot	1-2	Martin	3353	4	6	12	7					2	11		9	3	10	1			5				8	
40		4	Huddersfield Town	1-0	Bryant	3488	4	6		7					2		1	10	3	9				5			8	11	
41		8	DONCASTER ROVERS	0-0		2793	4	6							2		1		3	9			10	5			8	11	
42		11	Hartlepool United	2-0	McGowan 2	2844	4	6	11	7					2		1		3	9			10	5			8		
43		15	Barnsley	3-2	Farrington, Christie, Reilly	3434	4	6	11	7					2		1		3	9			10	5			8		
44		22	SWANSEA CITY	3-1	Christie, Reilly, Robertson	4865	4	6	11	7					2		1		3	9			10	5			8	12	
45		25	DARLINGTON	2-2	McGowan, Reilly	3181		6	11	7					2	4	1		3	9			10	5			8		
46		29	York City	3-0	Reilly 2, Williams	1389		6	11	7					2	4	1		3	9			10	5			8	12	
			Apps				34	41	43	44	11	10	3	18	27	20	25	25	38	32	10	1	44	38	2	28	28	7	6
			Goals				2	2	9	7		1			2			7	1	6			21	3		1	1		

F.A. Cup

		Date	Opponent	Score	Scorers	Att	Best WJB	Bryant SP	Christie DHM	Farrington JR	Gamham SE	Hall JL	Haywood RJ	Geidmintis AJ	Liddle DN	Litt SE	Jayes CG	Martin D	Mead PS	McGowan A	Parton JJ	Poppy APC	Reilly GG	Robertson SJ	Stratford P	Tucker WB	Williams KD	Wassall KD	Lyon DG
R1	Nov	26	Tooting & Mitcham	2-1	Christie, Martin	3513		3	11	7		9			4	6	1	8					10	5		2			
R2	Dec	17	ENFIELD	0-2		5249	10	3	11	7					4	6	1	8					9	5		2	12		

F.L. Cup

		Date	Opponent	Score	Scorers	Att	Best WJB	Bryant SP	Christie DHM	Farrington JR	Gamham SE	Hall JL	Haywood RJ	Geidmintis AJ	Liddle DN	Litt SE	Jayes CG	Martin D	Mead PS	McGowan A	Parton JJ	Poppy APC	Reilly GG	Robertson SJ	Stratford P	Tucker WB	Williams KD	Wassall KD	Lyon DG
R1/1	Aug	13	Southend United	3-2	Farrington, Reilly, Williams	4654	6	3		7			10		4			11			1		9	5		2	8		
R1/2		16	SOUTHEND UNITED	2-1	Best, Martin	4395	6	3	12	7					4			10			1		9	5		2	8		
R2		30	Ipswich Town	0-5		15443	6	3	11	7	1				4			10		12			9	5		2	8		

		P	W	D	L	F	A	W	D	L	F	A	Pts
1	Watford	46	18	4	1	44	14	12	7	4	41	24	71
2	Southend United	46	15	5	3	46	18	10	5	8	20	21	60
3	Swansea City	46	16	5	2	54	17	7	5	11	33	30	56
4	Brentford	46	15	6	2	50	17	6	8	9	36	37	56
5	Aldershot	46	15	8	0	45	16	4	8	11	22	31	54
6	Grimsby Town	46	14	6	3	30	15	7	5	11	27	36	53
7	Barnsley	46	15	4	4	44	20	3	10	10	17	29	50
8	Reading	46	12	7	4	33	23	6	7	10	22	29	50
9	Torquay United	46	12	6	5	43	25	4	9	10	14	31	47
10	NORTHAMPTON TOWN	46	9	8	6	32	30	8	5	10	31	38	47
11	Huddersfield Town	46	13	5	5	41	21	2	10	11	22	34	45
12	Doncaster Rovers	46	11	8	4	37	26	3	9	11	15	39	45
13	Wimbledon	46	8	11	4	39	26	6	5	12	27	41	44
14	Scunthorpe United	46	12	6	5	31	14	2	10	11	19	41	44
15	Crewe Alexandra	46	11	8	4	34	25	4	6	13	16	44	44
16	Newport County	46	14	6	3	43	22	2	5	16	22	51	43
17	Bournemouth	46	12	6	5	28	20	2	9	12	13	31	43
18	Stockport County	46	14	4	5	41	19	2	6	15	15	37	42
19	Darlington	46	10	8	5	31	22	4	5	14	21	37	41
20	Halifax Town	46	7	10	6	28	23	3	11	9	24	39	41
21	Hartlepool United	46	12	4	7	34	29	3	3	17	17	55	37
22	York City	46	8	7	8	27	31	4	5	14	23	38	36
23	Southport	46	5	13	5	30	32	1	6	16	22	44	31
24	Rochdale	46	8	6	9	29	28	0	2	21	14	57	24

1978/79   19th in Division 4

#	Date	Opponent	Score	Scorers	Att	Ashenden RH	Bowen KB	Bryant SP	Cordice NA	Christie DHM	Farrington JR	Froggatt JL	Geidmintis AJ	Jayes CG	Liddle DN	Matthews PW	Mead PS	McCaffrey J	Reilly GG	Robertson SJ	Perkins GS	Saunders PB	Poole AJ	Waldock DH	Walker RP	Wassall KO	Woollett AH	Williams KO
1	Aug 19	Torquay United	1-0	Liddle	3125			6		11	7		2	1	10		3		9							5	4	8
2	23	HARTLEPOOL UNITED	1-1	Farrington	4288			6		11	7		2	1	10		3		9						12	5	4	8
3	26	Wimbledon	1-4	Reilly	2644		12	10		11	7			1		6	3		9	5						2	4	8
4	Sep 2	BRADFORD CITY	1-0	Cordice	3320			6	10	11	7		2	1			3		9	5							4	8
5	9	York City	0-1		2443			6	12	11	7	9	2	1			3		10	5							4	8
6	12	DARLINGTON	4-1	Christie, Froggatt 2, Reilly	3443			6	12	11	7	9	2	1					10	5							4	8
7	15	SCUNTHORPE UNITED	1-0	Bryant	3859			6		11	7	10	2	1					9	5							4	8
8	23	Huddersfield Town	0-1		3320			6		11	7	9	2				12		10	5			1				4	8
9	26	Port Vale	2-2	Farrington, Froggatt	3245			6		11	7	9	2				3		10	5			1				4	8
10	30	DONCASTER ROVERS	3-0	Mead, Robertson, Christie	3011			6	12	11	7	9	2				3		10	5			1				4	8
11	Oct 7	Barnsley	1-1	Farrington	10336			6		11	7	9	2				3			5			1		10		4	8
12	14	READING	2-2	Farrington, Mead	4694			6		11	7	9	2	1			3			5		12			10			8
13	17	Grimsby Town	3-4	Christie, Froggatt, Bryant	5777			6		11	7	9	2	1			3			5		10						8
14	21	STOCKPORT COUNTY	2-2	Froggatt, Mead	3867			6	12	11	7	9	2	1			3		10			5						8
15	28	Wigan Athletic	0-2		6264			6		11	7	9	2	1			3		10	5		4			12			8
16	Nov 4	NEWPORT COUNTY	3-1	Froggatt, Farrington, Reilly	3065	12		6			7	9	2	1			3		10	5						11	4	8
17	11	Bradford City	0-3		3361			6			7	9	2	1			3		10	5						11	4	8
18	18	WIMBLEDON	1-1	Geidmintis (p)	3625			6	9		7	10	2				3			5			1			11	4	8
19	Dec 2	PORTSMOUTH	0-2		3592	6			9		7	10	2	1			3		4	5					12	11		
20	9	Hereford United	3-4	Wassall, Farrington, Reilly	2879	6	12				7	9	4	1			3		10	5					2	11		
21	26	ALDERSHOT	2-3	Reilly, McCaffrey	3325			6			7	9	4	1			3	11	10	5					2	12		
22	30	HALIFAX TOWN	2-1	Reilly, McCaffrey	2208		12	6			7	9	4	1			3	11	10	5					2			
23	Feb 10	Doncaster Rovers	0-2		1922			6			7	9	4	1			3	11	10	5					2			
24	21	Bournemouth	0-0		3990			6			7	9	2	1			3	11	10	5							4	8
25	24	Reading	1-5	Reilly	6933			6		10	7	9	2	1			3	11	4	5		12						8
26	Mar 2	Stockport County	1-2	Reilly	2929			6			7	9	2				3	11	10	5		4	1		12			
27	6	HUDDERSFIELD T	2-3	Reilly 2	1823			6			7	9	2				3	11	10	5		4	1		12			
28	10	WIGAN ATHLETIC	2-4	Froggatt, Bryant	2275	12		6			7	9	2	1			3	11	10	5		8					4	
29	13	PORT VALE	1-0	Farrington	1572	12		3			7	9	2					11	10	5		6	1				4	
30	16	Newport County	1-2	Robertson	3018	12		3			7	9	2					11	10	5		6	1				4	
31	20	Scunthorpe United	3-0	Reilly 3	1868						7	9	2				3	11	10	5		6	1				4	8
32	24	TORQUAY UNITED	1-2	Robertson	2194						7	9	2				3	11	10	5		6	1				4	8
33	31	ROCHDALE	1-0	McCaffrey	1653						6	11	2	1		8	3	9	10	5		4						7
34	Apr 3	YORK CITY	1-0	Froggatt	1628						6	11	2	1		8	3	9	10	5		4						7
35	7	Portsmouth	0-1		8166	12					6	11	2	1		8	3	9	10	5		4						7
36	10	Crewe Alexandra	4-2	Robertson, Farrington, Froggatt, Williams	1291	12					6	11	2	1		8	3	9	10	5		4	1					7
37	14	Aldershot	0-2		4438						6	11	2	1			3		10	5		4				9		7
38	16	BOURNEMOUTH	4-2	Reilly 3, Froggatt	2253	12					6	11	2	1			3	9	10	5		4						7
39	17	CREWE ALEXANDRA	3-1	Reilly 2, Froggatt	2570	12					6	11	2	1			3	9	10	5		4						7
40	21	Halifax Town	2-2	McCaffrey, Froggatt	1172						6	11	2	1			3	9	10	5		4						7
41	24	GRIMSBY TOWN	1-2	Williams	3019						6	11	2	1			3	9	10	5		4						7
42	26	BARNSLEY	0-1		3305	12					6	11	2	1			3	9	10	5		4	1					7
43	28	HEREFORD UNITED	2-1	Robertson, McCaffrey	2001	8					6	11					3	9		5		4	1		10			7
44	May 5	Rochdale	1-4	Reilly	1751						6	11	4			7		9	10	5			1	3	2			7
45	14	Darlington	0-0		1333		10				6	11	2					9	4			5	1	3				7
46	17	Hartlepool United	0-2		1769		10				6	11	2					9	4		12	3	1	5				7
		Apps				13	5	28	8	15	46	42	45	29	3	13	39	25	43	38	1	27	17	3	13	13	23	44
		Goals						3	1	3	8	12	1		1		3	4	19	6						1		2

F.A. Cup

#	Date	Opponent	Score	Scorers	Att	Ashenden RH	Bowen KB	Bryant SP	Cordice NA	Christie DHM	Farrington JR	Froggatt JL	Geidmintis AJ	Jayes CG	Liddle DN	Matthews PW	Mead PS	McCaffrey J	Reilly GG	Robertson SJ	Perkins GS	Saunders PB	Poole AJ	Waldock DH	Walker RP	Wassall KO	Woollett AH	Williams KO
R1	Nov 25	Portsmouth	0-2		13338			12			7	9	2	1			3		10	5		6				11	4	8

F.L. Cup

#	Date	Opponent	Score	Scorers	Att	Ashenden RH	Bowen KB	Bryant SP	Cordice NA	Christie DHM	Farrington JR	Froggatt JL	Geidmintis AJ	Jayes CG	Liddle DN	Matthews PW	Mead PS	McCaffrey J	Reilly GG	Robertson SJ	Perkins GS	Saunders PB	Poole AJ	Waldock DH	Walker RP	Wassall KO	Woollett AH	Williams KO
R1/1	Aug 12	Cambridge United	2-2	Farrington, Reilly	4043			6		11	7		2	1	10		3		9	5							4	8
R1/2	16	CAMBRIDGE UNITED	2-1	Reilly, Christie	4721			6		11	7		2	1	10		3		9	5					12		4	8
R2/1	30	HEREFORD UNITED	0-0		3991			6		11	7		2	1			3		9	5		10			12		4	8
R2/2	Sep 6	Hereford United	1-0	Reilly	4205	12		6	10	11	7		4	1			3		9	5			2					8
R3	Oct 4	STOKE CITY	1-3	Reilly	11235			6	10	11	7		2				3		9	5			1		12		4	8

		P	W	D	L	F	A	W	D	L	F	A	Pts
1	Reading	46	19	3	1	49	8	7	10	6	27	27	65
2	Grimsby Town	46	15	5	3	51	23	11	4	8	31	26	61
3	Wimbledon	46	18	3	2	50	20	7	8	8	28	26	61
4	Barnsley	46	15	5	3	47	23	9	8	6	26	19	61
5	Aldershot	46	16	5	2	38	14	4	12	7	25	33	57
6	Wigan Athletic	46	14	5	4	40	24	7	8	8	23	24	55
7	Portsmouth	46	13	7	3	35	12	7	5	11	27	36	52
8	Newport County	46	12	5	6	39	28	9	5	9	27	27	52
9	Huddersfield Town	46	13	8	2	32	15	5	3	15	25	38	47
10	York City	46	11	6	6	33	24	7	5	11	18	31	47
11	Torquay United	46	14	4	5	38	24	5	4	14	20	41	46
12	Scunthorpe United	46	12	3	8	33	30	5	8	10	21	30	45
13	Hartlepool United	46	7	12	4	35	28	6	6	11	22	38	44
14	Hereford United	46	12	8	3	35	18	3	5	15	18	35	43
15	Bradford City	46	11	5	7	38	26	6	4	13	24	42	43
16	Port Vale	46	8	10	5	29	28	6	4	13	28	42	42
17	Stockport County	46	11	5	7	33	21	3	7	13	25	39	40
18	Bournemouth	46	11	6	6	34	19	3	5	15	13	29	39
19	NORTHAMPTON TOWN	46	12	4	7	40	30	3	5	15	24	46	39
20	Rochdale	46	11	4	8	25	26	4	5	14	22	38	39
21	Darlington	46	8	8	7	25	21	3	7	13	24	45	37
22	Doncaster Rovers	46	8	8	7	25	22	5	3	15	25	51	37
23	Halifax Town	46	7	5	11	24	32	2	3	18	15	40	26
24	Crewe Alexandra	46	3	7	13	24	41	3	7	13	19	49	26

1979/80 13th in Division 4

#	Date	Opponent	Score	Scorers	Att	Poole AJ	Byatt DJ	Reilly GG	Farmer KJ	Taylor A	Ward SC	Denyer PR	Ashenden RH	McCaffrey J	Bowen KB	Sargent GS	Waldock DH	Jayes CG	Walker RP	Saunders PB	Farrington JR	Townsend RN	Sandercock PJ	O'Donoghue MG	Sandy AVC	Williams KD	Gage WAJ	Leonard GE	Ingram GP	Heeley DM	Muir M
1	Aug 18	Doncaster Rovers	1-2	McCaffrey	4402	1	2	4	5	3	6	7	9	11	8	10	12														
2	22	BRADFORD CITY	1-2	Denyer	2555		2	9	5	3	6	7		11	8	10	4	1													
3	25	WALSALL	1-2	Bowen	3136			10	5	3	6	7	12	11	9	8	4	1	2												
4	Sep 1	Torquay United	2-2	Denyer, Ward	2825			9	4		6	7		11	10	8	5	1	2	3											
5	7	HALIFAX TOWN	0-0		2759			10	4		6	7	9	11	8		5	1	2	3											
6	15	Port Vale	0-5		2847			3	4		6	7	12	11	8		5	1	2		9										
7	18	Newport County	1-2	Waldock	3185			4		3	6	7	12	11	9	10	5	1	2		8										
8	22	PETERBOROUGH UTD.	1-0	Bowen	3680			4	12		6	7	3	11	10	9	5		2		8										
9	29	Crewe Alexandra	1-2	Waldock	1909	1		4	12		6	7		11	10	9	5		2		8		3								
10	Oct 2	NEWPORT COUNTY	3-2	Waldock, McCaffrey, Reilly	2346			5	12		6	7		9		10	4	1	2	11	8		3								
11	6	TRANMERE ROVERS	2-1	Reilly, Sargent	2324			9	6		4	7		10			5	1	2	11	8		3								
12	10	Bradford City	1-3	Reilly	4534		12	11	6		4	7		9		10	5	1	2		8		3								
13	13	Aldershot	0-2		3799		11	10	12		4	7		9		8	5	1	2	6			3								
14	20	HEREFORD UNITED	2-0	Farmer 2	2319		6	9	11			7		4		10	5	1	2	8			3								
15	23	HUDDERSFIELD T	4-2	Sargent, Farrington, Farmer 2	3210		4	10	11			7				9	5	1	2	6	8		3								
16	26	Rochdale	2-3	Farmer, Byatt	1468		4	10	11			7	12			9	5	1	2	6	8		3								
17	Nov 3	DONCASTER ROVERS	1-0	Sandercock	3427	1	4	9	11			7				10	5		2	6	8		3								
18	6	Huddersfield Town	0-5		6552	1	4	10	11	12		8				9	5		2	6	7		3								
19	10	Darlington	0-0		1559	1	4		11			8				9	5		2	6	7		3	10							
20	17	HARTLEPOOL UNITED	2-1	O'Donoghue, Farrington	2251	1	4	9				7		10		8	5		2		6		3	11							
21	Dec 1	Wigan Athletic	0-0		6158	1	4		10			7		11			5		2	8	6		3	9	12						
22	8	SCUNTHORPE UNITED	0-0		2120	1	4		10			7		11			5		2	8	6		3	9							
23	21	Bournemouth	2-2	Denyer 2	2335	1	4		10			7		11	9		5		2				3		6	8					
24	26	STOCKPORT COUNTY	2-0	Bowen 2	3054	1	4		10			7		11	9				2				3		6	8	5				
25	29	Portsmouth	1-6	Bowen	15579	1	4		10			7		11	9	12			2				3		6	8	5				
26	Jan 5	YORK CITY	2-0	Ward, Farmer	2095	1	4		10		8	7		11	9		5		2				3		6						
27	26	Walsall	1-5	Bowen	5646	1	4	9				7		11	10	12	5		2				3				5	8			
28	Feb 2	PORT VALE	3-1	Sargent, Gage, Bowen	1946	1	4				6	7		11	9	10			2				3			8	5				
29	9	Peterborough United	0-0		4960	1	4		8			9		7		11			2		6		3		10		5				
30	13	Lincoln City	0-0		3652	1	4		10			7		9		11			2		6		3		8		5				
31	16	CREWE ALEXANDRA	1-0	Saunders	1852	1	4		10			7		9		11			2	12	6		3		8		5				
32	23	ALDERSHOT	2-1	Farrington, Denyer	2592	1	4					7		9	10	11			2		6		3		8		5				
33	Mar 1	Hereford United	1-0	Bowen	2299	1	4					7		9	10	11			2		6		3		8		5				
34	4	Halifax Town	1-2	Byatt	1377	1	4					7		9	10	11			2		6		3		8		5				
35	8	ROCHDALE	0-0		2370	1	4					7		9	10	11			2		6		3		8		5				
36	14	Tranmere Rovers	1-1	Bowen	1500	1	4			11		7		9		10			2	8	6		3				5				
37	18	TORQUAY UNITED	3-0	Byatt, Bowen, Ingram	2659	1	4					6			10	8			2			7	3				5		11	9	
38	22	DARLINGTON	2-0	Bowen, Ingram	3209	1	4					6			10	8		4	2			7	3				5		11	9	
39	29	Hartlepool United	1-2	Ingram	1995	1	4					6			10	8			2			7	3				5		11	9	
40	Apr 4	Stockport County	0-2		2499	1	4					6			10	8		4	2			7	3				5		11	9	
41	7	LINCOLN CITY	0-0		3371	1	4		10			6				8			2			7	3				5		11	9	
42	8	BOURNEMOUTH	0-1		3175	1	4					6			8				2	10		12	3	7			5		11	9	
43	12	York City	2-1	Ingram, Sandercock	2161	1	4	9				6	7		8	10			2	12		10	3				5		11		
44	19	WIGAN ATHLETIC	1-1	Sargent	2378	1	4					7		9	8				2	4	6		3		10		5		11		
45	25	Scunthorpe United	0-3		1810	1	4					6	7		8	10			2	4			3		8		5		11	9	12
46	May 3	PORTSMOUTH	0-2		10713	1	4		11			6	7		8				2				3				5		10	9	
		Apps				32	33	18	34	4	14	46	5	32	24	40	28	14	38	12	29	13	38	4	22	3	21	1	10	8	1
		Goals					3	3	6		2	5		2	11	4	3			1	3		2	1			1		4		

F.A. Cup

R	Date	Opponent	Score	Scorers	Att	Poole	Byatt	Reilly	Farmer	Taylor	Ward	Denyer	Ashenden	McCaffrey	Bowen	Sargent	Waldock	Jayes	Walker	Saunders	Farrington	Townsend	Sandercock
R1	Nov 24	Hereford United	0-1		3384	1	4		9			7		12	10	8	5		2		6	11	3

F.L. Cup

R	Date	Opponent	Score	Scorers	Att	Poole	Byatt	Reilly	Farmer	Taylor	Ward	Denyer	Ashenden	McCaffrey	Bowen	Sargent	Waldock	Jayes	Walker	Saunders	Farrington	Townsend	Sandercock	O'Donoghue
R1/1	Aug 13	MILLWALL	2-1	Reilly 2	3559	1	2	9	5	3		7	12	11	8	10				6	4			
R1/2	15	Millwall	2-2	McCaffrey, Bowen	4218	1	2	4	5	3	6	7	9	11	8	10								
R2/1	28	OLDHAM ATHLETIC	3-0	Reilly 2, Ward	3053			10	4		6	7		11	9	8	5	1	2	3				
R2/2	Sep 5	Oldham Athletic	1-3	Denyer	4850			10	4	12	6	7	9	11		8	5	1	2	3				
R3	27	BRIGHTON & HOVE ALB.	0-1		7105	1		4	12		6	7	3	11	9	10	5		2					8

Division 4 final table

		P	W	D	L	F	A	W	D	L	F	A	Pts
1	Huddersfield Town	46	16	5	2	61	18	11	7	5	40	30	66
2	Walsall	46	12	9	2	43	23	11	9	3	32	24	64
3	Newport County	46	16	5	2	47	22	11	2	10	36	28	61
4	Portsmouth	46	15	5	3	62	23	9	7	7	29	26	60
5	Bradford City	46	14	6	3	44	14	10	6	7	33	36	60
6	Wigan Athletic	46	13	5	5	42	26	8	8	7	34	35	55
7	Lincoln City	46	14	8	1	43	12	4	9	10	21	30	53
8	Peterborough Utd.	46	14	3	6	39	22	7	7	9	19	25	52
9	Torquay United	46	13	7	3	47	25	2	10	11	23	44	47
10	Aldershot	46	10	7	6	35	23	6	6	11	27	30	45
11	Bournemouth	46	8	9	6	32	25	5	9	9	20	26	44
12	Doncaster Rovers	46	11	6	6	37	27	4	8	11	25	36	44
13	NORTHAMPTON TOWN	46	14	5	4	33	16	2	7	14	18	50	44
14	Scunthorpe United	46	11	9	3	37	23	3	6	14	21	52	43
15	Tranmere Rovers	46	10	4	9	32	24	4	9	10	18	32	41
16	Stockport County	46	9	7	7	30	31	5	5	13	18	41	40
17	York City	46	9	6	8	35	34	5	5	13	30	48	39
18	Halifax Town	46	11	9	3	29	20	2	4	17	17	52	39
19	Hartlepool United	46	10	7	6	36	28	4	3	16	23	36	38
20	Port Vale	46	8	6	9	34	24	4	6	13	22	46	36
21	Hereford United	46	8	7	8	22	21	3	7	13	16	31	36
22	Darlington	46	7	11	5	33	26	2	6	15	17	48	35
23	Crewe Alexandra	46	10	6	7	25	27	1	7	15	10	41	35
24	Rochdale	46	6	7	10	20	28	1	6	16	13	51	27

1980/81 10th in Division 4

League (Division 4)

No	Date	Opponent	Score	Scorers	Att.
1	Aug 16	Darlington	0-1		1763
2	23	Bournemouth	0-0		2875
3	Sep 6	Hartlepool United	3-2	Bowen, Farmer, Phillips	2435
4	13	DONCASTER ROVERS	0-2		2280
5	17	Bradford City	1-3	Phillips	2765
6	19	YORK CITY	2-0	Phillips, Saxby	1843
7	23	SOUTHEND UNITED	2-0	Carlton, Phillips	2337
8	27	Hereford United	1-4	Phillips (p)	2693
9	30	BRADFORD CITY	0-1		2293
10	Oct 3	STOCKPORT COUNTY	0-1		1902
11	7	Bury	2-1	Denyer, Waldock	1779
12	11	Scunthorpe United	2-0	Phillips 2	2650
13	17	CREWE ALEXANDRA	4-1	Phillips 2, Farmer 2	2179
14	21	ALDERSHOT	2-0	Gage, Heeley	3194
15	25	Lincoln City	0-8		4060
16	27	Mansfield Town	0-2		3560
17	31	HALIFAX TOWN	2-1	Phillips 2	2226
18	Nov 4	BURY	5-3	Denyer 3 (1p), Saunders 2	2229
19	8	Wimbledon	0-1		2029
20	12	Wigan Athletic	0-3		3375
21	15	DARLINGTON	2-2	Denyer, Phillips	1656
22	29	TRANMERE ROVERS	3-1	Phillips 2, Sandy	1487
23	Dec 6	Torquay United	3-3	Bowen, Williams	1975
24	20	ROCHDALE	3-2	Phillips, Denyer, Bowen	1705
25	26	Peterborough United	0-3		6265
26	27	PORT VALE	5-1	Farmer, Bowen 2, Sandercock, Denyer	2978
27	Jan 3	Aldershot	0-0		2992
28	10	MANSFIELD TOWN	0-1		2985
29	16	Tranmere Rovers	2-3	Bramhall (og), Bowen	1246
30	23	Southend United	0-0		6191
31	31	BOURNEMOUTH	0-1		2140
32	Feb 3	WIGAN ATHLETIC	1-1	Farmer	1708
33	6	Doncaster Rovers	1-1	Bowen	5680
34	14	HARTLEPOOL UNITED	3-1	Bowen 2, Denyer	2032
35	Mar 6	Stockport County	2-1	Phillips, Cooke	1945
36	13	SCUNTHORPE UNITED	3-3	Denyer 3 (1p)	2046
37	21	Crewe Alexandra	1-3	Williams	2120
38	28	LINCOLN CITY	1-1	Heeley	2424
39	Apr 4	Halifax Town	1-0	Phillips	1996
40	11	WIMBLEDON	1-1	Bowen	2121
41	14	HEREFORD UNITED	0-0		1380
42	18	Port Vale	1-1	Farmer	2371
43	21	PETERBOROUGH UTD.	2-2	Denyer, Phillips	3800
44	May 1	TORQUAY UNITED	1-0	Bowen	1562
45	3	Rochdale	1-0	Denyer	1474
46	5	York City	2-1	Bowen, Phillips	1167

Appearances and goals

	Poole AJ	Walker RP	Sandercock PJ	Byatt DJ	Gage WAJ	Heeley DM	Denyer PR	Sargent GS	Phillips SE	Bowen KB	Farmer KJ	Saunders PB	Sandy AVC	Williams KD	Carlton DG	Saxby GP	Waldock DH	Cooke PC	Leonard GE
Apps	46	2	31	14	31	36	45	3	45	32	39	28	36	39	39	34	23	5	1
Goals			1		1	2	13		19	13	6	2	1	2	1	1	1	1	

one own goal

F.A. Cup

	Date	Opponent	Score	Scorers	Att.
R1	Nov 22	PETERBOROUGH UTD.	1-4	Phillips	5542

F.L. Cup

	Date	Opponent	Score	Scorers	Att.
R1/1	Aug 8	READING	0-2		3294
R1/2	13	Reading	3-2	Denyer, Phillips 2	4357

Final Division 4 table

		P	W	D	L	F	A	W	D	L	F	A	Pts
1	Southend United	46	19	4	0	47	6	11	3	9	32	25	67
2	Lincoln City	46	15	7	1	44	11	10	8	5	22	14	65
3	Doncaster Rovers	46	15	4	4	36	20	7	8	8	23	29	56
4	Wimbledon	46	15	4	4	42	17	8	5	10	22	29	55
5	Peterborough Utd.	46	11	8	4	37	21	6	10	7	31	33	52
6	Aldershot	46	12	9	2	28	11	6	5	12	15	30	50
7	Mansfield Town	46	13	5	5	36	15	7	4	12	22	29	49
8	Darlington	46	13	6	4	43	23	6	5	12	22	36	49
9	Hartlepool United	46	14	3	6	42	22	6	6	11	22	39	49
10	NORTHAMPTON TOWN	46	11	7	5	42	26	7	6	10	23	41	49
11	Wigan Athletic	46	13	4	6	29	16	5	7	11	22	39	47
12	Bury	46	10	8	5	38	21	7	3	13	32	41	45
13	Bournemouth	46	9	8	6	30	21	7	5	11	17	27	45
14	Bradford City	46	9	9	5	30	24	5	7	11	23	36	44
15	Rochdale	46	11	6	6	33	25	3	9	11	27	45	43
16	Scunthorpe United	46	8	12	3	40	31	3	8	12	20	38	42
17	Torquay United	46	13	2	8	38	26	5	3	15	17	37	41
18	Crewe Alexandra	46	10	7	6	28	20	3	7	13	20	41	40
19	Port Vale	46	10	8	5	40	23	2	7	14	17	47	39
20	Stockport County	46	10	5	8	29	25	6	2	15	15	32	39
21	Tranmere Rovers	46	12	5	6	41	24	1	5	17	18	49	36
22	Hereford United	46	8	8	7	29	20	3	5	15	9	42	35
23	Halifax Town	46	9	3	11	28	32	2	9	12	16	39	34
24	York City	46	10	2	11	31	23	2	7	14	16	43	33

1981/82   22nd in Division 4

#	Date	Opponent	Score	Scorers	Att	Poole AJ	Brady PJ	Saunders PB	Farmer KJ	Denyer PR	Coffill PT	Carlton DG	Heeley DM	Phillips SE	Bowen KB	Alexander JE	Sandy AVC	Gage WAJ	Saxby GP	Taylor Andy	Buchanan J	Russell R	Mahoney AJ	Perrin SC	Kruse PK	Massey S	Bryant SP	Muir M	Belfon F
1	Aug 29	SCUNTHORPE UNITED	1-1	Heeley	2064	1	2	3	4	5	6	7	8	9	10	11	12												
2	Sep 4	York City	1-2	Phillips	2086	1	2		4	3	6	7	8	9	10	11	12	5											
3		12 HULL CITY	1-1	Denyer (p)	1938	1	2		4	3	6	7			10	9	11	8	5	12									
4		19 Wigan Athletic	1-3	Denyer	3996	1	2	12	4	7	6	3		9			11	8	5	10									
5		21 Mansfield Town	1-4	Brady	2612	1	2	3		4	6	7	8	9			11	10	5										
6		26 HEREFORD UNITED	2-3	Phillips 2	1552	1	2	12		7	6	3	10	9			11	8	5		4								
7		29 STOCKPORT COUNTY	0-0		1865	1	4			7	6			12	10		11	8	5	3	2	9							
8	Oct 2	Colchester United	1-5	Denyer (p)	2760	1	4			7	6	3		9			11	10	5		2	8							
9		10 Bournemouth	1-1	Denyer	5241	1	4			5	6	3	7	10			11	8		12	2	9							
10		13 BLACKPOOL	0-1		2376	1	4			5	7	3	6	9			11	10			2	8	12						
11		17 BRADFORD CITY	0-2		2053	1	11	12		5			3	7	10			8	4	6	2	9							
12		21 Torquay United	2-2	Heeley, Sandy	2526	1	5					6	7	10			11	8	4	3	2	9							
13		24 TRANMERE ROVERS	3-2	Buchanan 2, Bramhall (og)	1722	1	8			5			3	7	10			12	4	6	2	9	11						
14		31 Bury	1-7	Phillips (p)	3375	1	5					12	7	6	9			8	4	3	2	10	11						
15	Nov 3	SHEFFIELD UNITED	1-2	Phillips	4168	1	4	9				6	8		10				5	3	2	7	11						
16		8 CREWE ALEXANDRA	3-0	Phillips, Saxby, Brady	2794	1	5	7				9	8		10		12		4	3	2	6	11						
17		14 Hartlepool	1-3	Phillips	1641	1	5	6					8		10		9		4	3	2	7	11						
18		28 Peterborough United	0-1		5293	1	4	9					7		10			11	6	5	3	2	8						
19	Dec 5	DARLINGTON	0-1		1669	1	4	9					8		10				6	5	3	2	7	11					
20	Jan 23	Scunthorpe United	1-2	Perrin	1439	1	4	6				12		7	11	8		10	5	3	2			9					
21		30 WIGAN ATHLETIC	2-3	Denyer, Perrin	2418	1	5			7			2			11	6	4	3		8			10					
22	Feb 2	PORT VALE	3-5	Alexander, Phillips, Saxby	1644	1	4			6			2	11	10	7		5	3		8			9					
23		6 Hull City	1-0	Alexander	3627	1	4	3		7			2	6	9	11	12	5			8			10					
24		9 MANSFIELD TOWN	1-1	Alexander	1945	1	4	3		7			2	11	9	6		5			8			10					
25		14 COLCHESTER UNITED	1-2	Coffill	3102	1		3			6		2	9		11	8	5	4					10					
26		17 Blackpool	0-1		2231	1		3		11	7	8		9	10		6	5		2					4				
27		20 Hereford United	1-2	Phillips	2229	1		3		11	6	2	7	9			12	4			8			10	5				
28		23 Aldershot	1-2	Phillips (p)	1171	1	8	3			6	2	7	9		11		4			10				5				
29		27 BOURNEMOUTH	1-0	Gage	2125	1	2	3			6						9	4	8		11				5	7			
30	Mar 2	ROCHDALE	2-1	Massey, Gage	1916	1	2	3			8				12	10	6	4	11		7				5	9			
31		7 Bradford City	1-2	Perrin	4836	1	2	3			6	8	11				12	4	7					9	5	10			
32		9 TORQUAY UNITED	2-0	Massey, Alexander	1599	1	2	3			6					11		8	4	7				9	5	10			
33		13 Tranmere Rovers	2-0	Perrin, Saxby	1198	1	2	3			6						9	4	7		8			10	5	11			
34		16 Sheffield United	3-7	Massey 2 (1p), Perrin	15716	1	2	3			6						12	4	7		8			9	5	10			
35		20 BURY	1-0	Bradley (og)	2109	1	2				6	3	9				12	4	7		8			10	5	11			
36		23 YORK CITY	5-0	Buchanan 2, Czuczman (og), Perrin, Aitkin	2452	1	2				6	3					9	4	7		8			10	5	11			
37		27 Crewe Alexandra	2-2	Saxby 2	1801	1	2				6	3						4	8	7				10	5	11	9		
38	Apr 3	HARTLEPOOL UNITED	2-1	Saxby, Coffill	1890	1				2	6	3	11				12	4	7		8				5	10	9		
39		10 ALDERSHOT	0-0		2365	1				2	6	3					12	4	7		8			11	5	10	9		
40		12 Port Vale	0-1		3014	1				6	7	2					9	4	11	8						10	3		
41		17 Darlington	0-3		1729	1	2				6	3					11	4	7		8				5	10	9		
42		20 HALIFAX TOWN	0-1		1935	1	2	5			6	3					10	4	7		8					11	9	12	
43		24 PETERBOROUGH UTD.	1-0	Saxby	4975	1	2				6	3	11					4	7		8			9	5	10			
44		30 Stockport County	0-0		1658	1	2				6	3						4	7		8			11	5	10	9		
45	May 4	Halifax Town	1-2	Sandy	1730	1	12				7	2	6				10	4	9		8				5	11	3		
46		15 Rochdale	3-5	Heeley, Massey (p), Sandy	1056	1					7		6				10	4	2					9	5	11	3		8

| | | | | Apps | | 46 | 39 | 24 | 4 | 22 | 36 | 37 | 26 | 30 | 3 | 22 | 39 | 43 | 34 | 17 | 34 | 1 | 6 | 18 | 18 | 18 | 18 | 10 | 1 |
| | | | | Goals | | | 2 | | | 5 | 2 | | 3 | 10 | | 4 | 3 | 2 | 7 | | 4 | | | 6 | | 5 | | | |

Four own goals

F.A. Cup

R	Date	Opponent	Score	Scorers	Att	Poole AJ	Brady PJ	Saunders PB	Farmer KJ	Denyer PR	Coffill PT	Carlton DG	Heeley DM	Phillips SE	Bowen KB	Alexander JE	Sandy AVC	Gage WAJ	Saxby GP	Taylor Andy	Buchanan J	Russell R	Mahoney AJ	Perrin SC
R1	Nov 20	Weymouth	0-0		2600	1	5	6				8	9	10			12	4	3	2	7			11
rep	24	WEYMOUTH	6-2	Carlton, Phillips, Sandy, Gage 2, Mahoney	2613	1	4					7	9	10			6	5	3	2	8			11
R2	Dec 15	Bristol City	0-3		2901	1	2	4			6		8	10		12	9	5	3		7			11

F.L. Cup (The Milk Cup)

R	Date	Opponent	Score	Scorers	Att	Poole AJ	Brady PJ	Saunders PB	Farmer KJ	Denyer PR	Coffill PT	Carlton DG	Heeley DM	Phillips SE	Bowen KB	Alexander JE	Sandy AVC	Gage WAJ	Saxby GP	Taylor Andy	Buchanan J	Mahoney AJ
R1/1	Sep 1	HARTLEPOOL UTD.	2-0	Denyer, Alexander	1480	1	2		4	3	6	7	8	9	10	11			5			
R1/2	16	Hartlepool United	1-2	Denyer	1975	1	2		4	3	6	7			10	9	11	8	5			
R2/1	Oct 6	BRISTOL ROVERS	2-1	Phillips, Sandy	4476	1	4			7	6	3	8	10			11	9	5	2		
R2/2	27	Bristol Rovers	3-1	Heeley, Saxby, Mahoney	3543	1	5					10	7	8	9		6	4	3	2		11
R3	Nov 11	Manchester City	1-3	Mahoney	21139	1	5	7				9	8		10		12	6	4	3	2	11

1982/83   15th in Division 4

League (Division 4)

#	Date	Opponent	Score	Scorers	Att
1	Aug 28	Wimbledon	1-1	Syrett	1703
2	Sep 4	YORK CITY	1-1	Massey	2257
3	7	CHESTER	1-1	Saxby	2171
4	11	Hartlepool United	1-2	Gage	947
5	19	BRISTOL CITY	7-1	Syrett 4, Massey 2, Denyer	2967
6	21	BURY	0-3		2792
7	24	Stockport County	1-0	Massey	1621
8	28	SWINDON TOWN	0-1		2706
9	Oct 2	ALDERSHOT	1-1	Massey	1706
10	10	TRANMERE ROVERS	1-0	Massey	2433
11	16	Torquay United	1-3	Wilson (og)	2015
12	19	COLCHESTER UNITED	2-1	Denyer, Burrows	1955
13	23	Hull City	0-4		4317
14	30	PETERBOROUGH UTD.	0-0		3284
15	Nov 2	Rochdale	0-2		1019
16	6	Scunthorpe United	1-5	Massey	3412
17	13	BLACKPOOL	2-1	Denyer 2	1893
18	28	DARLINGTON	3-3	Massey 2 (1p), Burrows	2599
19	Dec 18	Hereford United	1-1	Massey	1679
20	27	CREWE ALEXANDRA	4-0	Burrows, Massey, Saxby, Belfon	7494
21	28	Mansfield Town	0-2		2843
22	Jan 1	PORT VALE	2-2	Massey, Syrett	3618
23	3	Bury	1-1	Syrett	3398
24	15	WIMBLEDON	2-2	Brady, Saunders	2290
25	22	Bristol City	3-1	Phillips, Syrett, Massey	4874
26	29	HARTLEPOOL UNITED	3-1	Syrett 2, Massey	2181
27	Feb 1	Halifax Town	0-2		1927
28	5	STOCKPORT COUNTY	2-3	Patching, Burrows	1982
29	12	Aldershot	0-3		1761
30	19	Tranmere Rovers	1-2	Syrett	1466
31	26	TORQUAY UNITED	2-0	Saxby, Massey	1817
32	Mar 1	Colchester United	1-3	Massey	2501
33	5	HULL CITY	1-2	Gage	2879
34	12	Peterborough United	0-2		3778
35	15	York City	2-5	Massey (p), Tucker	2802
36	20	SCUNTHORPE UNITED	2-1	Gage, Sandy	2634
37	26	Blackpool	0-0		2054
38	Apr 2	MANSFIELD TOWN	1-2	Saunders	1988
39	4	Crewe Alexandra	0-1		2197
40	10	HALIFAX TOWN	3-1	Buchanan 2, one og	2208
41	16	Chester	1-2	Tucker	1267
42	19	ROCHDALE	1-1	Tucker (p)	1728
43	23	HEREFORD UNITED	2-1	Sandy, Massey	2071
44	30	Darlington	0-2		1042
45	May 8	Swindon Town	5-1	Massey 2, Denyer, Jeffrey, Syrett	3554
46	14	Port Vale	2-1	Coffill, Tucker (p)	6761

Appearances / Goals (squad totals)

	Freeman N	Brady PJ	Phillips IA	Gage WAJ	Burrows AM	Coffill PT	Denyer PR	Saunders PB	Heeley DM	Perrin SC	Syrett DK	Saxby GP	Massey S	Buchanan J	Kendall MI	Belfon F	Tucker WB	Buchanan D	Key RM	Sandy AVC	Muir M	Patching M	Gleasure PF	Beavon DG	Jeffrey WG
Apps	22	12	42	40	43	33	34	34	22	4	38	28	42	35	11	6	37	5	2	7	11	6	11	2	9
Goals		1	1	3	4	1	5	2			12	3	20	2		1	4			2		1			1

Two own goals

F.A. Cup

Rd	Date	Opponent	Score	Scorers	Att
R1	Nov 20	WIMBLEDON	2-2	Burrows, Denyer	2832
rep	23	Wimbledon	2-0	Coffill 2	2097
R2	Dec 11	Gillingham	1-1	Saxby	4054
rep	14	GILLINGHAM	3-2	Massey, Belfon 2	4290
R3	Jan 8	ASTON VILLA	0-1		14529

F.L. Cup (The Milk Cup)

Rd	Date	Opponent	Score	Scorers	Att
R1/1	Aug 31	Millwall	2-0	Syrett, Saxby	2947
R1/2	Sep 14	MILLWALL	2-2	Massey 2	2855
R2/1	Oct 5	BLACKPOOL	1-1	Massey	2490
R2/2	26	Blackpool	1-2	Syrett	3219

R2/2 a.e.t.

Football League Trophy

Rd	Date	Opponent	Score	Scorers	Att
R1	Aug 14	Norwich City	0-3		1801
R1	16	Mansfield Town	2-1	Syrett, Massey	1485
R1	21	Peterborough United	2-5	Denyer, Syrett	2192

1983/84 — 18th in Division 4

#	Date	Opponent	Score	Scorers	Att	Gleasure PF	Tucker WB	Forster MG	Gage WAJ	Lewis R	Burrows AM	O'Neill T	Jeffrey WG	Syrett DK	Belfon F	Hayes AWP	Austin TW	Mundee BG	Muir M	Brough NK	Martinez E	Mann AG	Brown SF
1	Aug 27	Chester City	1-1	Belfon	1707	1	2	3	4	5	6	7	8	9	10	11	12						
2	Sep 3	DARLINGTON	2-0	O'Neill, Austin	2009	1	2	3	4	5	6	7	8		10	11	9						
3	6	TRANMERE ROVERS	0-0		2326	1	2	3	4	5	6	8	7	12	10	11	9						
4	10	Blackpool	3-2	Gage, Belfon, Austin	3216	1	2	3	4	5	6	8	7		10	11	9	12					
5	18	STOCKPORT COUNTY	0-0		3189	1	3	2	4	5	6	8	7	9	10	12			11				
6	24	Rochdale	1-1	O'Neill	1402	1	3	2	4	5	6	8	7	9	10	11							
7	27	Halifax Town	2-2	Jeffrey, Syrett	1519	1	3	2		5	6	8	7	9	10		11	4					
8	Oct 1	CHESTERFIELD	1-1	Belfon	2733	1	3	2		5	6	8	7	4	10	11	9						
9	9	READING	2-2	Gage, Austin	3825	1	8	2	4	5	6		7			10	11	9	3				
10	15	Colchester United	2-2	Austin, O'Neill	1964	1	3	2	4	5	6	8	7		9	12	11	10					
11	18	TORQUAY UNITED	2-1	Hayes, Tucker	2573	1	3	2	4	5	6	8	7		10	11	9	12					
12	22	Crewe Alexandra	2-3	Jeffrey, Gage	2107	1	3	2	4	5	6	8	7		9	10	11						
13	29	YORK CITY	1-2	Belfon	2956	1	3	2	4	5	6	8	7		9	10	11	12					
14	Nov 1	Aldershot	0-1		1711	1	11	2	4	5	6	8	7		10	12	9	3					
15	5	SWINDON TOWN	2-0	Austin 2	2354	1		2	4	5	6	8	7		10	11	9	3		12			
16	12	Hereford United	0-0		3007	1		2	4	5	6	8	7		10	11	9	3					
17	26	Wrexham	1-0	Austin	1234	1		2	4	5	6	8	7		10	11	9	3	12				
18	Dec 3	BRISTOL CITY	1-0	Belfon	2823	1		2	4	5	6	8	7		10	11	9	3	12				
19	18	MANSFIELD TOWN	2-1	Austin, Lewis	2628	1		2	4	5	6	8	7		10	11	9	3					
20	26	Doncaster Rovers	0-1		3827	1		2	4	5	6	8	7		10	11	9	3	12				
21	27	PETERBOROUGH UTD.	2-1	Jeffrey, Hayes	6464	1		2	4	5	6	8	7		10	11	9	3	12				
22	31	Hartlepool United	0-2		1706	1	8	2	4	5	6		7		10	11	9	3		12			
23	Jan 2	BURY	1-0	O'Neill	2525	1		2	4	5	6	8	7		10	11	9	3					
24	14	CHESTER CITY	2-1	Lewis, Belfon	2198	1		2	4	5	6	8	7		10	11	9	3	12				
25	20	Stockport County	0-1		1846	1	2		4	5	6	8	7		10	11	9	3					
26	Feb 4	Chesterfield	1-2	Hayes	3250	1	10	2	4	5	6	8	7			11	9	3	12				
27	11	ROCHDALE	1-1	Hayes	2022	1	2		4	5	6	8	7		10	11	9	3	12				
28	14	ALDERSHOT	1-4	Belfon	1573	1	2	12	4		5	7	6		10	11	9	3	8				
29	18	York City	0-3		3941	1	9	2	4	5	6	8	7		10	11		3					
30	25	CREWE ALEXANDRA	2-0	Gage, Hayes	1696	1		2	4	5	6	8	7			10	9	3			11		
31	28	Darlington	3-5	Hayes 2, Martinez	1278	1	4	2		5	6	8	7		12	10	9	3			11		
32	Mar 3	Torquay United	1-2	Martinez	2042	1	4	2		5	6	8	7			10	9	3	12		11		
33	6	Swindon Town	0-0		2798	1		2	4	5	6	8	7			10	9	3			11		
34	10	HEREFORD UNITED	0-3		1592	1		2	4	5	6	8	7			10	9	3	12		11		
35	17	Reading	0-3		3695	1		2	4	5		8	7		12	10	9	3	6		11		
36	20	BLACKPOOL	1-5	O'Neill	1337	1		2	4	5	6	8	7		12	10	9	3			11		
37	24	COLCHESTER UNITED	3-1	Austin, Gage, Belfon	1499	1		2	4	3	5	8	7			10	6	9			11		
38	30	Tranmere Rovers	0-1		1829	1			4	5	6	8	7		2	10	9	3			11		
39	Apr 7	HALIFAX TOWN	1-1	Hayes	1356	1	12	3	4	2	5	8	7			10	6	9			11		
40	10	HARTLEPOOL UNITED	1-1	Hayes	1109	1		3	4	2	5	8	7			10	6	9	12		11		
41	14	Bristol City	1-4	O'Neill (p)	6655	1		3	4	2	5	8	7		12	6	10	9	11				
42	21	DONCASTER ROVERS	1-4	Lewis	1912	1	6		4	2	5	8	7		12	9	10	3	11				
43	24	Peterborough United	0-6		3481	1	11		2	4	6	5				7	10	3			9		
44	28	WREXHAM	3-3	Belfon, Gage, Austin	1189	1	11		3	4	6	5	8	12		10		9	2	7			
45	May 5	Bury	2-1	Mundee, Lewis	1096	1			3		2	5	8	4		10		9	6	7		11	
46	12	Mansfield Town	1-3	Jeffrey	2143	1			3		2	5		4		10	8	9	6	7		11	12
		Apps				46	26	42	40	45	45	43	45	6	40	43	43	36	15	5	12	2	1
		Goals					1		6	4		6	4	1	9	9	10	1			2		

F.A. Cup

	Date	Opponent	Score	Scorers	Att	Gleasure PF	Tucker WB	Forster MG	Gage WAJ	Lewis R	Burrows AM	O'Neill T	Jeffrey WG	Syrett DK	Belfon F	Hayes AWP	Austin TW	Mundee BG	Muir M	Brough NK	Martinez E	Mann AG	Brown SF
R1	Nov 19	WATERLOOVILLE	1-1	Gage	2627	1	3	2	4	5	6	8	7		10	11	9		12				
rep	23	Waterlooville	1-1	Austin	3500	1		2	4	5	6	8	7		10	11	9	3	12				
rep2	28	WATERLOOVILLE	2-0	O'Neill, Mundee	3534	1		2	4	5	6	8	7			11	9	3	10				
R2	Dec 10	TELFORD UNITED	1-1	Austin	3903	1		2	4	5	6	8	7		10	11	9	3	12				
rep	14	Telford United	2-3	Jeffrey, Muir	3320	1		2	4	5	6	8	7		10	11	9	3	12				

F.L. Cup (The Milk Cup)

	Date	Opponent	Score	Scorers	Att	Gleasure PF	Tucker WB	Forster MG	Gage WAJ	Lewis R	Burrows AM	O'Neill T	Jeffrey WG	Syrett DK	Belfon F	Hayes AWP	Austin TW	Mundee BG	Muir M	Brough NK	Martinez E	Mann AG	Brown SF
R1/1	Aug 29	Millwall	0-3		4158	1	2		4	5	6	8	7	9	10	11	12						
R1/2	Sep 13	MILLWALL	1-2	Gage	2313	1	3	2	4	5	6	8	7		10	11	9		12				

Played in R1/1: IA Phillips (at 3).

Associate Members' Cup

	Date	Opponent	Score	Scorers	Att	Gleasure PF	Tucker WB	Forster MG	Gage WAJ	Lewis R	Burrows AM	O'Neill T	Jeffrey WG	Syrett DK	Belfon F	Hayes AWP	Austin TW	Mundee BG	Muir M	Brough NK	Martinez E	Mann AG	Brown SF
R1	Feb 21	Walsall	1-3	Austin	3190	1		2	4	5	6	8	7		10	11	9	3					

1984/85   23rd in Division 4

#	Date		Opponent	Result	Scorers	Att	Gleasure PF	Cavener P	Mundee BG	Barnes MF	Gage WAJ	Brough NK	Train R	Shirtliff PR	Lee TC	Bancroft PA	Hayes AWP	Benjamin IT	Lewis R	Belfon F	Scott GS	Mann AG	Poole K	Perry MA	Hutchinson CM	Brown SF	Donald WR	Thompson KA	Bushell MJ
1	Aug	25	Exeter City	0-5		3166	1	2	3	4	5	6	7	8	9	10	11	12											
2	Sep	1	CHESTERFIELD	1-3	Hayes (p)	2554	1	2	3	5		12	8	7	10	9	11	6	4										
3		8	Darlington	0-4		1110	1	2	3		4		6	7	12	10	11	8	5	9									
4		15	HALIFAX TOWN	0-1		1437	1	9	3	5	4		6	8		10	11	7	2	12									
5		18	ROCHDALE	0-0		1653	1	2	3		4		6		9	10	11	8	5	7									
6		22	Chester City	0-1		1845	1	9	3		4		6		10	8	11	7	2	12	5								
7		29	COLCHESTER UNITED	1-3	Hayes	1595	1	9	3		4		6			8	11	7	2	12	5								
8	Oct	1	Port Vale	3-0	Belfon, Cavener, Hayes	3235	1	7	3		4		6	8		10	11		2	9	5								
9		6	SCUNTHORPE UNITED	0-2		1813	1	7	3		4		6	8		10	11		2	9	5	12							
10		13	Southend United	1-2	Belfon	2265	1	2			5		6	7		10	11	12	3	9		8							
11		16	Wrexham	3-0	Benjamin 2, Gage	1748	1	2		5	4		6	7			11	10	3	9		8							
12		20	ALDERSHOT	4-0	Benjamin 3, Gage	1864	1	2		5	4		6	7	9		11	10	3			8							
13		27	Blackpool	1-2	Mann	3577	1	2		5	4		6		9		11	10	3		7	8							
14	Nov	3	BURY	0-1		2240	1	2		5	4		6		9		11	10	3			8							
15		6	Crewe Alexandra	2-3	Belfon, Benjamin	2154	1	2		5	4		6	7			11	10	3	9	12	8							
16		10	SWINDON TOWN	4-0	Benjamin, Gage, Hayes 2 (1p)	2274		2		5	4		6	7			11	10	3	9		8	1						
17		23	Tranmere Rovers	2-1	Belfon, Benjamin	1899			3	5	4		6	12	7		11	10	2	9		8	1						
18	Dec	1	HEREFORD UNITED	0-3		2523			3	12	4		6	2		8	11	10	7	9			1						
19		15	Hartlepool United	0-0		2207	1		3	5	4		6	7			11	10	2	9	4								
20		22	Mansfield Town	0-2		1783	1	9	12	5	4		7	8			11	10	2		3	6							
21		26	PETERBOROUGH UTD.	0-3		4350	1	9	3	5	4		6	7			11	8	2					10					
22		29	TORQUAY UNITED	3-1	Cavener 3 (1p)	1496	1	9		5	4		6	7		8	11		2		3			10					
23	Jan	1	Stockport County	2-4	Benjamin, Lewis	1726	1	11		5	4		6	2	7			10	3			8		9					
24		5	EXETER CITY	5-2	Benjamin 3, Cavener 2 (1p)	1475	1	11	3		4		6	7		8		10	2	12	5			9					
25		12	Chesterfield	1-2	Cavener (p)	3759	1	11	3		4		6	7		8		10	2	9	12	5							
26	Feb	1	Colchester United	1-4	Mundee	2314	1	11	3		4		6	7				10	2	9	5	8							
27		16	Rochdale	0-3		1228	1	11	3	5	4		6	7				10	2	9		8							
28		23	Bury	1-3	Barnes	2938	1	9	3	5	4		6	8		12	11	10	2		7								
29		26	Halifax Town	0-1		1009	1	11	3		4		6	2		9		10		5	7	8			12				
30	Mar	2	BLACKPOOL	0-1		1860	1	9	3		4		7	2			11	10		5	12	8			6				
31		5	WREXHAM	0-4		1223	1	11	3	12	4		6	2	7			10		5	9	8							
32		9	Aldershot	0-0		1955	1			12	4		6	2	7			10	3	5	9	8			11				
33		17	SOUTHEND UNITED	1-2	Belfon	1702	1			12	4		6	2	7			10	3	5	9	8			11				
34		19	CHESTER CITY	0-2		942	1		3		4		6	2	7	11		10		5	9	8							
35		22	Scunthorpe United	1-2	Benjamin	2024	1		3		4		6	2		11		10		5	9	8				7			
36		30	CREWE ALEXANDRA	1-3	Benjamin	1264	1		3		4		6	2				10		5	12	7				11	8	9	
37	Apr	2	Peterborough United	0-0		2482	1		3		4		6	2				10		5		7				11	8	9	
38		9	STOCKPORT COUNTY	4-0	Benjamin, Brown, Donald, Mann	1426	1		3		4		6					10		5		7				11	8	9	2
39		13	Swindon Town	0-2		3642	1		3		4		6	2				10		5		7				11	8	9	
40		15	HARTLEPOOL UNITED	2-0	Donald, Mundee	1181	1		3		4		6	2				10		5		7				11	8	9	
41		17	PORT VALE	1-0	Gage	1311	1		3		4		6	2				10		5		7				11	8	9	
42		20	TRANMERE ROVERS	2-0	Benjamin, Brown	1581	1		3		4		6	8				10		5						9	7	11	
43		23	DARLINGTON	2-1	Benjamin, Thompson	1838	1		3		4		6	2				10		5		7				11	8	9	
44		27	Hereford United	1-1	Brown	3266	1				4		6	2		3		10		5		8				11	7	9	
45		30	MANSFIELD TOWN	1-0	Train	2350	1				4		6	2				10		5	12	7				11	8	9	
46	May	6	Torquay United	2-0	Benjamin, Lewis	1181	1		3		4		6	2				10		5	9	7				11	8		
			Apps				43	28	33	19	43	7	46	29	24	16	20	44	44	31	17	38	3	4	2	14	11	10	1
			Goals					7	2	1	4		1				5	18	2	5		2				3	2	1	

F.A. Cup

#	Date		Opponent	Result	Scorers	Att	Gleasure PF	Cavener P	Mundee BG	Barnes MF	Gage WAJ	Brough NK	Train R	Shirtliff PR	Lee TC	Bancroft PA	Hayes AWP	Benjamin IT	Lewis R	Belfon F	Scott GS	Mann AG
R1	Nov	17	V.S. RUGBY	2-2	Train, Lee	4815	1	2		5	4		6	8			11	10	3	9	12	7
rep		21	V.S. Rugby	1-0	Gage	3561	1		3	5	4		6	8			11	10	2	9		7
R2	Dec	8	Brentford	2-2	Train, Lee	4449	1		3	5	4		6	7			11	10	2	9		8
rep		17	BRENTFORD	0-2		3610	1		3	5	4		6	7			11	10	2	9	12	8

F.L. Cup (The Milk Cup)

#	Date		Opponent	Result	Scorers	Att	Gleasure PF	Cavener P	Mundee BG	Barnes MF	Gage WAJ	Brough NK	Train R	Shirtliff PR	Lee TC	Bancroft PA	Hayes AWP	Benjamin IT	Lewis R
R1/1	Aug	27	Crystal Palace	0-1		3752	1	2	3	5	4		7	8	9	10	11	6	
R1/2	Sep	4	CRYSTAL PALACE	0-0		2979	1	7	3	5	4		6		9	10	11	8	2

A.M.C. (Freight Rover Trophy)

#	Date		Opponent	Result	Scorers	Att	Gleasure PF	Cavener P	Mundee BG	Gage WAJ	Train R	Shirtliff PR	Lee TC	Bancroft PA	Benjamin IT	Lewis R	Belfon F	Scott GS	Mann AG	Hutchinson CM
R1/1	Jan	29	Port Vale	1-1	Benjamin	1385	1	11	3	4	6	7			10	2	9	5	8	
R1/2	Feb	5	PORT VALE	1-2	Belfon	1407	1		3	4	6	8		12	10	2	9	7	5	11

R1/2 a.e.t.

1985/86 8th in Division 4

#	Date		Opponent	Score	Scorers	Att	Gleasure PF	Curtis PAE	Mundee BG	Dawes IM	Lewis R	Hill RW	Mann AG	Benjamin IT	Reed G	Morley TW	Cavener P	Chard PJ	Schiavi MA	Donald WR	Nebbeling GM	McPherson KA	Friar JP	Sugrue PA	Hamill SP	Garner TJ
1	Aug	17	Burnley	2-3	Morley, Reed	4279	1	2	3	4	5	6	7	8	9	10	11									
2		26	Exeter City	2-1	Morley, Benjamin	2392	1	2	3		5	6	7	8	9	10	11	4								
3		31	MANSFIELD TOWN	1-0	Cavener (p)	2739	1	2	3	12	5	6	7	8	9	10	11	4								
4	Sep	6	Swindon Town	2-3	Hill, Cavener (p)	4102	1	2	3		5	6	7	8	9	10	11	4								
5		10	PRESTON NORTH END	6-0	Benjamin 2, Hill 3, Morley	2171	1	2	3			6	7	8	9	4	10	11	5	12						
6		14	CREWE ALEXANDRA	0-1		2654	1	2	3		5	7	8	9	4	10	11	6	12							
7		18	Hartlepool United	1-2	Benjamin	2200	1	2	3		5	6	12	8	9	10	11	4	7							
8		21	STOCKPORT COUNTY	3-1	Benjamin, Hill, Morley	1954	1	2	3		5	6	12	8	9	10	11	4	7							
9		28	Rochdale	2-3	Hill, Benjamin	1954	1	2	3		5	6	12	8	9	10	11	4	7							
10	Oct	1	Wrexham	1-2	Hill	2234	1	2	3		5	6	12	8	9	10	11	4	7							
11		5	HEREFORD UNITED	1-3	Chard	1998	1	2	3	12	5	6	7	8	9	10		4	11							
12		12	Peterborough United	5-0	Chard, Mann 2, Cavener, Benjamin	3901	1	2	3		5	6	11	8	9	10	12	4		7						
13		19	Torquay United	1-1	Chard	1186	1	2	3	6	5		11	8		10	9	4		7						
14		22	CHESTER CITY	2-2	Morley, Benjamin	2323	1	2	3	6	5		11	8		10	9	4	12	7						
15		26	Colchester United	2-0	Chard, Mann	2872	1		3		5	9	11	8	2	10	12	4		7	6					
16	Nov	2	SCUNTHORPE UNITED	2-2	Benjamin, Cavener (p)	2343	1		3		5	7	9	11	2	10	12	6		8		4				
17		5	TRANMERE ROVERS	2-2	Donald, Benjamin	2005	1		3		5	9		8	2	10	7			11	6					
18		9	Aldershot	0-1		1556	1		3		5	9	11	8	2	10	7		12			4	6			
19		23	HALIFAX TOWN	4-0	Chard (p), Benjamin, Morley, Schiavi	1514	1		3		5	9		8	2	10		4	11	7	6					
20		30	Cambridge United	5-2	Benjamin 3 (1p), Schiavi, Morley	2235	1		3		5	9	12	8	2	10		4	11	7	6					
21	Dec	6	Southend United	4-0	Schiavi, Curtis, Benjamin 2	2527	1	2	3		5	9	4	8		10			11	7	6					
22		14	PORT VALE	2-2	Morley, Chard	3259	1	2	3		5	9		8		10		4	11	7	6					
23		21	Preston North End	1-1	Hill	2570	1		3		5	11		8	2	10		4	9	7	6					
24	Jan	11	Mansfield Town	0-1		3836	1		3		5	11		8	2	10		4	9	7	6					
25		18	BURNLEY	2-0	Morley, Hill	3095	1		3		5	11		8	2	10		4	9	7	6					
26		25	Crewe Alexandra	1-0	Morley	1856	1		3		5		11	8	2	10		4	9				6			
27	Feb	1	SWINDON TOWN	0-1		4449	1		3		5		11	8	2	10		4	9	7			6			
28		5	Chester City	3-2	Hill, Schiavi, Morley	3332	1		3		5	11	7	8	2	10		4	9				6			
29		21	Stockport County	0-1		2011	1		3		5	11	7	8	2	10		4	9				6			
30	Mar	1	ROCHDALE	1-0	Benjamin	2146	1	2	3		5	9	11	8		10		4		7						
31		4	Wrexham	0-1		1433	1	2	3		5		11	8		10		4	9	7						
32		8	Hereford United	0-3		2478	1	2			5		11	8		10		4	9	7			6	3		
33		11	HARTLEPOOL UNITED	3-0	Benjamin 2, Hill	1815	1				5	11	7	8		10		2	9	4			6	3		
34		15	PETERBOROUGH UTD.	2-2	Morley, Hill	3332	1				4	11	7	8	12	10		2	9	6			5	3		
35		18	Scunthorpe United	0-1		1355	1	2			5		11	8		10		9	7	4			6	3	12	
36		22	COLCHESTER UNITED	1-0	Donald	2035	1				4	11		9	2	10		5	8	7			6	3	12	
37		29	Orient	1-0	Benjamin	2920	1				5	11		9	2	10		7	4				6	3		
38		31	SOUTHEND UNITED	0-0		3527	1				5	11	12	8	2	10		9	7	4			6	3		
39	Apr	4	Tranmere Rovers	3-1	Hamill, Benjamin, Sugrue	1103	1	2				11		8		5	10	9	4				6	3	12	7
40		8	EXETER CITY	2-2	Donald, Hill	2213	1	2				11		9		4	10	8	6				5	3	12	7
41		12	ALDERSHOT	2-3	Sugrue, Chard (p)	2049	1	2				11	12	8	5	10		3	9				6	4		7
42		15	ORIENT	2-3	Morley, Hill	1731	1				5	11		8	2	10		9	7	4			6	3	12	
43		18	Halifax Town	0-2		1105	1	2			5		11	8		10		9	7	4			6	3	12	
44		26	CAMBRIDGE UNITED	0-2		2100	1	2			5	11	7	8	12	10							6	3	9	
45		29	TORQUAY UNITED	5-1	Hill 3 (1p), Schiavi, Compton (og)	1167		2			5	11	7	8	9				10	4				3		1
46	May	3	Port Vale	0-0		3873		2			5	11	7	8	9				6	10	4			3		1
			Apps				44	27	31	5	43	41	32	46	36	43	17	41	34	32	11	20	14	8	3	2
			Goals					1				17	3	21	1	13	4	7	5	3				2	1	

One own goal

F.A. Cup

	Date		Opponent	Score	Scorers	Att	Gleasure PF	Curtis PAE	Mundee BG	Dawes IM	Lewis R	Hill RW	Mann AG	Benjamin IT	Reed G	Morley TW	Cavener P	Chard PJ	Schiavi MA	Donald WR
R1	Nov	16	Gillingham	0-3		3991	1	2	3		5	9		8	6	10	11	4		7

F.L. Cup (The Milk Cup)

	Date		Opponent	Score	Scorers	Att	Gleasure PF	Curtis PAE	Mundee BG	Dawes IM	Lewis R	Hill RW	Mann AG	Benjamin IT	Reed G	Morley TW	Cavener P	Chard PJ	Schiavi MA	Donald WR
R1/1	Aug	21	Peterborough Utd.	0-0		3117	1	2	3		5	6	7	8	9	10	11	4		
R1/2	Sep	3	PETERBOROUGH UNITED	2-0	Cavener, Chard	2446	1	2	3	9	5	6	7	8		10	11	4	12	
R2/1		25	Oxford United	1-2	Benjamin	5664	1	2	3		5	6		8	9	10	11	4		7
R2/2	Oct	8	OXFORD UNITED	0-2		5076	1	2	3		5	6	11	8	9	10	12	4		7

A.M.C. (Freight Rover Trophy)

	Date		Opponent	Score	Scorers	Att	Gleasure PF	Curtis PAE	Mundee BG	Dawes IM	Lewis R	Hill RW	Mann AG	Benjamin IT	Reed G	Morley TW	Cavener P	Chard PJ	Schiavi MA	Donald WR	Nebbeling GM	McPherson KA	Friar JP	Sugrue PA	Hamill SP	Garner TJ
R1	Jan	21	COLCHESTER UNITED	2-1	Benjamin, Schiavi	1958	1		3		4	8	12	9	2	10		6	11	7	5					
R1	Mar	13	Southend United	3-1	Hill, Benjamin 2	683	1				5	11	7	8	12	10		2	9	4			6	3		
QF		27	Bristol City	2-3	Hill, Hamill	3038	1				5	11		8	2	10		6	9	4				3	12	7

1986/87 Champions of Division 4: Promoted

No	Date	Opponent	Score	Scorers	Att	Gleasure PF	Reed G	Chard PJ	Donald WR	Coy RA	McPherson KA	McGoldrick EJP	Gilbert DJ	Benjamin IT	Morley TW	Hill RW	Schiavi MA	Mann AG	Wilcox R	Gernon FAJ	Millar J	McMenemy PC	Logan D	Henry CA	Bunce PE
1	Aug 23	Scunthorpe United	2-2	Hill, Reed	2302	1	2	3	4	5	6	7	9	8	10	11	12								
2	31	TORQUAY UNITED	1-0	Benjamin	3558	1	2	3	4	5	6	7	9	8	10	11									
3	Sep 6	Rochdale	2-1	Benjamin, Chard	1606	1	2	3	4	5	6	7	9	8	10	11									
4	14	PETERBOROUGH UTD.	2-1	Morley, Chard (p)	5517	1	2	3	4	5	6	7	9	8	10	11									
5	17	TRANMERE ROVERS	2-0	McGoldrick, Hill	3873	1	2	3	4	5	6	7	9	8	10	11									
6	20	Swansea City	1-2	Chard	6902	1	2	3	4	5	6	7	9	8	10	11		12							
7	27	WOLVERHAMPTON W.	2-1	Morley, Hill	5713	1	2	3	4	5	6	7	9	8	10	11			12						
8	30	Halifax Town	6-3	Donald, Hill 3 (1p), Benjamin, Chard	1034	1	2	3	4	5	6	7	9	8	10	11									
9	Oct 4	ALDERSHOT	4-2	Hill 2, Morley, Chard	4304	1	2	3	4	5	6	7	9	8	10	11									
10	17	Cambridge United	3-2	McPherson, Chard (p), Morley	6283	1	2	3	4		6	7	9	8	10	11			5						
11	22	BURNLEY	4-2	Morley 2, Benjamin, Hill	5718	1	2	3	4		6	7	9	8	10	11			5						
12	25	HEREFORD UNITED	3-2	Morley, Benjamin, Hill	5336	1	2	3	4		6	7	9	8	10	11			5						
13	27	Stockport County	3-0	Hill 2, Morley	1729	1	2	3	4		6	7	9	8	10	11			5						
14	Nov 1	Hartlepool United	3-3	Chard (p), Hill 2	1657	1	2	3	4		6		9	8	10	11		7	5						
15	4	Orient	1-0	Benjamin	3496	1	2	3	4	7	6		9	8	10	11			5						
16	8	PRESTON NORTH END	3-1	Benjamin, McPherson, Hill	6537	1	2	3	4		6	12	9	8	10	11			5		7				
17	28	Crewe Alexandra	5-0	Benjamin, McPherson, Hill 3	2331	1	2				6	7	9	8	10	11		4	5	3					
18	Dec 2	EXETER CITY	4-0	Morley, McGoldrick, Hill 2	6639	1	2				6	7	9	8	10	11		4	5	3					
19	13	WREXHAM	2-2	Wilcox, Benjamin	6070	1	2		4		6	7	9	8	10	11			5	3					
20	21	LINCOLN CITY	3-1	Gilbert (p), McGoldrick, Benjamin	7063	1		2	4		6	7	9	8	10	11			5	3					
21	26	Southend United	4-0	Hill 2, Benjamin, Donald	8541	1		2	4	12	6		9	8	10	11		7	5	3					
22	28	CARDIFF CITY	4-1	Benjamin, Gilbert (p), Morley, Hill	11138	1		2	4		6	7	9	8	10	11			5	3					
23	Jan 1	COLCHESTER UNITED	3-2	Benjamin, Gilbert, Morley (p)	8215	1		2	4		6	7	9	8	10	11			5	3					
24	3	Exeter City	1-1	Hill	4331	1		2	4		6	7	9	8	10	11			5	3					
25	24	ROCHDALE	5-0	McMenemy 2, Chard, McGoldrick, Hill	5484	1	2	9	4		6	7		8		11			5	3		10			
26	31	Peterborough United	1-0	Benjamin	7911	1	2	3	4		6	7	9	8		11			5			10			
27	Feb 6	Tranmere Rovers	1-1	Hill	2583	1	2	3	4		6	7	9	8		11			5			10			
28	14	SWANSEA CITY	0-1		8288	1	2	3	4		6	7	9	8		11			5			10			
29	21	Wolverhampton Wan.	1-1	Chard	9991	1	2	10	4		6	12	9	8		11		7	5				3		
30	24	Torquay United	1-0	Donald	1780	1	2	10	4		6		9	8		11		7	5				3		
31	27	HALIFAX TOWN	1-0	Benjamin	6351	1	2	10	4	12	6	7	9	8		11			5				3		
32	Mar 4	HARTLEPOOL UNITED	1-1	Benjamin	5470	1		10	4	2	6	7	9	8		11			5				3		
33	11	SCUNTHORPE UNITED	1-0	Morley	5352	1	2				6	7	9	8	10	11		4	5				3		
34	14	CAMBRIDGE UNITED	3-0	Gilbert 2 (2p), Hill	6201	1	2		4		6		9	8	10	11			5				3	7	
35	17	Burnley	1-2	Henry	2691	1	2		4		6		9	8	10	11			5				3	7	
36	21	STOCKPORT COUNTY	2-1	Chard 2	5466	1	2	11	4		6	12	9	8	10				5				3	7	
37	Apr 3	Preston North End	0-1		16556	1	2	3	4		6	7	9	8		11			5				10		
38	8	Hereford United	2-3	Chard, Morley	2758	1	2	9	4		6	12	7	8	10	11			5				3		
39	12	ORIENT	2-0	Gilbert, McPherson	6711	1	2		4		6	7	9	8	10	11			5				3		
40	17	Colchester United	1-3	Logan	3676	1	2	12	4		6	7	9	8	10	11			5				3		
41	20	SOUTHEND UNITED	2-1	Hill, McPherson	7383	1	2		4		6	7	9	8	10	11			5				3		
42	26	Lincoln City	1-3	McGoldrick	4012	1	12	2	4		6	7	9	8	10	11			5				3		
43	29	CREWE ALEXANDRA	2-1	Gilbert (p), Hill	8890	1	2		4	5	6	7	9	8	10	11							3		
44	May 4	Cardiff City	1-1	Benjamin	2682	1	2		4		6	7	9	8	10	11							3		
45	6	Aldershot	3-3	Gilbert, Benjamin, Morley	3377	1	2	3	4	5	6	7	9	8	10	11									12
46	9	Wrexham	3-1	Bunce, Morley 2	2709	1		3	4	2	6		9	8	10	11			5						7
		Apps				46	37	40	41	17	46	39	45	46	37	45	1	8	35	9	1	4	15	4	2
		Goals					1	12	3		5	5	8	18	16	29			1			2	1	1	1

F.A. Cup

Rnd	Date	Opponent	Score	Scorers	Att	Gleasure PF	Reed G	Chard PJ	Donald WR	Coy RA	McPherson KA	McGoldrick EJP	Gilbert DJ	Benjamin IT	Morley TW	Hill RW	Schiavi MA	Mann AG	Wilcox R	Gernon FAJ	Millar J	McMenemy PC	Logan D	Henry CA	Bunce PE
R1	Nov 16	PETERBOROUGH UTD.	3-0	McGoldrick, Gilbert, Benjamin	9114	1	2				6	7	9	8	10	11		4	5	3					
R2	Dec 5	Southend United	4-4	Donald, Benjamin, Hill 2	7412	1	2	10	4		6	7	9	8		11			5	3					
rep	10	SOUTHEND UNITED	3-2	Gilbert 2, Benjamin	10603	1	2	3	4		6	7	9	8	10	11					5				
R3	Jan 21	Newcastle United	1-2	Hill	23177	1	2	9	4		6	7		8	10	11			5		3				

Played in R2: Gorman (at 12)

F.L. Cup (Littlewoods Cup)

Rnd	Date	Opponent	Score	Scorers	Att	Gleasure PF	Reed G	Chard PJ	Donald WR	Coy RA	McPherson KA	McGoldrick EJP	Gilbert DJ	Benjamin IT	Morley TW	Hill RW	Schiavi MA	Mann AG	Wilcox R	Gernon FAJ	Millar J	McMenemy PC	Logan D	Henry CA	Bunce PE
R1/1	Aug 25	Gillingham	0-1		2945	1	2	3		5	6	7	8	9	10	11		4							
R1/2	Sep 3	GILLINGHAM	2-2	Coy, Benjamin	2727	1	2	3	4	5	6	7	9	8	10	11									

A.M.C. (Freight Rover Trophy)

Rnd	Date	Opponent	Score	Scorers	Att	Gleasure PF	Reed G	Chard PJ	Donald WR	Coy RA	McPherson KA	McGoldrick EJP	Gilbert DJ	Benjamin IT	Morley TW	Hill RW	Schiavi MA	Mann AG	Wilcox R	Gernon FAJ	Millar J	McMenemy PC	Logan D	Henry CA	Bunce PE
PR	Dec 16	Gillingham	0-1		2046	1			4	2	6	7	9	8	10	11		12	5	3					
PR	Jan 5	NOTTS COUNTY	3-0	Gilbert, Hill, Mann	3500	1	2				6	7	9	8	10	11		4	5				3		
R1	26	Fulham	2-3	Chard, Benjamin	2080	1	10	2	4		6	7	9	8		11		12	5				3		

Played v. Gillingham: Gorman (at 14). In R1, GP Donegal (at 14).

1987/88   6th in Division 3

#		Date	Opponent	Res	Scorers	Att	Gleasure PF	Reed G	Logan D	Donald WR	Wilcox R	McPherson KA	Longhurst DJ	Benjamin IT	Morley TW	Chard PJ	Gilbert DJ	Senior S	McGoldrick EJP	Mann AG	Bunce PE	Culpin P	Singleton MD	Donegal GP	Sandeman BR	O'Donnell C	Williams B	Adcock AC	Wilson PA	Slack TC	Carter LR
1	Aug	15	Chester City	5-0	Morley, Chard, Wilcox, Longhurst, Gilbert	3453	1	2	3	4	5	6	7	8	10	11	9	12	14												
2		29	Walsall	0-1		5993	1	2	3	4	5	6	7	8	10	11	9	12	14												
3		31	BRIGHTON & HOVE ALB	1-1	Morley	7934	1	2	3	4	5	6	7	8	10				11												
4	Sep	5	Doncaster Rovers	2-0	Morley, Longhurst	1869	1	2	3	4	5	6	7	8	10		9		11												
5		9	BRENTFORD	2-1	Gilbert, Longhurst	5748	1	2	3	4	5	6	7	8	10	12	9		11												
6		12	NOTTS COUNTY	0-1		6023	1	2	3		5	6		8	10	4	9		11	7	12										
7		15	Preston North End	0-0		5179	1	2	3		5	6		8	10	4	9	7	11												
8		19	Bristol Rovers	2-0	Morley, Chard	3668	1	2	3		5	6		8	10	4	9		11		7										
9		26	PORT VALE	1-0	Chard	5072	1	2	3	12	5	6		8	10	4	9		11		7										
10		29	Southend United	1-1	Morley	3506	1	2	3		5	6		8	10	4	9	12	11		7										
11	Oct	3	BRISTOL CITY	3-0	Chard 2, Bunce	6234	1	2	3		5	6		8	10	4	9		11		7										
12		11	Rotherham United	2-2	Culpin, Morley	5173	1	2	3	4	5	6		12	10	11	9		7			8									
13		17	CHESTERFIELD	4-0	Morley, Culpin 2, Benjamin	5073	1	2	3	4	5	6		11	10		9		7			8									
14		20	Mansfield Town	1-3	Culpin	3646	1	2	3	4	5	6			10		9		7			8									
15		24	GRIMSBY TOWN	2-1	Gilbert (p), Culpin	5388	1	2	3	4	5	6	12		10	11	9		7			8									
16		31	Aldershot	4-4	Culpin, Roberts (og), Morley, Longhurst	3358	1	2		4	5	6	11		10	3	9		7			8									
17	Nov	4	YORK CITY	0-0		4950	1	2		4	5	6	11		10	3	9		7		12	8									
18		7	Fulham	0-0		6733	1	2	3	4	5	6	11		10		9		12				8	7							
19		21	GILLINGHAM	2-1	Morley, Wilcox	5151	1	2	12	4	5	6	11		10	3			9					7							
20		28	Blackpool	1-3	Longhurst	3593	1	2	12	4	5	6	11		10	3			9		14			7							
21	Dec	12	SUNDERLAND	0-2		7279	1	2	3	4	5	6	14		10	11			9		12		8	7							
22		19	Wigan Athletic	2-2	Donald, Singleton	2692	1		3	4	5	6	11		10	2			9				8	7							
23		26	Port Vale	1-1	Singleton	4446	1		3	4	5	6	11		10	2			9		12		8	7							
24		28	BURY	0-0		6067	1		3	4	5	6	11		10	2			9		8		7	12							
25	Jan	1	WALSALL	2-2	Chard, Donegal	6034	1	2	3	4	5	6	11		10	2	9		8		14		12	7							
26		2	Notts County	1-3	Morley (p)	8153	1	12	3	4	5	6	11		10	2	9		8					7							
27		9	Brentford	1-0	Chard	6025	1	2	3	4	5	6	11		10		9		8								12				
28		16	BRISTOL ROVERS	2-1	Gilbert, Donald	4473	1			4	5	6	11		10		9		8								12	2	3		
29		27	Preston North End	0-1		5052	1		3	4	5	6	11			2	9		8				7				12	10		
30		30	WIGAN ATHLETIC	1-1	Adcock	4825	1		3	4	5	6				2	9		8				7				11	10		
31	Feb	6	DONCASTER ROVERS	1-0	Adcock	4381	1	2	3	4	5	6					9		8				7				11	10		
32		13	Bury	0-0		2172	1	2	3	4	5						9		12			8	7				11	10	6	
33		20	CHESTER CITY	2-0	Adcock, Slack	4285	1	2	3	4	5						9		12			8	7				11	10	6	
34		27	Bristol City	2-2	Adcock, Chard	8578	1		3	4	5					2	9		12			8	7				11	10	6	
35	Mar	2	SOUTHEND UNITED	4-0	McGoldrick, Longhurst, Wilcox, Adcock	4249	1		3	4	5					2	9		11			8					7	10	6	
36		5	Chesterfield	2-0	McGoldrick, Gilbert	2400	1		3	4	5					2	9		11			8					7	10	6	
37		11	ROTHERHAM UNITED	0-0		5432	1		3	4	5					2	9		11			8					7	10	6	
38		19	ALDERSHOT	1-1	Adcock	4322	1	2	3		5						9	4	11		14	8				12	7	10	6	
39		26	Grimsby Town	2-2	Singleton, Culpin	3406	1	12	3	4	5		11				9		2		14	8	7					10	6	
40	Apr	2	FULHAM	3-2	Adcock, Stannard (og), Culpin	6211	1	12	3	4	5		11				9		2			8					7	10	6	
41		4	Gillingham	2-1	Culpin, Adcock	4131	1		3	4	5		11				9		2		12	8					7	10	6	
42		10	MANSFIELD TOWN	2-0	Wilcox, Kenworthy (og)	6917	1		3	4	5		11				9		2			8					7	10	6	
43		15	Brighton & Hove Albion	0-3		14455	1	12	3	4	5		11				9		2			8				14	7	10	6	
44		23	York City	2-2	Culpin, Wilson	2048	1		3	4	5		11				9		2			8				12	7	10	6	14
45		30	BLACKPOOL	3-3	Longhurst, Gilbert, Adcock	5730	1		3	4	5		11				9		2			8				12	7	10	6	
46	May	2	Sunderland	1-3	Adcock	29454	1		3	4	5		11				9		2			8					7	10	6	
			Apps				46	31	26	40	46	32	35	14	27	34	41	4	46	1	10	20	29	11	2	1	4	18	15	13	1
			Goals							2	4		7	1	10	8	6		2		1	10	3	1				10	1	1	

Three own goals

F.A. Cup

		Date	Opponent	Res	Scorers	Att	Gleasure PF	Reed G	Logan D	Donald WR	Wilcox R	McPherson KA	Longhurst DJ	Benjamin IT	Morley TW	Chard PJ	Gilbert DJ	Senior S	McGoldrick EJP	Bunce PE	Culpin P	Singleton MD	Donegal GP
R1	Nov	14	NEWPORT COUNTY	2-1	Morley, Chard	4581	1	2		4	5	6	11		10	3	9		12			8	7
R2	Dec	5	BRIGHTON & HOVE ALB.	1-2	Morley	6444	1	2	12	4	5	6	11		10	3	9		8	14			7

F.L. Cup (Littlewoods Cup)

		Date	Opponent	Res	Scorers	Att	Gleasure PF	Reed G	Logan D	Donald WR	Wilcox R	McPherson KA	Longhurst DJ	Benjamin IT	Morley TW	Chard PJ	Gilbert DJ	Senior S	McGoldrick EJP	Culpin P	O'Donnell C
R1/1	Aug	17	Port Vale	1-0	Longhurst	3398	1	2		4	5	6	7	8	10	11	9	3			
R1/2	Sep	2	PORT VALE	4-0	McPherson, Morley 3	4748	1	2	3	4	5	6	7	8	10		9		11		
R2/1		22	Ipswich Town	1-1	Gilbert	5645	1	2	3		5	6	7	8	10	4	9		11	12	
R2/2	Oct	7	IPSWICH TOWN	2-4	Morley, Donegal		1	2	3		5	6		8	10	4	9	12	11	7	14

R2/2 a.e.t.   Played in R2/1: C Scott (at 14).

A.M.C. (Sherpa Van Trophy)

		Date	Opponent	Res	Scorers	Att	Gleasure PF	Reed G	Logan D	Donald WR	Wilcox R	McPherson KA	Longhurst DJ	Benjamin IT	Morley TW	Chard PJ	Gilbert DJ	McGoldrick EJP	Culpin P	Donegal GP
PR	Oct	13	NOTTS COUNTY	0-1		2351	1	2	3	4	5	6		7	10			8	11	9
PR		28	BRENTFORD	1-0	Longhurst	3076	1	2		4	5	6	11		10	3	9	7	8	

1988/89   20th in Division 3

No	Date		Opponent	Score	Scorers	Att	Gleasure PF	Reed G	Thomas DR	Donald WR	McGoldrick EJP	McPherson KA	Singleton MD	Longhurst DJ	Gilbert DJ	Adcock AC	Donegal GP	Wilson PA	Sandeman BR	Flexney P	Culpin P	Garwood J	Preece AP	Cobb GE	Johnson I	Blair A	Berry SA	Williams Wayne	Anderson DE	Bodley MJ	Quow TS	Collins D	Wilcox R	Craig AH
1	Aug	27	Mansfield Town	1-1	Donegal	4042	1	2	3	4	5	6	7	8	9	10	11	14	12															
2	Sep	3	BRENTFORD	1-0	Wilson	4488	1	5	3	4	2		7		9	10	11	8			6	12												
3		10	Notts County	1-0	Culpin	6340	1	6	3	4	2		7		9	10				5	8	11												
4		17	CHESTERFIELD	3-0	Adcock 3	4520	1	6	3	4	2		7		9	10				5	8	11												
5		20	Sheffield United	0-4		11904	1	6	3	4	2		7		9	10	14	12		5	8	11												
6		24	BRISTOL ROVERS	1-2	Adcock	3886	1	6	3	4	2		7		9	10	12			5	8	11												
7	Oct	1	ALDERSHOT	6-0	Culpin 3, Gilbert, Adcock	3477	1		3	4	2	6	7		9	10		12		5	8	11												
8		4	Blackpool	1-3	Gilbert	3034	1		3	4	2	6	7	12	9	10	11	14		5	8													
9		8	HUDDERSFIELD T	1-3	Singleton	3975	1		3	4	2	6	7		9	10	8	11	14	5	12													
10		15	Swansea City	0-1		4583	1	5	3	4	2	6	7		9	10	8	12	14						11									
11		22	BRISTOL CITY	1-3	McGoldrick	3668	1	8	3	4	2	6	7		9	10	14	11		5			12											
12		25	Fulham	2-3	Sandeman, Adcock	4644	1		3	4	2	6			9	10	11	7			8			5										
13		29	READING	1-3	McGoldrick	4355	1		3	4	2	6			9	10			12	5	8						7	11						
14	Nov	5	Wigan Athletic	3-1	Berry, Adcock, Culpin	2472	1		3	4	2	6			9	10	11			5	8						12	7						
15		8	PORT VALE	1-3	Culpin	3796	1		3	4		6			9	10	11	7			8		5				2							
16		12	Cardiff City	0-1		3342	1		3	4	2	6			9	10	11	14			8						12	7	5					
17		26	Bolton Wanderers	1-2	Culpin	4446	1		3	4	11	6			9	10				5	8						7	2						
18	Dec	4	WOLVERHAMPTON W.	3-1	Williams, Thomas, Adcock	6907	1		3	4	5	6			9	10	11				8						7	2						
19		18	GILLINGHAM	1-2	Gilbert	3829	1		3	4	5	6			9	10	12	11	7		8		14				2							
20		26	Southend United	1-2	Adcock	5034	1		3		5	6			9	10	12	7	4		8						2	11						
21		31	Chester City	1-2	Culpin	2741	1		3	4	5	6			9	10	7				8						2	11						
22	Jan	2	PRESTON NORTH END	1-0	Thomas	4219	1		3	4	5	6			9	10	7				8						2	11						
23		7	BURY	2-0	Culpin, Sandeman	3463	1		3	4	5	6			9	10	7	12			8						2							
24		14	Brentford	0-2		6043	1		3	4		6			9	10	7	12			8						11	2			5	14		
25		21	NOTTS COUNTY	1-3	Adcock	3704	1			4		6			9	10		3			8						11	2	12		5	7		
26		28	Chesterfield	1-1	Craig	3920	1			4		6				10		3	12		8						11	2			5	9		7
27	Feb	4	Aldershot	1-5	Wignall (og)	2244	1			4		6			8	10		3	12								11	2			5	9	14	7
28		11	BLACKPOOL	4-2	Gilbert 2 (1p), Adcock, Berry	3303	1					6			9	10		3	4		8						11	2		7	5			
29		18	Huddersfield Town	2-1	Gilbert (p), Culpin	5802	1					6			9	10		3	4		8						11	2		7	5			
30		25	SWANSEA CITY	1-0	Thomas	3900	1			4		6			9	10		3			8						11	2		7	5			
31		28	FULHAM	2-1	Gilbert, Thomas	3948	1			4		6			9	10		3									11	2		7	5		8	
32	Mar	4	Bristol City	1-3	Walsh (og)	7197	1			4		6			9	10	14	3	12								11	2		7	5		8	
33		11	WIGAN ATHLETIC	1-1	Adcock	3443	1			4		6			9	10		3	12								11	2		7			8	
34		15	Reading	1-1	McPherson	3746	1			4	5	6			9	10		3			8						11	2		7				
35		18	MANSFIELD TOWN	2-1	Thomas, Donald	2821	1			4	5	6			9	10		3			8						11	2		7			12	
36		25	Preston North End	2-3	Thomas, Adcock	9138	1			4	5	6				10		3			8						11	2		7			9	
37		27	SOUTHEND UNITED	2-2	Adcock, Culpin	3707	1			4	5	6				10	14	3	12		8						11	2		7			9	
38	Apr	1	Gillingham	0-1		3447	1			4	5	6				10	12	3	7		8						11	2			14		9	
39		4	Bury	1-0	Quow	1965	1			4	5	6				10		3			8						11	2			7		9	
40		8	CHESTER CITY	0-2		2845	1			4	5	6				10		3			8						11	2			7	12	9	
41		15	SHEFFIELD UNITED	1-2	McPherson	5030	1			4	5	6				10	14	3	12		8						11	2		7			9	
42		22	Bristol Rovers	1-1	Adcock	5568	1			4	5	6				10	11		12		8						8	2		7			9	
43		29	CARDIFF CITY	3-0	Thomas 2, Berry	3194	1			4	5	6				10	11				8						7	2		3			9	
44	May	1	Port Vale	2-1	Culpin, Thomas	6604	1			4	5	6				10	11				8						7	2		3			9	
45		6	Wolverhampton Wan.	2-3	Wilcox, Donegal	15259	1			4	5	6				10	12	11	14		8						7	2		3			9	
46		13	BOLTON WANDERERS	2-3	Adcock, Culpin	3655	1			4	5	6				10		11			8						7	2		3			9	
					Apps		46	8	43	37	22	41	11	2	34	46	9	39	22	12	39	6	1	1	3	3	34	26	5	20	18	8	11	2
					Goals				9	1	2	2	1		7	17	2	1	2		13						3	1			1		1	1

Two own goals

F.A. Cup

	Date		Opponent	Score	Scorer	Att	Gle		Tho	Don	McG	McP			Gil	Adc	Dnl	Wil	San	Fle	Cul						Ber							
R1	Nov	19	Swansea City	1-3	Berry	4521	1		3	12	2	6			9	10	14	4	7	5	8						11							

F.L. Cup (Littlewoods Cup)

	Date		Opponent	Score	Scorers	Att	Gle	Ree	Tho	Don	McG	McP	Sin		Gil	Adc	Dnl	Wil		Fle	Cul	Gar												
R1/1	Aug	30	Colchester Utd.	0-0		1678	1	5	3	4	2		7		9	10	11				6	8												
R1/2	Sep	6	COLCHESTER UTD.	5-0	Singleton, Gilbert(p), Adcock 2, Culpin	3953	1	5	3	4	2		7		9	10		11			6	8												
R2/1		27	CHARLTON ATHLETIC	1-1	Culpin	5290	1	6	3	4	2		7		9	10				5	8	11												
R2/2	Oct	11	Charlton Athletic	1-2	Wilson	2782	1		3	4	2	6	7		9	10		11	8	5			12											

Played in R1/2: TC Slack (12)

A.M.C. (Sherpa Van Trophy)

	Date		Opponent	Score	Scorers	Att	Gle		Tho	Don	McG	McP			Gil	Adc	Dnl			Fle	Cul		Pre	Cob			Ber	Wms		Bod	Quo	Col		
PR	Nov	22	CAMBRIDGE UNITED	1-1	McGoldrick	1806	1		3	4	7	6			9	10				5	8						11	2						
PR	Dec	21	Peterborough Utd.	2-0	Adcock, Culpin	1754	1		3	4	5	6			9	10	12				8			2			7	11						
R1	Jan	17	SOUTHEND UNITED	2-1	Berry, 1 og	2539	1			4		6			9	10	12	3	7		8						11	2			5			
R2	Feb	21	Wolverhampton Wand.	1-3	1 og	16815	1		7			6			9	10		3	4		8		14				11	2			5		12	

R1 and R2 games a.e.t.

1989/90   22nd in Division 3: Relegated

#		Date	Opponent	Score	Scorers	Att	Gleasure PF	Williams Wayne	Wilson PA	Thomas DR	Wilcox R	McPherson KA	Quow TS	Culpin P	Donald WR	Adcock AC	Berry SA	Sandeman BR	Collins D	Scope DF	Donegal GP	Brown SF	Barnes DO	Gernon FAJ	Chard PJ	Singleton MD	McPhillips T	Terry SG	Leburn CW	Thorpe A	Johnson DD	Bell M
1	Aug	19	Walsall	0-1		5020	1	2	3	4	5	6	7	8	9	10	11	12	14													
2		26	Swansea City	1-1	Collins	3637	1		3	4	5	6	7		9	10	11	2	8													
3	Sep	2	BRISTOL CITY	2-0	Thomas, Adcock (p)	4088	1		3	4	5	6	7		9	10	11	2	8													
4		9	Wigan Athletic	0-0		2289	1		3	4	5	6	7	12	9	10	11	2	8													
5		16	SHREWSBURY TOWN	2-1	Collins, Adcock (p)	3084	1	12	3	4	5	6	7		9	10	11	2	8													
6		23	Crewe Alexandra	1-2	Collins	3165	1		3	4	5	6	7	12		10	11	2	8	9												
7		26	Cardiff City	3-2	Quow, Adcock, Thomas	2801	1	9	3	4	5	6	7			10	11	2	8		12											
8		30	BURY	0-1		3486	1	2	3	4	5	6	7	12	14	10	11		8	9												
9	Oct	7	PRESTON NORTH END	1-2	Collins	3039	1	2	3	4	5	6	7		9		11		8			10	12									
10		14	Birmingham City	0-4		8731	1		3	4	5	6	2		9		7		8			12	11	10								
11		17	BLACKPOOL	4-2	Donald, Wilcox, Barnes, Collins	3098	1		3	4	5	6	2			8	7	12	9			11	10									
12		21	Bristol Rovers	2-4	Brown, Barnes (p)	4920	1			4	5	6	2			8	7	12	9			11	10	3								
13		28	NOTTS COUNTY	0-0		3734	1			4	5	6	8				7		9			11	10	3	2							
14		31	Fulham	1-1	Barnes (p)	3518	1			4	5	6	8	12			7	14	9			11	10	3	2							
15	Nov	4	ROTHERHAM UNITED	1-2	Barnes	3598	1			4	5	6	8		11		7	14	9				10	3	2	12						
16		11	Huddersfield Town	2-2	Gernon, Barnes	4973	1			4	5	6	12		11		7	8	9				10	3	2	14						
17		25	BRENTFORD	0-2		3165	1			4	5	6	11		14		7	8	9				10	3	2		12					
18	Dec	2	Bolton Wanderers	3-0	Barnes 2, Donald	5501	1		3	4	5	6			8		7		9			11	10		2	12						
19		17	READING	2-1	Barnes, Collins	3025	1			4	5	6	12				7		9			11	10	3	2	8						
20		26	Leyton Orient	1-1	Barnes	4784	1			4	5	6	12				7		9			11	10	3	2	8						
21		30	Mansfield Town	2-1	Berry, Barnes	3210	1			4	5	6	12				7		9			11	10	3	2	8						
22	Jan	1	CHESTER CITY	1-0	Berry	3823	1			4	5	6	8				7		9			11	10	3	2							
23		13	SWANSEA CITY	1-1	Barnes	3944	1			4	5	6	8				7		9			11	10	3	2	12						
24	Feb	17	BOLTON WANDERERS	0-2		3432	1		3	4	5	6	8				7	2	9	12			10					11				
25		20	WALSALL	1-1	Collins	2617	1		3	4	5	6	8				7	2	9			11	10									
26		25	Brentford	2-3	Thomas, Collins	6391	1		3	4	5	6	8				7	2	9			11	10									
27	Mar	3	TRANMERE ROVERS	0-4		3147	1		3		5	6	8		14		7	4	9			12	10		2			11				
28		6	Bury	0-1		2327	1	12		4	5	6	8				7	11	9				10	3	2							
29		10	CARDIFF CITY	1-1	Barnes (p)	2574	1		3	4	5	6	8		11		7		9			12	10		2							
30		13	WIGAN ATHLETIC	1-1	Chard	2172	1		3	9	5	6	8				7	11					10		2				4			
31		17	Preston North End	0-0		5686	1		3	9	5	6	8				7	2					10			11			4			
32		20	BIRMINGHAM CITY	2-2	Terry, Wilcox	4346	1		3	9	5	6					7	2				12	10			11		8	4			
33		24	Blackpool	0-1		3296	1				5	6	8				7	2				12	10		3			4	9	11		
34		27	Bristol City	1-3	Barnes	11965	1		3		5	6			12		7		8				10		2			4	9	11		
35		31	BRISTOL ROVERS	1-2	Thorpe	3774	1		3		5						7	12	8				10		2			4	9	11		
36	Apr	3	Shrewsbury Town	0-2		2314	1	2	3		5						6			14			10					4	9	11	12	
37		7	FULHAM	2-2	Sandeman, Thorpe	2882	1	2	3		5						7	6	8			9	10					4		11		
38		10	Notts County	2-3	Terry, Barnes	5396	1	2			5	6	12				7	9				3	10			8		4		11		
39		14	Chester City	1-0	Barnes (p)	2242	1	2	3		5	6	8				7						10			9		4		11		
40		16	LEYTON ORIENT	0-1		3215	1	2	3		5	6	8				7	14	12				10			9		4		11		
41		21	Reading	2-3	Barnes (p), McPherson	3140	1				5	6	8				7	12	11				10		2			4	9		3	14
42		24	MANSFIELD TOWN	1-2	Wilcox	2119	1	2			5	6			9								10			8		4		11	3	7
43		28	HUDDERSFIELD T	1-0	Barnes	2388	1	2			5	6											10			8		4	9	11	3	7
44		30	CREWE ALEXANDRA	3-1	Barnes (p), Chard, Thorpe	2622	1	2			5	6											10		9			4		11	3	7
45	May	2	Tranmere Rovers	0-0		5363	1	2			5	6					12		14				10			8		4	9	11	3	7
46		5	Rotherham United	0-2		3420	1	2			5	6								12		14	10		8			4	9	11	3	7
			Apps				46	15	27	31	46	43	30	4	27	8	41	29	35	7	1	21	37	12	29	10	1	17	9	13	7	6
			Goals							3	3	1	1		2	3	2	1	8			1	18	1	2			2		3		

F.A. Cup

	Date	Opponent	Score	Scorers	Att	Gleasure PF	Williams Wayne	Wilson PA	Thomas DR	Wilcox R	McPherson KA	Quow TS	Culpin P	Donald WR	Adcock AC	Berry SA	Sandeman BR	Collins D	Scope DF	Donegal GP	Brown SF	Barnes DO	Gernon FAJ	Chard PJ	Singleton MD	McPhillips T	Terry SG	Leburn CW	Thorpe A	Johnson DD	Bell M
R1	Nov 18	Kettering Town	1-0	Thomas	6100	1			4	5	6	8				7		9			11	10	3	2							
R2	Dec 9	AYLESBURY UNITED	0-0		6098	1		3	4	5	6			8		7		9			11	10		2							
rep	13	Aylesbury United	1-0	Barnes	4895	1	11		4	5	6			8		7	9					10	3	2	12	14					
R3	Jan 6	COVENTRY CITY	1-0	Berry	14529	1			4	5	6	8				7		9			11	10	3	2							
R4	27	Rochdale	0-3		9048	1		3	4	5	6	8		14		7		9			11	10		2	12						

F.L. Cup (Littlewoods Cup)

	Date	Opponent	Score	Scorers	Att	Gleasure PF	Williams Wayne	Wilson PA	Thomas DR	Wilcox R	McPherson KA	Quow TS	Culpin P	Donald WR	Adcock AC	Berry SA	Sandeman BR	Collins D
R1/1	Aug 22	Mansfield Town	1-1	Adcock	3095	1	2	3	4	5	6	7	8	9	10	11	12	14
R1/2	Sep 5	MANSFIELD TOWN	0-2		3963	1	12	3	4	5	6	7	14	9	10	11	2	8

A.M.C. (Leyland DAF Cup)

	Date	Opponent	Score	Scorers	Att	Gleasure PF	Williams Wayne	Wilson PA	Thomas DR	Wilcox R	McPherson KA	Quow TS	Culpin P	Donald WR	Adcock AC	Berry SA	Sandeman BR	Collins D	Scope DF	Donegal GP	Brown SF	Barnes DO	Gernon FAJ	Chard PJ	Singleton MD	McPhillips T
PR	Nov 7	Colchester Utd.	3-0	Collins, Barnes, Chard	1780	1			4	5	6					7	9	12	11			10	3	2	8	
PR	28	MAIDSTONE UNITED	2-4	Wilcox, Gernon	1665	1	2	11	4	5	6					7	8	12				10	3	9		14
R1	Jan 17	Southend United	1-2	Collins	1346	1	12		4	5	6			11		7	2	9				10	3		8	

1990/91   10th in Division 4

League (Division 4)

No.	Date	Opponent	Score	Scorers	Att.	Adcock AC	Angus TN	Beavon MS	Berry SA	Barnes DO	Brown SF	Bell M	Beresford M	Chard PJ	Collins D	Campbell GR	Evans GJ	Fee GP	Gleasure PF	Gernon FAJ	Johnson DD	Hitchcock KJ	Scully PJ	Sandeman BR	Scope DF	Terry SG	Thorpe A	Wilson PA	Wilkin K	Williams Wayne	Quow TS	Wood D
1	Aug 25	Hereford United	2-1	Wilkin, Barnes	3187		7	9	10	11				2					1				5			4	12	3	8			6
2	Sep 1	Maidstone United	3-1	Wilson, Wood, Thorpe	2049		7	9	10	11				2					1				5			4	12	3	8			6
3	8	BLACKPOOL	1-0	Barnes	4544		6	7	9	10	11			2					1				5	12		4	14	3	8			
4	14	Aldershot	3-3	Wilkin, Barnes, Beavon	2741		6	7	9	10	11			2					1				5	14		4	12	3	8			
5	18	Scarborough	1-1	Barnes (p)	1525		6	7	9	10	11			2					1				5	14		4	12	3	8			
6	22	PETERBOROUGH UTD.	1-2	Barnes	5549		6	7	9	10	11	14		2					1				5			4	12	3	8			
7	29	HALIFAX TOWN	1-0	Collins	2977		6	7	12	10	11	9	1	2	14								5			4		3	8			
8	Oct 2	Burnley	0-3		6273		6	7	11	10		9	1	2		8					14		5			4		3	12			
9	6	Chesterfield	0-0		3826		6	7	11	10	14	9	1	2		8							5			4		3	12			
10	13	STOCKPORT COUNTY	1-0	Chard	3927		6	7	9	10	11	12	1	2		8	14						5			4						
11	19	WALSALL	5-0	Barnes, Terry, Campbell 2, Chard	4055		6	7		10	11	9	1	2		8							5			4	12	3				
12	23	Darlington	1-1	Barnes	4882		6	7	12	10		9	1	2		8					11		5			4	14	3				
13	27	Lincoln City	1-3	Terry	3352		6		7	10		9	1	2		8					11		5			4	12	3				
14	Nov 3	HARTLEPOOL UNITED	3-2	Wilson 2, Beavon	3342		6	7	12	10		9	1	2	14	8					11					4		3		5		
15	9	WREXHAM	1-0	Barnes	3855		7	14	10	11			1	2	12	8							5			4	9	3		6		
16	24	York City	1-0	Barnes	2202		6	7		10	11		1	2		8					12		5			4	9	3				
17	Dec 1	ROCHDALE	3-2	Chard 2, Beavon (p)	3809		6	7		10	11		1	2	12	8		5			14					4	9	3				
18	15	Carlisle United	1-4	Campbell	2872		6	7	9		11		1	2		8				5	12				14	4	10	3				
19	21	CARDIFF CITY	0-0		3033		6	7	10		11	9	1	2		8				5					12	4		3				
20	29	Gillingham	0-0		4969		6	7			11	12		2		8	9			5		1				4						
21	Jan 1	DONCASTER ROVERS	0-0		5270		6	7	14	10	11	8		2			9			5	3	1			12	4						
22	12	MAIDSTONE UNITED	2-0	Adcock, Barnes	3710	9	6	7		10	11	8		2						5	3	1			12	4						
23	19	HEREFORD UNITED	3-0	Chard, Beavon (p), Angus	3577	9	6	7		10	11	8		2								1			5	4	12	3				
24	26	ALDERSHOT	2-1	Adcock, Beavon (p)	3800	9	6	7		10	11	12		2								1			5	4	8	3				
25	Feb 1	SCARBOROUGH	0-2		4058	9	6	7	12	10	11	8		2								1		14	5	4		3				
26	5	Peterborough United	0-1		5952	9	6	7		10	11	8		2								1		12		4	14	3		5		
27	15	YORK CITY	2-1	Angus, Barnes	2685	9	6	7		10	11	8		2								1				4	12	3		5		
28	23	Wrexham	2-0	Terry, Barnes	1790	9	6			10	11	8		2							14	1				4	12	3		5	7	
29	Mar 2	Rochdale	1-1	Beavon (p)	1890	9	6	7		10	11	8		2							14	1				4	12	3		5		
30	5	Scunthorpe United	0-3		2852	9	6	7		10	11	8		2		14				5		1				4		3			12	
31	9	CARLISLE UNITED	1-1	Campbell	3216		6	7	10		11	8		2		9					14	1				4		3		12	5	
32	12	BURNLEY	0-0		3710		6	7	10		11			2		9					14	1				4	8	3		12	5	
33	15	Halifax Town	1-2	Brown	1347		6	7	10		11			2		9					14	1				4	8	3		12	5	
34	23	CHESTERFIELD	2-0	Chard, Beavon (p)	3379	9	6	7	10		11			2		8				5		1				4		3			5	
35	26	Torquay United	0-0		2745	9	6	7	10		11			2		8						1				4		3			5	
36	30	SCUNTHORPE UNITED	2-1	Terry, Beavon (p)	3728	9	6	7	10		11			2		8					12	1				4		3			5	
37	Apr 1	Cardiff City	0-1		4805	9	6	7	14	10	11			2					1		12					4		3			5	
38	6	GILLINGHAM	2-1	Berry, Chard	2993	10		7	6	9	8	11		2		14			1		12					4		3			5	
39	9	Stockport County	0-2		3707	14	6	7	11			10		2		8			1		12					4	9	3			5	
40	13	Doncaster Rovers	1-2	Beavon	2939	9	6	7	11	12	5	10		2		8			1		14					4	9	3				
41	16	TORQUAY UNITED	1-4	Adcock	2678	9	6	7	11	10	12			2					1	5	12					4	8	3				
42	20	Walsall	3-3	Barnes, Beavon, Terry	3345	8	5	6	11	9	14			2					1		12					4	7	3		10		
43	27	DARLINGTON	0-3		4884	9	6	7	8	10	11			2					1		14					4	5	3		12		
44	30	LINCOLN CITY	1-1	Berry	2544	9	6		8	10		14				12			1	5	11					4		3		2	7	
45	May 7	Blackpool	1-2	Terry	7298	9	6		8	10	11	14				12			1	5						4		3		2	7	
46	11	Hartlepool United	1-3	Brown	6957	9	6			10	11	8			7				1		12					4	14	3		2	5	
				Apps		21	42	41	27	43	40	28	13	43	8	25	2	1	16	8	25	17	15	5	7	46	27	44	9	14	13	2
				Goals		3	2	10	2	13	2			7	1	4										6	1	3	2			1

F.A. Cup

Rd	Date	Opponent	Score	Scorers	Att.	Adcock AC	Angus TN	Beavon MS	Berry SA	Barnes DO	Brown SF	Bell M	Beresford M	Chard PJ	Collins D	Campbell GR	Evans GJ	Fee GP	Gleasure PF	Gernon FAJ	Johnson DD	Hitchcock KJ	Scully PJ	Sandeman BR	Scope DF	Terry SG	Thorpe A	Wilson PA	Wilkin K	Williams Wayne	Quow TS	Wood D
R1	Nov 17	Littlehampton	4-0	Beavon, Barnes 2, Campbell	3800			7	12	10	11			2	14	8			1	5						4	9	3		6		
R2	Dec 8	Barnet	0-0		5022			7		10	11			2	9	8		5	1		6			12		4		3				
rep	12	BARNET	0-1		5387	14		7		10	11			2		8		5	1		6			12		4	9	3				

F.L. Cup (Rumbelows League Cup)

Rd	Date	Opponent	Score	Scorers	Att.	Adcock AC	Angus TN	Beavon MS	Berry SA	Barnes DO	Brown SF	Bell M	Beresford M	Chard PJ	Collins D	Campbell GR	Evans GJ	Fee GP	Gleasure PF	Gernon FAJ	Johnson DD	Hitchcock KJ	Scully PJ	Sandeman BR	Scope DF	Terry SG	Thorpe A	Wilson PA	Wilkin K	Williams Wayne	Quow TS	Wood D
R1/1	Aug 29	Brighton & Hove Albion	2-0	Wilkin 2	3834			7	9	10	11			2		12			1							4	14	3	8	5		6
R1/2	Sep 4	BRIGHTON & HOVE ALB.	1-1	Brown	4760		6	7	9	10	11			2					1							4	12	3	8	5		
R2/1	25	SHEFFIELD UNITED	0-1		6910		6	7		10	11	9		2		12			1					14		4		3	8	5		
R2/2	Oct 10	Sheffield United	1-2	Barnes	8679		6	7		10	9	11	12	2		8			1					14		4		3		5		

A.M.C. (Leyland DAF Cup)

Rd	Date	Opponent	Score	Scorers	Att.	Adcock AC	Angus TN	Beavon MS	Berry SA	Barnes DO	Brown SF	Bell M	Beresford M	Chard PJ	Collins D	Campbell GR	Evans GJ	Fee GP	Gleasure PF	Gernon FAJ	Johnson DD	Hitchcock KJ	Scully PJ	Sandeman BR	Scope DF	Terry SG	Thorpe A	Wilson PA	Wilkin K	Williams Wayne	Quow TS	Wood D
PR	Nov 7	Stoke City	1-1	Beavon	4339			7	12	10	11		1	2	14	8							5			4	9	3		6		
PR	27	MANSFIELD TOWN	1-2	Beavon	2186		6	7	5		11		1	2	12	8					14				10	4	9	3				
R1	Feb 19	Torquay United	0-2		2112		6			10	11	8		2								1			12	4	9	3			5	7

1991/92 — 16th in Division 4

No	Date	Opponent	Score	Scorers	Att	Aldridge MJ	Angus TN	Adcock AC	Bulzis RRB	Beresford M	Brown SF	Burnham JJ	Benton J	Bell M	Barnes DO	Beavon MS	Chard PJ	Campbell GR	Colkin L	Edwards DS	Farrell SP	Gernon FAJ	Johnson DD	Kiernan DJ	McClean CA	Parker S	Parsons MC	Quow TS	Richardson B	Scope DF	Terry SG	Thorpe A	Wilson PA
1	Aug 17	Halifax Town	1-0	Chard	1834		5	9		1	6	7		10			2	12				11						8			4		3
2	30	Wrexham	2-2	Angus, Thorpe	2196		5			1	6	7			10		2	9				3						8			4	11	
3	Sep 3	DONCASTER ROVERS	3-1	Ormsby (og), Thorpe, Brown	2742		5			1	6	7			10		2					3	12					8			4	11	9
4	7	BARNET	1-1	Barnes	4344		5			1	6	7		12	10		2					9						8			4	11	3
5	14	Rochdale	0-1		2631		5			1	6	7		12	10		2					9	14					8			4	11	3
6	17	Crewe Alexandra	1-1	Farrell (p)	3597		5			1	6	14			10		2				7	9	12					8			4	11	3
7	21	CARLISLE UNITED	2-2	Wilson, Barnes	2657					1	6	12		11	10		2				7	9						8			4	14	3
8	Oct 5	BLACKPOOL	1-1	Barnes	3318					1	6	5		12	10		2				7	9	14					8			4	11	3
9	12	Scarborough	1-2	Adcock	2023		5	7		1	6			11	10		2	12				9						8			4		12
10	15	CHESTERFIELD	1-1	Adcock	2430		5	11		1	6	3			10	8	2				7	9									4		12
11	19	SCUNTHORPE UNITED	0-1		2583		5	11		1	6				10	7	2					9						8		12	4		3
12	26	Gillingham	1-3	Campbell	2543		5	11		1	6	14			12	7	2	10				9						8			4		3
13	Nov 2	Rotherham United	0-1		3146		5	11		1		14		12		7	2	10				9						8			4		3
14	5	MANSFIELD TOWN	1-2	Adcock	2181		5	11		1	12	6		14		7	2	10				9						8			4		3
15	9	LINCOLN CITY	1-0	Adcock	2575		5	11		1	4	6				7	2					9	12	10				8					3
16	23	Cardiff City	2-3	Burnham 2	2922		5	11			14	6			10	8	2	7				4	3		9			12	1				
17	30	BURNLEY	1-2	Campbell	4020		5	11			6				10	8	2	7				4	3		9			12	1				14
18	Dec 7	SCARBOROUGH	3-2	Barnes, Adcock, Bell	1815		5	11			12	6		8	10	7	2	14							9				1		4		3
19	21	Chesterfield	2-1	McClean, Terry	3048		5	11			10	6		8		7	2	12					14		9				1		4		3
20	26	HALIFAX TOWN	4-0	Adcock 2, Chard, Barnes	3147		5	11			10	6		8	10	7	2	12							9				1		4		3
21	28	WREXHAM	1-1	Angus	3209		5	11			10	6		8		7	2	12							9				1		4		3
22	Jan 1	Doncaster Rovers	3-0	Chard, Campbell, Scope	1973		5					6		12		8	7	2				11	10		9				1	14	4		3
23	11	YORK CITY	2-2	Terry, Barnes	3361		5				10	6		9	8	7	2	11											1		4	9	3
24	18	Maidstone United	1-1	Terry	1364		5				10	6		8	7	2	14						12		11				1		4	9	3
25	28	Walsall	2-1	Beavon 2	2399		5				10	6		8	7	12	2								11				1		4		3
26	Feb 8	GILLINGHAM	0-0		3183		5				6		8		7	9						2	10		11				1		4		3
27	11	Burnley	0-5		8760		5				6		8		7	9						2	10	14	11	4			1				3
28	15	WALSALL	0-1		2480		5				6		8		7	12	9					2	10	14	11	4			1				3
29	22	York City	0-0		2065		5				10	6	12		7	8						2	4		11				1			9	3
30	29	HEREFORD UNITED	0-1		2430		5				10	6	8		7	11							12	14	2	4	1					9	3
31	Mar 3	MAIDSTONE UNITED	1-0	Brown	1784		5				10	6	8		7		4				9			11	2	1					3		
32	10	Mansfield Town	0-2		2854		5				10	6	8		7	4					9	9		11	2	1					3		
33	14	ROTHERHAM UNITED	1-2	Brown	2561		5				10	6	8		7	12	4				9	3		11	2	14	1						
34	21	Lincoln City	2-1	Bell, Beavon (p)	2486		5				10	6	8		7	4					9			11	2	1				3	12		
35	28	CARDIFF CITY	0-0		2678		5				10	6	8		7	4					9			11	2	1				3	4		
36	31	ROCHDALE	2-2	McClean 2	2010		5				10	6	8		7						9			11	2	1				3			
37	Apr 4	Barnet	0-3		2816	12	5	14			10	6	8		7	11					9				4	2		1		3			
38	11	CREWE ALEXANDRA	0-1		3300		5	12			10	6	8		7	11					9				2			1		3			
39	14	Scunthorpe United	0-3		2286	14		11			10	6	12	8	7			5				9			4	2		1		4			
40	18	Carlisle United	1-2	Benton	1935	12		14			10	5	6	8	7	11		3				9			2		1		3				
41	25	Blackpool	0-1		5915	10					5	6	8		7	11					9				2		1		3				
42	28	Hereford United	2-1	Bell 2	1294	10					5	6	8		7	11					9				2		1		3				
		Apps				5	37	14	4	15	35	40	5	30	18	33	29	22	3	7	4	27	16	9	19	6	13	27	27	5	37	12	16
		Goals					2	7			3	2	1	4	6	3	3	3			1				3					1	3	2	1

Played in game 13: D Wood (at 6). In game 41: CL Adams (12).

One own goal

F.A. Cup

Rd	Date	Opponent	Score	Scorers	Att	Aldridge MJ	Angus TN	Adcock AC	Bulzis RRB	Beresford M	Brown SF	Burnham JJ	Benton J	Bell M	Barnes DO	Beavon MS	Chard PJ	Campbell GR	Colkin L	Edwards DS	Farrell SP	Gernon FAJ	Johnson DD	Kiernan DJ	McClean CA	Parker S	Parsons MC	Quow TS	Richardson B	Scope DF	Terry SG	Thorpe A	Wilson PA
R1	Nov 16	Crawley Town	2-4	Adcock, Chard	3370		4	11			7	6		10			2	14				12			9			8	1		5		3

F.L. Cup (Rumbelows League Cup)

Rd	Date	Opponent	Score	Scorers	Att	Aldridge MJ	Angus TN	Adcock AC	Bulzis RRB	Beresford M	Brown SF	Burnham JJ	Benton J	Bell M	Barnes DO	Beavon MS	Chard PJ	Campbell GR	Colkin L	Edwards DS	Farrell SP	Gernon FAJ	Johnson DD	Kiernan DJ	McClean CA	Parker S	Parsons MC	Quow TS	Richardson B	Scope DF	Terry SG	Thorpe A	Wilson PA
R1/1	Aug 20	Leyton Orient	0-5		2954		5	9			6	7		10			2	12				11	14					8			4		3
R1/2	Sep 10	LEYTON ORIENT	2-0	Barnes 2	1437		5				6	7			10		2			9								8	1		4	11	3

Played in R1/1: PF Gleasure (at 1)

A.M.C. (Autoglass Trophy)

Rd	Date	Opponent	Score	Scorers	Att	Aldridge MJ	Angus TN	Adcock AC	Bulzis RRB	Beresford M	Brown SF	Burnham JJ	Benton J	Bell M	Barnes DO	Beavon MS	Chard PJ	Campbell GR	Colkin L	Edwards DS	Farrell SP	Gernon FAJ	Johnson DD	Kiernan DJ	McClean CA	Parker S	Parsons MC	Quow TS	Richardson B	Scope DF	Terry SG	Thorpe A	Wilson PA
PR	Nov 20	Reading	2-0	Adcock, McClean	1151		5	11			6				10	8	2	7				4	3		9			12	1				
PR	Dec 3	LEYTON ORIENT	1-2	Chard	1193		5	11			12	6			10	7	2	8					3		9			4	1				14
R1	Jan 14	Barnet	2-3	Thorpe 2	1422		5				10	6	14	8	7			11				12	2						1		4	9	3

1992/93 20th in the new Football League Division 3

#	Date		Opponent	Score	Scorers	Att	Richardson B	Parker S	Burnham JJ	Beavon MS	Angus TN	Terry SG	Bell M	Lamb PD	Scott MJ	Brown SF	Wilkin K	Chard PJ	Parsons MC	Colkin L	Aldridge MJ	Benton J	Curtis PAE	Harmon DJ	McParland IJ	Young SR	Tisdale PR	Gavin PJ	Holmes MA	Gillard KJ	Hawke WR	Fox MC
1	Aug	15	Gillingham	3-2	Brown, Scott, Chard	3869	1	2	3	4	5	6	7	8	9	10	11	12														
2		28	Crewe Alexandra	2-3	Brown, Terry	3608	1		3	4	5	6	7	8	9	10	11	12	2													
3	Sep	1	Cardiff City	1-2	Brown	7494	1		3	4	5	6	7		9	10	11	12	2													
4		6	HEREFORD UNITED	1-1	Beavon (p)	2668	1		12	4	5	6	7		9	10	11	3	2	8												
5		12	SCUNTHORPE UNITED	1-0	Wilkin	1961	1	9	7	4	5	6	12			10	11	3	2	8												
6		15	Barnet	0-3		2885	1	9	7	4	5	6	12	14		10	11	3	2	8												
7		19	Torquay United	0-1		2393	1	9	7	4	5	6	12	14		10	11	3	2	8												
8		26	HALIFAX TOWN	2-5	Wilkin, Brown	2021	1		7	4	5	6	12	14	9	10	11	3	2			8										
9	Oct	3	LINCOLN CITY	0-2		1929	1		7	4	5	6	8		12	10	11	3			9		2									
10		10	Scarborough	2-4	Terry, Aldridge	1539	1		7	4	5	6	8			10	11	3		12	9	14	2									
11		13	CHESTERFIELD	0-1		1922	1		7	4	5	6	8		14	10	11			3	9	12	2									
12		17	DONCASTER ROVERS	0-1		2138	1		7	4	5	6	11		12	10	8			3	9		2									
13		24	Wrexham	1-0	Bell	3095	1		7		5	6	11			10	8	12			3		2	4	9							
14		31	SHREWSBURY TOWN	0-0		2730	1		7	12	5	6				10	8	11			3		2	4	9							
15	Nov	3	DARLINGTON	1-2	Wilkin	1991	1		7		5	6				10	8	11			3		2	4	9							
16		21	YORK CITY	4-3	Angus, Curtis, Terry, Chard	2812	1		7	3	5	6	9			10	8	11					2	4								
17		28	Carlisle United	0-2		3607	1		7	3	5	6	9			10	8	11					12	2	4							
18	Dec	12	Bury	3-3	McParland, Terry, Bell	1954	1		7	3	5	6	12			10	8						9	2	4	11						
19		26	COLCHESTER UNITED	1-0	McParland	4962	1		7		5	6	9			10	8	3					2	4		11						
20		28	Walsall	0-2		5080	1		7		5	6	9			10	8	3					2	4		11						
21	Jan	8	BARNET	1-1	Wilkin	4253	1		7		5	6	9			10	8	3					2	4		11						
22		16	Halifax Town	2-2	Hammon, McParland	1323	1		7		5	6	9		12	10	8			2			3	4		11						
23		23	TORQUAY UNITED	0-1		3082	1		7		5	6	9	8		10	12			2			3	4		11						
24		26	CREWE ALEXANDRA	0-2		2510	1		7	14	5	6	9	8		10	12			2			3	4		11						
25		30	Chesterfield	3-1	Chard, Terry, Scott	3031	1		7	2	5	6	9	8		10		11					3	4								
26	Feb	6	GILLINGHAM	2-2	Brown, Bell	3812	1		12		5	6	9	8		10	11	2					3	4		7						
27		13	Hereford United	2-3	Young, Chard	2358	1		7		5	6	9	3		10	14	12					2	4		11	8					
28		19	CARDIFF CITY	1-2	Brown (p)	4522	1		7		5	6	9			10	12	3					2	14	4	11	8					
29		27	SCARBOROUGH	1-3	Bell	2455	1		7		5	6	9			10	12		3				2	14		11	8	4				
30	Mar	6	Lincoln City	0-2		3328	1		14	7	5	6	9			10	12						2			11	8	4	3			
31		9	Rochdale	3-0	Chard, Brown, Young	1446	1			7	5	6	9			10							2			11	8	4	3			
32		20	Darlington	1-3	Bell	2106	1		7			6	11			12	5	3		2								9	8	4	10	
33		23	CARLISLE UNITED	2-0	Gavin, Angus	2561	1			4	5	6	11				7	2						12				9	8	3	10	
34		26	York City	1-2	Gavin	3334	1				5	6	11		4	7	2									12		9	8	3	10	
35		30	Scunthorpe United	0-5		2307	1			14	5	6	11		4	7	2									10		9	8	3		12
36	Apr	2	ROCHDALE	1-0	Brown	3037	1				5	6	11		10	7	2								4			9		3	8	
37		6	BURY	1-0	Hawke	2878	1					6	11		10	7	5	2							4			9		3	8	
38		12	WALSALL	0-0		4177	1					6	11		10	7	5	2			12				4			9		3	8	
39		20	Colchester United	0-2		3519	1					6	11		10	7	5	2			12				4			9		3	8	
40		24	Doncaster Rovers	2-2	Brown, Aldridge	2111	1				12	6			10	7	5	2		11	8				4			9				
41		27	WREXHAM	0-2		7504	1		3			6	11		10	7	5	2			8				4			9				
42	May	8	Shrewsbury Town	3-2	Chard, Gavin 2	7278	1			7	5	6	11			8	10	2	3		9						12	4				
			Apps				42	4	31	24	37	42	39	3	17	38	41	34	19	13	9	5	22	25	11	8	5	14	6	9	7	1
			Goals							1	2	5	5		2	9	4	6			2		1	1	3	2		4			1	

F.A. Cup

	Date		Opponent	Score	Scorers	Att	Richardson B	Parker S	Burnham JJ	Beavon MS	Angus TN	Terry SG	Bell M	Lamb PD	Scott MJ	Brown SF	Wilkin K	Chard PJ	Parsons MC	Colkin L	Aldridge MJ	Benton J	Curtis PAE	Harmon DJ	McParland IJ
R1	Nov	14	FULHAM	3-1	Terry, Brown, Wilkins	4823	1		7	3	5	6	9			10	8	11					2	4	
R2	Dec	6	Bath City	2-2	Brown, Chard	3626	1		7	3	5	6	9			10	8	12					2	4	11
rep		15	BATH CITY	3-0	Bell, Wilkins, McParland	4106	1		7	3	5	6	9			10	8	4					2		11
R3	Jan	12	ROTHERHAM UNITED	0-1		7256	1		7		5	6	9	12		10	8			2			3	4	11

F.L. Cup (Coca Cola Cup)

	Date		Opponent	Score	Scorers	Att	Richardson B	Parker S	Burnham JJ	Beavon MS	Angus TN	Terry SG	Bell M	Lamb PD	Scott MJ	Brown SF	Wilkin K	Chard PJ	Parsons MC	Colkin L	Aldridge MJ
R1/1	Aug	18	Gillingham	1-2	1 og	2245	1	2	3	4	5	6	7	8	9	10	11	12			
R1/2	Sep	9	GILLINGHAM	0-2		2390	1		12	4	5	6	7		9	10	11	3	2	8	14

A.M.C. (Autoglass Trophy)

	Date		Opponent	Score	Scorers	Att	Richardson B	Parker S	Burnham JJ	Beavon MS	Angus TN	Terry SG	Bell M	Lamb PD	Scott MJ	Brown SF	Wilkin K	Chard PJ	Parsons MC	Colkin L	Aldridge MJ	Benton J	Curtis PAE	Harmon DJ	McParland IJ
R1	Dec	1	Colchester United	2-1	Beavon, Brown	1454	1		7	3	5	6	9			10	8					12	2	4	11
R1		9	BARNET	2-1	Scott, McParland	1591	1		7	3	5	6	12	14		10	8					9	2	4	11
R2	Jan	19	HEREFORD UNITED	4-0	Bell, Scott, McParland 2	1962	1		7	12	5	6	9	8		10	14			2			3	4	11
QF	Feb	2	Port Vale	2-4	Scott, Chard	4834	1		7	2	5	6	9	8				11	10	12			3	4	

1993/94 22nd in Division 3

						Richardson B	Parsons MC	Gillard KJ	Phillips LM	Terry SG	Wood D	Fleming TM	Wilkin K	Gilzean IR	Brown SF	Bell M	Chard PJ	Colkin L	Aldridge MJ	Harmon DJ	Francis SR	Burnham JJ	Sherwood S	Preston RJ	Hyslop CT	Sampson I	Patmore WJ	Harrison GM	Gallacher B	Elad DE	Warburton R	Fitzpatrick PJ	Cornwell JA
1	Aug 14	Bury	0-0		2540	1	2	3	4	5	6	7	8	9	10	11				12													
2	28	Colchester United	2-3	Brown, Gilzean	2874	1	2	3	4	5		7		9	10	11	6	8															
3	31	Crewe Alexandra	1-3	Gilzean	3155	1	2	3	4	5		7		9	10	11	6	8					12										
4	Sep 4	WALSALL	0-1		3278		2	3	4	5		7		9	10	11	6	8			12		1										
5	11	Hereford United	1-1	Gilzean	2260		2		4	5		7		9	10	11	6	8		12		3	1										
6	18	WIGAN ATHLETIC	0-2		2281		2	12	4	5				9	10	11	6	8		7		3	1										
7	25	Lincoln City	3-4	Aldridge, Brown, Harmon	2705		2		4	5		12		9	10	11		6	8	7		3	1										
8	Oct 2	DARLINGTON	1-0	Aldridge	2268		2	3	4	5				9	10	11	6		8	7		12	1										
9	9	WYCOMBE WANDERERS	1-1	Aldridge	5414		2	3	4	5				9	10	11	6		8	7			1										
10	12	MANSFIELD TOWN	5-1	Gilzean, Hammon, Terry, Brown 2	2842		2	3	4	5				9	10	11	6		8	7		12	1										
11	16	Scunthorpe United	0-7		2814		2	3	4	5		12		9	10	11	6		8	7			1										
12	23	CARLISLE UNITED	1-1	Aldridge	2886	1	2	3	4	5		12		9	10	11	6		8	7													
13	30	Doncaster Rovers	1-2	Gilzean	2227	1	2		4	5		12		9	10	11		3	8	7		6											
14	Nov 2	Torquay United	0-2		2704	1	2		4	5		7		9	10	11	6	3	12			8											
15	6	SHREWSBURY TOWN	0-3		2639	1			4	5		12		9	10	11	6	7	8			3		2									
16	20	Chester City	0-1		2650		2	3	4	5				9		11	6	12	8	7		10	1										
17	27	CHESTERFIELD	2-2	Gilzean, Aldridge	1866		2	3	4	5				9		11	6	7	8			10	1										
18	Dec 11	Mansfield Town	0-1		2491		2		4	5					10	11	7		8				1		3	6	9						
19	18	BURY	0-1		2369		2		4	5					10	11	7	14	12				1		3	6	9	8					
20	27	Gillingham	0-1		4573				4	5			7		10		2	11	12				1		3	6	9	8					
21	Jan 1	Rochdale	2-6	Gilzean, Harmon	2453		2		4	5			7	12	10			11	8	14			1		3	6	9						
22	3	CREWE ALEXANDRA	2-2	Gilzean, Colkin	3404				4	5			7	9	10			11	8	2			1		3	6							
23	8	Scarborough	1-2	Gilzean	1703	1				5		4	7	9	10	12		11	8	2					3	6							
24	22	Wycombe Wanderers	0-1		6737	1			4	5		2	7	9	10	11		12	8						3	6	14						
25	29	DONCASTER ROVERS	0-0		2900	1			4	5		2	7	9	10	11			8							6			3	12			
26	Feb 5	Carlisle United	1-0	Chard	4535	1						2	7	12	10	11	6			4					3		9			8	5		
27	12	SCARBOROUGH	3-2	Harmon, Fitzpatrick, Gilzean	2974	1		3				2	7	9		11	6			4										8	5	10	
28	19	COLCHESTER UNITED	1-1	Wilkin	3205	1		3				2	7	9		11	6			4							12			8	5		10
29	26	Walsall	3-1	Harmon, Wilkin, Patmore	4553	1				6		2	7	12		11	3			4							9			8	5		10
30	Mar 5	HEREFORD UNITED	0-1		5394	1				6		2	7	12		11				4		3					9			8	5		10
31	8	SCUNTHORPE UNITED	4-0	Harmon, Fleming(p), Aldridge, Wilkin	3192	1				6		2	7	9		11			12	4		3								8	5		10
32	12	Wigan Athletic	1-1	Cornwell	1855	1				6		2	7	9		11			8	4		3									5	12	10
33	15	PRESTON NORTH END	2-0	Fensome (og), Aldridge	3845	1				6		2	7	9		11			8	4		3									5		10
34	19	LINCOLN CITY	0-0		3868	1				6		2	7	9		11			8	4		3					12				5		10
35	26	Darlington	1-0	Warburton	3226	1				6		2	7	9		11	12		8	4		3									5		10
36	Apr 2	GILLINGHAM	1-2	Patmore	4628	1				6		2	7	9		11	12		8	4		3					14				5		10
37	4	Preston North End	1-1	Harmon	7517	1				6		2	7			11	3		8	4							9				5		10
38	9	ROCHDALE	1-2	Aldridge	3330	1				6		2	7			11	3		8	4							9				5		10
39	16	TORQUAY UNITED	0-1		3519	1				6		2	7			11	8		12	4							9		3		5		10
40	23	Shrewsbury Town	1-2	Wilkin	6512	1				6		2	7			11	8	9		4							12		3	14	5		10
41	30	CHESTER CITY	1-0	Wilkin	6432	1			10	6		2	7			11		9		4							12		3	8	5		
42	Ma 7	Chesterfield	0-4		5285	1			10	6		2	7					9	12	4							11		3	8	5		

Played in game 14: HS Stackman (at 14).

	Richardson B	Parsons MC	Gillard KJ	Phillips LM	Terry SG	Wood D	Fleming TM	Wilkin K	Gilzean IR	Brown SF	Bell M	Chard PJ	Colkin L	Aldridge MJ	Harmon DJ	Francis SR	Burnham JJ	Sherwood S	Preston RJ	Hyslop CT	Sampson I	Patmore WJ	Harrison GM	Gallacher B	Elad DE	Warburton R	Fitzpatrick PJ	Cornwell JA
Apps	27	19	14	26	39	1	31	24	33	24	38	27	20	29	31	1	17	16	1	8	8	17	2	5	10	17	2	13
Goals					1		1	5	10	4		1	1	8	7							2				1	1	1

One own goal

F.A. Cup

						Richardson B	Parsons MC	Gillard KJ	Phillips LM	Terry SG	Wood D	Fleming TM	Wilkin K	Gilzean IR	Brown SF	Bell M	Chard PJ	Colkin L	Aldridge MJ	Harmon DJ	Francis SR	Burnham JJ	Sherwood S	Preston RJ	Hyslop CT	Sampson I	Patmore WJ	Harrison GM	Gallacher B	Elad DE	Warburton R	Fitzpatrick PJ	Cornwell JA
R1	Nov 13	BROMSGROVE ROVERS	1-2	Aldridge	3382		2	3	4	5		12		9		11	6		8	7		10	1										

F.L. Cup (Coca Cola Cup)

						Richardson B	Parsons MC	Gillard KJ	Phillips LM	Terry SG	Wood D	Fleming TM	Wilkin K	Gilzean IR	Brown SF	Bell M	Chard PJ	Colkin L	Aldridge MJ	Harmon DJ	Francis SR	Burnham JJ	Sherwood S	Preston RJ	Hyslop CT	Sampson I	Patmore WJ	Harrison GM	Gallacher B	Elad DE	Warburton R	Fitzpatrick PJ	Cornwell JA
R1/1	Aug 18	Reading	0-3		3283	1	2	3	4	5	6	7		9	10	11				12	8	14											
R1/2	Sep 7	READING	0-2		1631		2		4	5		7		9	10	11	6	8	12			3	1										

A.M.C. (Autoglass Trophy)

						Richardson B	Parsons MC	Gillard KJ	Phillips LM	Terry SG	Wood D	Fleming TM	Wilkin K	Gilzean IR	Brown SF	Bell M	Chard PJ	Colkin L	Aldridge MJ	Harmon DJ	Francis SR	Burnham JJ	Sherwood S	Preston RJ	Hyslop CT	Sampson I	Patmore WJ	Harrison GM	Gallacher B	Elad DE	Warburton R	Fitzpatrick PJ	Cornwell JA
R1	Oct 19	Walsall	0-0		1897	1	2	3	4	5				9	10	11	6		8	7													
R1	Nov 9	HEREFORD UNITED	1-1	Aldridge	1062			3	4	5		12		9	10	11	6		8	7			1	2									
R2	Dec 1	Reading	1-4	Aldridge	1811		2	3	4	5				9	10	11	6		8			7	1										

1994/95   17th in Division 3

#	Date		Opponent	Score	Scorers	Att	Stewart WI	Pascoe J	Curtis R	Norton DW	Warburton R	Sampson I	Harmon DJ	Trott DD	Grayson N	Bell M	Wilkin K	Colkin L	Aldridge MJ	Robinson PJ	Williams GJ	Ovendale MJ	Skelly RB	Cahill OF	Turner GM	Harrison GM	Brown IO	Patmore WJ	Hughes DJ	Burns C	Smith NL	Thompson GL	Martin Dave	Daniels SC	Woodman AJ	O'Shea DE
1	Aug	20	Doncaster Rovers	0-1		2154	1	2	3	4	5	6	7		9	10	11	14	12																	
2		27	Scunthorpe United	1-1	Trott	2499	1	2		4	5	6	7		9	12	11	10	3																	
3		30	Torquay United	1-2	Sampson	3619	1	2	6	8	5	4	7		9	10	11		3	12																
4	Sep	3	Walsall	1-1	Trott	4249	1		6	2	5	4	7		9	10	11		3	12	8															
5		10	ROCHDALE	1-2	Trott	2887	1			2	5	4	7		9	10	11		3		6															
6		13	HARTLEPOOL UNITED	1-1	Aldridge	2466	1	8		2	5	4	7		9	10	11		3	12	6															
7		17	Mansfield Town	1-1	Aldridge	2557	1		6	2	5	4	7		9		11		3	10	8															
8		24	CARLISLE UNITED	2-1	Aldridge, Bell	3508	1		6	2	5	4	7		9		11		3	10	8															
9	Oct	1	Lincoln City	2-2	Harmon, Warburton	3248	1		6	2	5	4	7		9		11		3	10	8															
10		8	Exeter City	0-0		3015	1		6	2	5	4	7		9		11		3		8	10														
11		11	MANSFIELD TOWN	0-1		4993	1		6	2	5	4	7		9	14	11		3	12	8	10														
12		15	BARNET	1-1	Aldridge	7461	1	2			5	4	7		9	12	11		3	10	6	8														
13		22	WIGAN ATHLETIC	1-0	Grayson	6379	1	2	6		5	4	7		9				3	10	11	8			12											
14		29	Scarborough	0-0		1468	1	2			5	4	7		9	8			11	12	10	6	3													
15	Nov	5	FULHAM	0-1		7366	1	2		12	5	4	7		8				3	9	10	6			11											
16		19	Preston North End	0-2		7043	1	14		2	5	4	7		9		11		3	8	10	6		1	12											
17		26	HEREFORD UNITED	1-3	Cahill	5148	1			2	5	4	7		9	12			8	10	6		3	11												
18	Dec	10	DONCASTER ROVERS	0-0		4463	1	3		2	5	4	7		9							12		6			11	10								
19		16	SCUNTHORPE UNITED	0-1		3841	1	12		2	5	4	7		9	3		14	8		6						11	10								
20		26	Colchester United	1-0	Harmon (p)	5064	1	12	5	2		4	7		9				3								11			8	14					
21		27	CHESTERFIELD	2-3	Brown, Harmon (p)	6329	1	2	5	6		4	7		9				3								11			8	12					
22		31	Darlington	1-4	Grayson	2247	1		6	2	5	4			10				3	12							11		7	9						
23	Jan	7	Wigan Athletic	1-2	Colkin	1911	1	12	6	2	5	4					11		10		9		3						7	8						
24		14	GILLINGHAM	2-0	Harmon (p), Trott	5529	1			2	5	4	7	12	11				6	9							8		3	10						
25		28	SCARBOROUGH	0-3		5737	1			2	5	4	7		9		11										8		12	3	10					
26	Feb	4	Hereford United	1-2	Grayson	2443				2	5	6		14	9							1				11	8			12	7	4		3		
27		11	PRESTON NORTH END	2-1	Burns, Smith	5197				2	5	4		6	11							1					8			7	10	3		9		
28		14	Fulham	4-4	Aldridge 2, Brown, Grayson	3423				2	5	4		12	11							1					8			7	10	3		9	6	
29		18	Gillingham	1-3	Thompson	4072	1			2	5	4		12	11												8				10	3		9	6	
30		25	LINCOLN CITY	3-1	Brown (og), Grayson, Aldridge	4821				2	5	4		10	11							1					12				8	3		9	6	
31	Mar	4	Carlisle United	1-2	Martin	6744	13			2	5	4		12	11				3	7			14	1			8				10			9	6	
32		7	BURY	0-5		4208	1			2	5	4		12	11				3	7							8				10			9	6	
33		11	Rochdale	0-0		1894				2	5	4			11			12	14							7	8				10			3		
34		18	TORQUAY UNITED	2-0	Grayson, Brown	3957				2	5	4			11			12	7								8			9	10			3	6	
35		25	WALSALL	2-2	Grayson, Warburton	6282				2	5	4		14	11				6			12					8			9	10			3	6	1
36	Apr	1	Hartlepool United	1-1	Thompson	2113				2	5	4			11				12								8			9	10			3	7	1
37		8	DARLINGTON	2-1	Thompson, Grayson	4496				2	5	4			11				7								8			9	10			3	7	1	6
38		15	Chesterfield	0-3		4884		5		2		4		12	14	11			7								8			9	10			3	12	1	6
39		17	COLCHESTER UNITED	1-1	Brown	5011				12	5	4			11				7								8			9	10			3		1	6
40		22	Bury	0-5		2921					5	4	10	9	11				7								8			9	12			2	1	6
41		29	Barnet	3-2	Burns, Thompson, Warburton	2796				2	5	4			11				7	14							8			9	10			2	1	6
42	May	6	EXETER CITY	2-1	O'Shea, Sampson	6734				2	5	4			11				12								8			9	10			14	1	6
			Apps				27	15	13	38	39	42	33	22	38	12	4	33	27	14	15	6	3	8	4	5	23	4	13	17	6	15	7	8	10	7
			Goals								3	2	4	4	8	1		1	7					1			4			2	1	4	1			1

Played in game 20: BR Sedgemore (6). In game 20,21: AJ Flounders (10).
In games 1 and 2: R Byrne (8). In game 5: B McNamara (12).

One own goal

F.A. Cup

	Date	Opponent	Score		Att	Stewart WI	Pascoe J	Norton DW	Warburton R	Sampson I	Harmon DJ	Grayson N	Bell M	Aldridge MJ	Robinson PJ	Williams GJ	Ovendale MJ
R1	Nov 12	Peterborough Utd.	0-4		8739	1	2	11	5	4	7	9	8	3	12	10	6

F.L. Cup (Coca Cola Cup)

	Date	Opponent	Score	Att	Stewart WI	Pascoe J	Curtis R	Norton DW	Warburton R	Sampson I	Harmon DJ	Grayson N	Bell M	Wilkin K	Colkin L	Aldridge MJ	Robinson PJ	Williams GJ
R1/1	Aug 16	Bournemouth	0-2	2587	1	2	3	4	5	6	7	9	10	11	12			
R1/2	Sep 6	BOURNEMOUTH	0-1	3249	1		6	2	5	4	7	9	10	12	3		11	8

Played in R1/1: R Byrne (8).

A.M.C. (Auto Windscreen Shield)

	Date	Opponent	Score	Scorers	Att	Stewart WI	Pascoe J	Curtis R	Warburton R	Sampson I	Harmon DJ	Grayson N	Bell M	Wilkin K	Aldridge MJ	Robinson PJ	Williams GJ	Ovendale MJ	Skelly RB	Cahill OF	Turner GM	Harrison GM
R1	Oct 18	Cambridge United	3-1	Warburton, Grayson, Aldridge	1497		2	6	5	4	7	11		14	10			8	1	3	12	
R1	Nov 1	BARNET	3-1	Harmon, Grayson, Aldridge	2618		2		5	4	7	8			3	9	10	6	1		12	11
R2		29 SWANSEA CITY	0-1		2706	1	14		2	5	4	7	9	8			10	6		3	11	12

Played in first game: B McNamara (9).

1981/82: Division 4

1	Sheffield United	46	15	8	0	53	15	12	7	4	41	26	96
2	Bradford City	46	14	7	2	52	23	12	6	5	36	22	91
3	Wigan Athletic	46	17	5	1	47	18	9	8	6	33	28	91
4	Bournemouth	46	12	10	1	37	15	11	9	3	25	15	88
5	Peterborough Utd.	46	16	3	4	46	22	8	7	8	25	35	82
6	Colchester United	46	12	6	5	47	23	8	6	9	35	34	72
7	Port Vale	46	9	12	2	26	17	9	4	10	30	32	70
8	Hull City	46	14	3	6	36	23	5	9	9	34	38	69
9	Bury	46	13	7	3	53	26	4	10	9	27	33	68
10	Hereford United	46	10	9	4	36	25	6	10	7	28	33	67
11	Tranmere Rovers	46	7	9	7	27	25	7	9	7	24	31	60
12	Blackpool	46	11	5	7	40	26	4	8	11	26	34	58
13	Darlington	46	10	5	8	36	28	5	8	10	25	34	58
14	Hartlepool United	46	9	8	6	39	34	4	8	11	34	50	55
15	Torquay United	46	9	8	6	30	25	5	5	13	17	34	55
16	Aldershot	46	8	7	8	34	29	5	8	10	23	39	54
17	York City	46	9	5	9	45	37	5	3	15	24	54	50
18	Stockport County	46	10	5	8	34	28	2	8	13	14	39	49
19	Halifax Town	46	6	11	6	28	30	3	11	9	23	42	49
20	Mansfield Town	46	8	6	9	39	39	5	4	14	24	42	47
21	Rochdale	46	7	9	7	26	22	3	7	13	24	40	46
22	**NORTHAMPTON TOWN**	46	9	5	9	32	27	2	4	17	25	57	42
23	Scunthorpe United	46	7	9	7	26	35	2	6	15	17	44	42
24	Crewe Alexandra	46	3	6	14	19	32	3	3	17	10	52	27

1982/83 Division 4

1	Wimbledon	46	17	4	2	57	23	12	7	4	39	22	98
2	Hull City	46	14	8	1	48	14	11	7	5	27	20	90
3	Port Vale	46	15	4	4	37	16	11	6	6	30	18	88
4	Scunthorpe United	46	13	7	3	41	17	10	7	6	30	25	83
5	Bury	46	15	4	4	43	20	8	8	7	31	26	81
6	Colchester United	46	17	5	1	51	19	7	4	12	24	36	81
7	York City	46	18	4	1	59	19	4	9	10	29	39	79
8	Swindon Town	46	14	3	6	45	27	5	8	10	16	27	68
9	Peterborough Utd.	46	13	6	4	38	23	4	7	12	20	29	64
10	Mansfield Town	46	11	6	6	32	26	5	7	11	29	44	61
11	Halifax Town	46	9	8	6	31	23	7	4	12	28	43	60
12	Torquay United	46	12	3	8	38	30	5	4	14	18	35	58
13	Chester	46	8	6	9	28	24	7	5	11	27	36	56
14	Bristol City	46	10	8	5	32	25	3	9	11	27	45	56
15	**NORTHAMPTON TOWN**	46	10	8	5	43	29	4	4	15	22	46	54
16	Stockport County	46	11	8	4	41	31	3	4	16	19	48	54
17	Darlington	46	8	5	10	27	30	5	8	10	34	41	52
18	Aldershot	46	11	5	7	40	35	1	10	12	21	47	51
19	Tranmere Rovers	46	8	8	7	30	29	5	3	15	19	42	50
20	Rochdale	46	11	8	4	38	25	0	8	15	17	48	49
21	Blackpool	46	10	8	5	32	23	3	4	16	23	51	49
22	Hartlepool United	46	11	5	7	30	24	2	4	17	16	52	48
23	Crewe Alexandra	46	9	5	9	35	32	2	3	18	18	39	41
24	Hereford United	46	8	6	9	19	23	3	2	18	23	56	41

1983/84 Division 4

1	York City	46	18	4	1	58	16	13	4	6	38	23	101
2	Doncaster Rovers	46	15	6	2	46	22	9	7	7	36	32	85
3	Reading	46	17	6	0	51	14	5	10	8	33	42	82
4	Bristol City	46	18	3	2	51	17	6	7	10	19	27	82
5	Aldershot	46	14	6	3	49	29	8	3	12	27	40	75
6	Blackpool	46	15	4	4	47	19	6	5	12	23	33	72
7	Peterborough Utd.	46	15	5	3	52	16	3	9	11	20	32	68
8	Colchester United	46	14	7	2	45	14	3	9	11	24	39	67
9	Torquay United	46	13	7	3	32	18	5	6	12	27	46	67
10	Tranmere Rovers	46	11	5	7	33	26	6	10	7	20	27	66
11	Hereford United	46	11	6	6	31	21	5	9	9	23	32	63
12	Stockport County	46	12	5	6	34	25	5	6	12	26	39	62
13	Chesterfield	46	10	11	2	34	24	5	4	14	25	37	60
14	Darlington	46	13	4	6	31	19	4	4	15	18	31	59
15	Bury	46	9	7	7	34	32	6	7	10	27	32	59
16	Crewe Alexandra	46	10	8	5	35	27	6	3	14	21	40	59
17	Swindon Town	46	11	7	5	34	23	4	6	13	24	33	58
18	**NORTHAMPTON TOWN**	46	10	8	5	32	32	3	6	14	21	46	53
19	Mansfield Town	46	9	7	7	44	27	4	6	13	22	43	52
20	Wrexham	46	7	6	10	34	33	4	9	10	25	41	48
21	Halifax Town	46	11	6	6	36	25	1	6	16	19	64	48
22	Rochdale	46	8	9	6	35	31	3	4	16	17	49	46
23	Hartlepool United	46	7	8	8	31	28	3	2	18	16	57	40
24	Chester City	46	7	5	11	23	35	0	8	15	22	47	34

1984/85 Division 4

1	Chesterfield	46	16	6	1	40	13	10	7	6	24	22	91
2	Blackpool	46	15	7	1	42	15	9	7	7	31	24	86
3	Darlington	46	16	4	3	41	22	8	9	6	25	27	85
4	Bury	46	15	6	2	46	20	9	6	8	30	30	84
5	Hereford United	46	16	2	5	38	21	6	9	8	27	26	77
6	Tranmere Rovers	46	17	1	5	50	21	7	2	14	33	45	75
7	Colchester United	46	13	7	3	49	29	7	7	9	38	36	74
8	Swindon Town	46	16	4	3	42	21	5	5	13	20	37	72
9	Scunthorpe United	46	14	6	3	61	33	5	8	10	22	29	71
10	Crewe Alexandra	46	10	7	6	32	28	8	5	10	33	41	66
11	Peterborough Utd.	46	11	7	5	29	21	5	7	11	25	32	62
12	Port Vale	46	11	8	4	39	24	3	10	10	22	35	60
13	Aldershot	46	11	6	6	33	20	6	2	15	23	43	59
14	Mansfield Town	46	10	8	5	25	15	3	10	10	16	23	57
15	Wrexham	46	10	6	7	39	27	5	3	15	28	43	54
16	Chester City	46	11	3	9	35	30	4	6	13	25	42	54
17	Rochdale	46	8	7	8	33	30	5	7	11	22	39	53
18	Exeter City	46	9	7	7	30	27	4	7	12	27	52	53
19	Hartlepool United	46	10	6	7	34	29	4	4	15	20	38	52
20	Southend United	46	8	8	7	30	34	5	3	15	28	49	50
21	Halifax Town	46	9	3	11	26	32	6	2	15	16	37	50
22	Stockport County	46	11	5	7	40	26	2	3	18	18	53	47
23	**NORTHAMPTON TOWN**	46	10	1	12	32	32	4	4	15	21	42	47
24	Torquay United	46	5	11	7	18	24	4	3	16	20	39	41

1985/86 Division 4

1	Swindon Town	46	20	2	1	52	19	12	4	7	30	24	##
2	Chester City	46	15	5	3	44	16	8	10	5	39	34	84
3	Mansfield Town	46	13	8	2	43	17	10	4	9	31	30	81
4	Port Vale	46	13	9	1	42	11	8	7	8	25	26	79
5	Orient	46	11	6	6	39	21	9	6	8	40	43	72
6	Colchester United	46	12	6	5	51	22	7	7	9	37	41	70
7	Hartlepool United	46	15	6	2	41	20	5	4	14	27	47	70
8	**NORTHAMPTON TOWN**	46	9	7	7	44	29	9	3	11	35	29	64
9	Southend United	46	13	4	6	43	27	5	6	12	26	40	64
10	Hereford United	46	15	6	2	55	30	3	4	16	19	43	64
11	Stockport County	46	9	9	5	35	28	8	4	11	28	43	64
12	Crewe Alexandra	46	10	6	7	35	26	8	3	12	19	35	63
13	Wrexham	46	11	5	7	34	24	6	4	13	34	56	60
14	Burnley	46	11	3	9	35	30	5	8	10	25	35	59
15	Scunthorpe United	46	11	7	5	33	23	4	7	12	17	32	59
16	Aldershot	46	12	5	6	45	25	5	2	16	21	49	58
17	Peterborough Utd.	46	9	11	3	31	19	4	6	13	21	45	56
18	Rochdale	46	12	7	4	41	29	2	6	15	16	48	55
19	Tranmere Rovers	46	9	1	13	46	41	6	8	9	28	32	54
20	Halifax Town	46	10	8	5	35	27	4	4	15	25	44	54
21	Exeter City	46	10	4	9	26	25	3	11	9	21	34	54
22	Cambridge United	46	12	2	9	45	38	3	7	13	20	42	54
23	Preston North End	46	7	4	12	32	41	4	6	13	22	48	43
24	Torquay United	46	8	5	10	29	32	1	5	17	14	56	37

1986/87 Division 4

1	**NORTHAMPTON TOWN**	46	20	2	1	56	20	10	7	6	47	33	99
2	Preston North End	46	16	4	3	36	18	10	8	5	36	29	90
3	Southend United	46	14	4	5	43	27	11	1	11	25	28	80
4	Wolverhampton Wan.	46	12	3	8	36	24	12	4	7	33	26	79
5	Colchester United	46	15	3	5	41	20	6	4	13	23	36	70
6	Aldershot	46	13	5	5	40	22	7	5	11	24	35	70
7	Orient	46	15	2	6	40	25	5	7	11	24	36	69
8	Scunthorpe United	46	15	3	5	52	27	3	9	11	21	30	66
9	Wrexham	46	8	13	2	38	24	7	7	9	32	27	65
10	Peterborough Utd.	46	10	7	6	29	21	7	7	9	28	29	65
11	Cambridge United	46	12	6	5	37	23	5	5	13	23	39	62
12	Swansea City	46	13	3	7	31	21	4	8	11	25	40	62
13	Cardiff City	46	6	12	5	24	18	9	4	10	24	32	61
14	Exeter City	46	11	10	2	37	17	0	13	10	16	32	56
15	Halifax Town	46	10	5	8	32	32	5	5	13	27	42	55
16	Hereford United	46	10	6	7	33	23	4	5	14	27	38	53
17	Crewe Alexandra	46	8	9	6	38	35	5	5	13	32	37	53
18	Hartlepool United	46	6	11	6	24	30	5	7	11	20	35	51
19	Stockport County	46	9	6	8	25	27	4	6	13	15	42	51
20	Tranmere Rovers	46	6	10	7	32	37	5	7	11	22	35	50
21	Rochdale	46	8	8	7	31	30	3	9	11	23	43	50
22	Burnley	46	9	7	7	31	35	3	6	14	22	39	49
23	Torquay United	46	8	8	7	28	29	2	10	11	28	43	48
24	Lincoln City	46	8	7	8	30	27	4	5	14	15	38	48

1987/88 Division 3

1	Sunderland	46	14	7	2	51	22	13	5	5	41	26	93
2	Brighton & Hove A.	46	15	7	1	37	16	8	8	7	32	31	84
3	Walsall	46	15	6	2	39	22	8	7	8	29	28	82
4	Notts County	46	14	4	5	53	24	9	8	6	29	25	81
5	Bristol City	46	14	6	3	51	30	7	6	10	26	32	75
6	**NORTHAMPTON TOWN**	46	12	8	3	36	18	6	11	6	34	33	73
7	Wigan Athletic	46	11	8	4	36	23	9	4	10	34	38	72
8	Bristol Rovers	46	14	5	4	43	19	4	7	12	25	37	66
9	Fulham	46	10	5	8	36	24	9	4	10	33	36	66
10	Blackpool	46	13	4	6	45	27	4	10	9	26	35	65
11	Port Vale	46	12	8	3	36	19	6	3	14	22	37	65
12	Brentford	46	9	8	6	27	23	7	6	10	26	36	62
13	Gillingham	46	8	9	6	45	21	6	8	9	32	40	59
14	Bury	46	9	7	7	33	26	6	7	10	25	31	59
15	Chester City	46	9	8	6	29	30	5	8	10	22	32	58
16	Preston North End	46	10	6	7	30	23	5	7	11	18	36	58
17	Southend United	46	10	6	7	42	33	4	7	12	23	50	55
18	Chesterfield	46	10	5	8	25	28	5	5	13	16	42	55
19	Mansfield Town	46	10	6	7	25	21	4	6	13	23	38	54
20	Aldershot	46	12	3	8	45	32	3	5	15	19	42	53
21	Rotherham United	46	8	8	7	28	25	4	8	11	22	41	52
22	Grimsby Town	46	6	7	10	25	29	6	7	10	23	29	50
23	York City	46	4	7	12	27	45	4	2	17	21	46	33
24	Doncaster Rovers	46	6	5	12	25	36	2	4	17	15	48	33

1988/89 Division 3

1	Wolverhampton Wan.	46	18	4	1	61	19	8	10	5	35	30	92
2	Sheffield United	46	16	3	4	57	21	9	6	8	36	33	84
3	Port Vale	46	15	3	5	46	21	9	9	5	32	27	84
4	Fulham	46	12	7	4	42	28	10	2	11	27	39	75
5	Bristol Rovers	46	9	11	3	34	21	10	6	7	33	30	74
6	Preston North End	46	14	7	2	56	31	5	8	10	23	29	72
7	Brentford	46	14	5	4	36	21	4	9	10	30	40	68
8	Chester City	46	12	6	5	38	18	7	5	11	26	43	68
9	Notts County	46	11	7	5	37	22	7	6	10	27	32	67
10	Bolton Wanderers	46	12	8	3	42	23	4	8	11	16	31	64
11	Bristol City	46	10	3	10	32	25	8	6	9	21	30	63
12	Swansea City	46	11	8	4	33	22	4	8	11	18	31	61
13	Bury	46	11	7	5	27	22	5	6	12	28	45	61
14	Huddersfield Town	46	10	8	5	35	25	7	1	15	28	48	60
15	Mansfield Town	46	10	8	5	32	22	4	9	10	16	30	59
16	Cardiff City	46	10	9	4	30	16	4	6	13	14	40	57
17	Wigan Athletic	46	9	5	9	28	22	5	9	9	27	31	56
18	Reading	46	10	6	7	37	29	5	5	13	31	43	56
19	Blackpool	46	10	6	7	36	29	4	7	12	20	30	55
20	**NORTHAMPTON TOWN**	46	11	2	10	41	34	5	4	14	25	42	54
21	Southend United	46	10	9	4	33	26	3	6	14	23	49	54
22	Chesterfield	46	9	5	9	35	35	5	2	16	16	51	49
23	Gillingham	46	7	3	13	25	32	5	1	17	22	49	40
24	Aldershot	46	7	6	10	29	29	1	7	15	19	49	37

1989/90 Division 3

		P	W	D	L	F	A	W	D	L	F	A	Pts
1	Bristol Rovers	46	15	8	0	43	14	11	7	5	28	21	93
2	Bristol City	46	15	5	3	40	16	12	5	6	36	24	91
3	Notts County	46	17	4	2	40	18	8	8	7	33	35	87
4	Tranmere Rovers	46	15	5	3	54	22	8	6	9	32	27	80
5	Bury	46	11	7	5	35	19	10	4	9	35	30	74
6	Bolton Wanderers	46	12	7	4	32	19	6	8	9	27	29	69
7	Birmingham City	46	10	7	6	33	19	8	5	10	27	40	66
8	Huddersfield Town	46	11	5	7	30	23	6	9	8	31	39	65
9	Rotherham United	46	12	6	5	48	28	5	7	11	23	34	64
10	Reading	46	10	9	4	33	21	5	10	8	24	32	64
11	Shrewsbury Town	46	10	9	4	38	24	6	6	11	21	30	63
12	Crewe Alexandra	46	10	8	5	32	24	5	9	9	24	29	62
13	Brentford	46	11	4	8	41	31	7	3	13	25	35	61
14	Leyton Orient	46	9	6	8	28	24	7	4	12	24	32	58
15	Mansfield Town	46	13	2	8	34	25	3	5	15	16	40	55
16	Chester City	46	11	7	5	30	23	2	8	13	13	32	54
17	Swansea City	46	10	6	7	25	27	4	6	13	20	36	54
18	Wigan Athletic	46	10	6	7	29	22	3	8	12	19	42	53
19	Preston North End	46	10	7	6	42	30	4	3	16	23	49	52
20	Fulham	46	8	8	7	33	27	4	7	12	22	39	51
21	Cardiff City	46	6	9	8	30	35	6	5	12	21	35	50
22	NORTHAMPTON TOWN	46	7	7	9	27	31	4	7	12	24	37	47
23	Blackpool	46	8	6	9	29	33	2	10	11	20	40	46
24	Walsall	46	6	8	9	23	30	3	6	14	17	42	41

1990/91 Division 4

		P	W	D	L	F	A	W	D	L	F	A	Pts
1	Darlington	46	13	8	2	36	14	9	9	5	32	24	83
2	Stockport County	46	16	6	1	54	19	7	7	9	30	28	82
3	Hartlepool United	46	15	5	3	35	15	9	5	9	32	33	82
4	Peterborough Utd.	46	13	9	1	38	15	8	7	9	29	30	80
5	Blackpool	46	17	3	3	55	17	6	7	10	23	30	79
6	Burnley	46	17	5	1	46	16	6	5	12	24	35	79
7	Torquay United	46	14	7	2	37	13	4	11	8	27	34	72
8	Scunthorpe United	46	17	4	2	51	20	3	7	13	20	42	71
9	Scarborough	46	13	5	5	36	21	6	7	10	23	35	69
10	NORTHAMPTON TOWN	46	14	5	4	34	21	4	8	11	23	37	67
11	Doncaster Rovers	46	12	5	6	36	22	5	9	9	20	24	65
12	Rochdale	46	10	9	4	29	22	5	8	10	21	31	62
13	Cardiff City	46	10	6	7	26	23	5	9	9	17	31	60
14	Lincoln City	46	10	7	6	32	27	4	10	9	18	34	59
15	Gillingham	46	9	9	5	35	27	3	9	11	22	33	54
16	Walsall	46	7	12	4	25	17	5	5	13	23	34	53
17	Hereford United	46	9	10	4	32	19	4	4	15	21	39	53
18	Chesterfield	46	8	12	3	33	26	5	2	16	14	36	53
19	Maidstone United	46	9	5	9	42	34	4	7	12	24	37	51
20	Carlisle United	46	12	3	8	30	30	1	6	16	17	59	48
21	York City	46	8	6	9	21	23	3	7	13	24	34	46
22	Halifax Town	46	9	6	8	34	29	3	4	16	25	50	46
23	Aldershot	46	8	7	8	38	43	2	4	17	23	58	41
24	Wrexham	46	8	7	8	33	34	2	3	18	15	40	40

1991/92 Division 4

		P	W	D	L	F	A	W	D	L	F	A	Pts
1	Burnley	42	14	4	3	42	16	11	4	6	37	27	83
2	Rotherham United	42	12	6	3	38	16	10	5	6	32	21	77
3	Mansfield Town	42	13	4	4	43	26	10	4	7	32	27	77
4	Blackpool	42	17	3	1	48	13	5	7	9	23	32	76
5	Scunthorpe United	42	14	5	2	39	18	7	4	10	25	41	72
6	Crewe Alexandra	42	12	6	3	33	20	8	4	9	31	37	70
7	Barnet	42	16	1	4	48	23	5	5	11	33	38	69
8	Rochdale	42	12	6	3	34	22	6	7	8	23	31	67
9	Cardiff City	42	13	3	5	42	26	4	12	5	24	27	66
10	Lincoln City	42	9	5	7	21	24	8	6	7	29	20	62
11	Gillingham	42	12	5	4	41	19	3	7	11	22	34	57
12	Scarborough	42	12	5	4	39	28	3	7	11	25	40	57
13	Chesterfield	42	6	7	8	26	28	8	4	9	23	33	53
14	Wrexham	42	11	4	6	31	26	3	5	13	21	47	51
15	Walsall	42	5	10	6	28	26	7	3	11	20	32	49
16	NORTHAMPTON TOWN	42	5	9	7	25	23	6	4	11	21	34	46
17	Hereford United	42	9	4	8	31	24	3	4	14	13	33	44
18	Maidstone United	42	6	9	6	24	22	2	9	10	21	34	42
19	York City	42	6	9	6	26	23	2	7	12	16	35	40
20	Halifax Town	42	7	5	9	23	35	3	3	15	11	40	38
21	Doncaster Rovers	42	6	2	13	21	35	3	6	12	19	30	35
22	Carlisle United	42	5	9	7	24	27	2	4	15	17	40	34

1992/93 Division 3 (of the "new" Football League)

		P	W	D	L	F	A	W	D	L	F	A	Pts
1	Cardiff City	42	13	7	1	42	20	12	1	8	35	27	83
2	Wrexham	42	14	3	4	48	26	9	8	4	27	26	80
3	Barnet	42	16	4	1	45	19	7	6	8	21	29	79
4	York City	42	13	6	2	41	15	8	6	7	31	30	75
5	Walsall	42	11	6	4	42	31	11	1	9	34	30	73
6	Crewe Alexandra	42	13	3	5	47	23	8	4	9	28	33	70
7	Bury	42	10	7	4	36	19	8	2	11	27	36	63
8	Lincoln City	42	10	6	5	31	20	8	3	10	26	33	63
9	Shrewsbury Town	42	11	3	7	36	30	6	8	7	21	22	62
10	Colchester United	42	13	3	5	38	26	5	2	14	29	50	59
11	Rochdale	42	10	3	8	38	29	6	7	8	32	41	58
12	Chesterfield	42	11	3	7	32	28	4	8	9	27	35	56
13	Scarborough	42	7	7	7	32	30	8	2	11	34	41	54
14	Scunthorpe United	42	8	7	6	38	25	6	5	10	19	29	54
15	Darlington	42	5	6	10	23	31	7	8	6	25	22	50
16	Doncaster Rovers	42	6	5	10	22	28	5	9	7	20	29	47
17	Hereford United	42	7	9	5	31	27	3	6	12	16	33	45
18	Carlisle United	42	7	5	9	29	27	4	6	11	22	38	44
19	Torquay United	42	6	4	11	18	26	6	3	12	27	41	43
20	NORTHAMPTON TOWN	42	6	5	10	19	28	5	3	13	29	46	41
21	Gillingham	42	9	4	8	32	28	0	9	12	16	36	40
22	Halifax Town	42	3	5	13	20	35	6	4	11	25	33	36

1993/94 Division 3

		P	W	D	L	F	A	W	D	L	F	A	Pts
1	Shrewsbury Town	42	10	8	3	28	17	12	5	4	35	22	79
2	Chester City	42	13	5	3	35	18	8	6	7	34	28	74
3	Crewe Alexandra	42	12	4	5	45	30	9	6	6	35	31	73
4	Wycombe Wanderers	42	11	6	4	34	21	8	7	6	33	32	70
5	Preston North End	42	13	5	3	46	23	5	8	8	33	37	67
6	Torquay United	42	8	10	3	30	24	9	6	6	34	32	67
7	Carlisle United	42	10	4	7	35	23	8	6	7	22	19	64
8	Chesterfield	42	8	8	5	32	22	8	6	7	23	26	62
9	Rochdale	42	10	5	6	38	22	6	7	8	25	29	60
10	Walsall	42	7	5	9	28	26	10	4	7	20	27	60
11	Scunthorpe United	42	9	7	5	40	26	6	7	8	24	30	59
12	Mansfield Town	42	9	3	9	28	30	6	7	8	32	35	55
13	Bury	42	9	6	6	33	22	5	5	11	22	34	53
14	Scarborough	42	8	4	9	29	28	7	4	10	26	33	53
15	Doncaster Rovers	42	8	6	7	24	26	6	4	11	23	31	52
16	Gillingham	42	8	8	5	27	23	4	7	10	17	28	51
17	Colchester United	42	8	4	9	31	33	5	6	10	25	38	49
18	Lincoln City	42	7	4	10	26	29	5	7	9	26	34	47
19	Wigan Athletic	42	6	7	8	33	33	5	5	11	18	37	45
20	Hereford United	42	6	4	11	34	33	6	2	13	26	46	42
21	Darlington	42	7	5	9	24	28	3	6	12	18	36	41
22	NORTHAMPTON TOWN	42	6	7	8	25	23	3	4	14	19	43	38

1994/95 Division 3

		P	W	D	L	F	A	W	D	L	F	A	Pts
1	Carlisle United	42	14	5	2	34	14	13	5	3	33	17	91
2	Walsall	42	15	3	3	42	18	9	8	4	33	22	83
3	Chesterfield	42	11	7	3	26	10	12	5	4	36	27	81
4	Bury	42	13	7	1	39	13	10	4	7	34	23	80
5	Preston North End	42	13	3	5	37	17	6	7	8	21	24	67
6	Mansfield Town	42	10	5	6	45	27	8	6	7	39	32	65
7	Scunthorpe United	42	12	2	7	40	30	6	6	9	28	33	62
8	Fulham	42	11	5	5	39	22	5	9	7	21	32	62
9	Doncaster Rovers	42	9	5	7	28	20	8	5	8	30	23	61
10	Colchester United	42	8	5	8	29	30	8	5	8	27	34	58
11	Barnet	42	8	7	6	37	27	7	4	10	19	36	56
12	Lincoln City	42	10	7	4	34	22	5	4	12	20	33	56
13	Torquay United	42	10	8	3	35	25	4	5	12	19	32	55
14	Wigan Athletic	42	7	6	8	28	30	7	4	10	25	30	52
15	Rochdale	42	8	6	7	25	23	4	8	9	19	44	50
16	Hereford United	42	9	6	6	22	19	3	7	11	23	43	49
17	NORTHAMPTON TOWN	42	8	5	8	25	29	2	9	10	20	38	44
18	Hartlepool United	42	9	5	7	33	32	2	5	14	10	37	43
19	Gillingham	42	8	7	6	31	25	2	4	15	15	39	41
20	Darlington	42	7	5	9	23	24	4	3	14	18	33	41
21	Scarborough	42	4	7	10	26	31	4	3	14	23	39	34
22	Exeter City	42	5	5	11	25	36	3	5	13	11	34	34

NORTHAMPTON'S RECORD AGAINST THE OTHER LEAGUE CLUBS

	P	HOME					AWAY					TOTALS		
		W	D	L	F	A	W	D	L	F	A	F	A	% Won
Aberdare Athletic	12	5	0	1	16	6	1	2	3	8	14	24	20	50.00
Accrington Stanley	2	1	0	0	2	1	0	0	1	2	3	4	4	50.00
Aldershot	78	25	9	5	93	41	7	12	20	39	73	132	114	41.03
Arsenal	2	0	1	0	1	1	0	1	0	1	1	2	2	0.00
Aston Villa	2	1	0	0	2	1	1	0	0	2	1	4	2	100.00
Barnet	6	0	3	0	3	3	1	0	2	3	8	6	11	16.67
Barnsley	18	6	2	1	22	10	2	2	5	12	19	34	29	44.44
Barrow	14	7	0	0	21	0	3	1	3	7	9	28	9	71.43
Birmingham C	4	1	1	0	4	3	0	0	2	0	7	4	10	25.00
Blackburn Rovers	4	2	0	0	4	2	0	0	2	1	9	5	11	50.00
Blackpool	20	5	2	3	18	17	1	1	8	7	18	25	35	30.00
Bolton Wanderers	8	2	0	2	8	6	2	1	1	6	3	14	9	50.00
Bournemouth	78	21	8	10	83	48	7	12	20	39	71	122	119	35.90
Bradford C	16	3	0	5	11	11	1	1	6	8	17	19	28	25.00
Bradford PA	12	5	0	1	15	4	5	0	1	12	9	27	13	83.33
Brentford	56	14	8	6	54	29	5	3	20	28	59	82	88	33.93
Brighton & Hove Alb.	72	20	10	6	64	33	9	9	18	46	71	110	104	40.28
Bristol C	56	15	4	9	58	38	5	5	18	34	58	92	96	35.71
Bristol Rovers	64	16	8	8	67	36	8	11	13	46	59	113	95	37.50
Burnley	10	2	1	2	8	6	0	0	5	4	17	12	23	20.00
Bury	38	8	3	8	21	21	5	7	7	25	38	46	59	34.21
Cambridge U	14	3	1	3	13	11	5	1	1	17	11	30	22	57.14
Cardiff C	36	12	4	2	28	8	3	3	12	20	43	48	51	41.67
Carlisle U	20	3	7	0	15	10	3	0	7	10	17	25	27	30.00
Charlton Athletic	26	7	3	3	17	11	1	8	4	14	23	31	34	30.77
Chelsea	2	0	0	1	2	3	0	0	1	0	1	2	4	0.00
Chester C	36	11	4	3	30	17	5	4	9	25	28	55	45	44.44
Chesterfield	22	4	3	4	18	13	3	3	5	11	16	29	29	31.82
Colchester U	48	15	6	3	47	22	5	5	14	31	50	78	72	41.67
Coventry C	42	11	6	4	47	28	6	6	9	21	31	68	59	40.48
Crewe Alexandra	50	14	5	6	45	21	9	3	13	37	40	82	61	46.00
Crystal Palace	70	21	11	3	81	30	11	10	14	49	64	130	94	45.71
Darlington	44	11	6	5	43	28	3	8	11	20	42	63	70	31.82
Derby Co.	6	0	1	2	2	5	0	2	1	5	6	7	11	0.00
Doncaster Rov.	36	9	5	4	23	14	4	3	11	23	28	46	42	36.11
Everton	2	0	0	1	0	2	0	0	1	2	5	2	7	0.00
Exeter C	90	27	14	4	112	51	10	13	22	55	83	167	134	41.11
Fulham	18	4	2	3	19	17	2	3	4	17	17	36	34	33.33
Gateshead	4	2	0	0	3	0	1	0	1	4	5	7	5	75.00
Gillingham	84	29	6	7	81	35	14	6	22	60	80	141	115	51.19
Grimsby T	22	7	1	3	26	12	4	2	5	15	19	41	31	50.00
Halifax T	30	9	2	4	31	15	6	3	6	24	22	55	37	50.00
Hartlepool U	46	16	6	1	51	22	3	5	15	23	46	74	68	41.30
Hereford U	30	5	2	8	17	26	3	4	8	18	28	35	54	26.67
Huddersfield T	18	5	1	3	16	13	4	2	3	9	12	25	25	50.00
Hull C	10	2	2	1	9	5	1	0	4	2	13	11	18	30.00
Ipswich T	26	8	3	2	22	17	2	4	7	15	28	37	45	38.46
Leeds U	4	1	0	1	2	4	0	1	1	1	6	3	10	25.00
Leicester C	2	0	1	0	2	2	0	1	0	1	1	3	3	0.00
Leyton Orient	54	17	6	4	63	25	5	8	14	26	46	89	71	40.74
Lincoln C	34	8	7	2	20	13	2	7	8	21	38	41	51	29.41
Liverpool	2	0	1	0	0	0	0	0	1	0	5	0	5	0.00
Luton T	36	11	3	4	31	19	0	3	15	15	43	46	62	30.56
Maidstone U	4	2	0	0	3	0	1	1	0	4	2	7	2	75.00
Manchester City	4	2	0	0	4	1	1	0	1	2	3	6	4	75.00
Manchester Utd.	2	0	1	0	1	1	0	0	1	2	6	3	7	0.00
Mansfield T	46	12	3	8	34	20	2	3	18	17	49	51	69	30.43
Merthyr Town	20	8	2	0	28	5	2	2	6	11	17	39	22	50.00
Middlesbrough	4	1	1	0	4	3	0	0	2	0	2	4	5	25.00
Millwall	54	11	5	11	47	42	4	2	21	23	52	70	94	27.78
Newcastle U	6	2	1	0	6	3	1	0	2	3	9	9	12	50.00
Newport County	80	27	4	9	94	43	11	10	19	47	65	141	108	47.50
Norwich C	58	15	10	4	52	29	5	8	16	40	63	92	92	34.48

Team	P	W	D	L	F	A	W	D	L	F	A	F	A	%
Nottm Forest	6	0	3	0	5	5	1	2	0	4	3	9	8	16.67
Notts County	34	7	5	5	29	21	2	1	14	16	36	45	57	26.47
Oldham Ath.	14	3	2	2	14	8	3	2	2	8	7	22	15	42.86
Oxford U	4	1	1	0	2	1	0	0	2	0	2	2	3	25.00
Peterborough U	38	6	7	6	26	29	5	3	11	18	30	44	59	28.95
Plymouth Argyle	36	12	4	2	36	17	4	3	11	21	34	57	51	44.44
Port Vale	44	12	7	3	44	27	6	7	9	26	32	70	59	40.91
Portsmouth	22	4	3	4	14	17	1	3	7	12	26	26	43	22.73
Preston North End	22	6	0	5	18	15	0	5	6	8	17	26	32	27.27
QPR	58	20	3	6	62	39	6	4	19	36	55	98	94	44.83
Reading	82	18	9	14	83	63	4	8	29	36	93	119	156	26.83
Rochdale	38	10	6	3	34	18	4	7	8	26	36	60	54	36.84
Rotherham U	20	4	2	4	13	14	4	2	4	11	12	24	26	40.00
Scarborough	10	2	0	3	7	12	0	2	3	5	9	12	21	20.00
Scunthorpe U	44	13	4	5	31	18	5	6	11	23	44	54	62	40.91
Sheffield Utd.	6	0	0	3	2	5	0	1	2	5	13	7	18	0.00
Sheffield Wed.	4	0	1	1	0	2	0	0	2	2	5	2	7	0.00
Shrewsbury T	34	10	5	2	39	23	4	1	12	18	41	57	64	41.18
Southampton	18	6	2	1	17	8	1	0	8	6	27	23	35	38.89
Southend U	86	22	12	9	98	56	12	6	25	46	84	144	140	39.53
Southport	22	6	4	1	15	8	5	1	5	14	16	29	24	50.00
Stockport County	42	12	7	2	42	17	5	5	11	19	31	61	48	40.48
Stoke C	2	1	0	0	1	0	0	0	1	2	6	3	6	50.00
Sunderland	6	2	0	1	7	4	1	0	2	3	6	10	10	50.00
Swansea	34	8	2	7	26	18	2	6	9	20	32	46	50	29.41
Swindon T	84	23	9	10	77	37	7	7	28	40	99	117	136	35.71
Thames	4	1	0	1	4	5	1	0	1	3	2	7	7	50.00
Torquay U	94	27	11	9	83	44	12	9	26	54	90	137	134	41.49
Tottenham Hotspur	2	0	0	1	0	2	0	1	0	1	1	1	3	0.00
Tranmere Rovers	26	7	3	3	21	17	3	4	6	16	18	37	35	38.46
Walsall	64	17	7	8	74	40	10	6	16	45	58	119	98	42.19
Watford	78	19	8	12	67	40	10	11	18	42	74	109	114	37.18
West Bromwich Alb.	2	0	0	1	3	4	0	1	0	1	1	4	5	0.00
West Ham Utd.	2	1	0	0	2	1	0	1	0	1	1	3	2	50.00
Wigan Ath.	18	1	5	3	10	14	1	4	4	8	14	18	28	11.11
Wimbledon	8	0	3	1	4	7	0	1	3	2	8	6	15	0.00
Wolves	6	2	0	1	5	6	0	1	2	3	5	8	11	33.33
Workington	20	7	2	1	20	6	0	2	8	6	24	26	30	35.00
Wrexham	22	3	3	5	19	17	6	2	3	19	13	38	30	40.91
Wycombe Wan.	2	0	1	0	1	1	0	0	1	0	1	1	2	0.00
York City	32	9	5	2	33	16	6	3	7	22	25	55	41	46.88

Complete League Record:

	HOME						AWAY					TOTALS		
P	W	D	L	F	A	W	D	L	F	A	F	A	Pts.
3004	813	352	337	2852	1665	336	340	826	1718	2860	4570	4525	3194

Consisting of:

	P	W	D	L	F	A	W	D	L	F	A	F	A	Pts.
Division 1	42	8	6	7	31	32	2	7	12	24	60	55	92	33
Division 2	126	32	15	16	100	80	16	16	31	71	114	171	194	127
Division 3	368	86	49	49	330	210	46	44	94	223	310	553	520	402
Division 4	1134	281	145	141	956	623	133	131	303	647	1028	1603	1651	1263
Division 3(S)	1334	406	137	124	1435	720	139	142	386	753	1348	2188	2068	1369

The new Football League Division 3 records are included with the old Division 4

F.A. Cup Record in Non-League Seasons

Players appearances and goals are included in the A-Z section only if they also made a League appearance.

1898/1899

					Att											
Q1	Oct	1	Hinckley T	2-1	Lawrence, Clipstone		Whiting	Byles	Sargeant	Minney	Howard	Warner R	Brawn	Warner F	Lawrence	Clipstone	Dunckley
Q2		24	Wellingborough T	1-2	Lawrence		Whiting	Byles	Sargeant	Minney	Howard	Warner R	Brawn	Warner F	Lawrence	Clipstone	Dunckley

Q2 followed a void game at Wellingborough that Northampton won 2-0.

1899/1900

Q1	Sep	30	WELLINGBOROUGH T	1-2	Unknown		Bullimer	Byles	Hendry	Foster	Shortland	Warner R	Handley	Dunkley	Lawrence	Miles	Braun

1900/01

Q3	Nov	3	Hinckley Town	0-2			Clarke	Warner R	Hendry	Pell	Howe	Murrell	Frost J	Warner F	Stewart	Scrivens	Pendred

1901/02

Q3	Nov	2	Gresley Rovers	2-0	Chapman, Coleman		Cooke	Bennett	Turner	Pell	Murrell	Howe	Frost	Chapman	Farrell	Coleman	Lawrence
Q4		20	Burton United	0-0			Cooke	Bennett	Turner	Pell	Murrell	Howe	Frost	Chapman	Farrell	Coleman	Lawrence
rep		25	BURTON UNITED	2-0	Morrell, Farrell		Cooke	Bennett	Turner	Pell	Murrell	Howe	Frost	Chapman	Farrell	Coleman	Lawrence
Q5		30	Kettering	2-2	Pell, Chapman	3000	Cooke	Bennett	Turner	Pell	Murrell	Howe	Frost	Chapman	Farrell	Coleman	Lawrence
rep	Dec	2	KETTERING	2-0	Morrell, Farrell		Bullimer	Bennett	Turner	Pell	Murrell	Howe	Frost	Chapman	Farrell	Coleman	Lawrence
IR		16	DARWEN	4-1	Pell, Coleman 2, Lawrence	2000	Cooke	Bennett	Turner	Pell	Murrell	Howe	Frost	Chapman	Farrell	Coleman	Lawrence
R1	Jan	22	SHEFFIELD UNITED	0-2		15000	Cooke	Bennett	Turner	Pell	Murrell	Neale	Frost	Chapman	Farrell	Coleman	Lawrence

1902/03

Q3	Nov	1	Burton United	0-2		2000	Cooke	Bennett	Durber	Murrell	Dainty	Howe	Frost	Crump	Benbow	Brown H	Wilson

1903/04

Q3	Oct	31	Wellingborough T	0-2		8000	Perkins	Clarke	Durber	Neale	Benbow	Howe	Frost	Garfield	Brown H	Brown G	Murray

1904/05

Q3	Oct	27	Burton United	3-2	Chapman 2, Brown G	2000	Perkins	Clarke	Durber	Neale	Chadwick	Howe	Frost	Smith	Chapman	Brown G	Marriott
Q4	Nov	12	Kettering	2-0	Smith, Marriott	3000	Perkins	Clarke	Durber	Neale	Chadwick	Howe	Frost	Smith	Benbow	Chapman	Marriott
Q5		26	LEICESTER FOSSE	2-2	Benbow 2	4000	Perkins	Clarke	Durber	Neale	Chadwick	Howe	Frost	Smith	Benbow	Chapman	Marriott
rep	Dec	1	Leicester Fosse	0-2		3000	Perkins	Clarke	Benbow	Neale	Chadwick	Howe	Frost	Smith	Chapman	Brown G	Marriott

1905/06

Q4	Dec	9	West Stanley	1-1	Dilkes	5000	Perkins	Drennan	Tirrell	Neale	Chadwick	Howe	Dilkes	Platt	Gooing	Cole	Turner
rep		14	WEST STANLEY	3-0	Gooing, Springthorpe 2		Perkins	Drennan	Kerridge	Neale	Chadwick	Tirrell	Frost G	Platt	Gooing	Springthorpe	Dilks
R1	Jan	13	New Brompton	1-2	Springthorpe	3500	Perkins	Drennan	Kerridge	Neale	Chadwick	Cole	Frost J	Batson	Gooing	Springthorpe	Hartwell

1906/07

Q5	Dec	8	SOUTHPORT CENTRAL	2-1	Platt 2	2000	Gooch	Drennan	Hartshorne	Neale	Tirrell	Dunkley	Frost J	Platt	Watkins	Springthorpe	Freeman
R1	Jan	12	Middlesbrough	2-4	Platt, Watkins	15000	Gooch	Drennan	Henry	Neale	Dunkley	Tirrell	Springthorpe	Platt	Vann BW	Watkins	Freeman

1907/08

Q5	Dec	7	SUTTON	10-0	See below	7000	Gooch	Drennan	Lloyd Davies	Tirrell	McCartney	Hickleton	Badenoch	Platt	Lowe	Chapman	McDiarmid
R1	Jan	11	BRISTOL ROVERS	0-1		10000	Gooch	Drennan	Lloyd Davies	Tirrell	McCartney	Hickleton	Badenoch	Freeman	Lessons	Chapman	McDiarmid

Scorers in Q5: Tirrell, Badenoch 3, Platt 3, Lowe, Chapman 2

1908/09

Rd	Date	Opponent	Att	Score	Scorers	1	2	3	4	5	6	7	8	9	10	11
R1	Jan 16	DERBY COUNTY	14798	1-1	McDiarmid	Gooch	Bonthron	Lloyd Davies	Manning	McCartney	Hickleton	McDiarmid	Walker	Lessons	Lewis	Freeman
rep	20	Derby County	11250	2-4	McCartney, Lewis	Gooch	Bonthron	Lloyd Davies	Dunkley	McCartney	Manning	McDiarmid	Walker	Lessons	Lewis	Freeman

1909/10

Rd	Date	Opponent	Att	Score	Scorers	1	2	3	4	5	6	7	8	9	10	11
R1	Jan 15	SHEFFIELD WED.	12000	0-0		Thorpe	Bonthron	Brittain	Whittaker	Lloyd Davies	Manning	McDiarmid	Walker	Lessons	Lewis	Freeman
rep	18	Sheffield Wednesday	18533	1-0	Walker	Thorpe	Bonthron	Brittain	Whittaker	McCartney	Manning	McDiarmid	Walker	Lessons	Lewis	Freeman
R2	Feb 5	NOTTM. FOREST	15000	0-0		Thorpe	Bonthron	Brittain	Whittaker	McCartney	Manning	McDiarmid	Walker	Lessons	Lewis	Freeman
rep	9	Nottm. Forest	15000	0-1		Thorpe	Bonthron	Brittain	Whittaker	McCartney	Manning	McDiarmid	Walker	Lessons	Lewis	Freeman

1910/11

Rd	Date	Opponent	Att	Score	Scorers	1	2	3	4	5	6	7	8	9	10	11
R1	Jan 14	LUTON TOWN	15000	5-1	Bradshaw, Lessons 3, Lewis	Thorpe	Brittain	Clipston	Manning	Lloyd Davies	Hampson	Walden	Bradshaw	Lessons	Lewis	McDiarmid
R2	Feb 4	Newcastle United	42023	1-1	Bradshaw	Thorpe	Brittain	Clipston	Manning	Lloyd Davies	Hampson	Walden	Bradshaw	Lessons	Lewis	McDiarmid
rep	8	NEWCASTLE UNITED	29880	0-1		Thorpe	Brittain	Clipston	Manning	Lloyd Davies	Hampson	Walden	Bradshaw	Lessons	Lewis	McDiarmid

1911/12

Rd	Date	Opponent	Att	Score	Scorers	1	2	3	4	5	6	7	8	9	10	11
R1	Jan 13	BRISTOL CITY	14000	1-0	Lewis	Thorpe	Clipston	Lloyd Davies	Manning	Hampson	Tomkins	Walden	King	Lessons	Lewis	Freeman
R2	30	Darlington	7200	1-1	King	Thorpe	Clipston	Lloyd Davies	Manning	Hampson	Tomkins	Walden	King	Lessons	Lewis	Freeman
rep	Feb 4	DARLINGTON	7000	2-0	King, Lessons	Thorpe	Clipston	Lloyd Davies	Manning	Hampson	Tomkins	Walden	King	Lessons	Lewis	Freeman
R3	24	Fulham	32035	1-2	Lewis	Thorpe	Clipston	Lloyd Davies	Manning	Hampson	Tomkins	Walden	King	Lessons	Lewis	Freeman

1912/13

Rd	Date	Opponent	Att	Score	Scorers	1	2	3	4	5	6	7	8	9	10	11
R1	Jan 11	Blackburn Rovers	23623	2-7	Walden, Lewis	Thorpe	Clipston	Lloyd Davies	Manning	Langham	Tomkins	Walden	Freeman	King	Lewis	Hughes

1913/14

1914/15

Rd	Date	Opponent	Att	Score	Scorers	1	2	3	4	5	6	7	8	9	10	11
R1	Jan 17	Derby County	15000	0-1		Thorpe	Clipston	Lloyd Davies	Manning	Lessons	Tull	Birtles	Freeman	King	Bellamy	Hughes

1919/20

Rd	Date	Opponent	Att	Score	Scorers	1	2	3	4	5	6	7	8	9	10	11
R1	Jan 9	Grimsby Town	5000	3-0	Smith, Lockett, Freeman	Thorpe	Clipston	Lloyd Davies	Tull	Manning	Tomkins	Hughes	Smith	Lockett	Bellamy	Freeman
R2	30	Hull City	8000	1-2	Freeman	Thorpe	Clipston	Lloyd Davies	Tull	Manning	Tomkins	Hughes	Smith	Lockett	Bellamy	Freeman

Rd	Date	Opponent	Att	Score	Scorers	1	2	3	4	5	6	7	8	9	10	11
Q6	Dec 20	BRISTOL ROVERS	9000	2-2	Sproson, Pease	Thorpe	Sproson	Lloyd Davies	Manning	Grendon	Tomkins	Pease	Freeman	Whitworth	Lockett	Freeman
rep	24	Bristol Rovers	14000	2-3	Pease, Whitworth	Thorpe	Sproson	Thompson WD	Grendon	Lloyd Davies	Tomkins	Pease	Burkinshaw	Whitworth	Lockett	Freeman

1945/46

Rd	Date	Opponent	Att	Score	Scorers	1	2	3	4	5	6	7	8	9	10	11
R1/1	Nov 17	CHELMSFORD CITY		5-1	Morrall 2, Hughes 2, Roberts	Scott	Smalley	Barron	Lowery	Sankey	Yarker	Roberts	Heaselgrave	Morrall	Hughes	Fowler
R1/2	24	Chelmsford City	6700	5-0	Morrall 2, Fowler, Roberts, Smith	Scott	Smalley	Barron	Lowery	Dennison	Yarker	Roberts	Smith	Morrall	Hughes	Fowler
R2/1	Dec 8	NOTTS COUNTY	10000	3-1	Morrall 2, Blunt	Scott	Smalley	Barron	Lowery	Dennison	Yarker	Roberts	Blunt	Morrall	Haycock	Fowler
R2/2	15	Notts County	17000	0-1		Scott	Smalley	Welsh	Lowery	Dennison	Sankey	Roberts	Blunt	Morrall	Hughes	Fowler
R3/1	Jan 5	MILLWALL	15384	2-2	Blunt, Hughes	Scott	Smalley	Barron	Lowery	Sankey	Yarker	Roberts	Blunt	Morrall	Hughes	Fowler
R3/2	7	Millwall	14000	0-3		Scott	Smalley	Barron	Lowery	Sankey	Yarker	Roberts	Blunt	Morrall	Hughes	Fowler

Cup ties played over two legs for this season only

1939/40 Season

The season was abandoned on the outbreak of World War Two. Players appearances and goals are not included in the A-Z section.

Rd	Date	Opponent	Att	Score	Scorers	1	2	3	4	5	6	7	8	9	10	11
1	Aug 26	SWINDON TOWN	8315	1-0	Ellwood	Clifford JC	McCullough K	Strathie WJ	Blunt E	Simons RR	Miller HS	King FAR	Jennings HW	Melaniphy E	Ellwood RJ	Barron W
2	28	EXETER CITY	5000	1-2	Melaniphy (p)	Clifford JC	McCullough K	Strathie WJ	Garvey J	Simons RR	Miller HS	King FAR	Jennings HW	Melaniphy E	Ellwood RJ	Barron W
3	Sep 2	Bournemouth	3000	0-10		Clifford JC	Smith A	Strathie WJ	McCullough K	Simons RR	Miller HS	King FAR	Jennings HW	Melaniphy E	Ellwood RJ	Barron W

Player			D.O.B	Place of Birth	Died	First Season	Last Season	Previous Club	Next Club	Appearances				Goals			
										League	FAC	FLC	Other	League	FAC	FLC	Oth.
Adams	CJ	Craig	09/11/74	Northampton		1991			VS Rugby	1	0	0	0	0	0	0	0
Adams	DF	Don	15/02/31	Northampton	1994	1951	1955		Bedford T	23	0	0	0	7	0	0	0
Adcock	AC	Tony	27/02/63	Bethnal Green		1987	1989	Manchester City	Bradford City	107	2	7	6	40	1	3	2
						1990	1991	Bradford City	Peterborough U								
Adey	TW	Thomas	22/02/01	Hetton-le-Hole	1986	1926		Swindon Town	Durham City	10	1	0	0	0	0	0	0
Aitken	JG	John	19/09/1897	Glasgow	1967	1927		Norwich City	Kilmarnock	10	0	0	0	5	0	0	0
Aldridge	MJ	Martin	06/12/74	Northampton		1991	1994		Oxford United	70	2	3	5	17	1	0	4
Aldridge	NH	Norman	23/02/21	Coventry		1948		West Bromwich A.	Oxford United	2	0	0	0	0	0	0	0
Alexander	JE	John	03/10/55	Liverpool		1981		Reading		22	1	4	0	4	0	1	0
Allan	CE	Charles	01/01/10	Darlington		1932	1933	Darlington	Darlington	15	0	0	0	0	0	0	0
Allen	AR	Robert	11/10/16	Bromley-by-Bow		1946		Brentford	Colchester Utd.	5	0	0	0	0	0	0	0
Allen	PW	Percy	02/07/1895	West Ham	1969	1925	1926	Lincoln C	Peterborough U	44	1	0	0	3	0	0	0
Allen	RSL	Ralph	30/06/06	Newburn	1981	1936	1938	Reading	Torquay United	52	2	0	3	41	0	0	3
Allen	T	Tommy	01/05/1897	Moxley	1968	1933		Accrington Stanley	Kidderminster H.	19	6	0	0	0	0	0	0
Allon	TG	George	27/08/1899	Blyth	1983	1926	1931	Coventry City	Wigan Borough	185	7	0	0	7	0	0	0
Ambridge	FW	Frederick	01/01/00	Wellingborough		1921		(Navy)	Wellingborough	13	4	0	0	0	0	0	0
Anderson	DE	Doug	29/08/63	Hong Kong		1988		Plymouth Arg. (loan)		5	0	0	1	0	0	0	0
Anderson	GL	Gary	20/11/55	Bow		1974	1975	Tottenham H	Barking	14	0	2	0	0	0	0	0
Anderson	JL	John	05/04/28	Glasgow		1953		Partick Thistle	Exeter City	14	1	0	0	5	0	0	0
Angus	TN	Terry	14/01/66	Coventry		1990	1992	VS Rugby	Fulham	116	6	7	9	6	0	0	0
Ansell	W	William 'Jack'	04/08/21	Bletchley	1947	1951		Bletchley Brick Wks	Oxford United	131	11	0	0	0	0	0	0
Anthony	C	Charles	1903	Mansfield		1929	1931	Mansfield Town	Mansfield Town	81	3	0	0	0	0	0	0
Armitage	JH	Jack	21/08/1897	Chapeltown		1930		Southend Utd.	Halifax Town	4	0	0	0	0	0	0	0
Ashenden	RH	Russell	04/02/61	South Ockendon		1978	1979		Wycombe Wan.	18	0	4	0	0	0	0	0
Asher	SJ	Sid	24/12/30	Portsmouth		1956		Hastings	Bedford	21	1	0	0	11	0	0	0
Ashworth	A	Alec	01/10/39	Southport	1995	1962		Luton Town	Preston NE	30	1	3	0	25	0	1	0
Austin	TW	Terry	01/02/54	Isleworth		1983		Doncaster Rovers	Stamford	43	5	2	1	10	2	0	1
Bailey	RR	Ray	16/05/44	St Neots		1971		Gillingham (loan)		1	0	0	0	0	0	0	0
Baines	SN	Stan	28/07/20	Syston		1946		Leicester City		1	0	0	0	0	0	0	0
Baker	TW	Tommy	17/08/05	Shotton	1975	1934		Brentford	Rochdale	13	0	0	1	0	0	0	0
Bancroft	PA	Paul	10/09/64	Derby		1984		Derby County	Nuneaton	16	0	1	0	0	0	0	0
Bannister	JH	Jack	01/02/29	Chesterfield		1958		Shrewsbury Town	Aldershot	24	1	0	0	0	0	0	0
Barnes	DO	David 'Bobby'	17/12/62	Kingston		1989	1991	Bournemouth	Peterborough Utd.	98	9	5	6	37	3	3	1
Barnes	MF	Michael	17/09/63	Reading		1984		Reading	Basingstoke	19	4	2	0	1	0	0	0
Baron	KP	Kevin	19/07/26	Preston	1971	1958		Southend Utd.	Gravesend	25	2	0	0	4	0	0	0
Barratt	AG	Alf	13/04/20	Corby		1938			Stewarts & Lloyds	1	0	0	0	0	0	0	0
Barron	RW	Roger	30/06/47	Northampton		1967	1968		Bedford T	17	0	2	0	0	0	0	0
Barron	W	Bill	26/10/17	Houghton-le-Spring		1938	1950	Charlton Ath.	Kettering	166	23	0	0	4	0	0	0
Bartram	JL	James	01/01/11			1935		Falkirk	Queen of the South	12	0	0	2	3	0	0	3
Baxter	LR	Larry	24/11/31	Leicester		1952	1953		Norwich City	17	0	0	0	2	0	0	0
Baxter	WA	Bill	23/04/39	Edinburgh		1972		Hull City	Nuneaton	41	1	1	0	4	0	0	0
Beavon	DG	David	08/12/61	Nottingham		1982		Lincoln City (loan)		2	0	0	0	0	0	0	0
Beavon	MS	Stuart	30/11/58	Wolverhampton		1990	1992	Reading	Newbury	98	6	6	9	14	1	0	3
Bedford	SG	Syd	01/01/01	Northampton		1920	1923		Brighton & Hove A.	70	7	0	0	1	1	0	0
Belfon	F	Frank	18/02/65	Wellingborough		1981	1984		Wellingborough	78	9	3	3	15	2	0	1
Bell	M	Mickey	15/11/71	Newcastle		1989	1994		Wycombe Wan.	153	5	9	11	10	1	0	1
Bell	T	Tommy	09/11/06	Seaham Colliery	1983	1934	1937	Luton Town	Wellingborough	73	5	0	1	31	0	0	0
Bellamy	BW	Ben	22/04/1901	Wollaston	1985	1920		Wollaston	Kettering	3	3	0	0	0	0	0	0
Benjamin	IT	Ian	11/12/61	Nottingham		1984	1987	Peterborough Utd.	Cambridge Utd.	150	9	12	9	58	3	2	5
Bennett	J	Jesse		Dronfield		1933	1935	Coventry City		56	2	0	7	0	0	0	0
Benton	J	James	09/04/75	Wexford		1991	1992			10	0	0	2	1	0	0	0
Beresford	M	Marlon	02/09/69	Lincoln		1990		Sheffield Wed. (loan)		28	0	0	2	0	0	0	0
						1991		Sheffield Wed. (loan)									
Berridge	R	Reginald		Northampton		1929			Wellingborough	1	0	0	0	0	0	0	0
Berry	SA	Steve	04/04/63	Walton		1988	1990	Aldershot	Maidstone Utd.	102	7	5	9	7	2	0	1
Best	WJB	Billy	07/09/43	Glasgow		1963	1967	Pollock	Southend Utd.	243	10	18	0	49	1	6	0
						1973	1977	Southend Utd.	Bedford								
Billingham	J	Jack	03/12/14	Daventry	1981	1935			Bristol City	3	0	0	0	0	0	0	0
Blair	A	Andy	18/12/59	Bedworth		1988		Aston Villa	Naxxar (Malta)	3	0	0	0	0	0	0	0
Blencowe	AG	Arthur	05/11/16	Brackley		1937		Brackley	Banbury	2	0	0	1	0	0	0	0
Blunt	E	Eddie	21/05/18	Tunstall		1937	1948	Port Vale	Accrington Stanley	87	8	0	2	2	3	0	0
Bodley	MJ	Mike	14/09/67	Hayes		1988		Chelsea	Barnet	20	0	0	2	0	0	0	0
Book	K	Kim	12/02/46	Bath		1969	1971	Bournemouth	Doncaster Rovers	78	11	6	0	0	0	0	0
Bosse	PL	Percy	18/10/14	Cardiff		1937	1938	Arsenal		34	1	0	3	3	0	0	0
Bowen	DL	David	07/06/28	Maesteg	1995	1947	1948		Arsenal	34	1	0	0	1	0	0	0
						1959		Arsenal									
Bowen	EC	Eddie 'Ted'	01/07/03	Goldthorpe		1927	1931	Arsenal	Bristol City	162	10	0	0	114	6	0	0
Bowen	KB	Keith	26/02/58	Northampton		1976	1981		Brentford	65	2	9	0	24	0	1	0
Bowker	K	Keith	18/04/51	West Bromwich		1976		Cambridge U (loan)		4	0	0	0	0	0	0	0
Boyd	MS	Malcolm		Harpole		1926			Rushden	2	0	0	0	0	0	0	0
Boyle	TW	Thomas	27/02/1897	Sheffield		1930	1934	Manchester Utd.	Scarborough	142	7	0	2	33	2	0	0
Bradshaw	H	Harold				1925				2	0	0	0	0	0	0	0
Brady	PJ	Paul	26/03/61	Birmingham		1981	1982	Birmingham City	Crewe Alexandra	51	7	8	3	3	0	0	0
Braidford	L	Lowington	1898	Scotland		1923		Hartlepool Utd.		5	0	0	0	1	0	0	0
Branston	TG	Terry	25/07/38	Rugby		1960	1966		Luton Town	246	8	17	0	2	0	0	0
Brett	FB	Frank	10/03/1899	King's Norton	1988	1923	1929	Aston Villa	Brighton & Hove A.	254	19	0	0	4	0	0	0
Brewer	AP	Anthony	20/05/32	Edmonton		1958	1960	Millwall		87	2	1	0	0	0	0	0
Bright	G	Gerry	02/12/34	Northampton		1956	1957		Wellingborough	4	0	0	0	0	0	0	0
Briscoe	JER	James	23/04/17	St Helens	1981	1946	1948	Preston NE	Wolverton	53	7	0	0	17	1	0	0
Broadfoot	J	Joe	04/03/40	Lewisham		1965		Ipswich Town	Millwall	17	1	0	0	1	0	0	0
Brodie	CTG	Charles 'Chic'	22/02/37	Duntocher		1961	1963	Wolves	Brentford	87	4	6	0	0	0	0	0
Brookes	E	Eric	03/02/44	Mapplewell		1969	1970	Barnsley	Peterborough Utd.	80	11	7	0	1	0	2	0
Brooks	JT	John	23/08/47	Paddington		1967		Ipswich Town	Guildford	1	0	0	0	0	0	0	0
Brough	NK	Neil	22/12/65	Daventry		1983	1984		Long Buckby	12	0	0	1	0	0	0	0
Brown	A	Alf	22/02/07	Chadderton		1933	1935	Oldham Athletic	Mansfield Town	55	3	0	4	1	0	0	0
Brown	AR	Roy	14/02/11	Pegswood		1934	1935	QPR	Nottm. Forest	79	5	0	7	23	0	0	4
Brown	DJ	Dennis	08/02/44	Reading		1966	1968	Swindon Town	Aldershot	46	0	2	0	10	0	1	0

Player			D.O.B	Place of Birth	Died	First Season	Last Season	Previous Club	Next Club	Appearances				Goals			
										League	FAC	FLC	Other	League	FAC	FLC	Oth.
Brown	IO	Ian	11/09/65	Ipswich		1994		Bristol City	Sudbury	23	0	0	0	4	0	0	0
Brown	L	Laurie	22/08/37	Shildon		1960		Darlington	Arsenal	33	3	2	0	22	3	0	0
Brown	RH	Bobby	02/05/40	Streatham		1963	1966	Watford	Cardiff City	50	2	4	0	22	1	1	0
Brown	SF	Steve	06/07/66	Northampton		1983	1993		Wycombe Wan.	173	11	10	11	22	2	1	1
Brown	WDF	Bill	08/10/31	Arbroath		1966		Tottenham H	Toronto Falcons	17	1	3	0	0	0	0	0
Brown	WY	Billy		South Inch		1922			Portsmouth	2	0	0	0	0	0	0	0
Bruck	DJ	Dietmar	19/04/44	Danzig		1972	1973	Charlton Ath.	Nuneaton	41	1	2	0	0	0	0	0
Bryant	SP	Steve	05/09/53	Islington		1976	1981	Birmingham City	Portsmouth	107	2	8	0	5	0	0	0
Buchanan	D	David	23/06/62	Newcastle		1982		Leicester City (loan)		5	0	1	0	0	0	0	0
Buchanan	J	John	19/09/51	Dingwall		1970	1974	Ross County	Cardiff City	183	15	8	3	30	3	1	0
						1981	1982	Cardiff City	Wolverton								
Buck	AR	Tony	18/08/44	Whitwell, Oxon.		1972	1973	Rochdale	Bedford	17	1	0	0	3	0	0	0
Buckby	LC	Leonard	1905	Wellingborough		1926			Wellingborough	4	0	0	0	0	0	0	0
Bukowski	DJ	David	02/11/52	Northampton		1971	1972		Blyth Spartans	12	0	0	0	0	0	0	0
Bulzis	RRB	Riccardo	22/11/74	Bedford		1991			Wellingborough	4	0	0	0	0	0	0	0
Bunce	PE	Paul	07/01/67	Coalville		1986	1987	Leicester City	Weymouth	12	0	2	0	2	0	0	0
Burn	RG	Ralph	09/11/31	Alnwick		1950			Crewe Alexandra	1	0	0	0	0	0	0	0
Burnand	WT	Walter	04/10/1894	Northampton		1920	1921		Rushden	25	1	0	0	5	0	0	0
Burnham	JJ	Jason	08/05/73	Mansfield		1991	1993		Chester City	88	6	6	8	2	0	0	0
Burns	C	Chris	09/11/67	Manchester		1994		Swansea City		17	0	0	0	2	0	0	0
Burrows	AM	Adrian	16/01/59	Sutton-in-Ashfield		1982	1983	Mansfield Town	Plymouth Argyle	88	10	5	3	4	1	0	0
Burt	JHL	Jimmy	05/04/50	Harthill		1972		Aldershot	Rochdale	21	0	1	0	0	0	0	0
Bushell	MJ	Mark	05/06/68	Northampton		1984			Corby	1	0	0	0	0	0	0	0
Byatt	DJ	Dennis	08/08/58	Hillingdon		1979	1980	Peterborough Utd.	Wealdstone	47	2	4	0	3	0	0	0
Byrne	J	John	25/05/39	Cambuslang		1967	1968	Peterborough Utd.	Addington (SA)	40	2	2	0	4	0	0	0
Byrne	R	Ray	04/07/72	Newry		1994		Nottm. Forest		2	0	1	0	0	0	0	0
Cahill	OF	Ollie	29/09/75	Clonmel		1994			Clonmel	8	0	0	3	1	0	0	0
Campbell	GR	Greg	13/07/65	Portsmouth		1990	1991	Plymouth Argyle		47	4	2	5	7	1	0	0
Candlin	MH	Maurice	11/11/21	Jarrow	1992	1949	1952	Partick Thistle	Shrewsbury Town	139	13	0	0	1	1	0	0
Canning	L	Larry	01/11/25	Cowdenbeath		1956		Kettering	Nuneaton	2	0	0	0	0	0	0	0
Carlton	DG	David	24/11/52	Stepney		1973	1976	Fulham	Brentford	180	6	8	0	7	1	0	0
						1980	1981	Brentford									
Carr	WG	Graham	25/10/44	Newcastle		1962	1967		York City	85	2	9	0	0	0	0	0
Carson	AM	Alec	12/11/42	Glasgow		1960	1961		Aldershot	8	0	0	0	0	0	0	0
Carter	LR	Lee	22/03/70	Dartford		1987			Boreham Wood	1	0	0	0	0	0	0	0
Cave	W	William	01/01/07	Northampton		1927	1936			93	6	0	5	0	0	0	0
Cavener	P	Phil	02/06/61	Tynemouth		1984	1985	Gillingham	Peterborough Utd.	45	2	6	1	11	0	1	0
Cegielski	W	Wayne	11/01/56	Bedwellty		1974		Tottenham H (loan)		11	0	0	0	0	0	0	0
Chambers	L	Leonard		Northampton		1920	1921	Rushden	Rushden	28	1	0	0	0	0	0	0
Chapman	WJ	Walter		Rothwell		1924		Rothwell	Rothwell	8	1	0	0	0	0	0	0
Chard	PJ	Phil	16/10/60	Corby		1985	1987	Peterborough Utd.	Wolves	277	19	18	16	46	3	1	4
						1989	1993	Wolves	Kettering								
Chatterley	LC	Lew	15/02/45	Birmingham		1971		Aston Villa	Grimsby Town	23	4	0	0	2	0	0	0
Cherry	J	James		Wigan		1933		Wigan Borough	Walsall	10	0	0	0	2	0	0	0
Christie	DHM	Derrick	15/03/57	Bletchley		1973	1978		Cambridge Utd.	138	6	12	0	18	1	2	0
Churchman	EA	Ernest	1891	Northampton		1920			Wellingborough	2	0	0	0	1	0	0	0
Civil	H	Harry		Northampton		1922				2	0	0	0	0	0	0	0
Clapton	DP	Dennis	12/10/39	Hackney		1961		Arsenal		1	0	0	0	0	0	0	0
Clarke	JL	John	23/10/46	Northampton		1966	1974			233	17	12	0	1	0	0	0
Claypole	AW	Anthony	13/02/37	Weldon		1956	1961		Cheltenham	116	6	3	0	1	0	0	0
Clifford	JC	John				1938		Crystal Palace	Bournemouth	11	0	0	0	0	0	0	0
Cobb	GE	Gary	06/08/68	Luton		1988		Luton Town (loan)		1	0	0	0	0	0	0	0
Cochrane	AF	Sandy	08/08/03	Glasgow		1933	1934	Chesterfield	Swindon Town	42	4	0	6	7	1	0	0
Cockburn	GW	George	01/01/07	Gateshead		1926			West Ham Utd.	1	0	0	0	0	0	0	0
Cockcroft	VH	Vic	25/02/41	Harbourne		1962	1966	Wolves	Rochdale	47	2	5	0	1	0	0	0
Cockle	ES	Ernest	12/09/1896	East Ham	1966	1924	1927	Luton Town	Wigan Borough	97	7	0	0	46	0	0	0
Coe	NC	Norman	06/12/40	Swansea		1960	1965	Arsenal	King's Lynn	58	3	2	0	0	0	0	0
Coffill	PT	Peter	14/02/57	Romford		1981	1982	Torquay United	Wellingborough	69	6	8	1	3	2	0	0
Coleman	GJ	Geoff	13/05/36	Bedworth		1955	1958	Bedworth	Leamington	18	0	0	0	0	0	0	0
Coley	WE	William	17/09/16	Wolverhampton		1947	1950	Torquay United	Exeter City	104	9	0	0	7	0	0	0
Colkin	L	Lee	15/07/74	Nuneaton		1991	1994			69	1	3	1	2	0	0	0
Collins	BV	Ben	09/03/28	Kislingbury		1948	1958			213	11	0	0	0	0	0	0
Collins	D	Darren	24/05/67	Winchester		1988	1990	Petersfield	Aylesbury	51	6	4	6	9	0	0	2
Connell	PM	Peter	26/11/27	East Kilbride		1951		Morton		13	0	0	0	0	0	0	0
Conway	T	Thomas		Belfast		1932		Burnley		3	0	0	0	0	0	0	0
Cook	C	Colin	08/01/09	North Shields		1936	1937	Luton Town		12	0	0	0	3	0	0	0
Cook	J	Jack	27/07/1891	Sunderland		1924		Notts County		20	0	0	0	2	0	0	0
Cooke	BA	Barry	1961	Wolverhampton		1959	1961	West Bromwich A.	Wisbech	58	3	3	0	1	0	1	0
Cooke	PC	Peter		Northampton		1980				5	0	0	0	1	0	0	0
Corbett	R	Robert		North Walbottle		1957		Middlesbrough		8	0	0	0	1	0	0	0
Cordice	NA	Neil		Amersham		1978		Tooting & Mitcham	Wealdstone	8	1	2	0	1	0	0	0
Cornwell	JA	John	13/10/64	Bethnal Green		1993		Southend Utd. (loan)		13	0	0	0	1	0	0	0
Cottrell	AT	Alfred						Bristol City		1	0	0	0	0	0	0	0
Cowen	JE	James	1928	Heningham	1950	1927	1928	Nelson	Southport	1	1	0	0	0	1	0	0
Coy	RA	Bobby	30/11/61	Birmingham		1986		Chester City	Aylesbury	17	0	2	1	0	0	1	0
Craig	AH	Albert	3/1/62	Glasgow		1988		Newcastle Utd. (loan)		2	0	0	0	1	0	0	0
Craven	J	Joseph	1935	Glasgow		1934	1935	St. Mirren		2	0	0	2	0	0	0	0
Crawford	GW	George	1906	Sunderland		1930			Bournemouth	2	0	0	0	0	0	0	0
Crilly	T	Tom	1934	Stockton	1960	1933	1934	Crystal Palace	Scunthorpe U	46	10	0	3	1	0	0	0
Cross	J	Jack	5/2/27	Durham		1953		Bournemouth	Sheffield Utd.	10	2	0	0	8	1	0	0
Croy	J	John	1954	Falkirk	1980	1951	1954	Third Lanark	Corby	25	1	0	0	0	0	0	0
Culpin	P	Paul	08/02/62	Kirby Muxloe		1987	1989	Coventry City	Peterborough Utd.	63	3	5	6	23	0	2	1
Curtis	LH	Leslie		Yorkshire		1938		Barnsley		2	0	0	0	1	0	0	0
Curtis	PAE	Paul	01/07/63	Woolwich		1985	1992	Charlton Ath.	Corby T	49	5	4	4	2	0	0	0
Curtis	R	Robbie	21/05/72	Mansfield		1994		Boston	King's Lynn	13	0	2	2	0	0	0	0
Daly	J	Joseph	28/12/1899	Lancaster		1927		Notts County	Luton Town	33	4	0	0	4	3	0	0
Daniels	SC	Scott	22/11/69	Benfleet		1994		Exeter City	Dover	8	0	0	0	0	0	0	0

Player			D.O.B	Place of Birth	Died	First Season	Last Season	Previous Club	Next Club	Appearances				Goals			
										League	FAC	FLC	Other	League	FAC	FLC	Oth.
Danks	PD	Derek	15/02/31	Cheadle		1954			Corby	1	0	0	0	0	0	0	0
Davids	NG	Neil	22/09/55	Bingley		1975		Norwich City (loan)		9	0	0	0	0	0	0	0
Davie	JG	James	07/09/22	Newton		1950	1952	Preston NE	Shrewsbury Town	75	1	0	0	1	0	0	0
Davies	AT	Arthur		Nelson		1921			Nelson	10	2	0	0	1	0	0	0
Davies	FP	Frank	01/08/03	Swansea	1970	1930	1933	Nantwich	Burton	144	18	2	2	7	6	0	0
Davies	LJ	Llewellyn	01/01/1894	Northampton	1965	1921				1	0	0	0	0	0	0	0
Davies	OT	Oliver		St Albans		1933			St. Albans	1	0	0	0	0	0	0	0
Dawes	AG	Bert	23/04/07	Frimley Green	1973	1929	1933	Frimley Green	Crystal Palace	164	18	2	0	82	16	5	0
Dawes	FW	Fred	02/05/11	Frimley Green	1989	1929	1935	Frimley Green	Crystal Palace	162	18	2	5	1	3	0	0
Dawes	IM	Ian	05/01/65	Aldershot		1985			Newcastle United	5	0	1	0	0	0	0	0
Dawson	W	William	05/02/31	Glasgow		1954	1955	Glasgow Ashfold	Corby	14	0	0	0	7	0	0	0
Deacon	R	Dicky	26/06/11	Glasgow	1986	1935		Chelsea	Lincoln City	3	1	0	0	0	1	0	0
Deakin	MRF	Mike	25/10/33	Birmingham		1959	1960	Crystal Palace	Aldershot	44	2	2	0	31	0	0	0
Dennison	RS	Bob	06/03/12	Amble		1946	1947	Fulham		55	12	0	0	0	0	0	0
Denyer	PR	Peter	26/11/57	Haslemere		1979	1982	Portsmouth	Kettering T	147	6	14	2	28	1	4	1
Dickinson	A	Alfred	01/01/15	Lancashire		1937	1938	Everton		19	0	0	3	5	0	0	1
Dixon	A	Arthur	17/11/21	Middleton		1949	1951	Hearts	Leicester City	68	9	0	0	21	5	0	0
Dixon	CH	Cecil	28/03/35	Trowbridge		1961		Newport County	Wisbech T	15	0	0	0	4	0	0	0
Docherty	J	James	21/04/26	Clydebank		1950		Celtic	Stirling Albion	1	0	0	0	0	0	0	0
Dodgin	N	Norman	01/11/21	Gateshead		1951	1952	Reading	Exeter City	19	0	0	0	1	0	0	0
Donald	WR	Warren	07/10/64	Hillingdon		1984	1989	West Ham Utd.	Colchester U	188	10	10	12	13	1	0	0
Donegal	GP	Glen	20/06/69	Northampton		1986	1989		Maidstone Utd.	21	1	2	2	3	0	1	0
Dowsey	J	John	01/05/05	Gateshead	1942	1931	1933	Notts County		86	11	2	0	5	5	1	0
Draper	RW	Richard	26/09/32	Leamington Spa		1955	1956	Leamington	Rugby T	49	3	0	0	20	2	0	0
Duckhouse	E	Ted	09/04/18	Walsall	1980	1950	1951	Birmingham City	Rushden	68	3	0	0	0	0	0	0
Dunkley	MEF	Maurice	19/02/14	Kettering	1989	1936	1937		Manchester City	30	0	0	1	5	0	0	0
						1949		Kettering T	Corby T								
Dutton	CA	Charles	10/04/34	Rugeley		1955	1956	Coventry City	Leamington	10	0	0	0	2	0	0	0
East	KMG	Keith	31/10/44	Southampton		1970		Bournemouth	Crewe Alexandra	29	0	6	0	7	0	2	0
Eccles	J	Joe	01/02/06	Stoke-on-Trent	1970	1928		West Ham Utd.	Coventry City	15	3	0	0	1	0	0	0
Edelston	M	Maurice	27/04/18	Hull	1976	1952	1953	Reading	(retired)	40	5	0	0	17	0	0	0
Edwards	DS	Dean	25/02/62	Wolverhampton		1991		Exeter City	(Hong Kong)	7	0	0	0	0	0	0	0
Edwards	EJ	Evan	14/12/1898	Merthyr Tydfil		1926		Swansea City	Halifax Town	11	1	0	0	2	0	0	0
Edwards	RH	Bob	22/05/31	Guildford		1960	1961	Norwich City	King's Lynn	23	1	0	0	10	0	0	0
Edwards	SC	Sydney	16/08/12	Northampton		1934	1935	Wellingborough	Rushden	4	0	0	2	1	0	0	1
Elad	DE	Efon	05/09/70	Hillingdon		1993		FC Cologne	Cambridge Utd.	10	0	0	0	0	0	0	0
Ellwood	RJ	Reginald	01/01/19	Worcester		1938		Worcester	Guildford	19	0	0	2	2	0	0	0
Elvy	R	Reg	25/11/20	Leeds	1991	1956	1958	Blackburn Rovers	(retired)	67	5	0	0	0	0	0	0
English	J	Jack	19/03/23	South Shields	1985	1947	1959		Gravesend	301	20	0	0	135	8	0	0
Etheridge	BG	Brian	04/03/44	Northampton		1961	1965		Brentford	17	1	4	0	1	0	0	0
Evans	CJH	Charles	31/01/1897	Cardiff		1924		Cardiff City	Grimsby Town	17	0	0	0	2	0	0	0
Evans	GJ	Gareth	14/01/67	Coventry		1990		Rotherham Utd. (loan)		2	0	0	0	0	0	0	0
Everitt	MD	Mike	16/01/41	Clacton		1960	1966	Arsenal	Plymouth Argyle	207	8	12	0	15	1	1	0
Eyre	FMB	Fred	29/09/03	Northampton		1930		Wolverton	Rushden	1	0	0	0	0	0	0	0
Facer	A	Albert	15/07/01	Northampton		1923			Higham T	2	0	0	0	0	0	0	0
Fagan	B	Bernard	29/01/49	Houghton-le-Spring		1969		Sunderland	Scarborough	6	2	0	0	0	0	0	0
Fairbrother	J	John	12/02/41	Cricklewood		1967	1971	Peterborough Utd.	Mansfield Town	140	14	10	0	56	4	2	0
Fairfax	RJ	Ray	13/01/41	Smethwick		1968	1970	West Bromwich A.	Onley T	116	14	8	0	2	0	0	0
Fairhurst	WS	Bill	01/01/02	New Delaval	1979	1932		Nelson	Hartlepool Utd.	13	2	2	0	0	2	0	0
Farmer	KJ	Kevin	24/01/60	Ramsgate		1979	1981	Leicester City	Bedworth	77	1	9	0	12	0	0	0
Farr	FE	Fred		Bristol		1935		Bristol City	Southampton	2	0	0	0	0	0	0	0
Farrell	SP	Sean	28/02/69	Watford		1991		Luton Town (loan)		4	0	1	0	1	0	0	0
Farrington	JR	John	19/06/47	Lynemouth		1974	1979	Cardiff City	Leamington	232	8	13	0	29	0	2	0
Faulkes	BK	Brian	10/04/45	Abingdon		1967	1968	Reading	Torquay United	52	3	4	0	2	0	0	0
Fee	GP	Greg	24/06/64	Halifax		1990		Sheffield Wed.(loan)		1	0	0	0	0	0	0	0
Feehan	I	Ignatius 'Sonn	17/09/26	Dublin	1995	1950	1951	Manchester Utd.	Brentford	39	1	0	0	0	0	0	0
Felton	GM	Graham	01/03/49	Cambridge		1966	1975	Cambridge U	Barnsley	254	19	13	0	25	2	0	0
Ferrari	FW	Fred	22/05/01	Stratford	1970	1925		Leyton Town	Sheffield Wed.	18	0	0	0	0	0	0	0
Fisher	PM	Peter	17/02/20	Edinburgh		1947			Shrewsbury Town	8	0	0	0	0	0	0	0
Fitzpatrick	PJ	Paul	05/10/65	Liverpool		1993		Hamilton	Rushden	2	0	0	0	1	0	0	0
Fleming	TM	Terry	05/01/73	Marston Green		1993		Coventry City	Preston NE	31	1	2	1	1	0	0	0
Flexney	P	Paul	18/01/65	Glasgow		1988		Clyde	Kilmarnock	12	1	4	1	0	0	0	0
Flounders	AJ	Andy	13/12/63	Hull		1994		Halifax T	(Hong Kong)	2	0	0	0	0	0	0	0
Flowers	R	Ron	28/07/34	Edlington		1967	1968	Wolves	Telford U	62	2	3	0	4	0	0	0
Folds	RJ	Bob	18/04/49	Bedford		1971		Gillingham	Telford U	30	1	1	0	0	0	0	0
Foley	TC	Theo	02/03/37	Dublin		1961	1966	Exeter City	Charlton Ath.	204	6	10	0	8	2	1	0
Forbes	FJ	Fred	05/08/1894	Leith		1932		Leith	Airdrie	35	10	2	0	3	10	0	0
Forrest	J	James 'Jack'		Shildon		1922		Leyton Orient	Spennymoor U	2	1	0	0	0	0	0	0
Forster	MG	Martyn	01/02/63	Kettering		1983		Kettering T	Corby T	42	5	1	1	0	0	0	0
Fotheringham	JG	Jim	19/12/33	Hamilton	1977	1959		Arsenal		11	1	0	0	0	0	0	0
Fowler	T	Tommy	16/12/24	Prescot		1946	1961	Everton	Aldershot	521	31	0	0	84	4	0	0
Fox	MC	Matthew	13/07/71	Birmingham		1992		Birmingham City		1	0	0	0	0	0	0	0
Francis	SR	Sean	01/08/72	Birmingham		1993		Birmingham City		1	0	1	0	0	0	0	0
Fraser	WC	William	3/07/07	Cowpen		1926	1927	East Stirling	Aldershot	20	3	0	0	5	0	0	0
						1933		Fuham	Hartlepools Utd.								
Freeman	E	Edwin	05/06/1886	Northampton	1945	1920				25	22	0	0	2	2	0	0
Freeman	N	Neil	16/02/55	Northampton		1982		Peterborough Utd.	(retired)	22	5	3	0	0	0	0	0
Freeman	NF	Neville	25/01/25	Brixworth		1950			Wellingborough	1	0	0	0	0	0	0	0
French	JR	Jim	27/01/26	Stockton		1951		Middlesbrough	Darlington	1	0	0	0	0	0	0	0
Friar	JP	Paul	06/06/63	Glasgow		1985		Charlton Ath. (loan)		14	0	0	2	0	0	0	0
Friedmanis	E	Eddie	22/02/20	Latvia	1993	1948	1949	Peterborough U	Nuneaton	19	0	0	0	4	0	0	0
Froggatt	JL	John	13/12/45	Sutton-in-Ashfield		1978		Port Vale	Boston U	42	1	0	0	12	0	0	0
Frost	SD	Stan	19/10/22	Northampton		1946		Leicester C	Leicester C	6	0	0	0	1	0	0	0
Gage	WAJ	Wakeley	05/05/58	Northampton		1979	1984	Desborough T	Chester City	218	17	13	5	17	4	1	0
Gale	CM	Colin	31/08/32	Pontypridd		1955	1960	Cardiff City	Wisbech T	211	9	2	0	0	1	0	0
Gallacher	B	Bernard	22/03/67	Johnstone		1993		Brighton & Hove A.	Bromsgrove Rov.	5	0	0	0	0	0	0	0
Garner	TJ	Tim	30/03/61	Hitchin		1985		Leamington	Aylesbury	2	0	0	0	0	0	0	0

Player			D.O.B	Place of Birth	Died	First Season	Last Season	Previous Club	Next Club	Appearances				Goals			
										League	FAC	FLC	Other	Leagu	FAC	FLC	Oth.
Garnham	SE	Stuart	30/11/55	Selby		1974		Wolves (loan)		12	0	1	0	0	0	0	0
						1977		Peterborough U (loan)									
Garrett	ACE	Archie	17/06/19	Lesmahagow	1994	1946	1947	Hearts	Birmingham City	94	5	0	0	50	6	0	0
						1948	1950	Birmingham C	Wisbech T								
Garwood	J	Jason	23/03/69	Birmingham		1988		Leicester City (loan)		6	0	1	0	0	0	0	0
Gavin	PJ	Pat	05/06/67	Hammersmith		1992		Barnet	Wigan Ath.	14	0	0	0	4	0	0	0
Geidmintis	AJ	Tony	30/07/49	Stepney	1993	1977	1978	Watford	Halifax Town	63	1	5	0	1	0	0	0
George	HS	Herbert	1905	Wellingborough		1924	1927	Wellingborough	Rushden	22	4	0	0	2	2	0	0
Gernon	FAJ	Frederick'Irvin	30/12/62	Birmingham		1986		Ipswich Town (loan)		56	8	1	6	1	0	0	1
						1989	1991	Reading	Kettering T								
Gilbert	DJ	David	22/06/63	Lincoln		1986	1988	Boston	Grimsby Town	120	6	10	9	21	3	2	1
Gillard	KJ	Ken	30/04/72	Dublin		1992	1993	Luton Town	Chesham	23	1	1	3	0	0	0	0
Gillespie	P	Pat	05/07/28	Bellshill		1947		Watford	Doncaster Rovers	1	0	0	0	0	0	0	0
Gilligan	JJ	John	02/05/57	Abingdon		1976		Swindon Town (loan)		5	0	0	0	1	0	0	0
Gilzean	IR	Ian	10/12/69	London		1993		Tottenham H	Ayr	33	1	2	3	10	0	0	0
Gleasure	PF	Peter	08/10/60	Luton		1982	1991	Millwall	Hitchin	344	25	25	18	0	0	0	0
Gormlie	WJ	Bill	01/04/11	Blackpool	1976	1935	1938	Blackburn Rovers	Lincoln City	138	3	0	7	0	0	0	0
Gould	TR	Trevor	05/03/50	Coventry		1970	1972	Coventry City	Bedford T	105	4	1	0	6	0	0	0
Graham	W	William		Preston		1921	1923	Lancaster T	Wrexham	45	4	0	0	10	0	0	0
Gray	GR	George		Sunderland		1923		Bury		11	1	0	0	0	0	0	0
Grayson	N	Neil	01/11/64	York		1994		Chesterfield		38	1	2	3	8	0	0	2
Gregory	JC	John	11/05/54	Scunthorpe		1972	1976		Aston Villa	187	7	9	0	8	1	1	0
Grendon	FJW	Frank	05/09/1891	Farnham	1984	1920	1921		Rushden T	38	5	0	0	0	0	0	0
Griffin	FA	Frank	28/03/28	Pendlebury		1959		West Bromwich A.	Wellington S	16	1	0	0	0	0	0	0
Groome	JPG	Joseph	01/09/01	Apsley	1956	1926		Apsley T	Watford	13	0	0	0	6	0	0	0
Gunn	K	Kenneth	1941	Dunfermline	1991	1937	1938	Port Vale	(retired)	74	2	0	3	1	0	0	0
Gunnell	RC	Richard	10/04/1889	Harpenden	1977	1926		Hertford	Bedford	11	2	0	0	0	1	0	0
Hails	W	Billy	19/02/35	Nettlesworth		1962	1963	Peterborough Utd.	Luton Town	59	1	3	0	13	0	0	0
Hall	JL	Jim	02/03/45	Northampton		1963	1967		Peterborough Utd.	124	5	12	0	35	0	4	0
						1974	1977	Peterborough Utd.	Cambridge C								
Hamill	SP	Stewart	22/01/60	Glasgow		1985		Leicester City	Scarborough	3	0	0	1	1	0	0	1
Hammond	L	Leonard	12/09/01	Rugby	1983	1924	1932	Rugby T	Notts County	301	24	2	0	0	1	0	0
Harmon	DJ	Darren	30/01/73	Northampton		1992	1994	Shrewsbury Town	Kettering T	89	5	3	9	12	0	0	1
Harrington	JW	Jack		Hednesford		1928		Wolves	Brierley Hill	8	0	0	0	0	0	0	0
Harrison	GM	Gary	12/03/75	Northampton		1993	1994	Aston Villa	King's Lynn	7	0	0	1	0	0	0	0
Harron	J	Joe	14/03/00	Langley Park	1961	1921		Hull City	Sheffield Wed.	18	2	0	0	1	0	0	0
Harvey	BR	Bryan	26/08/38	Stepney		1963	1967	Blackpool	Kettering T	165	3	13	0	0	0	0	0
Haskins	AJ	Anthony	26/07/35	Northampton		1959	1961		Cheltenham T	8	0	0	0	0	0	0	0
Hatton	RJ	Bob	10/04/47	Hull		1968		Bolton Wanderers	Carlisle Utd.	33	3	0	0	7	11	0	0
Hawke	WR	Warren	20/09/70	Durham		1992		Sunderland (loan)		7	0	0	0	1	0	0	0
Hawkings	B	Barry	07/11/31	Birmingham		1957	1958	Lincoln City	Gravesend	65	5	0	0	25	2	0	0
Hawkins	PM	Peter	18/12/51	Swansea		1968	1973		Bedfford	61	3	2	0	10	1	0	0
Hawtin	LC	Leonard	02/07/1892	Northampton		1920	1922			10	2	0	0	0	0	0	0
Haycox	JH	Jack	01/01/10	Cheltenham		1938		Torquay United	Peterborough U	17	1	0	1	6	0	0	0
Hayes	AWP	Austin	15/07/58	Hammersmith	1986	1983	1984	Millwall	Barnet	63	9	4	2	14	0	0	0
Haywood	RJ	Ray	12/01/49	Dudley		1976	1977	Shrewsbury Town	Kidderminster H.	16	0	1	0	2	0	0	0
Hazledine	D	Don	10/07/29	Derby		1954		Derby County	Boston U	22	1	0	0	4	0	0	0
Heaselgrave	SE	Sammy	01/10/16	Smethwick	1975	1946	1947	West Bromwich A.	Boston U	42	4	0	0	4	1	0	0
Heeley	DM	Mark	08/09/59	Peterborough		1979	1982	Arsenal	Aylesbury	92	7	8	3	5	0	1	0
Henry	CA	Charlie	13/02/62	Acton		1986		Swindon Town (loan)		4	0	0	0	1	0	0	0
Henson	GH	George	25/12/11	Stony Stratford		1932	1934	Wolverton	Wolves	43	6	0	2	23	1	0	2
Heslop	B	Brian	04/08/47	Carlisle		1970	1971	Sunderland	Workington	50	4	1	0	0	0	0	0
Hewison	R	Bob	25/03/1889	Backworth	1964	1920	1924	Newcastle United		99	9	0	0	8	1	0	0
Hewitt	JJ	John 'Joss'	01/07/11	Evenwood		1935	1938	Norwich City	Southport	83	2	0	5	14	1	0	0
Hicks	TG	Thomas	01/01/03	Trehafod		1928		Nottm. Forest	Chester	5	0	0	0	0	0	0	0
Higgins	T	Thomas		Glasgow		1934		Hearts	Scunthorpe U	3	0	0	0	0	0	0	0
Hill	DR	David	28/09/53	Kettering		1970			Kettering	1	0	0	0	0	0	0	0
Hill	RW	Richard	20/09/63	Hinckley		1985	1986	Nuneaton	Watford	86	5	6	6	46	3	0	3
Hinson	RH	Ronald	09/10/15	Chelveston		1933	1935	Irchester	Rushden	8	2	0	0	4	0	0	0
Hitchcock	KJ	Kevin	05/10/62	Custom House		1990		Chelsea (loan)		17	0	0	1	0	0	0	0
Hobbs	EC	Ernest	01/01/12	Wellingborough		1934	1935	Wellingborough	Exeter City	9	1	0	4	0	1	0	2
Hobbs	RV	Ralph		Toddington		1923		Toddington		1	0	0	0	0	0	0	0
Hold	JD	John	28/03/48	Southampton		1971	1972	Bournemouth	Weymouth	44	0	1	0	11	0	0	0
Holmes	MA	Mick	09/09/65	Blackpool		1992		Carlisle Utd.	Telford U	6	0	0	0	0	0	0	0
Holt	D	David		Northampton		1936				1	0	0	0	0	0	0	0
Holton	CC	Cliff	29/04/29	Oxford		1961	1962	Watford	Crystal Palace	62	3	3	0	50	3	1	0
Horne	AT	Alf	06/09/26	Brixworth		1948			Corby T	1	0	0	0	0	0	0	0
Hoten	RV	Ralph	27/12/1896	Pinxton	1978	1924	1929	Luton Town	QPR	197	16	0	0	75	9	0	0
Hoult	AA	Alfred	09/07/15	Ashby-de-la-Zouch		1937		Notts County		9	1	0	0	0	0	0	0
Hudson	GA	George	14/03/37	Manchester		1965	1966	Coventry City	Tranmere Rovers	18	0	2	0	6	0	0	0
Huffer	P	Phil	23/01/32	Bedworth		1954		Derby County		1	0	0	0	0	0	0	0
Hughes	DJ	Darren	06/10/65	Prescot		1994		Port Vale		13	0	0	0	0	0	0	0
Hughes	TG	Gwyn	07/05/22	Blaenau Ffestiniog		1946	1955		Bedford T	225	20	0	0	15	4	0	0
Hunt	RR	Bobby	01/10/42	Colchester		1963	1965	Colchester Utd.	Millwall	45	0	2	0	13	0	2	0
						1972		Charlton Ath. (loan)									
Hurel	E	Eli	10/04/15	Jersey		1938		Everton		12	0	0	2	2	0	0	0
Hurrell	WT	Billy	15/09/55	Newcastle		1972				5	0	0	0	0	0	0	0
Hutchinson	CM	Mark	02/11/63	Stoke-on-Trent		1984		Leicester City	Nuneaton	2	0	0	1	0	0	0	0
Hyslop	CT	Chris	14/06/72	Watford		1993		Southend Utd. (loan)		8	0	0	0	0	0	0	0
Inglis	WW	Bill	02/03/1897	Kirkcaldy	1969	1930	1931	Manchester Utd.	(retired)	62	5	0	0	0	0	0	0
Ingram	GP	Godfrey	26/10/59	Luton		1979		Luton Town (loan)		10	0	0	0	4	0	0	0
Isaac	WH	William	16/05/35	Pontypridd		1959		Stoke City	Hereford U	8	0	0	0	0	0	0	0
Jackson	LW	Len	06/09/22	Birmingham		1948		Birmingham City		2	0	0	0	0	0	0	0
James	R	Ron	16/03/22	Birmingham		1948		Birmingham City	Kidderminster H	4	0	0	0	1	0	0	0
Jayes	CG	Carl	15/03/54	Leicester		1977	1979	Leicester City	Leamington	68	3	6	0	0	0	0	0
Jeffrey	WG	Billy	25/10/56	Clydebank		1982	1983	Blackpool	Kettering	54	5	2	1	5	1	0	0
Jeffs	TE	Thomas	03/08/00	Peterborough	1971	1921	1927	Rugby		143	17	0	0	0	0	0	0

Player			D.O.B	Place of Birth	Died	First Season	Last Season	Previous Club	Next Club	Appearances				Goals			
										League	FAC	FLC	Other	League	FAC	FLC	Oth.
Jenkins	RJ	Randolph	05/09/23	Sligo		1946	1947	Walsall	Fulham	18	3	0	0	6	1	0	0
Jennings	HW	Bill	07/01/20	Norwich	1969	1938	1946		Ipswich Town	11	0	0	1	2	0	0	0
Jennings	W	Bill	25/02/1891	Bulwell		1926		Luton Town		3	0	0	0	0	0	0	0
Jobey	G	George	01/07/1885	Heddon	1962	1920	1921	Leicester City	Wolves (mgr)	78	5	0	0	2	2	0	0
John	M	Malcolm	09/12/50	Bridgend		1973		Bristol Rovers (loan)		41	2	0	0	8	0	0	0
						1974		Bristol Rovers	Trowbridge								
Johnson	DD	David	10/03/67	Northampton		1989	1991		Rushden	48	2	1	4	0	0	0	0
Johnson	I	Ian	14/02/69	Newcastle		1988		Gateshead	Weymouth	3	0	0	1	0	0	0	0
Johnson	PR	Percy	13/12/1899	Northampton	1983	1921	1922		Wellingborough	11	0	0	0	0	0	0	0
Johnston	WJ	Willie	03/09/48	Sunderland		1967			Durham	1	0	0	0	0	0	0	0
Jones	B	Bernard	10/04/34	Coventry		1953	1955		Cardiff City	43	4	0	0	16	0	0	0
Jones	BR	Bryn	20/05/31	Swansea	1990	1963		Bournemouth	Watford	7	0	0	0	0	0	0	0
Jones	H	Herbert		Wolverton		1926			Wolverton	5	0	0	0	0	0	0	0
Jones	JT	John	25/11/16	Holywell		1938	1947	Port Vale	Oldham Athletic	71	8	0	2	0	0	0	0
Jones	RS	Bobby	28/10/38	Bristol		1966		Bristol Rovers	Swindon Town	17	1	0	0	1	0	0	0
Jordan	G	Gerry	04/04/49	Seaham		1966				1	0	0	0	0	0	0	0
Kane	P	Peter	04/04/39	Petershill		1959		Queen's Park	Arsenal	46	1	2	0	24	1	0	0
						1963		Arsenal	Crewe Alexandra								
Kavanagh	PJ	Peter	1911	Ireland		1932		Celtic		1	0	0	0	0	0	0	0
Kendall	MI	Mark	10/12/61	Nuneaton		1982		Aston Villa	Birmingham City	11	0	1	3	0	0	0	0
Key	RM	Richard	13/04/56	Coventry		1982		Cambridge Utd. (loan)		2	0	0	0	0	0	0	0
Kiernan	DJ	Daniel	16/12/73	Northampton		1991			Ayr	9	0	0	0	0	0	0	0
Kiernan	J	Joe	22/10/42	Coatbridge		1963	1971	Sunderland	Kettering T	308	19	25	0	13	0	1	0
Kilkelly	TF	Tom	22/08/55	Galway		1974		Leicester City (loan)		4	0	0	0	0	0	0	0
Kilsby	RH	Reginald	23/08/10	Wollaston		1934		Wellingborough	Scunthorpe U	1	0	0	0	0	0	0	0
King	FAR	Fred 'Bobby'	19/09/19	Northampton		1937	1938		Wolves	98	2	0	1	23	0	0	0
						1947	1949	Wolves	Rushden								
Kirkup	BA	Brian	16/04/32	Slough		1958	1959	Reading	Aldershot	26	2	0	0	7	2	0	0
Knight	BM	Brian	28/03/49	Dundee		1969		Huddersfield T	Cambridge C	12	1	0	0	0	0	0	0
Knox	T	Tommy	05/09/39	Glasgow		1967	1968	Mansfield Town	St. Mirren	30	1	2	0	0	1	0	0
Kruse	PK	Pat	30/11/53	Biggleswade		1981		Brentford (loan)		18	0	0	0	0	0	0	0
Krzywicki	RL	Dick	02/02/47	Penley		1973		Huddersfield T (loan)		8	0	0	0	3	0	0	0
Kurila	J	John	10/04/41	Glasgow		1962		Celtic	Bristol City	148	3	11	0	4	0	0	0
						1963	1967	Bristol City	Southend								
Laird	DS	David	11/02/36	Rutherglen		1960		St. Mirren	Folkestone	12	1	1	0	1	0	0	0
Lamb	PD	Paul	12/09/74	Plumstead		1992			Buckingham	3	0	1	0	0	0	0	0
Large	F	Frank	26/01/40	Leeds		1962	1963	QPR	Swindon Town	220	17	13	0	88	5	3	0
						1966	1967	Oldham Ath.	Leicester City								
						1969	1972	Fulham	Chesterfield								
Lauderdale	JH	Jock	27/11/08	Dumfries	1965	1936	1938	Coventry City	Nuneaton	47	1	0	1	10	0	0	0
Leaburn	CW	Carl	30/03/69	Lewisham		1989		Charlton Ath. (loan)		9	0	0	0	0	0	0	0
Leck	DA	Derek	08/02/37	Northbourne		1958	1965	Millwall	Brighton & Hove A.	246	10	12	0	45	3	1	0
Lee	TC	Trevor	03/07/54	Lewisham		1984		Cardiff City	Fulham	24	4	2	2	2	0	0	0
Leek	K	Ken	26/07/35	Ynysybwl		1955	1957		Leicester City	87	6	0	0	31	2	0	0
						1964	1965	Birmingham C	Bradford C								
Leonard	GE	Gary	23/03/62	Northampton		1979	1980		Kettering T	2	0	0	0	0	0	0	0
Lewis	R	Russell	15/09/56	Blaengwynfi		1983	1985	Swindon Town	Kettering T	132	10	7	6	6	0	0	0
Liddle	DN	David	21/05/57	Bedford		1977	1978		Bedford	30	2	5	0	3	0	0	0
Lincoln	A	Andy	17/05/02	Seaham Harbour	1977	1928		Millwall	Stockport Co.	2	0	0	0	0	0	0	0
Lindsay	DM	Duncan	01/01/07	Cambuslang		1933		Bury	Hartlepool U.	1	0	0	0	0	0	0	0
Lines	B	Barry	16/05/42	Bletchley		1960	1969	Bletchley U	Milton Keynes	266	10	18	0	48	1	1	0
Litt	SE	Steve	21/05/54	Carlisle		1977		Minnesota Kicks	Minnesota Kicks	20	2	0	0	0	0	0	0
Little	J	Jack	18/09/04	Dunston-on-Tyne	1988	1935	1937	Chester City	Exeter City	57	1	0	1	1	0	0	0
Livesey	CE	Charlie	06/02/38	West Ham		1964	1965	Watford	Brighton & Hove A.	28	1	4	0	4	0	2	0
Llewellyn	HA	Herbert	05/02/39	Golborne		1962	1963	Port Vale	Walsall	1	0	1	0	0	0	0	0
Loasby	AA	Alan	19/03/37	Wellingborough		1958		Luton Town	Wellingborough	2	0	0	0	0	0	0	0
Loasby	H	Harry		Wellingborough		1927	1929		Gillingham	27	3	0	0	25	3	0	0
Lockett	WC	William	23/04/1893	Tipton	1974	1920	1925	Wolves	Kidderminster H.	185	20	0	0	68	9	0	0
Logan	D	David	05/12/63	Middlesbrough		1986	1987	Mansfield Town	Halifax Town	41	1	3	1	1	0	0	0
Longhurst	DJ	David	15/01/65	Northampton	1990	1987	1988	Halifax Town	Peterborough Utd.	37	2	3	1	7	0	1	1
Lovatt	HA	Harry	01/02/06	Audley		1931		Notts County	Macclesfield	14	4	0	0	7	4	0	0
Lowery	H	Harry	26/02/18	Moor Row		1946	1948	West Bromwich A.	Bromsgrove	76	16	0	0	2	0	0	0
Lyman	CC	Colin	09/03/14	Northampton	1986	1934	1937	Southend Utd.	Tottenham H	86	2	0	5	29	0	0	1
Lyon	DG	David	18/01/51	Northwich		1977		Cambridge Utd.	Cambridge C	6	0	0	0	0	0	0	0
Mabee	GL	Gary	01/02/55	Oxford		1974	1975	Tottenham H	(retired)	33	1	4	0	13	0	0	0
McAleer	J	Joseph	08/03/10	Blythswood		1933		Rochdale	Lincoln City	8	0	0	0	6	0	0	0
McCaffrey	J	Jim	12/10/51	Luton		1978	1979	Portsmouth	(retired)	57	1	5	0	6	0	1	0
McCartney	JJ	Jimmy	30/03/09	Washington	1976	1938		Millwall	South Shields	22	0	0	2	7	0	0	0
McClean	CA	Christian	17/10/63	Colchester		1991		Swansea City	Chelmsford	19	1	0	2	3	0	0	1
McCoy	W	Wilf 'Tim'	04/03/21	Birmingham		1948	1949	Portsmouth	Brighton & Hove A.	60	8	0	0	0	0	0	0
McCulloch	ABR	Adam	04/06/20	Crossford		1949	1951	Third Lanark	Shrewsbury Town	89	10	0	0	36	3	0	0
McCulloch	T	Tommy	25/12/21	Dumfries		1949		Queen of the South	Bradford City	2	0	0	0	0	0	0	0
McCullough	K	Keillor		Larne		1937	1938	Manchester City		35	0	0	2	1	0	0	1
McFarlane	J	John		Shettleston		1932		Halifax Town	Kiddermister H.	3	8	2	0	1	8	1	0
McGleish	JJ	John	09/11/51	Airdrie		1970	1972		Wellingborough	8	0	0	0	0	0	0	0
McGoldrick	EJP	Eddie	30/04/65	London		1986	1988	Nuneaton	Crystal Palace	107	9	7	7	9	1	0	1
McGowan	A	Andy	17/05/56	Corby		1975	1977	Corby	Irthlingborough	105	1	5	0	14	0	0	0
McGuire	JP	James	01/01/11	Edinburgh		1932	1935	Celtic	Brooklyn Wan.	70	12	0	3	0	0	0	0
McIlvenny	P	Paddy	01/01/00	Belfast		1928		Shelbourne	Boston	8	0	0	0	2	0	0	0
McKechnie	JP	John		Inverness		1920		Newcastle United	Exeter City	11	0	0	0	0	0	0	0
McKee	RT	Ray	16/06/26	Finchley		1946		Finchley T		5	0	0	0	0	0	0	0
McKenna	MJ	Mike	03/11/16	Darkley	1974	1946		Bromsgrove		4	0	0	0	0	0	0	0
Mackie	JA	Alex	23/02/03	Belfast	1984	1935	1936	Portsmouth	(retired)	19	0	0	0	0	0	0	0
Mackin	J	John	18/11/43	Glasgow		1965	1968		Lincoln City	101	4	7	0	11	0	2	0
McLachlan	ER	Edwin	24/09/03	Glasgow	1970	1930		Mansfield T	Mansfield T	11	0	0	0	1	0	0	0
McLain	T	Tom	19/01/22	Linton	1995	1952	1955	Sunderland	Wellingborough	96	5	0	0	11	0	0	0

Player			D.O.B	Place of Birth	Died	First Season	Last Season	Previous Club	Next Club	Appearances				Goals			
										League	FAC	FLC	Other	League	FAC	FLC	Oth.
McMenemy	F	Frank	01/01/10	Rutherglen		1933	1935	Airdrie	Crystal Palace	57	3	0	5	3	0	0	0
McMenemy	PC	Paul	05/11/66	Farnborough		1986		West Ham Utd. (loan)		4	0	0	0	2	0	0	0
McNamara	B	Brett	08/07/72	Newark		1994		Stamford	King's Lynn	1	0	0	1	0	0	0	0
McNaughton	WF	Bill	08/12/05	Poplar	1980	1928	1929	Peterborough	Gateshead	11	1	0	0	2	0	0	0
McNeil	R	Richard 'Dixie'	16/01/47	Melton Mowbray		1969	1971	Corby T	Lincoln City	85	11	6	0	33	5	0	0
McParland	IJ	Ian	04/10/61	Edinburgh		1992		Lincoln City	(Hong Kong)	11	3	0	3	3	1	0	3
McPartland	D	Des	05/10/47	Middlesbrough		1969		Carlisle Utd.	Hartlepool Utd.	6	0	0	0	0	0	0	0
McPherson	KA	Keith	11/09/63	Greenwich		1985	1989	West Ham Utd.	Reading	182	12	9	13	8	0	1	0
McPhillips	T	Terry	01/10/68	Manchester		1989		Halifax Town (loan)		1	1	0	1	0	0	0	0
Mahoney	AJ	Tony	29/09/59	Barking		1981		Fulham (loan)		6	0	2	0	0	0	0	0
Malcolm	AA	Alex	13/02/56	Hamilton		1976		Luton Town	Dunstable	2	0	0	0	0	0	2	0
Maloney	RJH	Robert		Thringstone	1981	1926	1931	Peterborough U	Shelbourne	2	0	0	0	0	0	0	0
Mann	AG	Adrian	12/07/67	Northampton		1983	1987		Newport County	183	11	0	0	4	0	0	0
Marston	M	Maurice	24/03/29	Trimdon		1953	1956	Sunderland	Kettering T	81	5	4	6	5	0	0	1
Martin	D	Don	15/02/44	Corby		1962	1967		Blackburn Rovers	149	3	0	0	2	0	0	0
						1975	1977	Blackburn Rovers	Hitchin	228	6	18	0	70	1	11	0
Martin	D	Dave	25/04/63	East Ham		1994		Bristol City (loan)		7	0	1	0	0	0	0	0
Martinez	E	Eugene	06/07/57	Chelmsford		1983		Newport Co. (loan)		12	0	0	0	2	0	0	0
Massey	S	Steve	28/03/58	Denton		1981	1982	Peterborough Utd.	Hull City	60	5	4	3	25	1	3	1
Matthews	PW	Paul	30/09/46	Leicester		1978		Rotherham U (loan)		13	0	0	0	0	0	0	0
Maxwell	K	Ken	11/02/28	Glasgow		1950		Kilmarnock	Bradford	2	0	0	0	0	0	0	0
Mayes	AK	Alan	11/12/53	Edmonton		1975		Watford (loan)		10	0	0	0	4	0	0	0
Mead	PS	Peter	09/09/56	Luton		1977	1978	Luton Town	Hitchin	77	1	6	0	4	0	0	0
Melville	J	Jim	15/03/09	Barrow	1961	1934	1935	Hull City		20	0	0	4	0	0	0	1
Millar	J	John	08/12/66	Coatbridge		1986		Chelsea (loan)		1	1	0	2	0	0	0	0
Miller	RL	Roger	18/08/38	Northampton		1956	1958		Wellingborough	4	0	0	0	1	0	0	0
Mills	RWG	Roly	22/06/33	Daventry		1954	1963			305	16	6	0	30	1	2	0
Mitchell	A	Andrew	20/04/07	Coxhoe	1971	1933		Hull City	Rossendale U	18	4	0	2	3	0	0	0
Mitchell	AJ	Bert	22/01/22	Stoke-on-Trent		1949	1950	Blackburn Rovers	Luton Town	81	9	0	0	21	8	0	0
Molloy	W	William	01/01/00	Gateshead		1924			Ashington	3	0	0	0	0	0	0	0
Moore	G	Graham	07/03/41	Hengoed		1965	1966	Manchester Utd.	Charlton Ath.	53	0	5	0	10	0	2	0
Moore	J	John	21/12/43	Harthill		1974		Luton Town	Hitchin	14	0	2	0	0	0	0	0
Moran	J	Jimmy	06/03/35	Wishaw		1960	1961	Norwich City	Darlington	24	1	0	0	6	1	0	0
Morley	TW	Trevor	20/03/61	Nottingham		1985	1987	Nuneaton	Manchester City	107	6	10	7	39	2	4	0
Morrall	AD	Alf	01/07/16	Duddeston		1946	1947		Newport County	34	11	0	0	11	8	0	0
Morritt	GR	Gordon	08/02/42	Rotherham		1968	1969	Doncaster Rovers	York City	42	3	1	0	0	0	0	0
Morrow	HJE	Hugh	09/07/30	Larne		1956		Leamington	Kettering	30	0	0	0	3	0	0	0
Mortimer	R	Bob	01/04/08	Bolton		1931	1932	Bolton Wanderers	Brentford	62	8	2	0	22	7	0	0
Muir	M	Malcolm		Campbeltown		1930		Aberdeen		3	0	0	0	0	0	0	0
Muir	M	Maurice	19/03/63	Wimbledon		1979		Crystal Palace	Leamington	28	8	1	0	0	1	0	0
						1981	1983	Banbury	Kettering								
Mulgrew	T	Tommy	13/04/29	Motherwell		1950	1952	Morton	Newcastle United	8	0	0	0	1	0	0	0
Mundee	BG	Brian	12/01/64	Hammersmith		1983	1985	Bournemouth	Cambridge Utd.	100	8	6	4	3	1	0	0
Murphy	E	Eddie	13/05/24	Hamilton		1949	1950	Morton	Barnsley	71	9	0	0	15	1	0	0
Myers	EC	Colin	1894	Chapeltown		1922	1924	Aberdare Ath.	QPR	72	3	0	0	29	3	0	0
Neal	G	George	29/12/19	Wellingborough		1946				3	0	0	0	0	0	0	0
Neal	PG	Phil	20/02/51	Irchester		1968	1974		Liverpool	187	12	9	0	28	1	1	0
Nebbeling	GM	Gavin	15/05/63	Johannesburg, SA		1985		Crystal Palace (loan)		11	0	0	1	0	0	0	0
Needham	GW	George		Staveley		1923	1924	Gillingham		35	1	0	0	1	0	0	0
Newman	R	Ron	01/05/33	Pontypridd		1954	1955		Coventry City	18	0	0	0	5	0	0	0
Newton	F	Frank	01/01/02	Romiley		1922	1923	Bradford City	Halifax T	41	4	0	0	0	0	0	0
Norris	OP	Ollie	01/04/29	Derry		1958		Bournemouth	Ashford	14	1	0	0	1	0	0	0
Norton	DW	David	03/03/65	Cannock		1994		Hull City		38	1	2	1	0	0	0	0
Oakley	JE	James	10/11/1901	Tynemouth		1931	1932	Reading	Kettering T	33	0	0	0	0	0	0	0
Oakley	K	Ken	09/05/29	Rhymney		1954		Cardiff City	Ebbw Vale	13	0	0	0	6	0	0	0
Odell	GW	George	16/1/01	Hoddesdon	1971	1927	1931	St. Albans	Wigan Borough	147	11	0	0	10	0	0	0
O'Donnell	C	Chris	26/05/68	Newcastle		1987		Ipswich Town (loan)		1	0	0	0	0	0	0	0
O'Donnell	W	Willie	09/08/24	Clydebank		1951	1953	Partick Thistle	Shrewsbury Town	105	4	0	0	44	0	0	0
O'Donoghue	MG	Mike	13/09/56	Redhill		1979		Southampton (loan)		4	0	0	0	1	0	0	0
Olah	B	Bela	08/06/38	Hungary		1958	1960	Bedford	Wisbech T	42	1	0	0	8	0	0	0
Oman	AJ	Alan	06/10/52	Northampton		1970	1974		Wellingborough	88	7	1	0	3	0	0	0
O'Neil	J	Joe	15/08/31	Glasgow		1957	1958	Leicester City	Bath C	28	0	0	0	4	0	0	0
O'Neill	T	Tommy	02/02/58	Glasgow		1983		Cambridge Utd.	Royston	43	5	2	1	6	1	0	0
O'Rourke	J	John		Bolton		1935	1938	Bury		14	0	0	2	1	0	0	0
O'Rourke	P	Peter	14/03/03	Newmains		1925		Bradford	Norwich C	2	0	0	0	0	0	0	0
O'Shea	DE	Danny	26/03/63	Kennington		1994		Cambridge Utd.		7	0	0	0	1	0	0	0
Ovendale	MJ	Mark	22/11/73	Leicester		1994		Wisbech T		6	0	0	2	0	0	0	0
Owen	R	Bobby	17/10/47	Farnworth		1976		Carlisle U (loan)		5	0	0	0	0	0	0	0
Oxley	RL	Richard	01/01/1895	Wallsend	1953	1924		QPR		1	0	0	0	0	0	0	0
Oxley	W	William		Wallsend		1926		Merthyr T	Durham	3	0	0	0	1	0	0	0
Page	LA	Louis	27/03/1899	Kirkdale	1959	1922	1924	Stoke City	Burnley	122	7	0	0	24	2	0	0
Page	W	William	19/09/1896	Lancashire	1981	1922		Cardiff C	Bideford T	13	0	0	0	1	0	0	0
Park	O	Ossie	7/02/05	Darlington		1931	1933	Newcastle United	Hartlepool Utd.	75	7	2	0	5	0	0	0
Park	RC	Bobby	03/07/46	Edinburgh		1972	1973	Peterborough Utd.	Hartlepool Utd.	24	0	1	0	0	0	0	0
Parker	S	Sean	23/08/73	Newcastle		1991	1992		Rushden	10	0	1	0	0	0	0	0
Parris	JE	Eddie	31/01/11	Chepstow		1937	1938	Luton Town	Cheltenham T	25	0	0	1	7	0	0	0
Parsons	MC	Mark	24/02/75	Luton		1991	1993		Kettering T	51	2	3	4	0	0	0	0
Parton	JJ	Jeff	24/02/53	Swansea		1975	1977	Burnley	Irthlingborough	25	1	4	0	0	0	0	0
Partridge	AE	Albert	13/2/01	Birmingham	1966	1933		Bradford City		2	0	0	0	0	0	0	0
Pascoe	J	Jason	15/02/70	Jarrow		1994		Clipston	King's Lynn	15	1	1	2	0	0	0	0
Patching	M	Martin	01/11/58	Rotherham		1982		Watford (loan)		6	0	0	0	0	0	0	0
Patmore	WJ	Warren	14/08/71	Kingsbury		1993	1994	Millwall	Yeovil T	21	0	0	0	2	0	0	0
Patterson	RL	Ron	30/10/29	Gateshead		1952	1961	Middlesbrough	Rothwell	300	17	0	0	5	0	0	0
Payne	IEH	Irving 'Joe'	29/06/21	Briton Ferry		1951		Scunthorpe Utd.	(coach)	32	1	0	0	6	1	0	0
Peacock	RJ	Robert	18/12/37	Rushden		1957		Rushden T	Kettering T	2	1	0	0	0	0	0	0
Pease	WH	Billy	30/09/1898	Leeds	1955	1920	1925	Leeds City	Middlesbrough	246	21	0	0	45	6	0	0
Perkins	GS	Glen	12/10/60	Little Billing		1978			Kettering T	1	0	0	0	0	0	0	0

Player			D.O.B	Place of Birth	Died	First Season	Last Season	Previous Club	Next Club	Appearances				Goals			
										League	FAC	FLC	Other	League	FAC	FLC	Oth.
Perrin	SC	Steve	13/02/52	Paddington		1981	1982	Hillingdon	Wycombe	22	3	1	2	6	1	0	0
Perry	MA	Mick	04/04/64	Wimbledon		1984		West Brom. Alb. (loan)		4	0	0	0	0	0	0	0
Perryman	G	Gerry	03/10/47	West Haddon		1966			Colchester Utd.	1	0	0	0	0	0	0	0
Phillips	IA	Ian	23/04/59	Edinburgh		1982	1983	Peterborough Utd.	Colchester Utd.	42	5	5	3	1	0	0	0
Phillips	LM	Les	07/01/63	Lambeth		1993		Oxford United	Marlow	26	1	2	3	0	0	0	0
Phillips	R	Ralph	09/08/33	Houghton-le-Spring		1958	1960	Middlesbrough	Darlington	83	4	2	0	1	0	0	0
Phillips	SE	Steve	04/08/54	Edmonton		1975	1976	Birmingham City	Brentford	126	5	10	0	38	2	3	0
						1980	1981	Brentford	Southend U								
Pickering	PB	Peter	24/03/26	York		1955	1957	Chelsea	(South Africa)	86	5	0	0	0	1	0	0
Pinchbeck	CB	Cliff	20/01/25	Cleethorpes		1951		Port Vale	Bath C	3	0	0	0	3	0	0	0
Platt	R	Richard		Huyton		1937	1938	Tranmere Rovers		3	0	0	2	0	0	0	0
Poole	AJ	Andy	06/07/60	Chesterfield		1978	1981	Mansfield Town	Wolves	141	5	11	0	0	0	0	0
Poole	K	Kevin	21/07/63	Bromsgrove		1984		Aston Villa (loan)		3	0	0	0	0	0	0	0
Poole	KJ	Ken	02/07/33	Blaencwm		1956		Swansea City		4	0	0	0	0	0	0	0
Poppy	APC	Arthur	06/01/61	Yeovil		1977				1	0	0	0	0	0	0	0
Postlethwaite	TW	Tom	4/09/09	Haverthwaite		1937	1938	Bradford	Watford	61	1	0	3	1	0	0	0
Potter	FL	Len		Bedford		1934	1935	Bedford	Wellingborough	20	0	0	0	6	0	0	0
Potts	HJ	Henry	23/01/25	Carlisle		1950		Pegasus	Kettering T	10	0	0	0	0	0	0	0
Poyntz	WI	Bill	18/03/1894	Tylorstown	1966	1924		Doncaster Rovers	Bradford	29	1	0	0	4	0	0	0
Preece	AP	Andy	27/03/67	Evesham		1988		Evesham U	Worcester C	1	0	1	1	0	0	0	0
Preston	RJ	Richard	07/05/76	Basildon		1993			Corby T	1	0	0	1	0	0	0	0
Price	E	Eric	03/09/05	Hemsworth	1976	1927		Norwich City	Torquay United	4	0	0	0	2	0	0	0
Price	RJ	Ray	30/11/48	Northampton		1966	1967		Corby T	7	0	0	0	0	0	0	0
Quinney	HJ	Jesse	15/10/22	Rugby		1946		Wolves	Banbury U	3	0	0	0	0	0	0	0
Quow	TS	Trevor	28/09/60	Peterborough		1988	1991	Gillingham	(Hong Kong)	88	4	4	4	2	0	0	0
Radford	B	Bernard	1907	West Melton		1931		Sheffield Utd.		8	0	0	0	0	0	0	0
Ramscar	FT	Fred	24/01/19	Salford		1951	1954	Preston NE	Millwall	139	7	0	0	55	4	0	0
Rankmore	FEJ	Frank	21/07/39	Cardiff		1968	1970	Peterborough Utd.	(retired)	103	14	9	0	15	4	0	0
Rawlings	JSD	Syd	05/05/13	Wombwell	1956	1936	1937	West Bromwich A.	Millwall	48	2	0	0	18	0	0	0
Reed	G	Graham	24/06/61	Doncaster		1985	1988	Barnsley	VS Rugby	112	7	12	7	2	0	0	0
Reid	J	John	20/08/32	Newmains		1961	1963	Bradford City	Luton Town	85	1	4	0	14	0	2	0
Reilly	GG	George	14/09/57	Bellshill		1976	1979	Corby T	Cambridge Utd.	127	4	13	0	45	0	9	0
Richardson	B	Barry	05/08/69	Willington Quay		1991	1993	Stockport Co.	Preston NE	96	5	4	8	0	0	0	0
Riches	LE	Len	1910	Broughton		1929	1937	Kettering T	Kettering T	136	12	0	3	8	1	0	0
Riddick	GG	Gordon	06/11/43	Watford		1972	1973	Leyton Orient	Brentford	28	0	1	0	3	0	0	0
Riley	H	Harry	22/11/09	Hollinwood	1982	1936	1937	Cardiff City	Exeter City	22	0	0	0	4	0	0	0
Rioch	NG	Neil	13/04/51	Paddington		1971		Aston Villa (loan)		14	0	0	0	4	0	0	0
Roberts	DG	Gordon	30/05/25	Foleshill		1946	1948	Wolves	Brighton & Hove A.	57	12	0	0	7	6	0	0
Roberts	JG	John	11/09/46	Abercynon		1967	1968	Swansea City	Arsenal	62	4	0	0	11	2	0	0
Roberts	JT	John	24/03/44	Cessnock, Australia		1972		Southend Utd.		13	0	0	0	0	0	0	0
Robertson	SJ	Stuart	16/12/46	Nottingham		1972	1978	Doncaster Rovers	Bedford T	254	11	16	0	27	1	1	0
Robinson	LStJ	Les	02/05/1898	Romford	1965	1925	1926	West Ham Utd.	Norwich City	73	6	0	0	32	6	0	0
Robinson	M	Maurice	09/11/29	Newark		1957		Kettering T	Bedford T	11	1	0	0	2	0	0	0
Robinson	PJ	Phil	06/01/67	Stafford		1994		Huddersfield(loan)		14	1	0	2	0	0	0	0
Robinson	TE	Tommy	11/02/09	Coalville	1982	1935		Lincoln City	Gillingham	5	0	0	2	2	0	0	0
Robinson	TH	Terry	08/11/29	Woodhams		1957		Brentford	QPR	13	1	0	0	0	0	0	0
Robson	T	Tom		Morpeth		1934	1937	Yeovil T	Kettering T	38	3	0	5	0	0	0	0
Robson	TH	Tommy	31/07/44	Gateshead		1961	1965		Chelsea	74	1	7	0	20	0	1	0
Rodger	CC	Colin		Ayr		1937	1938	Manchester City		35	0	0	2	4	0	0	0
Rogers	E	Eamonn	16/04/47	Dublin		1972		Charlton Ath. (loan)		4	0	0	0	1	0	0	0
Ross	I	Ian	26/11/47	Glasgow		1976		Aston Villa (loan)		2	0	0	0	0	0	0	0
Ross	WE	Eric	19/09/44	Belfast		1969	1971	Newcastle United	Hartlepool U	57	10	4	0	5	0	0	0
Russell	CH	Colin		Pottersbury		1931			Wolverton	7	0	0	0	8	0	0	0
Russell	GH	George	01/08/02	Atherstone		1927	1930	Watford	Bristol Rovers	53	4	0	0	0	0	0	0
Russell	R	Roger	20/11/57	Corby		1981				1	0	0	0	0	0	0	0
Russell	SEJ	Sid	01/01/11	Feltham		1935	1938	QPR	(retired)	109	3	0	5	0	0	0	0
Sampson	I	Ian	14/11/68	Wakefield		1993		Sunderland (loan)		50	1	2	3	2	0	0	0
						1994		Sunderland									
Sandeman	BR	Bradley	24/02/70	Northampton		1987	1990		Maidstone Utd.	58	3	5	7	3	0	0	0
Sandercock	PJ	Phil	21/06/53	Plymouth		1979	1980	Huddersfield T	Kettering T	69	2	2	0	3	0	0	0
Sanders	RJ	Roy	22/09/40	Stepney		1962		Romford	Romford	15	1	3	0	2	0	0	0
Sandy	AVC	Adam	22/09/58	Peterborough		1979	1982	Wolverton	Wolverton	104	4	5	0	6	1	1	0
Sankey	J	Jack	19/03/12	Winsford	1985	1946	1947	West Bromwich A.	Hereford U	42	8	0	0	0	0	0	0
Sargent	GS	Gary	11/09/52	Turvey		1979	1980	Peterborough Utd.	Barnet	43	1	7	0	4	0	0	0
Saunders	PB	Paul	17/12/59	Watford		1978	1982	Watford	Aylesbury	125	4	9	3	5	0	0	0
Saxby	GP	Gary	11/12/59	Mansfield		1980	1982	Mansfield Town	Stamford	96	9	6	3	11	1	2	0
Schiavi	MA	Mark	01/05/64	City of London		1985	1986	Bournemouth	Cambridge Utd.	35	0	2	3	5	0	0	1
Scope	DF	David	10/05/67	Newcastle		1989	1991	Blyth Spartans		19	2	0	1	1	0	0	0
Scott	DP	David	06/06/18	Belfast	1977	1946	1947		Oxford U	11	7	0	0	0	0	0	0
Scott	GS	Geoff	31/10/56	Birmingham		1984		Middlesbrough	Cambridge Utd.	17	3	0	2	0	0	0	0
Scott	J	Jack	5/02/08	Sunderland		1931		Nottm. Forest	Exeter City	22	3	0	0	0	0	0	0
Scott	MJ	Morrys	17/12/70	Swansea		1992		Plymouth Argyle	Slough	17	1	2	3	2	0	0	3
Scully	PJ	Pat	23/06/70	Dublin		1990		Arsenal (loan)		15	0	0	1	0	0	0	0
Seabrook	A	Arthur	1897	Luton		1921	1923	Luton Clarence	Halifax T	36	2	0	0	9	0	0	0
Seddon	S	Syd		Kettering		1926		Rushden	Rushden	1	0	0	0	0	0	0	0
Sedgemore	BR	Ben	05/08/75	Wolverhampton		1994		Birmingham C (loan)		1	0	0	0	0	0	0	0
Senior	S	Steve	15/05/63	Sheffield		1987		York City	Wigan Ath.	4	0	2	0	0	0	0	0
Shaw	WH	William	1902	Durham		1925	1930	Barcelona	Kettering T	74	6	0	0	15	0	0	0
Sherwood	S	Steve	10/12/53	Selby		1993		Grimsby Town	Grimsby Town	16	1	1	2	0	0	0	0
Shipley	AG	Arthur		Kettering		1926		Desborough	Wellingborough	1	0	0	0	0	0	0	0
Shirtliff	PR	Paul	03/11/62	Hoyland		1984		Sheffield Wed.	Frickley Ath.	29	0	1	0	0	0	0	0
Simpson	WS	Billy	01/05/07	Cowdenbeath		1936		Aston Villa	Walsall	42	1	0	1	0	0	0	0
Singleton	MD	Martin	02/08/63	Banbury		1987	1989	West Bromwich A.	Walsall	50	4	4	2	4	0	1	0
Sissons	AE	Albert	05/07/03	Kiveton Park	1975	1929		Southport		19	2	0	0	4	1	0	0
Skeet	SC	Stuart	06/07/48	Cheshunt		1968		Tottenham H (loan)		1	0	0	0	0	0	0	0
Skelly	RB	Richard	24/03/72	Norwich		1994		Newmarket T	King's Lynn	3	0	0	2	0	0	0	0
Slack	TC	Trevor	26/09/62	Peterborough		1987	1988	Grimsby Town	Chesterfield	13	0	1	0	1	0	0	0

Player			D.O.B	Place of Birth	Died	First Season	Last Season	Previous Club	Next Club	Appearances				Goals			
										League	FAC	FLC	Other	League	FAC	FLC	Oth.
Smalley	T	Tom	13/01/12	Kinsley	1984	1946	1950	Norwich City	Gornell	200	26	0	0	2	0	0	0
Smith	D	David	12/10/15	Durham		1946	1950	Newcastle United		128	14	0	0	31	2	0	0
Smith	EWA	Eddie	23/03/29	London		1954	1955	Watford	Colchester Utd.	53	3	0	0	12	1	0	0
Smith	HC	Charles		Lichborough		1920	1925		Higham	173	8	0	0	0	1	0	0
Smith	HR	Ray	13/09/34	Hull		1962	1963	Peterborough Utd.	Luton Town	23	0	1	0	7	0	1	0
Smith	JO	John	04/09/28	Leicester		1950	1959			187	9	0	0	9	0	0	0
Smith	NL	Nicky	28/01/69	Berkeley		1994		Sudbury (loan)		6	0	0	0	1	0	0	0
Smith	TG	Tom	01/10/00	Whitburn	1934	1927	1929	Manchester Utd.	Norwich City	112	9	0	0	22	0	0	0
Smith	WH	Bill	07/09/26	Plymouth		1948		Reading	Birmingham City	26	2	0	0	6	2	0	0
Sorenson	IM			Northampton		1923				1	0	0	0	0	0	0	0
Southam	JH	James 'Jack'	19/08/17	Willenhall	1982	1949	1954	Birmingham City	Walsall (coach)	145	11	0	0	1	1	0	0
Spelman	RE	Ron	22/05/38	Blofield		1960	1961	Norwich City	Bournemouth	34	4	0	0	3	0	0	0
Sproson	A	Albert	1889	Northampton	1934	1920			Desborough	5	0	0	0	0	0	0	0
Stackman	HS	Scott	16/11/75	Arizona, USA		1993			Bedworth	1	0	0	0	0	0	0	0
Stanton	SH	Sid	16/06/23	Dudley		1947	1948	Birmingham C		7	0	0	0	0	0	0	0
Starling	AW	Alan	02/04/51	Barking		1971	1976	Luton Town	Huddersfield T	238	11	9	0	1	0	0	0
Starocsik	F	Felix	20/05/20	Poland (Silesia)		1951	1954	Third Lanark	Bedford	49	1	0	0	19	0	0	0
Stewart	WI	Billy	01/01/65	Liverpool		1994		Chester City	Chester City	27	1	2	1	0	0	0	0
Strang	R	Richard		Rutherglen		1932		Halifax T	Darlington	7	0	0	0	0	0	0	0
Stratford	P	Paul	04/09/55	Northampton		1972	1977		(retired)	172	7	9	0	59	1	1	0
Strathie	WJ	James	12/02/13	Beancross	1976	1946		Luton Town	Kettering T	6	0	0	0	0	0	0	0
Sugrue	PA	Paul	06/11/60	Coventry		1985		Portsmouth	Newport County	8	0	0	1	2	0	0	0
Syrett	DK	Dave	20/01/56	Salisbury		1982	1983	Peterborough Utd.	Brackley T	44	1	4	3	13	0	2	2
Taylor	A	Tony	06/09/46	Glasgow		1979		Portsmouth		4	0	3	0	0	0	0	0
Taylor	A	Andy	04/04/63	Stratford-on-Avon		1981		Aston Villa	Alvechurch	17	2	3	0	0	0	0	0
Taylor	JW					1930				1	0	0	0	0	0	0	0
Tebbutt	RS	Robert	10/11/34	Irchester		1956	1959		Bedford T	55	3	0	0	21	1	0	0
Terry	PA	Pat	02/10/33	Lambeth		1961		Gillingham	Millwall	24	3	1	0	10	1	0	0
Terry	SG	Steve	14/06/62	Clapton		1989	1993	Hull City	Walton & Hersham	181	9	10	11	17	1	0	0
Thayne	W	Billy	1912	West Hartlepool		1935	1938	Luton Town	Walsall	133	3	0	2	0	0	0	0
Thomas	DR	Dean	19/12/61	Bedworth		1988	1989	Achen	Notts County	74	6	6	5	12	1	0	0
Thomas	WS	William		Croydon		1920			Millwall	21	3	0	0	2	0	0	0
Thompson	GL	Garry	07/10/59	Birmingham		1994		Cardiff City		15	0	0	0	4	0	0	0
Thompson	H	Harry	29/04/15	Mansfield		1946	1948	York City	Oxford U	38	7	0	0	2	1	0	0
Thompson	KA	Keith	24/04/65	Birmingham		1984		Coventry City (loan)		10	0	0	0	1	0	0	0
Thompson	WJ	Walter	1910	Croydon		1933	1935	Aston Villa	Scarborough	9	0	0	0	0	0	0	0
Thorpe	A	Adrian	25/11/63	Chesterfield		1989	1991	Walsall	Kettering T	52	2	3	4	6	0	0	2
Thorpe	T	Thomas	19/5/1881	Kilnhurst	1953	1920		Barnsley	Barnsley	22	20	0	0	0	0	0	0
Tilson	SF	Fred	01/01/03	Barnsley	1972	1937	1938	Manchester City	York City	41	1	0	0	10	1	0	0
Tisdale	PR	Paul	14/01/73	Malta		1992		Southampton (loan)		5	0	0	0	0	0	0	0
Tolland	D	Donal 'Danny'	19/03/05	Ireland		1933	1937	Ayr U	Bristol Rovers	138	12	0	10	26	1	0	3
Tomkins	EF	Eric	18/12/1892	Rushden		1920	1926	Rushden	Rushden	82	14	0	0	0	0	0	0
Townsend	NR	Neil	01/02/50	Long Buckby		1968	1971		Southend Utd.	67	4	1	0	1	1	0	0
Townsend	RN	Russ	17/01/60	Reading		1979		Barnet	Barnet	13	1	1	0	0	0	0	0
Train	R	Ray	10/02/51	Nuneaton		1984		Oxford United	Tranmere Rovers	46	4	2	2	1	2	0	0
Tresadern	J	Jack	26/09/1890	Leytonstone	1959	1925	1926	Burnley		34	7	0	0	1	0	0	0
Trott	DD	Dean	13/05/67	Barnsley		1994		Boston U	Gateshead	22	1	2	1	4	0	0	0
Tucker	KJ	Ken	15/07/35	Merthyr Tydfil		1959	1960	Shrewsbury Town	Merthyr	10	2	1	0	3	0	0	0
Tucker	WB	Barry	28/08/52	Swansea		1971	1977		Brentford	277	12	13	0	8	0	0	0
						1982	1983	Brentford									
Tumbridge	RA	Ray	06/03/55	Hampstead		1974		Charlton Ath. (loan)		11	0	0	0	0	0	0	0
Turner	G	George	1910	Mansfield		1935	1936	Luton T		22	0	0	1	3	0	0	0
Turner	GM	Mark	04/10/72	Bebington		1994		Wolves	Telford U	4	0	0	1	0	0	0	0
Tysoe	J		13/11/1902	Northampton		1920				1	0	0	0	0	0	0	0
Upton	F	Frank	18/10/34	Ainsley Hill		1952	1953	Nuneaton	Derby County	17	0	0	0	1	0	0	0
Vickers	P	Peter	06/03/34	Kilnhurst		1959		Lincoln C		2	0	0	0	0	0	0	0
Wainwright	RK	Robin	09/03/51	Luton		1973	1974	Millwall	Milton Keynes C	32	2	1	0	5	0	0	0
Walden	FI	Frederick 'Fanny'	1/3/1888	Wellingborough	1949	SL		Wellingborough	Tottenham H	20	9	0	0	1	1	0	0
						1926		Tottenham H									
Walden	HB	Harry	22/12/40	Walgrave		1964	1966	Luton Town	Kettering T	76	1	7	0	3	0	0	0
Waldock	DH	Des	04/12/61	Northampton		1978	1980			54	2	4	0	4	0	0	0
Walker	DCA	Clive	24/10/45	Watford		1966	1968	Leicester City	Mansfield Town	72	2	6	0	1	0	0	0
Walker	RP	Ricky	04/04/59	Northampton		1978	1980	Coventry City	Corby T	53	1	7	0	0	0	0	0
Wallace	J	James	17/02/33	Kirkintilloch		1955		Aberdeen	Aberdeen	1	0	0	0	0	0	0	0
Wallbanks	J	Jimmy	12/09/09	Platt Bridge	1979	1934		Norwich City	Millwall	2	0	0	0	0	0	0	0
Walsh	W	William	04/12/23	Easington		1953		Sunderland	Darlington	19	0	0	0	0	0	0	0
Walton	RP	Ronnie	12/10/45	Newcastle		1964		Rotherham Utd.	Crewe Alexandra	1	0	0	0	0	0	0	0
Warburton	R	Ray	07/10/67	Rotherham		1993 / 1994		York City (loan) / York City		56	1	2	3	4	0	0	1
Ward	JR	Richard	16/09/40	Scunthorpe		1959		Scunthorpe Utd.	Millwall	6	0	0	0	0	0	0	0
Ward	RA	Bob	04/08/53	West Bromwich		1976		West Brom. A. (loan)		8	0	0	0	0	0	0	0
Ward	SC	Steve	21/07/59	Derby		1979		Brighton & Hove A.	Halifax Town	14	0	4	0	2	0	1	0
Warren	E	Ernest	14/9/10	Sunderland		1933		Southampton	Hartlepool Utd.	2	0	0	1	1	0	0	0
Wassell	KD	Kim	09/06/57	Wolverhampton		1977	1978	West Bromwich A.	Aldershot	20	1	2	0	1	0	0	0
Watson	WJ	William		Carlisle		1920	1928			326	26	0	0	4	2	0	0
Watson	WJB	Jimmy	01/01/14	Durham	1979	1934		Bristol Rovers	Gillingham	7	1	0	0	3	0	0	0
Watts	D	Derek	30/06/52	Leicester		1973		Leicester City (loan)		5	0	0	0	0	0	0	0
Weaver	E	Eric	01/07/43	Rhymney		1967	1969	Notts County	Boston U	63	5	3	0	9	0	0	0
Webber	GM	George	28/06/25	Abercynon		1954		Torquay United	Ebbw Vale	13	0	0	0	0	0	0	0
Wells	TC	Tommy		Nunhead		1926	1934	Arsenal	Swindon T	277	34	2	3	73	20	0	1
Weston	CA			Kettering		1920	1921		Kettering T	4	0	0	0	0	0	0	0
Weston	JM	John		Halesowen		1928	1931	Burnley	Shelbourne	45	5	0	0	15	0	0	0
Wheeler	AJ	Alf		Bilston		1933		Brentford	Southampton	5	0	0	0	1	0	0	0
Whitworth	GH	George	14/07/1896	Northampton		1920	1921		Crystal Palace	67	9	0	0	42	5	0	0
Whyte	C	Campbell		Lochgelly		1930		Gillingham	Rochdale	5	0	0	0	0	0	0	0
Wilcox	R	Russell	25/03/64	Hemsworth		1986	1989	Frickley Ath.	Hull City	138	10	6	8	9	0	0	1
Wilkin	K	Kevin	01/10/67	Cambridge		1990	1994	Cambridge C	Rushden	78	4	7	5	11	2	2	0

Player			D.O.B	Place of Birth	Died	First Season	Last Season	Previous Club	Next Club	Appearances				Goals			
										League	FAC	FLC	Other	League	FAC	FLC	Oth.
Williams	B	Brett	19/03/68	Dudley		1987		Nottm. Forestt (loan)		4	0	0	0	0	0	0	0
Williams	DR	Roley	10/07/27	Swansea		1955	1956	Cardiff City	Bath C	15	0	0	0	0	0	0	0
Williams	E	Edgar	20/05/19	Sheffield		1948		Nottm. Forest		3	0	0	0	0	0	0	0
Williams	GJ	Gareth	12/03/67	Cowes		1994		Bournemouth		15	1	0	3	0	0	0	0
Williams	JS			Rugby		1921		Rugby T		2	0	0	0	0	0	0	0
Williams	KD	Keith	12/04/57	Burntwood		1976	1980	Aston Villa	Bournemouth	131	3	8	0	6	0	1	0
Williams	W	Billy	1896	Llantwit Vardre		1921	1926	Cardiff City	Newport County	187	16	0	0	3	0	0	0
Williams	W	Wayne	17/11/63	Telford		1988	1990	Shrewsbury Town (loan)		55	1	6	6	1	0	0	0
Wilson	F			Northampton		1926		Rothwell	Higham	1	0	0	0	0	0	0	0
Wilson	JA	James	28/06/22	Musselburgh		1951		Luton Town	Chesterfield	23	1	0	0	0	0	0	0
Wilson	JR	John 'Jock'		Blyth		1927	1929	Reading		24	2	0	0	1	0	0	0
Wilson	PA	Paul	02/08/68	Bradford		1987	1991	Norwich City	Halifax Town	141	8	10	9	6	0	1	0
Woan	AE	Alan	08/02/31	Liverpool		1956	1959	Norwich City	Crystal Palace	119	4	0	0	68	1	0	0
Wonnacott	CB	Clarence	31/12/09	Clowne	1989	1930	1931	Mansfield T	Shelbourne	13	0	0	0	4	0	0	0
Wood	AR	Alf	14/05/15	Aldridge		1951	1954	Coventry City	Coventry City	139	7	0	0	0	0	0	0
Wood	D	Darren	22/10/68	Derby		1990	1993	Reading	(retired)	4	0	2	0	1	0	0	0
Wood	EE	Edmund	10/02/03	King's Norton		1922	1924	Rhyl	Birmingham City	50	0	0	0	3	0	0	0
Wood	JT	John	1902			1921		Daventry		1	0	0	0	0	0	0	0
Wood	W	William	01/01/00	Parkgate		1923		Oldham Athletic	Swansea City	32	5	0	0	6	4	0	0
Woodman	AJ	Andy	11/08/71	Denmark Hill		1994		Exeter City		10	0	0	0	0	0	0	0
Woods	DE	Derek	23/03/41	Northampton		1961			Cambridge U	6	0	0	0	2	0	0	0
Woollard	AJ	Arnold	24/08/30	Bermuda		1950		(Bermuda)	Newcastle United	31	1	2	0	0	0	0	0
						1961	1962	Bournemouth	(retired)								
Woollett	AH	Alan	04/03/47	Wigston		1978		Leicester City	Corby T	23	1	4	0	0	0	0	0
Wright	ME	Mike	16/01/42	Newmarket		1959	1961	Newmarket	King's Lynn	26	0	2	0	7	0	0	0
Wright	RL			Kettering		1923			Kettering T	1	0	0	0	0	0	0	0
Yeoman	RI	Ray	13/05/34	Perth		1953	1958	St. Johnstone	Middlesbrough	169	7	0	0	4	0	0	0
York	R	Roland				1923		Higham	Higham	3	0	0	0	0	0	0	0
Yorke	AE	Andrew	1901	Blyth		1925	1926	Coventry City	Lincoln City	24	2	0	0	0	0	0	0
Young	JW	Joe	1906			1929		Luton T		2	0	0	0	2	0	0	0
Young	SR	Stuart	16/12/72	Hull		1992		Hull City	Scarborough	8	0	0	0	2	0	0	0

Played in F.A. Cup only

Player			D.O.B	Place of Birth	Died	First Season	Last Season	Previous Club	Next Club	League	FAC	FLC	Other	League	FAC	FLC	Oth.
Gorman	K	Keith	13/10/66	Bishop Auckland		1986		Ipswich T (loan)		0	1	0	1	0	0	0	0
Roe	J			Northampton		1920			Kettering T	0	1	0	0	0	0	0	0
Welsh	A	Andy	1918	Annfield		1945		Darlington		0	1	0	0	0	0	0	0
Wilson	S	Sam	16/12/31	Glasgow		1960		Millwall		0	1	0	0	0	1	0	0
Yarker	L					1945		(RAF)		0	5	0	0	0	0	0	0

Played in Football League Cup only

Player			D.O.B	Place of Birth	Died	First Season	Last Season	Previous Club	Next Club	League	FAC	FLC	Other	League	FAC	FLC	Oth.
Caine	B	Brian	20/06/36	Nelson		1961		Coventry C	Barrow	0	0	1	0	0	0	0	0
Linnell	J	John	02/01/44	Holcot		1966			Peterborough U	0	0	1	0	0	0	0	0
Parker	K	Ken	1954	Newcastle		1972			Milton Keynes	0	0	1	0	0	0	0	0
Scott	C	Chris	11/09/63	Wallsend		1987		Blyth Spartans	Lincoln C	0	0	1	0	0	0	0	0
Sharpe	C	Colin	1944	Bugbrooke		1963			King's Lynn	0	0	2	0	0	0	0	0

Played in Miscellaneous Games Only

Player			D.O.B	Place of Birth	Died	First Season	Last Season	Previous Club	Next Club	League	FAC	FLC	Other	League	FAC	FLC	Oth.
Cuff	J			Lancs.		1938		Everton	Tranmere Rov.	0	0	0	1	0	0	0	0
Hewitt	E	Edwin				1936		Aston Villa		0	0	0	1	0	0	0	0
Jones	H			Wolverton		1935		Wolverton		0	0	0	1	0	0	0	1
Smith	A			Northampton		1938				0	0	0	1	0	0	0	0
Wallbanks	F	Fred	1909	Wigan		1936		Nottm. Forest		0	0	0	1	0	0	0	0

Played in Abandoned Season 1939/40 only

Player			D.O.B	Place of Birth	Died	First Season	Last Season	Previous Club	Next Club
Garvey	J	Jim	04/06/19	Paisley		1939			Leicester City
Melaniphy	E	Eugene 'Ted'	5/2/13	Westport		1939		Cardiff City	
Miller	HS	Harold	20/5/02	St. Albans		1939		Chelsea	
Simons	RR	Reuben	16/10/08	Swansea		1939		Swansea Town	Swansea Town
Smith	A					1939			

Managers of Northampton Town

	From	To	Honours
Herbert Chapman	May 1907	May 1912	Southern League 1909
Walter Bull	June 1912	Dec 1912	
Fred Lessons	June 1913	June 1915	
Bob Hewison	May 1920	May 1925	
Jack Tresadern	May 1925	Oct 1930	
Jack English Snr	Feb 1931	Feb 1935	
Sid Puddefoot	Mar 1935	Mar 1937	
Warney Cresswell	Apr 1937	Sep 1939	
Tom Smith	Sep 1939	Mar 1949	
Bob Dennison	Mar 1949	July 1954	
Dave Smith	July 1954	July 1959	
Dave Bowen	July 1959	Sep 1963	Division 3, 1963
Jack Jennings (caretaker)	Sep 1963	Oct 1963	
Dave Bowen	Oct 1963	Sep 1967	
Tony Marchi	Sep 1967	May 1968	
Ron Flowers	May 1968	May 1969	
Dave Bowen	May 1969	May 1972	
Bill Baxter	May 1972	May 1973	
Bill Dodgin	Jun 1973	June 1976	
Pat Crerand	July 1976	Jan 1977	
John Petts	July 1977	Jan 1978	
Mike Keen	Feb 1978	Mar 1979	
Clive Walker	May 1979	Oct 1980	
Bill Dodgin	Oct 1980	Feb 1982	
Clive Walker	Feb 1982	May 1984	
Tony Barton	July 1984	Apr 1985	
Graham Carr	Apr 1985	May 1990	Division 4, 1987
Theo Foley	May 1990	Apr 1992	
Phil Chard	Apr 1992	Sep 1993	
John Barnwell	Sep 1993	Dec 1994	
Ian Atkins	Jan 1995		

The first 5 managers and Dave Bowen, Ron Flowers, Bill Baxter and Phil Chard were player managers at some stage.